THE
WINNING
OF
INDEPENDENCE

THE
WINNING
OF
INDEPENDENCE

Marshall Smelser

NEW VIEWPOINTS
A Division of Franklin Watts, Inc.
New York / 1973

Library of Congress Cataloging in Publication Data

Smelser, Marshall.
    The winning of independence.

    Original ed. issued as no. 3 of the Quadrangle
bicentennial history of the American Revolution.
    Bibliography: p.
    1. United States–History–Revolution.
I. Title. II. Series: The Quadrangle bicentennial history
of the American Revolution, 3.
[E208.S64 1973]   973.3   73-3104
ISBN 0-531-06490-5 (pbk)

First NEW VIEWPOINTS edition published 1973 by
Franklin Watts, Inc.

Manufactured in the United States of America

TO

Carson I. A. Ritchie

PREFACE

This book attempts to tell the story of the course of the War for Independence from the breakdown of British civil authority in 1774 until the peace of 1783. I hope I have told the story in a way which will satisfy lay readers; I do not think I have written anything that would surprise or instruct a professional scholar of the Revolution. The military history of this much-studied war has been well written, and Edmund Cody Burnett has thoroughly explained the Continental Congress as an institution. If there is anything original in this book it results from my attempt to weave the intercolonial and interstate military and civilian threads into one tapestry (I have left provincial and state affairs to others).

I wish here to thank the Notre Dame Committee on Grants for Arts and Humanities for underwriting considerable clerical costs, and the staff of the Notre Dame Memorial Library for every kind of help. Leonard W. Levy has been wise and kind in advice. I owe a special debt to Gerard F. McCauley. Former students Arnold Klingenberg, James F. Sefcik, and Ralph Pastore—now fellow tillers of this field—gave drudging but ungrudging help. Carmela Rulli and her corps of expert and good-humored manuscript typists in the Notre Dame faculty stenographic pool earned commendation for service much above and beyond the call of duty. My note files show that I have learned more from the Institute of Early American History and Culture at Williamsburg than from any other single institution, for which I thank its competent editors. Anna Smelser, my wife, read every word and tried to persuade me to let light through opaque sentences and to sharpen the outlines of fuzzy images; hence failures are to my discredit only. It is a valiant woman who will see her husband through eight literary confinements in twenty-three years.

M. S.

Notre Dame, Indiana, 1971

LIST OF MAPS

CONTENTS

THE
WINNING
OF
INDEPENDENCE

PROLOGUE

On Monday, July 1, the Continental Congress sat as Committee of the Whole and drudged through a good deal of paperwork. On Tuesday the Congress convened itself again, heard the report of its own work, and made six decisions: it settled some financial accounts, ordered the publication of a letter which had been lying on the table, referred some papers to the Board of War, and told the Marine Committee to look into complaints against its operations. And it resolved to declare the independence of the United States.[1] A statement of independence had been in preparation for many days; approval of the wording was a task that absorbed most congressional attention on July 3.

Thursday, July 4, was a pleasant day in Philadelphia. Thomas Jefferson, a lanky, loose-jointed young Congressman from Virginia whose curiosity ranged far enough to include meteorology, noted that his thermometer registered 68 degrees at six o'clock in the morning; it rose to a high of 76 degrees at one o'clock. Such fine weather seems to have invigorated Jefferson and his colleagues, which was just as well because there was plenty of work to do. By the end of the day the Congress had made seventeen formal decisions, including an order to design a great seal of the United States and one to send a man searching at public expense for stone suitable for musket flints. One of the seventeen resolutions approved the final draft of the Declaration of Independence.

The document was not done hastily. Not until Saturday, July 6, did the *Pennsylvania Evening Post* print the Declaration, as signed by John Hancock, president of the Congress, and attested by Charles Thomson, secretary (no other signatures were published until the next year). On the next Monday the Congress proclaimed the Declaration from a stage in the yard of the State House. Such troops as were nearby paraded, and spent much of their perilously short supply of gunpowder in exuberantly firing salutes, while the bells of Philadelphia, including the Liberty Bell in the State House tower, clanged all that day and far into the night. The local rebels added a clownish touch to the parade by dressing a well-known streetwalker in unaccustomed finery topped by the kind of headdress then affected by the loyalist ladies of Philadelphia.[2]

The Congress ordered General George Washington to have the Declaration read to the troops who were at the moment rather nervously preparing to defend New York City from the largest expeditionary force ever sent out of Britain, a great army which even then was debarking on Staten Island. The American officers read the Declaration to their men on July 9, and, as Washington soberly put it, "the measure seemed to have their most hearty assent; the Expressions and behaviour of both Officers and Men testifying their warmest approbation of it."[3] Although the harbor was a forest of enemy masts, some of the civilians of New York testified their own support by going to the Bowling Green and pulling the equestrian statue of George III from its fifteen-foot pedestal. The figure was of gilded lead, which made it easy to decapitate and useful to melt down for bullets.

The news moved up and down the coast. In Newport the Declaration proved its psychological value by shocking the Reverend Mr. Ezra Stiles (a future president of Yale) into the realization, for the first time, that the United States were actually independent. In Providence the ship masters celebrated by firing thirteen volleys of ships' guns, while local rebels tore the King's arms from a government office and the identifying crown from the Crown Coffee House, and burned both. In Boston the Declaration sounded from pulpits as the trumpet of the Lord of Hosts. In Baltimore an effigy of George III rode through town and perished in flames. The word reached Savannah on August 10 and was greeted with mixed solemnity and joy. The Declaration was read aloud in three places and thrice saluted by muskets and field guns, after which governor, council, gentlemen, and militia (a nice distinction) "dined under the cedar trees, and cheerfully drank to the united, free, and independent states of America." That night the Savannah citizens illuminated the town for a cortege which buried the effigy of George III in a grave dug in front of the courthouse.[4] London learned of the Declaration about a fortnight after Savannah had the news, and a French translation was printed on the continent on August 30. The King's friends might have been excused if they had confined themselves to the language

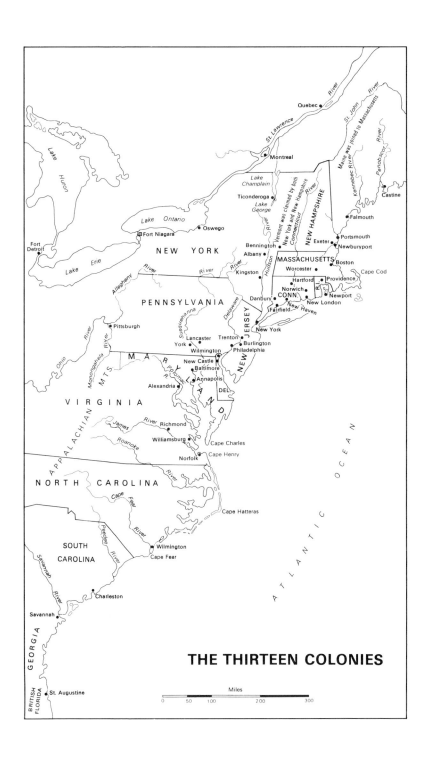

Quebec

Montreal

Lake Champlain

Ticonderoga

Lake George

Lake Huron

Lake Ontario

Oswego

Fort Niagara

NEW YORK

Fort Detroit

Lake Erie

Allegheny River

River

River

Hudson River

Kingston

Albany

Bennington

Worcester

MASSACHUSETTS

Hartford

CONN.

Danbury

New Haven

Fairfield

New London

Newport

R.I.

Providence

Cape Cod

Norwich

Vermont was claimed by both New York and New Hampshire

Connecticut River

NEW HAMPSHIRE

Exeter

Portsmouth

Newburyport

Falmouth

Boston

St. Lawrence River

St. John River

Maine was joined to Massachusetts

Kennebec River

Penobscot River

Castine

PENNSYLVANIA

Pittsburgh

Ohio River

Monongahela River

APPALACHIAN MTS.

Susquehanna River

Delaware River

Lancaster

York

Wilmington

New Castle

NEW JERSEY

Trenton

Burlington

Philadelphia

New York

MARYLAND

Baltimore

Annapolis

Alexandria

Potomac R.

DEL.

VIRGINIA

James River

Roanoke

Richmond

Williamsburg

Cape Charles

Norfolk

Cape Henry

NORTH CAROLINA

Cape Fear River

River

Cape Hatteras

SOUTH CAROLINA

Pee dee River

Wilmington

Cape Fear

Savannah River

Charleston

Savannah

GEORGIA

BRITISH FLORIDA

St. Augustine

ATLANTIC OCEAN

THE THIRTEEN COLONIES

Miles

0   50   100   200   300

of scorn, but at least one (in America) tried a rational criticism, to wit, the Declaration cut the ground from under American sympathizers in Parliament, and was a poor tactical response to the pro-American speeches of such men as Chatham and Richmond.[5] As for the government of Great Britain, about the most interesting event of July 4, 1776, in the home islands was the conferring of a pair of honorary degrees by the Chancellor of Oxford, Frederick North, M.A., LL.D., D.C.L., known by courtesy as Lord North and by royal appointment as First Lord of the Treasury. The recipients were Thomas Hutchinson and Peter Oliver, lately governor and chief justice of Massachusetts. They both had Harvard degrees already, but they would not see Harvard again.

⫾
═══════════

An Assembly of the Angry

☆ The War for Independence began long before the Declaration of Independence. The Declaration simply announced the existence of a loose confederation which had already assumed the power and authority of a sovereign state. Men who were angered at a series of British laws which the Parliament enacted to punish Massachusetts for its contumacious Tea Party of 1773, set in train the events which led to the Declaration. The indignant Americans called these laws the "Intolerable Acts." The Acts rather insultingly proposed to protect Crown officials from hostile local courts, made the government of Massachusetts less popular and more authoritarian, and closed the port of Boston. The most infuriating of these statutes was the Boston Port Act, which closed the port until somebody paid the tea tax and made it up to the owners of the tea for their losses dumped in Boston harbor. The Act was to become effective on June 1, 1774. The Bostonians asked their fellow Americans whether Boston was not suffering for all, and suggested that other colonies might attempt economic reprisals against the British. Thus the Port Act stimulated the line of thinking that led to the First Continental Congress.

Colonial neighbors had not been callous to Boston's pains. The Providence Town Meeting, the Committees of Correspondence of Philadelphia and New York, and the Virginia House of Burgesses had shuddered as one, realizing that what could be done to Massachusetts could be done to every colony. Providence, New York, and Philadelphia had proposed, in May 1774, a general meeting of the colonies; Virginia, on motion of Thomas Jefferson, resolved that June 1 be observed as a day of fasting and prayer.[1] The men who composed these bodies were not fierce revolutionaries. The New York Committee, for example, were upper-middle-class men, 40 per cent of whom chose loyalism when the final break with England came.[2] The Burgesses of Virginia were the firmly established magnates of the Old Dominion; yet, when dissolved by the governor for expressing sympathy for Massachusetts, and upon receiving angry comments on the Boston Port Act from Boston, Philadelphia, and Annapolis, the twenty-five Burgesses still in Williamsburg met unofficially on May 27 and suggested the formation of an intercolonial congress to meet annually. Massachusetts, on June 17, 1774, much relieved by this outpouring of fellow feeling, invited all colonies to meet at Philadelphia on September 1, and must have been pleased to learn that Connecticut and Rhode Island had already appointed delegates in anticipation. All colonies except Georgia chose delegates in one way or another within a few weeks.

Since the Boston Port Act had not arrived in Boston until May 10, 1774 (three days before General Thomas Gage came to succeed Thomas Hutchinson as governor), the organization of near-unanimous protest had been swift. Food and relief funds arrived in Boston at the same time as the expressions of political solidarity. The movement was of the heart, not merely a tactical baiting of Britain. The American colonies were mature, self-reliant, and optimistic. British leaders had failed to see that such people could not be controlled by coercion. Instead, coercion brought a unity not previously credible. Although the Crown and the separate colonies had learned how to live together, the intervention of Parliament, beginning in the 1760's, had wrecked the ancient relationship and required the Crown to confront the angry new extra-legal provincial and continental congresses of the 1770's.[3] The arrangement of intra-imperial harmony would have to be done all over, if it were done at all. It was not done. The colonies had maintained a corps of agents in England to deal with executive officers, but from the middle of the 1760's their influence steadily declined, partly because their respective instructions from home reflected the increasing bitterness of the colonial assemblies toward British legislation.[4] By 1774 American and British officials were hardly on speaking terms.

The Continental Congress of 1774 had a much better representation than the earlier Stamp Act Congress of 1765, which had been ignored by the leaders of four colonies. Only Georgia was unrepresented in 1774; its governor did not press hard for money from Georgia's assembly, and the constant danger from Georgia's unfriendly Indian neighbors showed the value of British military power.[5] The other colonies chose delegates in their assemblies, in committees of safety, or in simple mass meetings. Thus the Congress was an extra-legal convention of delegations of angry local politicians. Although the delegates were chosen in many different ways, and mostly by the organizers of resentment, they were rather more wise and understanding than one would expect. The new governor of Massachusetts, General Gage, whose job was to cow the province, inaccurately described the Congress as a "motley crew" which could only talk and threaten.[6] In a different way Ezra Stiles underestimated the Congress when he feared that British agents would infiltrate and corrupt the body. The Ministry lacked imagination for such a congenial policy or it would have begun to pension and ennoble potent moderates and royalists earlier.

The Congress was a moderate convocation. A few radicals might have been willing to try something really drastic, but they knew the moderates were not ready and kept quiet. Furthermore, unity might be illusory: there were old intersectional suspicions. Finally, a few royalists came only to try persuasion, and could never agree to commit a rebellious act. Republican sentiment waited on the Second Continental Congress. The meeting of 1774 was a meeting of men who resented Britain's policy, not its monarchy.

Although the political poll had not yet been invented, the opinions of the leaders of 1774 are traceable. Probably Samuel Adams of Massachusetts would have liked a violent response, but no other member was as much inclined to precipitate a crisis. The delegates generally were reticent on the subject of the regulation of seaborne commerce, and quite outspoken on the internal fiscal and political restrictions introduced by British Ministries since 1764. At present they were unwilling to speak of independence but willing at least to *think* of fighting. Joseph Hawley of Massachusetts exercised the American prerogative and wrote to his Congressmen: they would have to fight if there was no other way to rid themselves of Parliament's taxes and Parliament's remodeling of their governments. Otherwise in twenty years the new imperial system which had been poured into the American mold would have cooled and set, and would be unbreakable. But these sentiments, however widely shared, were not yet public.

The Congress which met in 1774 had a good many strong-minded characters. Space does not permit sketching each, but a few of the more influential and persevering may be portrayed to give an idea of the quality of the group. George Washington and Richard Henry Lee, the Virginia luminaries, may well be left until later.

A forgotten hero of this and every later Continental Congress was Charles Thomson of Philadelphia, never an elected voting member, and always the elected secretary. Thomson had long-standing credentials as a Pennsylvanian anti-British obstructionist. Born in Ireland, he arrived in America as an orphan aged ten. Friends saw to it that he received a classical education. He prospered in business and gained a reputation for probity which extended as far as the frontier Indians, who called him "Man Who Tells Truth." He was long active in Pennsylvania politics, firmly opposed British policy from the passage of the Stamp Act, and continued as a Philadelphia leader of the anti-British opposition until the winning of independence. Although Thomson was no colorful, magnetic incendiary, John Adams called him "The Sam Adams of Philadelphia," an accurate epithet, intended to be complimentary. He was both intellectual and politician, and in later life was the first American to translate the Bible from the Greek. Royalist Joseph Galloway had blocked Thomson's election to the Congress, but friends arranged to put him in the middle of things by choosing him secretary, a task he worked at faithfully until the institution of the federal Congress in 1789.[7]

Samuel Adams, the archetype of American revolutionary agitator, had no real career except as a revolutionary. While neglecting his family and his material interests he achieved excellence as an agitating propagandist who hammered on the theme of the dangers of centralized power, a position based on his Harvard reading which had sensitized him to tyranny. He had more enemies than intimate friends; indeed, he seemed to prefer collaborators to friends. His associates found him severe and opinionated, but persuasive.

The best mind in the First Continental Congress belonged to John

An Assembly of the Angry

Adams. In early manhood he was torn between popularity and probity, poise and awkwardness, an introverted wallowing in hurt feelings and a necessity to appear self-disciplined. Marriage to Abigail Smith, who became his balance wheel, much matured him.[8] To say his small talk was sometimes grotesque, his temper explosive, his vanity large, and his judgment of men's motives poor, is to catalogue all his vices (except his habit of chewing tobacco). He was short, thick, vigorous, and not yet fat in 1774. With round head, wide forehead, and usually mild eyes, he made a striking appearance but managed dignity without stiffness. His independent spirit gave him a weakness for heated language, but he was always coolly brave in deed. Despite—or because of—his virtues, he was a rather lonely man. His trip to Philadelphia in 1774 was his first outside New England. Suspicious at first, he was pleased to learn that his new colleagues agreed in opposing England, even if they differed about the means.[9]

Two Connecticut notables who served long in successive Congresses were Roger Sherman and Eliphalet Dyer. Sherman was one of the few Continental leaders who had worked with his hands. He graduated to the bar and the Congress, combining a Puritan manner and practical ambitions supported by genuine ability, perhaps aided by a farmerish pose. Dyer was a veteran of the French and Indian War (Europe knew it as the Seven Years' War) and of the Stamp Act Congress, and learned politics in the Connecticut Council. He later declined a general's commission in favor of continuing in the Congress, where he was thought wise but rather windy. He also compiled a generous expense account.

A brace of colorful Pennsylvanians, Thomas McKean and Thomas Mifflin, spent most of their revolutionary years in the Congress. McKean served on thirty-five committees, yet found time to be a fierce radical in Pennsylvania's internal revolution. Despite his vanity and bad manners, even his enemies admitted his energy, honesty, and ability. The very popular Mifflin spent the beginning and end of the war as a Congressman, and the interim as a major general—for which he was expelled from the Society of Friends. He was president of the Congress when Washington, for whom he had no great admiration, resigned his commission. Mifflin was a handsome man of middle height who kept up with fashion in men's clothes, spent freely, entertained lavishly, and died (in 1800) flat broke.

A turbulent disposition made large Samuel Chase of Maryland a natural rebel until he achieved authority himself. He served in the Congress until 1778 when he was implicated in a flour scandal (he was re-elected in 1780). Nicknamed "Bacon Face," he was once described as a double for Dr. Samuel Johnson in almost every way.

South Carolina sent two Rutledges, John and Edward, both educated to the law in England. John sat in the Congress only at the beginning and end of the war, preferring South Carolina politics. He showed courage, tact, energy, a deep conviction of the rightness of the cause, and an occasionally detonating temper. Edward, the younger brother, was a less impressive man. He served in the Congress from 1774 to November 1776. He was contemptuous of democracy and haunted by a dread of Yankee democrats. As an inflexibly conservative rebel he was a fairly typical phenomenon of the 1770's.[10]

The letters and diaries of the First Continental Congress are full of references to food and drink. John Adams feared he would be killed by the hospitality of "the nobles of Pennsylvania," but, though stuffed with wines and delicacies, he managed to "hold it out surprisingly."[11] On one occasion the grandees of Philadelphia dined nearly five hundred at once, and toasts to the King, Queen, Prince of Wales, and the union of the colonies were "drunk with applause."[12] Adams once privately observed Benjamin Harrison and Richard Henry Lee as "very high." Lee, supplied by John Dickinson, "drank Burgundy the whole afternoon."[13]

The ability of Americans to manage their own affairs was quite well illustrated in the organization of the First Congress. The debates, for intelligence and dignity—and occasional pettiness—matched those of the House of Commons.[14] The Congress met in Carpenters' Hall, mainly because Joseph Galloway, speaker of the Pennsylvania assembly, offered the State House, and the bitterness of Pennsylvania politics required his opponents to block whatever he suggested. On the second day of meeting the members resolved to keep their proceedings private and not to publish them until ordered by majority vote. On that same day they decided that each state should have one vote, though the members formally denied they were setting a precedent. Some argued for voting in proportion to white free population, and others for formulating a weight per state by somehow combining population and property, to which spokesmen of small colonies responded by saying they might be small but were risking everything, and a small colony's everything was as important as a large colony's everything. The question was settled one state, one vote, simply because of the Congress "not being possess'd of, or at present able to procure proper materials for ascertaining the importance of each Colony."[15] The solution seems to have been the only one possible in an age when nobody could have authenticated the populations or property values of the colonies.

The first serious resolution of the Congress was to endorse some fiery resolves of a convention of the people of Suffolk County (in which Boston lies), which had been written by Joseph Warren and carried to Philadelphia by Paul Revere for congressional consideration. The endorsement was unanimous, and encouraged continued opposition to "these wicked ministerial measures." The Congress also unanimously urged all colonies to continue to relieve the distress of Bostonians, and ordered Suffolk's defiance, with Congress's supporting statements, to be published in the newspapers. Galloway in his later recollections unconsciously hinted at an explanation of the American Revolution when he observed that the rebellious spirit burned most hotly in the neighborhood of the British Army. This action of the First Congress, supporting Boston and Suffolk County, stated the philosophical theme of what was to become the American Revolution: the Intolerable Acts, because intolerable, were null and void.

II

The endorsement of the Suffolk Resolves showed a current of feeling which, if not deflected, would flow strongly enough to erode every foundation of loyalty. A royalist with the help of moderates—that is, with the help of men only moderately exasperated—tried to turn the stream with a constructive plan for an institution able to prevent insufferable British behavior in the future. The royalist was Joseph Galloway, the same who had frustrated Thomson's election and had been rebuffed in his offer of the State House as a meeting place.

Galloway suggested on September 28, 1774, what is known as the Galloway Plan, which would have provided for an Anglo-American legislature in America representing all North American colonies and dealing only with intercolonial affairs. The King would appoint its president general and the assemblies would elect its legislators, known collectively as the Grand Council, for terms of three years. This body would be an "inferior and distinct branch of the British legislature," and the assent of both the Parliament in England and the Grand Council in America would be required to make statutes that were binding in America.[16] Inasmuch as the president general would have some executive authority and would be named by the King, Galloway was proposing to unite the angry Americans in a kind of viceroyalty.

Joseph Galloway was a respected lawyer who had served twenty years in the assembly where with Benjamin Franklin he had joined the movement to dispossess the Penn family and to royalize the province. In the obscurity that nowadays shrouds even the most eminent of loyalists, he stands as a pathetic figure who loved both King and country and who made the painful choice of George III over America when he had to choose irrevocably. In 1765 he had foreseen that "Democratic notions in America may lead to the independence of the Colonies from England."[17] Writing to Governor William Franklin of New Jersey (Benjamin Franklin's illegitimate son) on the eve of the First Continental Congress, he told much about his temperament when he casually referred to England as "Home."[18]

In a later explanation of his motives for offering his plan, Galloway said he entered the Congress to seek a means of reconciliation, but he found the Congress more inflammatory than conciliatory. The Congress was then considering two proposals, first, a demand for a return to the status of 1763, which was a generalized and indecisive proposition specifying neither grievances nor reforms, and, second, an economic boycott of Britain, which would be at once illegal and provocative of more British reprisals. Galloway's plan tried to be both precise and soothing.[19]

Galloway's design aroused considerable and respectable support. The best remembered of his allies were James Duane and John Jay of New York, and Edward Rutledge of South Carolina. Duane was a successful lawyer, and no coward. On the Stamp Act issue he had alienated New York radicals, and was elected to the First Continental Congress over their opposition. When he had to face the break with Britain he chose rebellion and worked hard in the Congress thereafter. He was often suspected of softness toward loyalism, though he spent himself almost wholly in the service of congressional committees. Jay always stood by him, and Duane won the confidence of New York radicals in the long run, at least so far as his devotion to independence was concerned.

Edward Rutledge, acting in character, said he came to the Congress to get a Bill of Rights and some plan of permanent relief from British domineering. He thought Galloway's plan was almost perfect and could be made agreeable to everybody.[20]

For Galloway to succeed required that the members of the Congress tremble with fear of Britain, or feel much gratitude to Britain for past favors. It would also have helped if Galloway himself had been a highly popular politician. As for fear of Britain, men easily frightened would not have come to the Congress. Gratitude? Patrick Henry was probably representative of his peers when he said the British had been well repaid for any help to America by the profits from their monopoly of American trade. As usual when once uncorked, Henry fizzed over. He went on to say that any new legislative body set up in imitation of the House of Commons would be bribed like the House of Commons, because the British claimed bribery to be part of their system of government. Actually the Galloway Plan suffered more from the conservative reputation of its author than from any intrinsic demerits. Galloway's Pennsylvania adversaries managed to convince the outlanders that he belonged to the category of loyalists that each delegate most despised in his home province. Galloway's proposition was dead on the day he introduced it, but the Congress let it linger by resolving to postpone, six states to five states, and did not kill the scheme overtly until late in October.

Franklin, who appears to have had a genuine respect for Galloway's character, was in London in the winter of 1774–1775. He commented on the plan to Galloway in February, perhaps concealing irony beneath a solemnity of manner. He argued somewhat as Patrick Henry had argued, that a closer union with Britain would corrupt America. He advised Galloway not to bring his plan forward again unless circumstances changed radically. The proposed union could not succeed, he wrote, unless Parliament repealed the Declaratory Act of 1765 (which announced Parliament's complete authority over America), and repealed all duties applicable to America, all statutes altering colonial charters, and all laws restraining manufactures. Then the new union could re-enact the Navigation Acts and their necessary regulatory duties, which would be collected by colonials and paid into colonial treasuries.[21]

As well ask the Royal Navy to convert to birchback canoes.

Thus died the faint and only hope of reconciliation. What the Ministry might have done with Galloway's conception cannot be known, but the rejection of the plan led Galloway to decline membership in the next Congress. Our measure of greatness in that generation is success. By that criterion Joseph Galloway was a minor figure, but if he had succeeded in 1774 tourists might now throng some place associated with him, as pilgrims to a shrine.

III

By mid-October the Congress was ready to speak out strongly, and speak it did in the Declaration and Resolves, a statement which went about as far as possible short of war itself. It denounced the "impolitic, unjust, and cruel" Coercive Acts, repudiated practically all revenue measures since 1763, denied the validity of changing the jurisdictions of courts and the powers of assemblies, and damned the presence of a standing army. The rights of the colonists appeared in ten resolutions, of which the most memorable claimed "life, liberty, and property," and reserved exclusive power of "taxation and internal polity" to the colonial assemblies. The Congress specifically listed thirteen Acts of Parliament that were "infringement and violations of the rights of the colonists. . . ." The document concluded with the threat of an economic boycott of Britain, the promise of further apologetics addressed to the British and American publics, and notice that "a loyal Address to His Majesty" was in preparation.[22]

Notable omissions from the inventory of evils were any references to the Navigation Acts or to the practice of paying the salaries of the governors from royal funds. The strongest resolution included was by John Adams, saying that participation in lawmaking was the foundation of free government, that it was physically impossible for Americans to sit in Parliament, hence legislation for Americans could be enacted only by American legislatures. Although this might be misread as complete independence, the Congress let it stand. The

Quebec Act was one of the thirteen British statutes condemned. Duane noticed a cynical motive for its listing: it would meet "the popular clamor in England"[23] where the Ministry had been most savagely criticized for giving even half a loaf to the papistic idolaters of Canada. The whole statement, though phrased legalistically, was pretty wroth. No doubt the authors remembered that in the tumults since 1763 no Crown defenders had died, but six Crown opponents had been killed.

The Congress next attacked the British economy, proving the sincerity of the American dissent by drafting a self-denying agreement known as the Association.[24] The delegates accepted it with remarkable unanimity. The purpose was to provoke the British merchants who traded with America into pressing their own government to quit annoying the Americans. In the eighteenth century it was widely believed that Europe was economically dependent on America, because America was such an important source of raw materials and provided such a profitable market for European manufactures. Believing this, the American dissidents were surely wise in urging the application of such leverage. The Association—which resembled a project drafted some weeks earlier by irritated Virginians—pledged the colonies through their delegates to buy nothing from Great Britain. It also proposed the abolition of the maritime slave trade, and the promotion of sheep husbandry to relieve America of its reliance upon the British textiles industry. The signatories revealed a puritanical heritage by promising "to discountenance and discourage every species of extravagance and dissipation," from gambling to having fun at funerals. The closing paragraphs provided ways to heap public odium on those who did not comply with the Association.

There is no evidence of any congressional disagreement on the Association. It appears to have been signed on October 22. Two members who were absent had signed the preliminary draft, and another absentee ordered his name appended. Six were absent and did not sign. Apparently all of the others signed.

The adoption of the Association had a strong psychological impact. In the minds of those to whom the Association was intended to apply, it probably had the effect of establishing the Congress as a government, whether legitimate or tyrannical, and a government which was (or pretended to be) above the government of Britain.

For enforcement the Congress relied upon the extra-legal anti-British bodies abounding in the colonies, mostly Committees of Correspondence. The enforcers were not always gentle with those who bought British. This placing of neighbor over neighbor as overseers of private conduct provoked the first continental crisis of loyalism versus rebellion. Local magnates who held back from joining the Association sometimes found it necessary to flee to the protection of the King's armed forces. Lesser folk who would not sign often suffered neighborhood ostracism at the least. Ridicule was a weapon. Mercy Warren used it when she wrote a poem satirizing women who felt an irrestistible need for imported manufactures. The puritanism written into the Association was an ominous portent, for a puritanical strain has shown itself at the outset of almost every modern revolution.

The Association was rather hard on the great merchants, but merchants were not loved and trusted by the agrarian leaders of 1774, who greatly outnumbered the seaport personages in the protest against British policy. As Thomas Jefferson later put it, merchants had no country. On the other hand, the invisible self-blockade encouraged an impulse toward manufacturing because of the obvious necessity of making what the colonists refused to import legally and could not smuggle freely, and because manufacturing relieved the country of dependence on merchants.[25] The precise economic effect on Great Britain could not be measured for lack of statistical skills, but, as usual, men made their own estimates of reality and then guided themselves by those estimates. Edmund Burke thought the United Kingdom escaped economic disaster only by good luck. He estimated the North American trade as a seventh of the whole trade of the United Kingdom. To lose that fraction would have been very painful except that the end of East European turbulences and a newly made Balkan peace opened markets which made up for the American export losses. Furthermore, the immediate increase of British military spending helped manufactures, and the chartering of troop transports helped shipping. The Association swelled one branch of British wholesale trade, because supplies for the West Indies which were formerly bought in North America now came from Europe.[26] One benefit to British creditors was unforeseen: Americans seem to have paid the larger part of their debts to British merchants while they were abstaining from buying anything.[27] The British merchants did not know it, but it would be years before the remaining debts were paid.

The Congress also drafted an invitation to the people of Quebec to make common cause with their neighbors to the south, which few ever did. The address told the Canadians they too suffered from tyranny and invited them to send delegates to the next Congress. This approach to the French Canadians was the least successful of congressional gambits, simply because the governor general of Canada prevented the circulation of the statement. There is no reason to think the address would have made much impress if it had been nailed to every barn in Lower Canada. Its rhetoric and philosophy were strange to *les habitants* who had their own quite different complaints about the administration of the Empire. But the address to the Canadians had an effect on the American rebels, for it became a kind of building block in the structure of American political philosophy, and the rebel press drew on it later as a good explanation of the principles of liberty.[28]

Before adjournment the delegates wrote a sincere and respectful petition to their King, asking him to remedy their evils. John Dickinson was its principal author, though Richard Henry Lee and Patrick Henry wrote drafts that had some influence on the final text. To show their high regard for the services of secretary Charles Thomson, the delegates voted to give him a piece of plate to cost fifty pounds sterling, and to show their high regard for their own lives and limbs they resolved that if anyone seized or tried to seize any person in America to take him overseas for trial of any offense alleged to have been committed in any American county, he could expect "to meet with resistance and reprisal."[29] This was the first hint that the Congress might try systematically to organize the use of force. Then they adjourned, agreeing to meet again on May 10, 1775, unless they received a redress of grievances. The choice of May 10 can be used to support either the accidental or the providential interpretation of history. It was to fall exactly twenty-two days after the shot heard round the world from Concord Bridge, and was to give the Congress exactly the time needed to assemble to systematize the use of force in 1775.

The First Continental Congress, although biased against the Coercive Acts, provided a better sample of American opinion than any later Continental Congress, because warm royalists would not be seen in later congresses. A more artful British Ministry might have come to an understanding with these men by trading some of the glittering marks of imperial majesty in exchange for a strengthening of the economic bonds of empire, to the mutual advantage of both the realm and the dominions beyond the seas. But Frederick North's Ministry and Frederick North's King lacked the necessary imagination. They missed this chance, and it never came again. Joseph Galloway had two attributes of a prophet. He lacked honor among about half the people of his home town, and he correctly predicted that the measures of this Congress "tended to incite America to sedition & terminated in Independence."[30]

CHAPTER

2

From Ink to Blood

Pamphlet warfare was the normal condition of political life in the English-speaking world during the eighteenth century. In the dispute over the relations of Great Britain and the North American colonies, the argument was a constitutional argument which relied strongly on political philosophy. The antagonists had to rely on political philosophy since there were few legal precedents on which to lean. It may be questioned whether political philosophy is a selfless search for abstract truth or a rationalization of the secret wishes of the thinkers and their allies. After all, the number of political philosophers who have sketched ideal political systems in which political philosophers would have no share of power must be very small. But regardless of the ultimate purposes of the writers, they appealed to settled convictions (or prejudices) on both sides and thus gave us samples of the logic (or watchwords) that leaders thought would help their causes.

After the Boston Tea Party of 1773 British pamphleteers canvassed their theories of empire, and most of them predictably affirmed the dependence of the colonies and the supremacy of Parliament. Colonials replied most effectively in the resolutions of the First Continental Congress, which were not so much arguments as bluntly stated axioms, but they also brought out their own counter-tracts.

The exchange of literary salvos pinned the polemicists of both sides in positions from which they could not retreat.

In August, before the meeting of the First Continental Congress, James Wilson of Pennsylvania produced his *Considerations on the Nature and Extent of the Legislative Authority of the British Parliament*.[1] The gist of his argument follows: The idea that men might lose their liberty by leaving Britain was not only ignominious but dangerous. Surely the British would be shocked at any notion of making the House of Commons independent of *them*, but the Americans are required "to trust the security of our liberties" to British "veneration for the dictates of natural justice"—a very shaky support. The arrangement was not only illogical but illegal. As early as the reign of Richard III all judges agreed that Parliament did not bind the Irish, although the Irish were personally subject to the King in the same way as the people of the King's French holdings. The only contrary right the British could claim would be the right of conquest, which did not apply to their American colonies. And the Commons could give no right to bind their fellow and equal subjects. In America all government was in the name of the King, not Parliament, and Americans rightly acknowledged their dependence on him. So far as trade was concerned, its regulation was properly a function of the Crown.

Wilson thus made each American—that is, each white American— the equal of an Englishman, with whom he shared a king in common. It may have seemed revolutionary, but it was not novel. He had gone all the way back to *Calvin's Case* (1608), which concerned the relations of England and Scotland under one king. Wilson's concluding pages were merely a collection of ideas and quotations from a case argued while the first colonists were starving at Jamestown.[2]

Thomas Jefferson was not a delegate to the Congress, but his teeming mind was represented in the polemic literature of the moment by his *Summary View of the Rights of the British Colonies*.[3] Like Wilson, Jefferson argued that the only union of Britons and Americans was through the Crown. The tone of his essay was that of a voice which presumed to speak for the colonies as a unit. Since his piece appeared shortly before Wilson's, he must be credited as first to utter the federal principle on which the colonies ultimately united as states under the federal constitution.[4] And, again like Wilson, he denounced the regulation of trade by Parliament—a view of the place of Parliament in the Empire which even parliamentary friends of America could not accept. Parliament's right to regulate the trade of the Empire was the last claim it would surrender.

John Adams had concluded that Britain's monopoly of imperial trade was acceptable so far as it helped the common good, even though it made prices higher than Americans would pay if they could shop the world. The difference he saw as a tax on America for the common good.[5] He could have added that the "tax" went into private pockets, and that Parliament might have been more innocently employed in taxing the profits of the sellers than in taxing the buyers.

Back home in Massachusetts, after the Congress adjourned, Adams found cause to mutter over a series of letters in a Boston newspaper by Daniel Leonard, signing himself "Massachusettensis" and praising the Anglo-American way of life. Adopting the pen name "Novanglus,"[6] Adams dipped his quill and went for Leonard. Where, he demanded angrily, did the Parliament of the United Kingdom get any rights at all in these matters? Every colony (except Georgia) existed before the Act of Union of 1707 brought Parliament into being. The Stuarts could as reasonably have governed America through the Scottish Parliament. As for American representation in Parliament, the colonists would need 250 seats for equitable representation. And what of Ireland, India, Jamaica, Africa? And then transoceanic peers? And what if Americans came to outnumber all others?

Political philosophy, masked as constitutional controversy, seemed to raise more questions than answers. The deadlock of empire was approaching. Looking back at the argument it is not at all clear that the British proved that the ability to pay confers a right to demand payment, which is a fair statement of their case as proclaimed in America. Earlier Americans accepted taxes to regulate external trade. In the 1760's they protested the Stamp Act as an *internal* tax, then fought the Townshend Duties as *revenue* measures, and, finally, after the Coercive Acts, opposed all parliamentary taxation, regulatory or revenue-producing, internal or external. And what is not described in the polemics is the outrageous behavior of the lower-level British administrators in America whose very presence came to be personally obnoxious. The American response to the problem of empire had been to ask the entire removal of Parliament from American affairs. This asked more of Englishmen than they could give, because it revived the memory of the Stuart claims to a broad royal prerogative. Englishmen who gloried in the memory of the reduction of the monarchy to manageable size in the Glorious Revolution had to insist on the supremacy of the blended institution they called the King-in-Parliament. They could not separate the crown of King from the mace of Commons. The structure of British politics barred a solution of the American problem.

II

The Coercive Acts not only failed to daunt Massachusetts but brought on a state of armed deadlock in the province which made it impossible for the new governor, General Thomas Gage, to govern.[7] Leaders of the native opposition frustrated the organization of the new courts which were contemplated by the Massachusetts Government Act. Events of the autumn proved that Gage could rule in Boston because he had an army, but he could not rule elsewhere in Massachusetts unless he sent his army wherever he wished a royal writ to run. Indignant at the "Intolerable Acts," town meetings busied themselves with refitting and invigorating their neighborhood militia companies. Gage tried to thwart the towns' military preparations, but the response to his counter-measures only showed the heat of the opposition. For example, on September 1, 1774, he sent men across the Charles River from Boston to Charlestown where they seized 250 barrels of gunpowder and then marched to Cambridge and took two field guns recently acquired by the town militia. The detachment met no forcible opposition, but rumor ran wild with the false report of the killing of six Americans at Charlestown. The news reached Shrewsbury, forty miles away, at midnight, and by nightfall of September 2 four thousand armed men had assembled in the vicinity. On the next day Israel Putnam heard that the Royal Navy had bombarded Boston. About forty thousand armed men were moving toward Boston before they learned the rumors of bloodshed and naval bombardment were untrue.[8]

In such a state of public feeling Massachusetts was ungovernable outside the town of Boston, which by now was merely a British Army post. Royal authority extended no farther than the range of royal artillery. As in so many instances of the application of a scourging policy, the parliamentary attempt to hold the dignity of a province for ransom had stimulated resistance, enlivened agitators, and, in the long run, seemed to scare the executors of the policy more than the victims.

Although Boston was thronged with unemployed men, Gage could not get workmen to repair his fortifications or build barracks for his troops. When a few laborers succumbed to job offers, a joint committee of the Boston Selectmen and the Committee of Correspondence persuaded them to quit. Committees in thirteen nearby towns said they looked on men who supplied or worked for the garrison as "most inveterate enemies."[9] To get the work done the governor had to import labor from Nova Scotia.

Gage had become a pessimist, with good reason. Several times in late 1774 he told his superiors in Britain he would need twenty thousand troops to reduce New England to obedience. The despairing reports from the Massachusetts governor merely lowered him in the eyes of the incredulous ministers and made them doubt his judgment and ability. Surely the government was properly warned, but Gage never had enough status to say "I told you so." In the many years that he had been senior officer in America, the Army in America decayed. Its officers lacked audacity and, in a few instances, simple honesty. Lodged among free-spirited white Americans the Army was becoming Americanized, partly through intermarriage and less regular arrangements. (Gage himself had an American wife, but she did not weaken his will to loyalty.) Life on the American station may have blunted the Army as the cutting edge of British policy.

Gage had dissolved the Massachusetts legislature after the summoning of the Continental Congress. In the fall of 1774 the towns held new elections, without new authorization from the governor. The new body met in Salem, awaited the governor's pleasure, and, when he did not appear, named itself the Provincial Congress. For executive it appointed a Committee of Public Safety, to which were added a Committee of Supplies, and officers to command the militia. The Committee of Supplies immediately took charge of feeding Boston through the port of Marblehead.

While the new Committee of Supplies began its corporal works of mercy, the new militia generals Artemas Ward and Seth Pomeroy had some merciless work to do. The first task was the political purification of the force. For example, the colonels of half of the province's thirty militia regiments were loyalists, as had been the previous commanding general. Starting with Worcester County in 1774, all of the officers resigned. The anti-British officers did it gladly, but the loyalists took a certain amount of persuasion. Each town then elected its own company officers, and the company officers elected the field officers. And thus the Provincial Congress assured the political soundness of the militia. At the same time the officers of each company listed some of their men who were to act at a minute's notice—the famed Minute Men (who were voted out of existence the next spring).[10] Nor did Massachusetts act alone. In the winter of 1774–75 Rhode Islanders took forty-two big guns from a public battery and carried them to Providence, while New Hampshire men forcibly seized field pieces, many barrels of gunpowder, and fifteen hundred muskets.

New England had become an unstable compound in real danger of detonation. Joseph Warren, Samuel Adams's able co-agitator, wrote to Arthur Lee, who served in London with Benjamin Franklin as joint agent for Massachusetts, to say that Yankee patience was running out after ten years of counteracting unconstitutional British plans. Reconciliation was yet possible, but if Gage tried to march his soldiery out to enforce the Coercive Acts "Great Britain may take her leave, at least of the New-England colonies, and, if I mistake not, of all America."[11] Within a fortnight it was Warren's turn again to deliver the annual oration commemorating the Boston Massacre, a ceremony devised by Adams, Warren, and company to encourage the good people of Massachusetts to keep their minds on tyranny. Warren began by warning orphans not to slip *"on the stones bespattered with your father's brains,"* dwelt on the "villains, traitorous alike to king and country" who badly counseled an otherwise "gracious prince," advised young men to study the British troops in order to learn to be soldiers, and closed with a reference to "the inhuman miscreant, who, to secure the loaves and fishes to himself, would breed a serpent to destroy his children."[12]

Warren's fiercely inflammatory language, at any time before the death of King James I, could have cost him his bowels and head for *lèse majesté* and incitement to treason. Forty-four days later the War for Independence began. And two months after that Warren was shot dead at the battle of Bunker Hill.

III

Frederick North, son of the Earl of Guilford and called by courtesy Lord North, was not at all a wicked man. King George's First Minister can be characterized by the adjectives humorous, procrastinating, lazy, loyal, flexible. In politics he thought the means were more important than the ends, that a good law was a law that passed with little wrangling. Several times when the going was rough he tried to resign, but King George needed fidelity and elasticity in the job and North provided both qualities. It was hard to dislike this chubby chap with the protruding eyes who could occasionally convulse the House with a spontaneous quip.

A man like North who so disliked contention ought really to have been more sensitive to its onset. Serious contention was forecast in the news of the First Continental Congress coming from America in the winter of 1774–1775, even though communications were slow, erratic, and biased. Nevertheless it is possible to write the history of the "American War" from the British side with very little reference to any Continental Congress. To the British administrators, North included, the Congresses seem to have been regarded as little more than nuisances. The Ministry's evaluation was fatally wrong. Intelligent reflection on the unprecedented proceedings of the First Continental Congress should have made it plain that Britain faced a serious problem. The Congress was unique in colonial history, its procedures were rational, its conclusions—despite the anger that stimulated the meeting—were founded more on logic than on passion, and its attitude, while conciliatory, was decidedly firm. Perhaps it is the clarity of hindsight that is so revealing, but, all things considered, it seems that the Ministry should at least have planned for the possibility of grave and forcible resistance.

But the First Continental Congress impressed Britons so little that its Address to the King was disregarded. Benjamin Franklin reported that he tried five times on his own to get the document moving through channels but failed.[13] Eventually he and the other American agents, who had become men of little influence, managed to get it into North's office, whence it went to Parliament after the

Christmas recess as a document numbered 149 in a great heap of papers which received no special consideration.[14] In any case, months had passed and much had happened to make it rather late to open a debate on a transatlantic petition for redress of grievances.

During the critical winter of 1774–1775 the Earl of Dartmouth, Secretary at State for the Colonies, carried on indirect negotiations with Franklin who learned for the hundredth time the theory that the British Empire could not exist without the doctrine of the supremacy of Parliament, and the colonists, like all British subjects, were either subordinate to Parliament or were independent. This was exactly contrary to the position advanced in the resolutions of the First Continental Congress, and as long as the Ministry held to this theory of empire it would be impossible to reconcile imperial control with local home rule. No alternatives remained for skeptical colonists except to submit, to resist forcibly, or to hurt Britain badly enough in the pocketbook to persuade the royal metaphysicians to re-examine their philosophical position. The colonists had begun the economic attack. If it failed, submission was unthinkable. But forcible resistance was thinkable.

The best offer Franklin received in these lectures on polity was a shapeless promise: virtual home rule linked to tacit recognition of the authority of Parliament if it were not exercised too vigorously. This was a cloudy proposition which ministers could very easily repudiate. Even so, it was more generous than any dream of Dartmouth's successor, Lord George Germain, to whom such a proposal would have seemed like a syllogism published in Bedlam Hospital.

To British political leaders who were bound by a theory of parliamentary supremacy there seemed to be no reason to yield a thing to the Americans. No Ministry had yet lost portfolios because of a dispute on a colonial issue, and the North Ministry was the strongest that had yet served King George III. The elections of 1774 proved there was a great trust in Lord North's leadership. He needed no support from any of the splinter groups in Parliament. The American colonial agents and the British merchants trading to America had once been a fairly effective lobby when working together, but in the winter of 1774–1775 it no longer seemed necessary for parliamentarians to consider the feelings of that uneasy and declining alliance. On the other hand, North himself was too easygoing to be intransigent. Although he was unwilling to weaken the power of Parliament over the colonies, he was much too amiable to prefer

From Ink to Blood

force over persuasion, and favored compromising specific issues if he could avoid compromising parliamentary authority.

William Pitt, Earl of Chatham, longtime friend of American local government but no enemy of parliamentary supremacy, took the floor on the first day after he had official access to the proceedings of the First Continental Congress (January 19, 1775) and moved to take the redcoats out of Boston. He lost by North's usual majority of three to one. North was too dilatory to bring out his own thoughts before Chatham again proposed an American solution (February 1), moving to recognize the Continental Congress, to pledge not to tax without consent of the colonial assemblies, to require American recognition of parliamentary supremacy, and to require the Continental Congress to vote a revenue for the Crown. The government defeated him as easily as before.

North had not been idle. In January he and the Cabinet agreed to offer the colonies exemption from all but regulatory taxes if they paid up methodically by committing themselves permanently to meet a colonial civil-service payroll. After brushing aside Chatham's four-point American program, North prepared the ground by successfully moving to proclaim a state of rebellion in Massachusetts (so Gage could use force), and then moved the exemption proposition. The Commons admired North's crafty scheme and voted for it 274 to 88 (February 27). It must have been fun, and it only cost them an empire. This ransom note went off to America four days later. North could not expect unanimous consent in America for his policy, but he could hope that at least one colony would take it, thus breaking the united front of the First Continental Congress.[15] By postal coincidence, the geniality of the American reception of "North's Conciliation" was marred by its arriving at the same time as two later acts of Parliament which barred Americans from fishing on the Grand Banks and from trading outside the Empire. North's pill was bitter-coated.

Benjamin Franklin, who had one of the keenest minds in the world, had been drearily dickering with official clods in London all winter. By the end of February he gave up. Of "North's Conciliation" he thought that such an arrangement was not "giving our own property freely" because it did not allow the Americans to judge their ability to pay. It was as if a highwayman had said, "Give me your purse, and then I will not put my hand into your pocket. But give me all your money, or I will shoot you through the head."[16]

29

Edmund Burke, the most memorably myopic member of the House of Commons, who wore spectacles most of the time, had a clearer vision of the state of the world than his colleagues. The disheveled Burke was prone to impatience, but when really moved he could be as clear and cool as ice. As agent employed by New York to represent its interests in Britain, he was especially well informed on American moods. On March 22 he delivered his famous oration on conciliation with America, stating the case in a manner which has carried conviction to posterity; but he failed to convince his contemporaries, in part because they left their benches empty while he spoke. The two ablest British minds of that generation, Chatham and Burke, had warned their colleagues of the folly of the government, but North's majorities remained as large after they spoke as they had been before. In addition to Chatham and Burke, the American parliamentary case may have had a third author, for it is possible that Burke drew on conversations with Benjamin Franklin.[17]

Parliament seemed to go out of its way to be mulish. On behalf of his New York employers, agent Burke presented a remonstrance against recent British policy. It was politely phrased and emphasized loyalty as much as disagreement. But the House of Commons voted adversely—not to table it, not to postpone consideration, either of which would be understandable if impolitic, but, more harshly, the House voted not even to receive the remonstrance. Surely the British parliamentary majority showed no sense of fraternity with their American fellow subjects. In fact, heterogeneous America had a more brotherly attitude toward Britain than Britain had toward America. If the hostility of the Parliament toward America in 1774 and 1775 had a rational ground it was probably a belief that Americans were ungrateful descendants of malcontents. There is no evidence that a majority of the ruling group had the slightest doubt of the justice and propriety of British policy toward America.

IV

Had there been a method of measuring public opinion in the winter of 1774–1775, it seems likely that anti-British feeling would have been recorded as warm in Virginia and heating up as the pollsters moved north. Anger positively blazed in Boston, where the feeling of the people toward their scarlet-coated garrison was ugly. Joseph Galloway had correctly noted that hostility to Britain was strongest wherever the British Army took its station.

The Provincial Congress of Massachusetts, self-created in Salem, moved its seat to Concord in February 1775, about the time the British Parliament was approving the proclamation to define the condition of Massachusetts as rebellion. Governor Gage kept a pair of spies in Concord. One was probably Dr. Benjamin Church, a member of the Committee of Safety, publicly a fiery radical, but privately burdened with an extra-marital second household, the lady of which found the cost of living high and put Dr. Church into such a position that espionage afforded welcome financial relief. The other spy, unknown, wrote his observations in schoolboy French, which hints that he may have been a British officer. Gage, from his agents or from the simple evidence of his own senses, knew the public temper was unfriendly. A man of transcendent genius might have worked out a plan to disarm the rapidly rearming militia and to disrupt the parallel extra-legal government which actually ruled in Massachusetts outside the town limits of Boston. But Gage was merely an adequate model of an eighteenth-century major general, and no wizard. He was lucky to keep the peace that winter.[18] A very clever man might have managed to fetter John Hancock. Instead Gage asked him to help persuade the workmen to put up barracks for the troops who were suffering a New England winter with inadequate shelter and no sympathy.

The countryside seemed to look forward with pleasure to the possibility of an attempt by Governor Gage to govern the province. Gage's secret agents reported the remarks of armed men—perhaps duck hunters?—who, when asked by friends what they were hunting, replied succinctly, "Redcoats," or who inquired whether there were any Tories around. Without knowing the whole story one may suspect that these were the remarks of village jokers who knew that strangers were eavesdropping. Even so, their conversation showed no reverence for the laws and servants of their anointed King. Gage's men were trying systematically to estimate the temper of the people, to take an inventory of the stores and munitions of the militia, and to learn the roads and terrain. In every town they found friends of the King to shelter them, but they also confirmed the reports of the baleful enmity of the populace.

While British agents and scouting parties roved the eastern counties of Massachusetts, the dissidents had no need to organize an espionage system. The Port Act filled the streets of Boston with unemployed and disaffected loungers who had nothing to do but keep their eyes on the hated garrison. It seems unlikely that a private soldier of the King could have scratched his nose unobserved. It has been said that American-born Margaret Gage fed headquarters facts to her fellow countrymen, but this is slander. Even if she chose to betray her spouse, she could have passed on little the neighbors could not learn for themselves—except, perhaps, her husband's private desolation.

For month after month eastern Massachusetts lived in a state of armed truce. Supplies for Boston, even scarce wood for fuel, had to be unloaded at Marblehead and hauled down in wagons—nicknamed North's Coasters. Month after month passed without news of any government effort to resolve the deadlock. The Ministry in England shrugged off Gage's advice to use *enough* force if force was to be the solution, and thought him old-maidish. Instead of raising his strength from three thousand to twenty thousand men (which would have been none too many), the ministers sent Gage some marines and three major generals. They came in a ship named *Cerberus*, which gave local wits a theme on which to improvise a dozen canine variations.

These new officers were no better than Gage, and each was fated to have a conspicuously inglorious career in America. William Howe, made Knight of the Bath while in America, was the senior of the three. His brother Richard was Admiral Lord Howe and simultaneously commander of the Royal Navy on the American station for several years. Another brother was affectionately remembered in America, having left a heroic reputation when he died a soldier's death in the French and Indian War. General Howe claimed to be a friend of America, and had a reputation for strength, activity, and reticence. Either the reputation for military activity was groundless, or later events changed his personality, though he certainly showed heterosexual activity. Howe was an excellent executive. The parallel may seem strained, but he appears to have a good deal in common—as a soldier only—with a later soldier remembered as a good executive, General George B. McClellan. Another of the trio, Sir Henry Clinton, small, overweight, and dull, did the strict letter of his duty, occasionally showed ability and energy but no spark of brilliance, and rose only to mediocrity. He had a feeling of being unappreciated, and may well have been seriously neurotic. John Burgoyne, the junior of the three, was a handsome military figure, persuasive, likable, and quite at home in the clubs, theaters, and great houses of the class into which he fitted as the son-in-law of an earl. He hoped to win a golden entry in the book of military fame, and was willing to intrigue to be in the right place at the right time to gain his glory. If drawn as a literary character, Gentleman Johnny would be a little overwritten. He had literary ability of his own, however, and in another day might have made himself a playwright, even an actor-manager, for there was a touch of the ham in his official statements. In a rationally ordered army he would have been assigned as assistant chief of staff at the highest, never as commanding general.

Having sent this weak and redundant reinforcement, the Ministry then sent something more important: a secret dispatch which ordered the beleaguered Gage to lay hands on the leaders of the Massachusetts opposition. This was an order to pick up quicksilver barehanded. Those around the Boston headquarters who knew both the public temper and the secret dispatch knew that the crisis was upon them. The secret dispatch was the signal for some kind of action. The only action Gage could perform was military action. The military clash that followed was therefore the result of the Ministry's misreading of the American news. It was not Thomas Gage's idea.

Lord Dartmouth's secret dispatch to Governor Gage, dated February 22, 1775, began sententiously with the advice that force should be repelled by force. Reinforcements were on the way, and Gage should raise a loyalist corps. With these added forces he could then act more decisively—which was not the most delicate way of saying that his administration gave the appearance of indecision. His explicit orders were "to arrest the principal actors and abettors in the Provincial Congress . . . though such a proceeding should be . . . a signal for hostilities. . . ."[19] Gage should move with vigor even if it brought war.

Thus the explosion of America in the spring of 1775 was no isolated event, but, like practically everything that happens in public life, part of something that was already going on. With his weak force Gage had done about all he could to govern a province which was in a state of fury. He had strength only to hold Boston and to collect intelligence. He had also warned his government and his official colleagues in America, including the Indian superintendents, the commandant at Fort Ticonderoga, and the officers of the Royal Navy on the American station, that tumult might be expected. Like Joseph Galloway, he had the qualities of a prophet. He was correct, and not respected by his own people.

V

With the force at his disposal General Gage could undertake no strategic offensive to destroy the organization that set itself against Britain. Hence he decided to raid the nearest important concentration of militia stores as a pre-emptive strike against the strongest target within his reach. This was a mark of his military impotence, since all such operations are essentially defensive. As for the "principal actors and abettors" of the Provincial Congress, the wording of his orders could not mean to try to bag the whole Congress. (If he had tried, we know now, the members would have scattered, and it would have been like setting a net to catch the wind.) The "principal actors" were the leaders, and only one important leader, the inflammatory Joseph Warren, was in town at the time. The others were out of sight and out of grasp. At the moment Gage received Dartmouth's secret dispatch it is unlikely that he knew with certainty where the other leaders were. Gage had learned, however, that Worcester was the central supply depot of the militia, and that Concord had a large collection, according to one of his spies who said he knew where the munitions were concealed. Very well. It was a long march to Worcester, but Concord might be despoiled in a day. If the Ministry wished him to strike a blow, Concord seemed the place to strike. If the operation were carefully timed and executed, it just might be carried off with no more unpleasantness than the seizure of the gunpowder of Charlestown and the ordnance of Cambridge. On the other hand, if the British met resistance it would be the fault of the Americans in obstructing the duly commissioned governor of Massachusetts in the performance of his duty. Or so it probably seemed to Gage as he frowned over his dispatch from England.

From Ink to Blood

If Concord was the place, when should be the time? Gage next learned that the Provincial Congress was sitting at Concord, and was to recess on April 15. To raid Concord immediately after that would be to move when the Congress could not act because its membership would be traveling to their homes; being neither at home nor in session, they would be unable to exercise their asserted leadership. The old story that Gage intended to scoop up John Hancock and Samuel Adams, who were staying at Lexington, may be true, but there is no evidence to support the conjecture.[20]

Unit commanders received orders to be ready, but a garrison surrounded by the sullen population of a crowded peninsula had no privacy. The troops could not hide their preparations—all those last-minute tasks of soldiers who have just experienced an alerting movement order. That the redcoats were about to sally was clear to the Bostonians, but a gunner could replace a swab and a musketeer make cartridges without themselves knowing where they were going. As in all military camps under such circumstances, there were probably a half-dozen contrary and plausible rumors afloat. For an enemy it would be safest to guess that Concord was the objective, but the route to be marched was a matter of some consequence.

Watchers saw troops marching to the waterfront on the evening of April 18. Warren took charge. He sent William Dawes along the south bank of the Charles River to cross at Cambridge and take the road to Lexington, warning the country, and, particularly, getting word to Hancock and Samuel Adams of their personal danger. To make doubly sure of the efficacy of the alarm, and to warn the people between Charlestown and Lexington, Warren sent for the equestrian silversmith Paul Revere at about ten o'clock. The lantern signal so famous in American poetry had already been agreed upon, and Revere arranged for a friend to climb the North Church tower and to flash the light when the troops embarked. Revere dressed for the ride, crossed to Charlestown, borrowed a mare, saw the lantern flicker, and set out for Lexington. Having a shorter road to ride, he beat Dawes to Lexington by thirty minutes, leaving an aroused yeomanry behind him along the route the British were to march. But Revere did not reach Concord. Gage, the prudent professional, had a mounted patrol on the road, which picked up Revere. Luckily the alarm bearer had fallen in with young Dr. Samuel Prescott who had been visiting his girl in Lexington. Prescott escaped the patrol by jumping his horse over a wall and carried the news to Concord.

The British force of about seven hundred men under Lieutenant Colonel Francis Smith had ferried across the Charles during the night and tramped off toward Concord. Ahead of them heavy guns boomed, church bells rang, and muskets popped warnings in the dark. Any dullard knew this was no secret mission. Colonel Smith realized he would meet armed opposition, and wisely sent back to Boston for reinforcements.

An inch of rain fell in those parts on April 18, and then the sky cleared. That night and the next day were dry and crisp, with a temperature range from about 46 to 52 degrees and fair-weather clouds marching eastward under a hard blue sky.[21] (A little chilly for the Minute Man of the sculpture to be out without a jacket.) The rain made it too wet to plow on April 19, and there was nothing to keep a man on his farm unless his woodpile was low. His wife and children could milk the cows and feed the animals. It would have been a good day for repairing stone walls, but that could wait. He was interested in another kind of reparation.

The men of the Lexington town militia put aside any thought of chores or wall mending and walked to the town center with muskets in hand to follow their elected captain, John Parker. It was an odd hour for militia drill, but they were supposed to rally when warned. They did not know the world was turning upside down, but they knew Britain had overturned the customary ways of Massachusetts. They were ordinary village men clustered on Lexington Green awaiting the dawn, the British Army, and their captain's orders. At their best they could form only a rather straggly line against professionals who fought by reflex and drilled-in habit and who were forbidden to take thought for themselves. In a private sense, each Lexington man who reported for duty made an irrational decision. The approaching foe was the peer of the imperialist world's mercenary soldiers; there could be no material profit from such a fight so far as Lexington was immediately concerned; and the villagers were singularly lacking in pomp and circumstance and heroic ambitions. They were there not because of logic but because of the passion of anger. Their British betters might do this sort of thing in other places to lesser breeds, but not in Middlesex County where generations of free white men, mostly of English descent, had minded their own business.

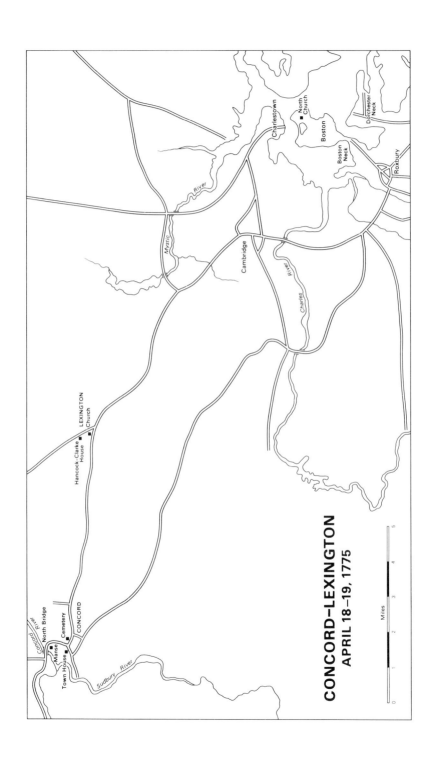

CONCORD–LEXINGTON
APRIL 18–19, 1775

The British troops trudged into view by the day's first light to see a mere seventy amateurs drawn up to oppose a thousand professionals. The militia position was ridiculous—a line in the open across the route the British intended to use. Captain Parker realized the futility of his gesture, and when Major John Pitcairn trotted forward to tell him to disperse his men he seemed about to comply. Then *somebody* fired a shot, other shots came, volleys blasted the militia company out of the way, and a world war had started. A fourth of the Lexington company were hit: eight dead, ten wounded. One British soldier received a wound.

Because of the political impact of the event, both sides denied having fired that first fatal shot and went on proving their innocence for years, until the puzzle became insoluble and a heap of contradictory documents accumulated.[22] Paul Revere, who was within earshot, thought someone had fired a shot "which appeared to be a pistol." A pistol would be the arm of a mounted man, hence a British officer, rather than a village musketeer. But he put it in writing twenty-five years later, a delay which reduced the weight of his testimony.[23]

The British marched on to Concord and occupied the village. Men of three light-infantry companies went to hold the rude bridge which arches the flood separating Concord from the neighbors north and west, in order to prevent those neighbors from interfering with what had by now become a futile enterprise. The well-warned Concordians had removed most of the military stores that Gage intended to confiscate. Colonel Smith's troopers could only spoil some barrels of flour, pull down the local Liberty Pole, and smash a few shovels and gun carriages. Meanwhile, three or four hundred farmers converged on the western approach to the bridge, most from the town of Lincoln. The British infantry, apparently rather nervous, fired several warning shots which frightened nobody. Then they fired a volley into the growing body of irate rustics on the far side of the bridge. Perhaps the commander of this detachment had panicked, for his volley was loosed at a range of seventy-five yards, which was about twenty-five yards farther than would be tactically effective. It killed only two Americans, and drew upon the bridge guard a rush of shooting men who killed one British soldier outright, mortally wounded two, and hit nine others. These attacking amateurs outnumbered the British about three to one. The skirmish lasted perhaps five minutes, during which the British lost the bridge and lost the first hotly contested "battle" of the War for Independence. It was a small engagement, but, as Emerson so indelibly observed, its echoes were heard round the world.

Having done what little the people of Concord left them to do, the regulars set out on the road to Boston at mid-day. It had been a long march out, with just a little butchery thrown in, but worse was coming. By this time the nearby militia all knew the British were out in force and were hurrying to do them harm. The militia had neither central command nor useful communications between units, but wherever cover—a clump of vegetation, a stone wall—and armed farmers coincided, there the road reddened with blood. By the time the regulars were a mile out of Concord the local men, shielded mostly by the ubiquitous stone walls, immersed the enemy in sniper fire. When the weary column was half a mile past Lexington, and perhaps half an hour short of exhaustion, Brigadier the Earl Percy met them with about fifteen hundred men and two pieces of artillery in answer to Colonel Smith's earlier request for help. Under this protection the tired troops rested, but every passing minute saw the number of their opponents increase. When they set out again, despite the work of British flanking parties paralleling the road, the snipers were more dangerous than before. The routine withdrawal had become a stumbling but orderly retreat which continued under harassing fire until the soldiery reached Charlestown. From there they crossed to Boston that night, their passage covered by fresh troops under Brigadier Robert Pigot. They might have returned via Cambridge rather than Charlestown. The use of the Charlestown route disappointed the militia of Cambridge, who filled the buildings of Harvard College and prepared to charge a high toll of casualties for British passage through the town.

The total of British troops engaged in this inglorious sally was from 1,500 to 1,800. The number of Americans who opposed them could hardly have been less than 3,500. The British suffered 73 killed, 174 wounded, and 26 missing, a total of 273. The Americans lost 49 killed, 39 wounded (a number so small as to suggest that many slight injuries were never counted), and 5 missing, or 93 in all.

By sending Percy to rescue Smith near Lexington, and Pigot to cover both at Charlestown, Gage must have reduced the Boston garrison to fewer than thirteen hundred men. The men of Massachusetts might have recovered their capital by storm from the land side, and by amphibious operations along shore, but it did not occur to them. What a disaster had Gage lost his base at that critical moment! And what had he accomplished? Tactically considered, he sent a strong force into the countryside and managed to save it from massacre at the hands of disorganized, poorly trained, small bodies of despised apple-knockers. His sally drew thousands of militia to his perimeter. They made their headquarters at Cambridge and composed themselves into a raggle-taggle army which sat down to besiege Boston. In short, Gage had started a war.

The immediate popular reaction to the affair of Lexington and Concord showed the timidity or weakness of loyalism outside of Boston. Safe within the British lines some Boston civilians were pretty bloody-minded on the subject of the King's foes, but the people outside either applauded the militia or kept silence. The only large and immediately noticeable effect on the population of eastern Massachusetts—apart from the accumulation of sons, husbands, brothers, and fathers in the siege lines—was the partial and temporary evacuation of some of the coastal towns[24] in fear of naval reprisals, which showed an instinctive understanding of the meaning of sea power. Much better remembered than anything else said that day (if indeed it was said) is the remark attributed to Samuel Adams when he heard the gunfire at Lexington as he was fleeing the town with Revere, Hancock, and a box of Hancock's papers: "O! What a glorious morning this is!"[25]

The British certainly did not look invincible. But it would have been an entirely different story if the Concord raid had been a cavalry raid. Barring the unimaginable, it is hard to think it could have been a failure. Alas for Gage, he had no cavalry. On the American side, had there been some single command of these scattered town companies they could have placed themselves between the British and Boston, obstructed the road with felled trees, destroyed the flanking parties, and prevented Percy's reinforcement. All of this was well within their capacity but for the lack of central direction. Except that the Americans would have been willing to take prisoners, the catastrophe could have been as great as Braddock's disaster of 1755. But these are only speculations on what might have been.

On what *did* happen, the Americans are open to serious criticism. Given their disorganization, their inexperience, their total lack of communications, they still should have been able to shoot their smooth-bore muskets. Assuming 3,500 Americans, it ought to be fair to estimate that from 3,500 to 75,000 rounds were fired, and struck home fewer than three hundred times. No matter how one measures it, it seems safe to say, "In all his day's work, only one man out of 15 hit anybody."[26] That was American military capacity at the moment: excellent morale, no command, no communications, wretched musketry.

VI

On the bright spring day when Gage's troops had such a miserable outing in the country, their harassed commander sent word to the senior officer in Canada, Sir Guy Carleton, telling him that Fort Ticonderoga on Lake Champlain should be reinforced immediately by sending a regiment there. But the rebellious colonials had thought about the Lake Champlain region and Canada much earlier, probably not later than the previous February. The Boston Committee of Correspondence, or perhaps Samuel Adams acting in its name, seems to have sent a Pittsfield lawyer named John Brown to spy out the land. In Canada he talked to some Old Subjects, that is, recently arrived English-speakers, who said they sympathized with the colonial grievances (perhaps they disliked the Quebec Act). They told Brown not to worry about the *habitants* helping the British, and that the Indians would be little inclined to aid Carleton in a crisis.

Brown sent back an optimistic report urging an attack on Fort Ticonderoga as soon as war started. He said the Green Mountain Boys of Vermont promised to take the weakly defended fort, which was filled with military stores and armed with useful heavy guns. If Crown Point could also be taken, the road to Canada would be open. When Brown left Montreal he left an espionage net behind him.[27] Brown's operation surely supports almost any conspiracy theory of the American Revolution which one could imagine. It all happened weeks before the Lexington-Concord blood-spilling. Brown assumed war to be inevitable, and an impartial grand jury could hardly avoid indicting him for treason if such a jury had ever been convened to study the matter. Gage's letter to Carleton of April 19 was pathetically tardy.

Shortly after the beginning of the siege of Boston, Benedict Arnold, merchant and sea captain of Connecticut, received permission from the Massachusetts Committee of Safety to recruit up to four hundred men for a surprise attack on the British on and near Lake Champlain. He had no authority to take over the command of any other officer's troops. When he went west he found Ethan Allen with a large body of tough Vermonters under his command, getting ready to move on Ticonderoga. Arnold joined as a volunteer. Ethan Allen was a consistent character: a braggart ready to back up his bravado with force, an intensely provincial patriot much moved by the prospect of real estate profits, a man prodigal of his physical and mental powers, a champion drinker, and a loyal servant of Vermont and his family's financial interests there while that region was an independent republic. Colonel Arnold did well to force no leadership issue with Colonel Allen, especially when Allen was surrounded by friends.

The little force marched swiftly to Lake Champlain, took all the boats they could find, crossed the lake, and entered Ticonderoga without meeting opposition. The garrison of the fort was made up of half a dozen Invalids (old or crippled soldiers unfit for field duty) commanded by a junior officer. Allen summoned the commander, though it is not agreed what he said. He either shouted for him to surrender "in the name of the Great Jehovah and the Continental Congress," or said, "I must have immediate possession of the fort and all the effects of George the Third," or cried, "Come out of there you damned rat."[28] Allen did not believe in the Great Jehovah, and later wrote a book to say so. He never had a course in military courtesy. The third form of summons is most in character.

Thus Ticonderoga fell on May 10. The same force took Crown Point on blue Lake George in the same way two days later. Arnold managed to raise fifty recruits of his own, laid hands on a schooner, sailed to the mouth of Lake Champlain, and took Fort St. John and an armed sloop lying there. More recruits gathered, enough for Arnold to found the Army's freshwater Navy on Lake Champlain. By this time his head had swelled to what would become its normal size, his popularity had declined, and he left for Cambridge to promote an ambitious and audacious scheme for a surprise attack against Quebec through the Maine woods.

The Continental Congress—now the *Second* Continental Congress—had convened. It received word of the fall of Ticonderoga as quickly as communications allowed. Who first reported it? Who took all the credit? Benedict Arnold.[29]

CHAPTER

3

Undeclared Independence

Borne on the racing hoofs of lathered horses, the word of the bloody encounter at Lexington on April 19 spread even before the redcoats reached Concord. A rider headed south at ten o'clock in the morning carrying a hasty dispatch to rally the disaffected: ". . . The bearer . . . is charged to alarm the Country quite to Connecticutt and all persons are desired to furnish him with fresh Horses as they are needed."[1] Private letters added their writers' stories. Jane Franklin Mecom told brother Ben that God intervened when Gage "sent out a party to creep out into the night and slaughter our own dear brethren for endeavoring to defend our own property." The frustrated British "coming in bringing their wounded men, caused such an agitation I believe none had much sleep" for fear the battle would carry right into the town.[2] Traveling immediately after the Lexington dispatch went the Concord news. The story passed speedily from Committee to Committee, reaching Charleston on May 7. From every coastal town the news flashed inland like an electric current. Minute Men flowed into Cambridge from Connecticut, Rhode Island, and New Hampshire. George Washington personally declared war, and Charleston raised two white regiments, apparently as furious as Bostonians. A convention in Mecklenburg County of North Carolina voted that all royal commissions in America were null. Gage reported to his government routinely, but the

43

rebels chartered a ship in ballast to carry their partisan account to Britain, where it arrived eleven days before Gage's and commanded all attention as a nine-days' wonder.

The Connecticut assembly tried for peace by sending members to Boston with a suggestion of truce and talks, but Gage would speak only of North's "conciliation." The Connecticut troops in Massachusetts, and the Massachusetts leaders, disdained further parley. New Yorkers made a similarly futile pacification try. Gage hoped the next Continental Congress would be conciliatory, a hope that flickered until he had to plan his attack in June on Breed's Hill. The times simply were not peaceable. New York, no furnace of rebellion, saw troops parading, and not for their King, while radicals blocked a military supply shipment intended for Boston and seized a thousand brown royal muskets.

The radical leaders of the British colonies faced new circumstances during this crisis. To make the Association work in the fall of 1774 had required only local leadership. After the fighting and bloodshed at Lexington and Concord, local Committees could not wage a larger war, because the problems of getting up the money, the men, and the supplies were more than local problems. Local Committees were great for passing handbills, scaring loyalists, and fighting in the streets, but such experience was not necessarily useful training for assuming continental leadership. Whether the Massachusetts uproar was to be an abortive insurrection or the launching of a successful war depended on the ability of the local radicals to produce a continentally responsible leadership. Such leaders could not be drawn from the old legal institutions which were interlarded with officers whose interest was to preserve the status quo, not to write new laws to create a new order.[3] As it turned out, in every colony the proper form of agency to do the job was some extra-legal assemblage—or treasonable band, depending on one's viewpoint—such as the Massachusetts Provincial Congress, which could provide the local force and send delegates to a continental coalition of provincial radical leaders, a good description of the Continental Congress.

Convinced radicals could hardly doubt the need for unity. By 1774 novel statutes, unwonted scarlet-coated garrisons, pluralism in office, alien courts, frustrations of ambition (perhaps heightened by envy)—all seemed to spell conspiracy against the liberty of American white male Protestants. Political philosophy may have governed, but few saw the questions of free elections and trial by jury as philosophical questions. To even a confirmed political theorizer the Concord raid meant that opponents of policy must defend themselves or the British would straightaway kill them.[4] In some American eyes the unlucky Gage had become the brutal agent of a callous despot.

By sheer coincidence the Continental Congress* met in this heated atmosphere. It had agreed to reconvene on May 10, 1775, if grievances were not righted. This purely coincidental choice of a date gave just enough time to let the delegates assemble after the Massachusetts outbreak. Philadelphia welcomed the members with all possible pomp. The Virginia delegation, on May 9, and the men from New England, on May 10, were escorted into town, serenaded, and subjected to oratory.

The Congress was to be more radical in tone than the First Congress. There would be no one sturdily opposed to armed resistance. Hereafter the debatable question was not whether to resist but whether to be independent, and the question of independence was not immediately before the Congress. Old faces, for example that of Joseph Galloway, were gone, and new faces appeared. We may well glance at a few of the new faces.

The Congress convened on May 10, this time in the State House instead of Carpenters' Hall. The members re-elected Peyton Randolph of Virginia and Charles Thomson of Philadelphia as president and secretary. Randolph resigned in a fortnight, to be succeeded by the newly arrived John Hancock of Boston. When Hancock was at the zenith of his popularity he may have been the best-liked man who ever lived in New England; but he outlived the trust and love of his peers, partly because he found it so hard to account for the finances of Harvard College when he was its treasurer in his later years. In 1764, at the age of twenty-seven, he had inherited the largest business in Boston and was worth about seventy thousand pounds sterling. In little more than a decade this man with every material interest in the stability of society, after unconscionable harassment by the British customs officers, became president of the Massachusetts Provincial Congress, from which it was a natural step to the presidency of the Continental Congress. These were his prime years as

* The Congress of 1774 has been called, above, the First Continental Congress. Hereafter this central organization will be referred to simply as the Congress.

a genius of political organization, when he was perhaps the strongest political figure of the continent. He not only served as president of the Congress from May 1775 through October 1777 but won election as governor of Massachusetts eleven times by overpowering majorities. His mind was rather shrewd than profound. He saw the presidency of the Congress as a singular dignity and lived up to it ostentatiously, dashing about Philadelphia in a glittering coach with an armed escort of mounted militia.

New Hampshire sent two new men. William Whipple was a sea captain, a former slave trader, and a politician. He sat in the Congress with few interruptions until 1779, an energetic committeeman adversely critical of the war effort but never skeptical of success. He was rather bloody-minded in urging the execution or exile of all loyalists. Perhaps it was a quarterdeck manner which moved him to call for ever greater vigor. His quieter colleague was John Langdon, who sprang from nowhere. Langdon had not even the exaltation of being a village selectman before election to the Congress.

Elbridge Gerry was a Massachusetts newcomer with legislative experience and the friendship of Samuel and John Adams (and later of Jefferson). Small, cultivated, popular with both sexes, he gave a false initial impression of hardness because of a habit of contracting his eyes in conversation (myopia?). Although sometimes indecisive, sometimes stubborn on trivialities, he was energetic and unquestionably honest. He stayed in the Congress until 1780 (and died in 1814 as Vice-President of the United States).

Studious Samuel Huntington of Connecticut taught himself Latin and law, won admission to the bar, served in the Congress from 1775 to 1784, and became its president in the years 1779–1781.

James Wilson of Pennsylvania was lawyer, pamphleteer, speculator, and something of a political philosopher. He moved to successively more conservative positions during the war. Defeats in the heated internal Pennsylvania revolution interrupted his service in the Congress. He is remembered more as a library democrat than a ballot box democrat, and like most such men he inclined to inflexibility and disliked compromise. John Dickinson also represented the conservatives of Pennsylvania. He tried hard for reconciliation. When the ultimate choice faced him he could not vote for independence, which ended his usefulness in the Congress for awhile; but when his militia regiment called him out he came.

Undeclared Independence

White-haired Benjamin Franklin, then most distinguished of Pennsylvanians and most famous of Americans, also served in the Congress in 1775. He arrived home (distracted by his recordings of the temperatures of the Gulf Stream) shortly after news of Concord reached Philadelphia. The next morning the Pennsylvania assembly unanimously elected him to the Congress. He thought Gage "began cutting of throats" before the colonists could adequately weigh Lord North's proposals.[5] Franklin was then in his seventies and had for years been America's chief spokesman in Britain where he was now regarded as a stranger and a spy. As he saw it, the Empire could survive only if free British subjects on both sides of the ocean were recognized as equals, but he had learned that persuasion in the chambers of British ministers would not win that recognition. The only recourse remaining, in his opinion, was forcible resistance. His reading of the portents was identical with that of the Adamses with whom he allied himself.

There were others in this Congress worth noticing, but this sampling suffices to illustrate the point that the Continental Congress was inferior to the House of Commons not in intellect but only in its ability to exert material force.[6]

II

The new Congress had barely enough of the conscious spirit of independence to estimate. The intention of the radicals was to continue opposition to British policy until a Ministry fell or changed its policy. In that sense this Congress was certainly stiffer of neck than its predecessor. In the fall of 1774 a majority would probably have settled for the political arrangements of the good old days before 1763, but in the spring of 1775 something more would be required to make them content. Their firm but friendly words of 1774 had been ignored. Blood had been shed, and blood was not something to spend idly.

In the strict letter of the law any order issued by this Congress would be a usurpation. Neither charter nor popular vote authorized it to act, but moral pressure to support New England was powerful, and moral pressure justified action in the eyes of men who admired natural law. The practical success of a self-created authority seemed to require that the Congress be nearly unanimous in any decision. Hence it moved slowly in the spring and summer of 1775, and was quite good at getting unanimity. As in 1774, the Congress worked in secret, except to publish propaganda statements. The sober private letters of the members prove they knew their job was serious and probably dangerous. As Joseph Hewes, now in his second Congress, wrote to one of the North Carolinians who had sent him, "You have been instrumental in putting a halter about our necks. . . ."[7]

The sobriety, the gravity, the secrecy were not marks of fear. The Congress was a truly audacious body. After all, it is possible for men to be carefully audacious as when, to use a modern phrase, they take a calculated risk. These men had not received uniform instructions, they had no constitutional authority to govern, and they lacked jurisdiction over any tract of green America. They had no money, no laws, and no agency to enforce any orders they issued. Nevertheless they plunged in to try to direct a society engaged in a revolution. To ministers and loyalists this was government by effrontery.

The Congress had some general advice to the colonies. Putting first things first, the call went out to collect all the military supplies in America and then to try to make gunpowder (which was almost a lost art). Next, each colony should quickly establish a provincial convention and appoint an executive committee to carry on between convention sessions. In effect this resolution ratified the existing system of Committees of Safety and thus established interim local governments with some color of legality. Radicals welcomed calls to common action from a harmonious center, and Massachusetts, with the largest bet already on the board, moved with alacrity to call a general assembly to meet on July 19.[8] Congress next evoked a feeling of psychological fraternity by naming July 20 as an intercolonial day of humiliation and prayer for the restoration of justice in America. The day was called "Congress Sunday," and many heads bowed in prayer, though more in towns than in the country.[9]

Of course the most important decision of 1775 was the election of George Washington as commanding general of the forces, but that matter deserves special attention, to be given later.

The Congress was instantly beset by military questions. Before any large plans could be made, the immediate problem of New York came before the group. Rumor said British troops were coming to New

York. New York asked what to do. The Congress answered in a matter of days: if the troops came, the colony should stay on the defensive and allow the soldiers to occupy their barracks so long as they were well-behaved. But if the British began building more fortifications or tried to cut New York off from its neighbors, the people should defend themselves "and repel force by force." They should meanwhile get all military stores out of reach of the British and embody enough men to protect the citizenry.[10] Virginia's Congressman George Washington helped to write this program.

The Congress had expected to meet briefly and draft some advice to the colonies. Instead, the smoke of New England combat and the possibility of other fire-fights enlarged its duties and puzzles far beyond anticipation. Obviously, if resistance was to continue, the Congress could not go home until the military situation was regularized. Should the Congress assist the army then besieging Boston? Could it do other? There was no eagerness to have a congressional army, but the army might dissolve if not supported from outside New England. Once the army dispersed it would be hard to reorganize. The answer was plain: adopt the army. The first actual assumption of responsibility for what became the Continental Army was a promise by the Congress to replace supplies sent to the troops by other colonies, and an exhortation to every state between Georgia and Connecticut to collect the materials needed to make gunpowder "for the use of the Continent." The Congress would pay the cost.[11] Within a few days the Congress initiated continental recruiting with a resolution to raise companies of riflemen for "the American continental army," and to write a code of military law.[12] John Adams reported a rumor that explained why other colonies were willing to send troops to New England. They feared New England would have all of the veteran soldiers and might some day "conceive Designs unfavourable to the other Colonies. This may be Justly thought whimsical."[13]

Once the army became continentalized, at least on paper, the Congress found itself with new problems arising from the change, such as the touchy question of a relative ranking of general officers, how to fill vacancies in the officer corps at lower levels, how much discretion a commanding general could have without becoming a Caesar, and who should pay for fortifying and arming harbor defenses.

While studying such questions the Congress received the news of the reduction of Fort Ticonderoga and Crown Point. The members recoiled at first, because such operations seemed rather more offensive than defensive. Finally they salved their consciences with the rationalization that the captures could be justified because they prevented invasion from Quebec. Nevertheless, just in case, they told the victors to inventory the forcibly acquired effects of King George so that restitution might be made when Britannia and her daughters became again a loving family.

If armed resistance to the Ministry was a good thing, the Congress made most of its decisions quite intelligently, but in the matter of supplies it walked into a field of choice in which it stumbled. By July the country was desperately short of military materials. Even if manufacturing was encouraged it could not do the job quickly enough. The handicap was the Association, which operated to isolate America from the British economy. On July 15 the Congress opened a temporary loophole: ships unloading certain military supplies could carry out colonial produce to the same value. The word went to the West Indies, but the Congress kept it out of the newspapers. *If* fighting was to continue, the true military necessity was to open the doors to all nations except Britain. Robert R. Livingston of New York argued in October for repealing the nonexportation clause of the Association, but he failed, and the members obtusely voted (November 1) to continue the complete embargo until February.[14]

Some reluctant revolutionaries wished to petition their King once more. Although many of their colleagues had no hope of winning redress that way, they went along (July 5) with one last effort to persuade the King to protect his subjects from Parliament. The document, written by John Dickinson, is known as the "Olive Branch." It is one of the gentlest statements brought out by the Congress and omitted any firm assertions of rights. The omission represented no softening of congressional hearts but merely appeased the well-liked and very anxious John Dickinson. Dickinson even asked permission to leave out the word "Congress," but in that he asked too much.[15] The delegates adopted the "Declaration on Taking Arms" on the next day after adopting the "Olive Branch."

If not always wise, the Congress was ever brave. The members continued the war knowing they might hang. To rally the country they published their reasons on July 6, 1775, in "A Declaration by the Representatives of the United Colonies of North America, now met in Congress at Philadelphia, setting forth the causes and necessity of their taking up arms,"[16] named more briefly in their journal as "Declaration on Taking Arms."[17] By now the Congress was a propaganda ministry. Indeed, both sides did much of their fighting throughout the war by hurling proclamations. An early propaganda step of the Congress had been to publish twenty depositions testifying to the guilt of the British in the Lexington-Concord raid.

The "Declaration on Taking Arms" was written by John Dickinson and Thomas Jefferson (who had succeeded to Peyton Randolph's seat). Washington was to publish it to the troops when he took command.[18] The "Declaration" insisted that the purpose of American resistance was not to separate from Great Britain nor to involve Britain in a foreign war, but was merely to defend Americans against attack "by unprovoked enemies" who offered "no milder conditions than servitude or death." "Servitude" was rather a strong word to describe the life of white male Americans who kept nearly half a million black slaves, but the Congress wished propaganda, not social analysis. The "Declaration" included a threat which probably received closer attention in England than the more philosophic parts of the paper: "Our internal resources are great, and, if necessary, foreign assistance is undoubtedly attainable."[19] The authors were pointing to the Bourbon cloud which had hovered on the British horizon since the seventeenth century.

Under British rule the colonies enjoyed a good postal service operated by Deputy Postmaster General Benjamin Franklin. Without it the Americans could not have nationalized their resistance to the ministers. As a precaution the Congress annexed the Post Office and kept Franklin as its nominal head, while cutting the cost of rebellion by reducing postal rates 20 per cent[20] (the Post Office had long shown a profit).

The First Congress had sent a *billet-doux* to Canada, but wise Governor Guy Carleton silently suppressed it. In May 1775 the Congress tried again with an address "To the Oppressed Inhabitants of Canada," which pleaded for *fraternité*. Disingenuously it said, among other things, ". . . from the commencement of the present plan for subjugating the continent, we have viewed you as fellow-sufferers with us."[21] After the uproar against the grant of legal recognition and a few narrowly drafted privileges to the Catholic Church in Canada by the religious provisions of the Quebec Act of 1774 (which the

Americans had mistakenly assumed were wholly acceptable to Catholics), this affirmation of fellowship does not stand close scrutiny. The text described the form of Canadian government as tyranny and presumed its readers would agree. The very intelligent John Jay of New York wrote the draft, or it might be called naive. The best one can say for the author and the Congress is that wishful thinking blinded them. In the next eight years only a few score French Canadians took up arms against the British.

The Congress also wished to cultivate the Indians, to keep them neutral. Three Indian agents, one for each of three newly defined departments, were to try to persuade the Indians not to be hostile, which was about the best the Congress could hope to achieve.

All of this deliberation took place in Philadelphia while the fighting went on in New England. The bloody battle of Bunker Hill occurred while the Congress sat in Philadelphia. The members thought about moving nearer to the war, but decided to stay in Philadelphia. However, when the Congress recessed on August 2 to reconvene on September 5, most members did not go directly home but hurried off toward Massachusetts to see with their own eyes how things had gone.

Quite apart from the battlefield, things had gone pretty far. In that century there were certain things that only sovereigns were to do, among them establishing military magazines, contracting for munitions, legitimizing local governments, designating national holidays, commissioning military officers, fortifying cities, recruiting soldiers, opening and closing ports, operating postal services, and—in America —tampering with the loyalties of Indians. The Congress, outside the royal sway, unchartered, without mandate, had done all of these things, and the only indication of dependence on their liege lord King George was their quite perfunctory "Olive Branch" petition. In the movement of human affairs there are moments when people arrive at points from which there is no returning, at decisions which can not be revoked, at transgression which can not be overlooked, at deeds which can not be repudiated. At any such moment a trend becomes a result, and a tendency becomes a condition. The Continental Congress knew it not, but it had put on the vestments of sovereignty, and "the United Colonies of North America" by August 1775 were practicing independence.

III

After the Ministry received Gage's official confirmation of the news of the Lexington-Concord raid, the King told Lord Dartmouth, then Colonial Secretary, that he had resolved on firmness. Lord George Germain belittled the causes of the violence (and later succeeded Dartmouth as Colonial Secretary). Through the year 1775 Germain believed parliamentary opposition to the American policy was merely a tactical maneuver to overthrow the Ministry, or at least to get some ministers fired and thus create vacancies for opportunists, and he also believed that any otherwise sound ministers who advised easing the policy feared the lily flag of France more than they loved America. Early in the winter Germain received an accurate description of the Continental Army as of November 1775,[22] when it was certainly a raggle-taggle host which should have frightened the Continental Congress more than the British government.

Contempt for the American military potential was almost universal in Britain. Lord Sandwich, First Lord of the Admiralty, said he thought the sound of artillery would panic Americans, and Franklin reported that a British officer said he could march the length of the country with a thousand grenadiers. Even as late as a few weeks before Burgoyne's catastrophic surrender in 1777, General James Murray described American soldiers as womanish.[23] A British officer who had heard the muskets pop on April 19 credited the militia exertions only to "enthusiasm and madness." (Enthusiasm then meant gross fanaticism, too tiring to last.) But Lord Percy, who had rescued the Concord raiders and who had previously believed the Americans were cowards, now changed his mind and said the "insurrection" was not a minor matter.[24]

Outside of the British government, heat against the Americans was not noticeable. The ministers liked to receive laudatory petitions from around the British Isles to continue controversial policies, but instead received several against their American policy and only one immediately favorable, which was organized by a man who wished Parliament to renew a patent.[25] Nevertheless, the rationalization of the Ministry's future policy appeared in an anonymous but obviously authoritative London pamphlet of early 1776, demanding American gratitude for the economic benefits of both motherly defense and production bounties. The writer pointed to the American payment of British customs dues since the 1630's, and even the payment of postage (as a kind of license fee).[26] Precedents they were, and they had been accepted. There would be no official yielding. While the Congress unconsciously practiced independence, the King-in-Parliament would consciously practice imperialism.

Nevertheless there were Britishers who sympathized with American resistance. The news from Lexington and Concord crowded the proceedings of the General Assembly of the Church of Scotland from the *Caledonian Mercury*, which had the largest circulation of any Scottish newspaper. So great was the interest in the American quarrel that good American coverage was essential to the circulation of every paper in Scotland. The interest was sympathetic enough to make it impossible for the Ministry to get a laudatory petition from Glasgow, and Edinburgh presented one very tardily.[27] In Ireland a literate Protestant recorded his sympathy for America: "Here we sympathize more or less with the Americans," wrote Charles O'Hara to his friend Burke. "We are in water colours, what they are in fresco."[28] But Irish Catholics owed their extra-legal toleration only to the government in England and therefore tended to favor the Ministry.[29]

Remarks favorable to America strengthened the voices of the opposition in Parliament. For example, Lord Keppel's secretary had a letter from an English friend in Massachusetts who marveled at American zeal and could not believe "that Arms will enforce obedience."[30] Similar sentiments echoed in speeches by members of the opposition, though not necessarily for reasons of altruism. The Duke of Grafton said English liberty could not survive the death of liberty in America; General Conway claimed to believe American fervor would substitute for military discipline; and John Wilkes said victory could only mean the permanent military occupation of a country in which the population was outstripping that of Britain. Half a dozen parliamentarians predicted war with both France and Spain. Confident Lord North, after lounging on the front bench and thinking these men more interested in getting Cabinet seats than in conciliation, replied that a Parliament with one Wilkes had one

Undeclared Independence

Wilkes too many, and scoffed at the danger of war with France and Spain. A war with the Bourbon powers was a real danger, and North knew it, but he or King George decided not to let that risk weigh very heavily.[31] They were overconfident of quick victory in America.

The British forensic sympathy for the American side soon appeared in print in America,[32] where it could hardly have discouraged Americans in arms. The best remembered of American sympathizers was Edmund Burke, who had the news of warfare in a private letter two weeks before Gage's report arrived. He wrote, "All our prospects of American reconciliation are, I fear, over." Some weeks later he added, "We are actually engaged in a civil war."[33] He had estimated the situation precisely.

Even before blood stained the grass of Lexington, the Ministry began to cramp America by restraining the trade of the colonies, except those in which loyalists were thought to abound. The government barely noticed the arrival of the "Olive Branch" petition. Richard Penn, a mild ex-governor of Pennsylvania, carried the petition to Britain where he handed in a copy at the Colonial Secretary's office on August 21, and the Congress's original draft on September 1. When Penn inquired about it the reply was, "As His Majesty did not receive it on the throne, no answer would be given."[34] Dartmouth let him know the British could not deal with the Congress but with individual colonies only. On August 23, two days after the copy of the "Olive Branch" first officially came to Dartmouth's attention, the Ministry published a royal Proclamation of Rebellion in America, and called for information leading to punishment of those in America and England who were encouraging the rebellion by exchanging news and information.[35] What had happened was the gory battle of Bunker Hill.* The Congress recorded no disquiet at the rejection of the "Olive Branch."

The origins of the insurrection were political, but hope of a political settlement was dead by the beginning of the summer of 1775. The Ministry was temperamentally unable to bring itself to lessen the power and authority of the King-in-Parliament over any acre where the Union Jack flew. The Declaratory Act of 1765 had defined Parliament's power as total, and no British leader in responsible office

---

* The battle of Bunker Hill is a subject of the next chapter.

had disapproved. When the colonials opposed musket fire to authority, North had either to resign or fight. He and most of his colleagues favored force. The Ministry arranged the Proclamation of Rebellion, began to raise troops, and went to war in earnest by August. The last regular mail sailed from Britain to America in October. Communication had been cut by command.

As noted before, Lord George Germain succeeded Dartmouth as Colonial Secretary in November. Germain, a cashiered lieutenant general, was fierce to crush the rebels because he believed the laxity of his predecessors had bred the troubles. He had supported the "Intolerable Acts" and all through 1775 he urged the use of flashing bayonets to compel obedience. Now he had a chance to redeem his military reputation after being convicted of disobedience in the Seven Years' War. The new post made him practically a minister of war and gave room to show his talent (if any) for military administration. He was quite eager and optimistic, anticipating victory in a single campaign; one decisive victory and the pressure of a blockade, he had written in July, would do the job.[36]

Edmund Burke continued his losing course. At the thought of Germain running a war he introduced a four-part bill which would repeal all acts offensive to the insurgent Americans, renounce parliamentary taxation, recognize the Continental Congress, and pardon all rebels. The vote came at a time when the independent gentlemen of the Commons were at hand (their harvests in), and was a good test of strength. The score (on what is known as Burke's second conciliation bill): government 210, opposition 105. It would be years before the opposition would score as well again.[37]

In America, Gage had begun to enlist loyalist troops (Boston was the worst place to try). He wisely prevented the war from becoming even more grisly by exchanging prisoners in May. This was good law-of-nations, but by British municipal law all of Gage's prisoners were traitors, liable to be hanged, drawn, and quartered, after which reprisals, of course, would have followed.[38] Gage also thought of using Indians to close the open Champlain corridor to Canada, and took note of the possibility of raising black troops but never acted on it—which may have been the gravest error of omission of the war. (Lord Dunmore, governor of Virginia, was recruiting a Royal Ethiopian regiment while Germain was still settling into office.) A promise of land and freedom might have raised fifty thousand Afro-American loyalist soldiers with a stake in the fighting greater than anyone else's.

During the spring of 1775 Gage at last received his reinforcements. By June he had 6,500 men. And in the middle of June, 1,054 of them shed blood on the grassy slopes below Bunker Hill.

4

Men at Arms, 1775-1776

George Washington, tall, squarely built, was tireless, firm, cool, and mostly just, but prone to blame other men for failures of his plans. Standing six feet plus, strongly muscled and large boned, weighing more than two hundred pounds, he excelled at horsemanship which was the athletics of his day. He avoided contention and took care to present himself to the world as a man of sobriety and gravity. Virginia sent him to the Congress in 1774 and 1775.

After the Congress adopted the army in Massachusetts it had to choose a commanding general and other general officers. Artemas Ward was senior in Massachusetts but not really equal to continental command. If John Adams observed him accurately, John Hancock had hopes. Charles Lee, an English ex-officer, had the most military experience available, but his relatively brief American residence ruled him out.

Eyes must have turned to the forty-three-year-old Washington who sat in the Congress wearing the uniform of his Virginia colonelcy of the 1750's. In the First Congress Washington served on no noteworthy committee nor did he make a memorable remark,[1] but the start of war apparently broke his silence. His appearance, his reputation, his real or assumed modesty, and his military conversation much impressed John Adams,[2] who was eager to enlarge the military commitment beyond New England limits. On June 15, 1775, the Congress decided to appoint a general "to command all the continental forces," and then by unanimous vote named George Washington.[3] John Adams took the credit, claiming to have lined up a majority for Washington which was easily swung to unanimity as a choice which "would command the approbation of all America. . . ."[4] Although Adams's maneuvering for a non-Yankee no doubt helped, it may have been unnecessary since the range of choice was narrow, and powerful Virginia, the most populous colony, thought so highly of Washington that he ranked second in votes cast for the seven Virginians chosen as delegates to the Congress.

The election of Washington to command could gratify Virginia economically as well as politically. Most Southern magnates were interested in western lands, and Virginia's western claims overlapped the claims of Massachusetts and Connecticut. It would take little persuading to round up Southern votes to place a distinguished Virginia land speculator in a high place in intercolonial councils.[5] Virginia's economic hopes coincided neatly with New England's need to continentalize the war. Why Washington and not some other Southerner? One can only speculate, but Charles Lee and Horatio Gates, former British officers who had settled in Virginia, visited Washington at Mount Vernon after the adjournment of the First Congress and before May 1775. Lee had been drafting a table of military organization. Among Lee's several outstanding flaws was garrulity. It is impossible to believe Lee spoke not of military matters over Mount Vernon nuts and Madeira, and everywhere else he visited that winter. It was probably understood in Virginia that Virginia's ranking native-born soldier, George Washington, had been talking with experienced men about how to organize an army.

In any event, Washington had a larger task than he knew, for he wrote to Martha that he would be home by Christmas. But the Ministry was not converted by the resolutions of the Congress, and he did not come home for Christmas to stay until seven years later.

Having begun to continentalize the Army, the Congress went on to elect two major generals, five brigadier generals, and a retinue of staff officers, secretaries, and aides. Artemas Ward, then commanding outside Boston, was the second-ranking major general, and Charles Lee the third. Actually, Washington, two subordinate major generals, and five brigadiers were plenty for warfare but not enough for politics. Four days after electing this nucleus, the Congress appointed more generals, to make the total four major generals and eight brigadiers, distributing the choices among the sections of the country in order to give local leaders a vested interest in the Army. Gates became the adjutant general. Of all these generals, only Philip Schuyler of New York and Nathanael Greene of Rhode Island ever amounted to much. Richard Montgomery, ranking fourth as brigadier, became the first martyr-hero when he was killed in Canada on New Year's Eve, 1775.[6]

General Washington has not always been clearly visible through the patriotic haze of early views of the American Revolution. His nineteenth-century exaltation was inevitable. If nationalism is necessary there must be at least one national hero. A biography for children by Mason L. Weems began the apotheosis. Weems illustrated Washington's character by incidents and anecdotes diligently hunted, some of which are no doubt essentially true. The book, nine times enlarged, ran to eighty printings, and the flood of print left a cherry tree and a hatchet on the national memory as the tide receded. In fairness it must be said that the pre-Weemsian French already thought Washington a leading world personage,[7] and the first French Minister to the United States knew him and approved his character and tactics.[8] Jared Sparks helped further to elevate Washington with an edition of his writings which consciously altered and omitted texts to put their author in an admirable light. Later writers accepted whatever Washington said as unqualified truth, without applying the ordered skepticism with which they scrutinized other men.[9] Luckily for the nation-state, the hero chosen by acclamation was not very vulnerable to deflation. There was a respectable opposition to the Revolution in America, the war was certainly not a parade of insurrectionary successes, the outcome was less certain than many nineteenth-century writers led their readers to believe, and the victory— while not Washington's alone—owed more to him than to any other one man.[10]

Washington's temperament was that of a born winner. Ambition kept him working at his best ability, which was above average. Pride made him sensitive to criticism, but he taught himself the patience that won the war.[11] As he gained in eminence he gained in serenity. He was acquisitive in every conventional way of his generation, and much interested in capital gains from ownership of western land. If, by genetic accident, he had been born in England, he would have fitted well into county social and civic life. British officials had thought well of him in Virginia. His consciously stoic conduct would now be described as inner-directed, and, according to shallow popularizers of Freudianism, would necessarily inhibit and repress him. But instead of becoming a neurotic he became a free, stolid, placid man. He was not much interested in abstractions and recorded no introspection, which makes his writings rather dull.[12]

Although no philosopher, Washington absorbed the rationalism of the day and his character remained unaffected by evangelical Christianity. He promoted cultural pluralism and protected ideological nonconformity, whether that of Catholics on the one hand or atheists on the other. He believed restriction of conscience to be cruel to the victims and even more injurious to the practitioners of spiritual tyranny. His toleration was more than condescension, as he proved by going out of his way to show respect for the convictions of Catholics, the pacificism of Quakers, and the dignity of Jews. He proved his regard for civil liberty by refusing in 1777 to prosecute a farmer who was charged with betraying the Army's countersign to the British but whose accuser could not come forward to testify publicly. Washington said no citizen should be arrested and confined in ignorance of his charge and his accuser.[13]

Washington apparently thought little about theology. In the forty volumes of his printed writings the name of Christ appears but once. When he named some power superior to man he used the word "Providence." But he believed in the social utility of institutionalized religion, in religious toleration, and in the separation of church and state. There was nothing original in these ideas, and nothing at all for black people as such, but the rise of such a man to first rank in the eyes of his fellows made the United States a more comfortable place for the white people of unconventional views. His own religious practices were those of contemporary social compliance. The Washington who prayed on his knees in some dark moment of the war is a myth. He belonged to the Anglican Church, and then to the Protestant Episcopal Church, attended services with some regularity, and served as vestryman. This was not hypocrisy, but was his contribution to social stability.

Since he read very little, his political thought was absorbed from Virginia society. He never claimed that he had been for independence before October 1775 when the King's Proclamation of Rebellion reached him. It is pointless to theorize that he prudently concealed a fire for independency before that time, because everything he ever did is consistent with everything he said he thought. What he *said* was that he entered the struggle to thwart the Ministry and the Parliament, and only came around to favor independence late in 1775. The treatment of Boston certainly angered him. On a hot afternoon in Philadelphia in 1774, John Adams heard about the speech of Washington in Virginia in which he had pledged to raise a thousand men at his own expense and to march at their head to the relief of Boston.[14] When fully committed to the struggle as its leader in the field, he was conscious of posterity and asked the Congress for a secretary and some copyists to put his papers in order.[15] Here was a man whose life was all of a piece.

His relations with his subordinates were reserved. Although he sat in his mess after dinner, cracking nuts, drinking, and talking a good deal, a junior messmate left a revealing note: Colonel Alexander Hamilton, who resigned from Washington's military family in a huff, explained that Washington was ill-tempered and uncivil.[16] (Hamilton was twenty-six years old.) Neither delicacy nor good temper in dealing with aides is rated near the top of any list of necessary qualifications of commanders-in-chief of near-desperate causes.

On balance we know that Washington was usually frank and generous, but sometimes less than candid. For most of his life he was hypersensitive to criticism and quite humanly in favor of putting himself in the best light. This led him to blame subordinates when his plans failed. The trait needs mention only because writers have tended to take his side in each such instance. Heavily outweighing this flaw were his personal bravery, his coolness in emergencies, and his perfect devotion to duty which riveted his attention to the job from first to last. There is plenty in him to admire without raising him to the status of a demigod.

The general of 1775 was the colonel of 1758 grown older. From 1753 to 1758 Washington commanded the Virginia Regiment, a provincial regular corps, but saw no later service and gained no more training. Apparently he did not follow closely the later campaigns of the French and Indian War, nor did he read anything of military arts thereafter. There had been no important war since then, so he had had to learn no new tactics. He had successfully assumed responsibility over subordinates chosen by others (often men of little military aptitude). He earned the respect, even affection, of his officers while learning the dangers of favoritism. He knew that desertion and drunkenness were the twin perennial dangers in the enlisted ranks. A valuable and peculiarly American lesson was that supply and transport demanded early and continuous attention, since frugality was a primary condition of American operations. Washington had never been able to stir enlisted men to a sense of responsibility, nor did recruits flock to him. He was prejudiced against militia. He never commanded more than a thousand men, and that number briefly, and for every minute of combat experience he spent hours of defensive patrolling. His election by the Congress was not the acclamation of a genius but the acceptance of a competent man by a treaty between sections.[17]

The choice was fortunate for the United States. No disinterested professional soldier scorned Washington, and his French colleagues admired him for making an army from individualists. He was not indispensable, but few in America had equal talents. The war might have been won without him, but probably by using different methods, and, perhaps, with anti-republican results. In practice Washington won often enough to show that his victories were more than lucky. He stood fast in adversity, his strategy was sound, his tactics occasionally sparkled, he was tactful with civil authorities and allies, he trained troops well, and he showed great energy and moral power. He was no Alexander, but he was good enough.

Washington knew his appointment was a continental political decision.[18] The wording of his commission left no doubt that he was the servant of the Congress and not its collaborator. His orders were to come from the Congress, and he held his authority at its pleasure.[19] He was an experienced politician himself, and knew that he could not allow himself to be provincially biased if he were to succeed. As a continental officer he early had to make it clear that purely local defense problems were problems for militia; his were larger responsibilities.[20]

His generally smooth relations with the civil authority stemmed from his experience as an officer subject to the authority of Virginia, and as a Virginia Burgess. One youthful attempt to teach the Virginia government how to use his regiment had provoked civilian hostility, and he never tried it again. Service in the Burgesses and in the Congress broadened his understanding, and taught him so well how to deal with legislators that he was more apt to err in battle than in politics. For administration he relied on the experience of managing a large farm, where he had to learn how to organize seasonal work. Yet he gained no fellow feeling for men who worked with their hands. He wished to know of adverse criticism in order to make his conduct "coincide with the wishes of mankind, as far as I can consistently."[21] He had rules of thumb for dealing with the Congress, which showed his respect for his erstwhile colleagues and for the chain of command. He had proved his intention of doing all he could for the cause, he knew that legislators absolutely needed information, and he intended to avoid blame for withholding useful facts. He sent quick reports of everything of importance except military secrets. He explicitly kept the Army subject to the Congress. To strengthen arguments in favor of what he thought would be correct policies, he supplemented his official correspondence by letters to friendly Congressmen in which he added what might be useful to them in persuasion. The Congress always knew it could expect obedience if possible, and if obedience were impossible, it immediately learned why. Washington never permitted himself any open disparagement of the Congress nor any imputation of unworthy motives.[22] This way of working allowed flexibility, for after 1776 he had no hesitance about acting on his own. If the Congress disapproved, he did not repeat the act. If the Congress were silent, silence gave consent.

Washington arrived in Cambridge to assume his command on July 2, 1775, and the provincial council lodged him in John Vassall's handsome house on leafy Brattle Street. The army in Massachusetts was in such poor condition that he wished the advice of the Congress in reshaping it, but the Congress declined to move closer or to send a committee to advise him. Washington thought his most pressing problem was how to communicate with the Congress.[23] Even New York seemed so remote that he left Schuyler there under direction of the Congress instead of himself. To keep in touch as best he could, Washington continuously corresponded with Congressman Benjamin Harrison as his go-between with the delegates. His need for advice was symptomatic of an initial reluctance to take complete charge. His congressional orders had been to consult his council of war in any unforeseen circumstance, and he chose to think his council must approve any action. The result was that in the first winter of Washington's command the Army was governed by majority vote of the generals, a poor arrangement since military councils have notoriously lacked daring.

George Washington, who had not grown in moral stature since his late twenties, was about to enter a fire which refined from dross and purified seven times. In youth he was ambitious and not very lovable, but his hard edges had softened as his ambitions neared satisfaction. His sense of justice for white men sharpened steadily—and certainly included attention to strict justice for himself. After his nerve steadied in the winter of 1776–1777, he had a firmness of character needed to handle the questioning kind of an army he commanded. There were men of greater intelligence in America, but probably none better fitted by judgment and physical courage for the post his peers gave him. He could appear optimistic in defeat and modest in victory. In the long run his personality made it possible for him to combine the qualities of a field commander, a secretary of a war ministry, and a chief of staff—precisely the combination needed for victory.

II

Before Washington left Philadelphia, Thomas Gage had bought a hill at a price in blood so high that one more victory at such a cost could have lost the war.

When the Lexington-Concord raiders returned and the rebels besieged Boston, Admiral Thomas Graves, the sea force commander, urged a constructive reply to the affronts of the rebels: fortify Bunker Hill, burn Charlestown and Roxbury, and fortify Roxbury Hill so as to command Dorchester Heights. He offered to lend seamen and marines for the shoveling. Gage rejected the plan and the muscle-power. In retrospect Graves seems to have had the right idea, especially since the British stayed on in Boston. General Gage thought he should keep his Army in one place, awaiting further reinforcements. He lacked men and ships to take New York, and to go to Halifax would be to strip the colonies of redcoats. So Boston it was, but

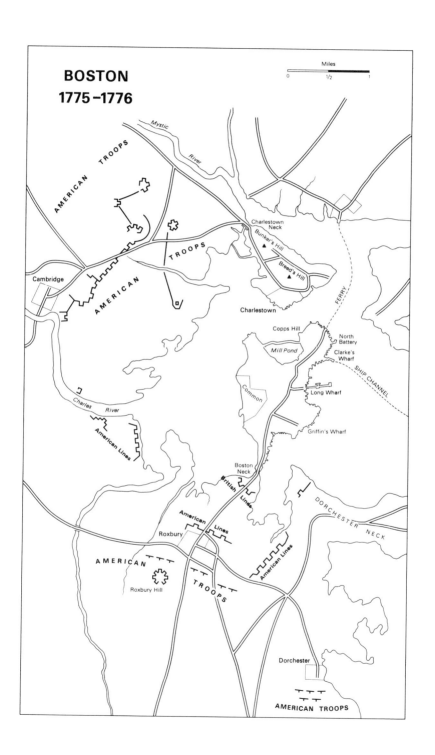

BOSTON
1775–1776

Miles
0   1/2   1

Mystic
River

AMERICAN TROOPS

TROOPS

AMERICAN

Cambridge

Charles   River

American Lines

Charlestown
Neck

Bunker's Hill

Breed's Hill

Charlestown

FERRY

Copps Hill

Mill Pond

North
Battery

Clarke's
Wharf

SHIP CHANNEL

Common

Long Wharf

Griffin's Wharf

Boston
Neck

British Lines

DORCHESTER NECK

American   Lines

Roxbury

AMERICAN

American Lines

Roxbury Hill

TROOPS

Dorchester

AMERICAN TROOPS

he neglected the approaches to the town, except to close Boston Neck to all but loyalists seeking refuge and radicals wishing to leave town permanently. After some weeks of rather sluggish thinking, Gage concluded on June 12 to protect Boston by occupying Dorchester Heights on the 18th, and then to move against Charlestown. Somebody talked. When the besiegers heard about it they decided to forestall Gage by being first to fortify Bunker Hill, which commanded Charlestown and much of the harbor.

Unopposed, Colonel William Prescott of the Massachusetts militia led his regiment and odds and ends of other units to the peninsula on the night of June 16, 1775. For some reason—perhaps the consistency of the soil of Bunker Hill, perhaps a loss of bearings in the dark—the troops went to the eastern end of the eminence, called Breed's Hill, and set manfully to digging. (The fight was properly for Breed's Hill, but the name Bunker Hill has stuck.) The men had no orders to be quiet, and the noise they made carried across the quiet waters to Boston where sentries reported the sounds. Sir Henry Clinton, second-ranking of three unasked-for generals sent to help Gage, was sensitive to the possible meanings of the racket, but his superiors were placid, perhaps out of contempt for the sodbusters and hayseeds who opposed them. Major General William Howe received the news as a signal to go to bed. No one alerted the redcoats. At first gray light of June 17 a lookout on a British warship in the harbor sighted a completed redoubt crowning Breed's Hill. British action was at last imperative. The ship and a land battery both opened fire on the hilltop,[24] but the spade-fresh entrenchments of sweet-smelling spring earth suffered little damage from British gunnery at such an awkward angle, and the men perched there were in little danger from the cannonade.

By the time the British saw them, Prescott's men were tired, hungry, and thirsty. They suggested that other men might well take over the fortification, but Prescott's command was the only American body ever under artillery bombardment, so he kept them while sending word to the rear that he needed men and supplies. There was no supply system, but men came. Connecticut and New Hampshire troops occupied a line from the hill northward to the Mystic River. General Joseph Warren of the Massachusetts militia, who served as a private, and Israel Putnam, a veteran of the French and Indian War with an inspiriting ability as a humorist, joined the troops. The Connecticut and New Hampshire men built flimsy breastworks which at least hid their legs. Gage convened a council which decided to attack. Although Clinton and Burgoyne demurred, Gage and Howe favored a simple march up the hill to push the diggers off and chase them to the mainland, which became the British plan. Howe received command upon the field. Although he gained no luster this day, he had seized the path to Quebec for Wolfe in 1759. Now, ferrying the infantry across Boston harbor took time, and when Howe crossed he took a careful look and sent for more men. It was after noon before he was ready to attack with his well-drilled regulars carrying full field packs so that they would be able to march inland in pursuit of fleeing Americans.

Howe was no fool. He had shown inventiveness in the development of light infantry, although he did not use such tactics on June 17. He did not expect to take the hill by a brute-strength smash but to engage the center while cracking the American left (those Connecticut and New Hampshire men) and then outflanking the hilltop from the north.

The British advanced uphill at their slow, long stride, like magnificent automatons aligned for parade. The Americans held their fire. When their muskets exploded at close range the firing was heavy and continuous. The redcoats fell as if mowed by machinery, and, at most places, the survivors rushed out of range to re-form. A second attack fell to the same butchery. Because the American left did not obligingly break, ninety-six British soldiers died of short-range fire at the extreme left of the American line—about 40 per cent of the redcoated dead. Drill or no drill, men can stand just so much; the surviving British in that part of the field ran. By this time Clinton had arrived with four hundred marines. Incendiary shells had set the village of Charlestown ablaze. Another assault at those points where the British tide had receded followed after careful realignment, deployment, and artillery fire. Again the slaughter was great, but the American firing died away for lack of gunpowder. The disorganized rebels did not panic but withdrew in fairly good order to Bunker Hill and then to the mainland. The exhausted British, pursuit unthinkable, camped on their hard-won summit in drying rills of blood, surrounded by the unburied dead.

The British had suffered a greater loss in proportion to men engaged than in any battle of the earlier Great War for Empire, and a sixth of the officers killed and wounded in the War for Independence were casualties of Bunker Hill. The figures: of 2,400 British engaged, 1,054 were hit, of whom 226 were killed outright. Ninety-two officers were killed or wounded. Howe had twelve aides with him; all were killed or wounded, and their blood stained the white of his uniform. Of the Fourth Regiment all men but four were killed or wounded; of the Twenty-third, all but three. Lord Percy wrote of his own regiment, "There are but 9 men left in my co, & not above 5 in one of the others."[25] Of the 1,600 Americans in the fight, 100 (including Joseph Warren) were killed, 267 wounded, and thirty captured. Two of the American dead were free black men. The American casualties nearly all came after the men ran out of gunpowder. Nathanael Greene reflected, "I wish we could sell them another hill at the same price."[26]

The Congress received a confused and incomplete report of the battle on June 22, and Washington left for the north with generals Lee and Schuyler before the full story reached Philadelphia. A more complete report, directed to John Adams, arrived at eleven o'clock of the night of June 24. About a hundred men came to Adams's lodgings to hear the news. Two hours later the brace of Adamses and John Hancock went out to beg gunpowder from the Philadelphia Committee, which collected ninety quarter-casks and sent them northward immediately. John Adams finally got to bed at about three o'clock.[27] He soon became annoyed in the Congress at the persistence of John Dickinson in pressing the passage of the Olive Branch petition (adopted nineteen days after Bunker Hill), believing the Americans should instead take over the whole continent, build a navy, open the ports to foreigners, take the loyalists into custody, and only then talk about peace negotiations; no more petitioning as respectful subjects.[28] Despite the loss of the hill, most Americans exulted in the results and regarded the battle as a victory.

More serious than the loss of this piece of real estate was the death of Dr. Joseph Warren, politician and revolutionary, who had helped to organize the Massachusetts provisional government, to mobilize the brave amateurish army, to win the support of other colonies, and to feed the hungry of Boston during the seige. His fellows regarded him as a martyr, and a later poet predicted that the rocks would raise their heads to commemorate his deeds, as happened with the erection of the Bunker Hill Monument.

In Britain, Germain showed his usual perspicacity by describing the hemorrhage as a "most decisive blow against the Bostonians,"[29] and the King continued in his view that the colonials must submit before conciliation. No minister who believed that the King-in-Parliament was not supreme in the Empire could have held office for twenty-four hours. The only division of opinion among the majority of Parliament was on the means of making the authority effective. The bloodshed only strengthened those who urged strong measures.

As its first step in moving with stronger measures against America, the Ministry recalled poor Gage, promoted Howe in his place, and opened negotiations to rent soldiers from avaricious continental princelings. The promotion of Howe indicated no new readiness. Officers intensified home recruitment (with little success), and let large military contracts for food and equipment. Running through British comment in those months—in direct contradiction of the evidence of Lexington, Concord, and Bunker Hill—was the theme that the colonials were cowardly. This was not so much wishful thinking as it was the exaggeration and bluster of professional fighters discussing amateurs. The Americans lacked organization, drill, and supplies, but they did not lack heart. The British officers still expected to fight formal parade-ground battles, and looked on the Americans as police estimate a mob. Even Edmund Burke was willing to believe Bunker Hill was something of a British victory; he called it "only a successful sally of a besieged garrison."[30]

Washington, with usual good judgment, was very dubious of the possibility of reconciliation when he had the full story of Bunker Hill and learned how the British received the news. And Thomas Gage saw things clearly when he concluded that George III should either send a mighty, overwhelming force or be content to blockade America. The battle of Bunker Hill had channeled the current of events toward war. Earlier clashes had left no strain on the relationship of Britannia and her daughters which could not, with good will, be relaxed, but from now on it was dead serious war. The scarlet-stained grass of Breed's Hill seeded a continent.

III

While the British generals in Boston were making the series of judgments that led to the great bloodletting on Breed's Hill, the Congress very gingerly considered the prospect of adding Canada as a four-teenth colony. The Congress had nothing to do with taking Ticonder-oga, Crown Point, and St. John's, but certainly welcomed the valuable military stores captured. The way appeared open to Canada, and Benedict Arnold was eager to lead legions in that province, but on June 1 the Congress refused to authorize an invasion. The resolution was more postponement than decison, being one of those very human recoilings from surprising propositions which require large commit-ments. After four weeks of reflection—and several days of digesting the news of Bunker Hill—the delegates reversed themselves and authorized General Schuyler, commanding in New York, to conquer Canada "if . . . it will not be disagreeable to the Canadians. . . ."[31] Schuyler's command was nominal, since New York port itself seemed in peril. Brigadier Richard Montgomery was to be Schuyler's deputy at the head of the thrust, while Benedict Arnold was to try to force his way through the thickets and over the highlands of wilderness Maine to surprise Quebec. The reversal of the congressional decision made sense on the basis of evidence available. The reconnoitering John Brown had reported Canadian sympathy before Lexington and Concord, and Quebec sent a thousand bushels of wheat in relief when the Port Act paralyzed Boston. In October Washington confirmed the optimism of the Congress by reporting Canada's defenses as weak, Canadians as favorably inclined to the cause of the united colonies, and—what must have stimulated the Congress considerably—that Quebec had "the largest Stock of Ammunition ever Collected in America."[32]

A better-organized and more expert "government" than the Con-tinental Congress might actually have made friends for itself in Can-ada by first preparing the ground politically and socially. Canadian clergy and landlords proved unexpectedly loyal to the new regime, and the attitude of the clergy, with their revised statutory authority under the Quebec Act to tithe their parishioners willy-nilly, pro-voked anti-clericalism almost to the point of schism. The loyalist at-titude of the landlords began their long decline from leadership of French Canadian public life. The American Revolution stirred the imaginations of the Canadians and started them talking politics in 1775, and they have never stopped, but the English-speaking coloni-als to the southward had no understanding of the structure of Cana-dian society, and were probably too provincial to have exploited its

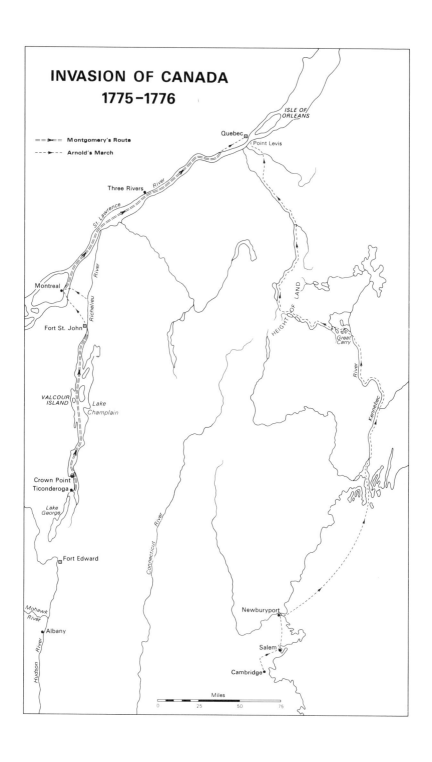

INVASION OF CANADA
1775–1776

═══► Montgomery's Route

- - -► Arnold's March

ISLE OF ORLEANS

Quebec

Point Levis

Three Rivers

St. Lawrence River

Richelieu River

Montreal

Fort St. John

HEIGHT OF LAND

Great Carry

Kennebec River

VALCOUR ISLAND

Lake Champlain

Crown Point

Ticonderoga

Lake George

Fort Edward

Connecticut River

Mohawk River

Albany

Hudson River

Newburyport

Salem

Cambridge

Miles

0   25   50   75

divisions had they been informed. What they needed was some efficient anti-clerical agitation in Canada, but tribal Protestantism saw Catholicism as a monolith even though the writings of the *philosophes* of France circulated in America and proved the contrary. It was too bad for the colonials that Franklin had not spent his many years abroad in Paris instead of London. *He* might have thought of some way to prepare the ground. But the solution attempted was military.

Arnold's men suffered every imaginable hardship which could torment an ill-trained force crossing an unmapped northern wilderness in severe fall weather. After a painful October and November they arrived on the banks of the St. Lawrence near Quebec in bad physical condition and without surprising the enemy. Montgomery's column had a somewhat easier march inasmuch as its route was the fairly well-known corridor between the St. Lawrence and Hudson valleys, with no topographical surprises. Montreal was unguarded, and Montgomery took it easily. That was the last success.

The British commander, General Sir Guy Carleton, probably the ablest British officer in North America during the whole of the war, had a difficult defense problem. When Arnold appeared before Quebec the town had a garrison of about seventy infantry and a handful of gunners. Carleton borrowed thirty-seven marines and 271 seamen from the Royal Navy, and activated a militia unit of eighty men named the Royal Highland Emigrants, all former regular soldiers of the King. He scraped up enough British and French militia, in a ratio of two British for each three French, to bring his total garrison to twelve hundred. His proportion of trained to unskilled fighters was about four to seven, and some of the veterans were probably on the arthritic side. The total was not really enough to man the walls properly.

Like Washington, Carleton could not inspire recruiting. The *habitants* remained cool to his summons despite—or because of—his use of the French feudal form for rallying vassals. Jean Briand, the Bishop of Quebec, proved himself an old-fashioned legitimist by urging his flock to help Carleton and promising to excommunicate any who helped the united colonies. But his decretal left his nominal followers as cold as Carleton's archaic writ, and they stayed on their farms, no doubt prayerfully meditating on the happy years between the victory of Wolfe and the passage of the Quebec Act, years when the

Bishop had to live by passing the collection basket instead of levying tithes backed up by the force of King-in-Parliament. Nevertheless, despite Canadian apathy, the shell of Quebec could not be cracked by the two American leaders who collected their small forces before it in the early winter snows.

Montgomery's and Arnold's men had enlisted for the calendar year 1775, which was drawing to a close. It would obviously be better—speaking militarily—to spend them in fighting than to issue discharges, so Montgomery and Arnold put together an assault of Quebec on New Year's Eve, 1775. Arnold and a part of the force broke into the town but could not maintain themselves. The enemy killed Montgomery and captured some of Arnold's men. That was the practical end of the campaign, though Arnold surrounded Quebec with a thin line for the next few months, and the expedition survived with much suffering from poor diet, hard weather, inadequate clothing, and, finally, the ugly ravages of smallpox. The prime reason for the failure was that the invaders were too few. When the Congress in Philadelphia received news on January 17 of Montgomery's death the American cause had its first eminent martyr (Warren was not a Continental officer). Someone suggested visible tokens of mourning, but others swept the idea aside on the ground that Montgomery's memory was "already embalmed in the Heart of every good American and that such Proceeding may cause too much alarm at such a critical Juncture."[33] It was indeed "a critical juncture." Washington's council at Cambridge advised him to raise New England regiments to march to the north, which he did, but he showed his steady deference to the Congress by offering to countermand the order instantly if the Congress demurred.[34] Meanwhile, the sickly survivors in Canada were enduring one of the worst of recent winters.[35]

The Canadian disaster of 1775–1776 surprised the Congress because it was the result of optimistic, even wishful, planning. To find out for themselves what had happened the delegates sent a mission to the scene. They chose Benjamin Franklin, then aged seventy, Congressman Samuel Chase of Maryland, and two men who were not members of the Congress, Charles Carroll of Carrollton and his brother the ex-Jesuit John Carroll, most respected of the few Catholic priests of the colonies. The delegates also intended to send, immediately, another complete army under command of Charles Lee, but nothing came of this proposal. Charles Carroll had a French education and was a Catholic. He was also one of the richest men in the united colonies, with one of North America's largest holdings of slaves. If Bishop Briand had shown any hint of wavering in his allegiance, the Carroll brothers would have been the correct agents to send, but otherwise their value is hard to imagine. They shared nothing with the commoners of Quebec except Catholicism, which has never been a political cement. Nevertheless, the mission served a useful purpose by exposing the painful results of half-baked plans, since it found the troops inadequately supplied and learned that every such expedition must be regarded as hazardous. That was the first lesson of a course of study which the Congress took years to master. Samuel Chase was characteristically outspoken. To Richard Henry Lee he wrote that the Congress was not fit to act as a council of war: "Pray divide your business into different departments."[36] (The Congress did—five years later.) The commissioners wrote jointly from Montreal that hard money was necessary in Canada, and if it were not available it would be better to withdraw from Canada and to fortify the lakes.[37] That became the policy, but its execution was tortuous.

The fiasco was not without indirect profit to the united colonies. It pinned Carleton, the wisest of British soldiers, in Canada where he could do less harm to the Continental Army than his inferior colleagues did in the following years. The invasion so interested the government in England that troops intended for Howe went to Quebec instead, delaying the attack on the middle colonies. The well-fought rear-guard actions, mostly by Arnold, prevented Carleton from overrunning New York, but that, of course, was not to be entered in the profit column, since the defense of northern New York was a desperate result of a disaster and not at all a part of the intentions of the original invasion of Canada.

5

The Balance of Obstinacy, 1775-1776

The Congress that had met shortly after the bloodshed of the Lexington and Concord raid and had warmly endorsed the behavior of the Massachusetts rebels expected that a short war would convince the government of Great Britain to change its policy. Through most of 1775 the delegates made only short-range plans and took short views. But the reaction of the British government showed that Americans' thinking was wishful thinking, for King George III and his obedient servant Frederick Lord North led Parliament to approve ever stricter punishments of the rebels. Slowly the Americans came to realize they had waded into a sea of troubles. They were every bit as angry as the British rulers, and began to behave as a sovereign nation. On their own soil they began to grope toward a rational and permanent table of organization of their Army. They founded a navy. And they began to seek help abroad from the ancient enemies of Britain in Europe. Both Britons and Americans were equally obstinate. Not being clairvoyant, they could not foresee that the only resolutions of the deadlock could be a smashing British conquest of America or the emergence of an independent United States.

The Balance of Obstinacy, 1775–1776

After its recess, the Continental Congress of 1775 reconvened on September 12 with no sign of fear or even of irresolution. Perhaps Benjamin Rush, not yet a Congressman but certainly *au courant*, best wrote of the antagonistic spirit in an unsigned letter to England, dated October 29: "Nothing short of a total repeal of all the Acts complained off [*sic*] last year will now satisfy the most timid of the delegates. . . . Britain & america [*sic*] *will* hereafter be distinct empires."[1] The British intercepted the letter and the London *Morning Post* printed it in a rather inaccurate transcription. But the meaning was clear, and in none of its decisions did the Congress prove that Rush overstated the situation.

The colonies had been seething since the Concord raid. Loyalists claimed the rebels were only a minority, but in the twelve months after Concord every royal or proprietary governor lost his place except the governor of New York, who had to be maintained by the Royal Navy in his harbor. Many assemblies found themselves replaced or paralleled by revolutionary provincial congresses. These extra-legal deliberative bodies barred conservatives, or the conservatives voluntarily stood aside in delicate disdain, which opened careers to rebels, some of whom could not previously vote or who had at best exerted negligible political influence.

British stubbornness meanwhile showed itself in proclamations and acts which ended all hope of peace. In August the King proclaimed rebellion in America. In October the King's speech to Parliament spoke of "desperate conspiracy" and "general revolt" "for the purpose of establishing an independent empire," which must be met by arms. In November Parliament responded with the Prohibitory Act to blockade America, allow seizure of American property at sea, and put captured American seamen in the Royal Navy.[2] In pacification the government promised to send commissioners to America to absolve the contrite. Many Americans read the Prohibitory Act as expulsion from the Empire.

From May until the end of 1775, as the demands of the resistance became visible, it is remarkable how the Congress maintained its high degree of optimism in the face of prospects which could well have dismayed other groups. Because the Congress ultimately won the contest, we do not usually ask whether its perseverance, despite royal threats, was rash. The intellectual heritage of these American leaders of opinion made them optimistic. Nature was trustworthy (and on their side). Man was usually rational and master of his destiny. The united colonies might well be the nucleus of earthly paradise. These notions saturated the political air and sparkled in the rhetoric. Instead of being awed by the power of British arms—of which they had been so proud in 1760—the rebels were rather more confident than circumstances justified. The horrors of the Thirty Years' War were not much more remote from them in time than the horrors of the Civil War of the 1860's are from us, and reflection on that terrible epoch might well have given them pause. But they pressed on almost blithely.

A study of public attitudes, or at least of the leaders' attitudes, is easily made from the toasts proposed at public dinners from the mid-1760's to the mid-1770's. Every newspaper published long lists of them, and a serial reading shows a shift of opinion that cannot be misunderstood. Toasts praised leaders or public bodies, or, in epigrammatic form, expressed hopes and beliefs. The shift is exquisitely symmetrical. From King and royal family, to parliamentary opposition, to condemnation of American loyalists, to praises of constitutional writers who argued that Americans had all of the rights of Englishmen, to American military heroes—the line is straight and clear. The royalty disappear, parliamentary opposition drops out because it did not help, the loyalists need no condemnation when at the mercy of provincial congresses, the constitutional philosophers withdraw in favor of the military officers because the appeal has been carried from legal parchment to cartridge paper.[3] The British ignored every friendly gesture from across the sea, while the Ministry declared its intention of restoring the total authority of King-in-Parliament by every force it commanded or could hire. These attitudes are understandable, but must be rated as gross blunders of what passed for statecraft in Britain. It was almost as Newton had said—for every British action there was an American reaction, and vice versa. Mechanist philosophy has few friends nowadays, but the interaction of Anglo-American politics in the eighteenth century was almost the acting out of the behavior of the clockwork universe described by that century's natural philosophers.

Although conservatives were no longer prominent, the Congress was a middle-class group, drawn mostly from landowners, city leaders, and lawyers. It was no body of climbers but a group of delegates determined to preserve the status they had already gained. Their ideology was not a new extremism but what is properly called Whiggery, most simply defined as a profound distrust of executive power by men themselves powerful. Whether farmers or "planters," lawyers or shipping magnates, believers in a Holy Trinity or an omnipotent, omniscient Unity, they spoke the language of English Whiggery, altered slightly to American conditions (for example, American Whigs need not boggle at slavery). Whiggery—white, Protestant, male, Anglo-Saxon, and aromatic with the incense offered at shrines of seventeenth-century regicides—was the spirit of all but a few arch-conservative or democratic colonists.[4] In it there was practically nothing of democracy; the few democrats were given supporting roles.

A galaxy of new luminaries had joined the Congress at the first session of 1775: Jefferson, Franklin, John Hancock (promptly elected president), Robert R. Livingston (the untitled Hudson Valley duke), Philip Schuyler (who went away with Washington to be a soldier), and James Wilson. In the September session another famous man came, George Wythe of Virginia, Jefferson's law tutor. Of middle height, well-framed, straightforward and courteous in manner, he was the leading scholar of Virginia. He stayed only through 1776, but that was the critical year for his influence to be most usefully felt, because, as Jefferson said, he was not "higgling on half-way principles" but "he took his stand on the solid ground that the only link between us and Great Britain was the identity of our executive; that that nation and its Parliament had no more authority over us, than we had over them, and that we were coordinate nations with Great Britain and Hanover."[5] (It is easy to see here one of the sources of Jefferson's *Summary View*.) Carrying Wythe's view logically forward, it is clear that if loyalty to the King faltered, independence would be at hand.

The Congress had been several days late in reconvening after the recess. In all the years it existed, whenever it recessed or moved to another place the Congress lost more working days than anticipated, not because of apathy but because the delegates always estimated their travel time too optimistically. Three days after the beginning of the September session the united colonies became the thirteen colonies when the first Georgia delegation appeared. The Georgia Congressmen were Archibald Bullock, John Houston, and the Reverend Mr. Johannes Joachim Zubly, who much impressed John Adams as "a clergyman of independent persuasion" from Switzerland, fluent in at least four languages.[6] (To be candid, Georgia was so new, so poor, and so isolated that no Georgia Congressman was essential to the winning of independence.) Hope of Canada's becoming the fourteenth colony was quite alive, since the Montgomery and Arnold columns were on the march. But, though they did not know it, with the arrival of Georgia the family of political entities that became the United States was complete.

What was not complete—and not to be completed soon—was a plan to use the armed forces in such a way as to cause Britain to revise its colonial policy. To arrive at such a plan absolutely required consultation with Washington, so the delegates discussed whether the Continental Congress might take up a permanent seat nearer the Army. Looking backward, we can see that it would have been administratively awkward and psychologically uncomfortable (at least to the Continental Army) to have the Congress breathing down Washington's neck. But a practical reason also carried weight. The movement of the whole Congress overland to some site near the Army in New England would be physically very tiresome. To move the delegates in a body by water would expose them to the risk of capture by the Royal Navy. In a typical compromise, they decided to send a committee to represent the Congress in dealing with the Army.[7]

Taking up military problems was surely putting first things first. While the colonies were rich in food and timber, they had almost nothing else useful to armies. It was a real question whether they could continue to resist by force of arms. If the delegates had tried to answer the question solely in accord with principles of accountancy, they would have quit in the fall of 1775 for lack of both war materials and money.

The select committee to maintain liaison between the Congress and the Army was to investigate the needs of the Army and to make recommendations in concert with Washington and with the civil "governments" of the New England colonies. Its mission was to consult with Washington on the state of the forces, and with the de facto rulers of Rhode Island, Connecticut, Massachusetts, and New Hampshire on ways and means of continuing the struggle.

The committee's members were Thomas Lynch of South Carolina, Benjamin Harrison, the fat Virginian ancestor of Presidents (so respected by Washington and so despised by John Adams for sloth), and Franklin. A different committee wrote the instructions for these travelers, and rather naively. The visitors were to suggest driving the British out of Boston by the end of December (when enlistments expired). If additional men were needed, the Minute Men could be summoned (the Congress did not know that the Minute Men no longer existed as a formal organization). If expulsion of the redcoats seemed impractical, the number of troops should be reduced and those who chose to re-enlist should be rewarded with a pay cut. One is driven to ask, was cost accounting to prevail?

The Congress had adopted the Army bravely but had not reckoned on a prolonged war. Washington's expressed hope to finish the job by Christmas illustrated the optimism of the delegates. By fall the bills were beginning to come in, and the pendulum of hopes and fears had swung from audacity to depression. The timorous instructions to the select committee to visit the Army represented an ebb tide of congressional confidence as the once falsely bright future turned murky and opaque. Because the Congress had taken charge of the soldiery of the several colonies, it was obliged to pay for them. It entered on the field of military finance with an air of quaking. Its question was the central question of every legislative body: Where is the money coming from? The delegates could not long postpone an answer, yet *any* answer would take the form of an act of an independent nation.

After conferring in Cambridge with the visiting committee from the Congress, Washington saw that *he* must phrase the questions for the Congress to answer, and not the other way around. The Army encamped around Cambridge cost $275,000 a month, a figure the Congress could hardly ignore. The paymaster general of the troops was unable to accept offers of cash in exchange for bills drawn on the Congress in Philadelphia, because the Congress had not delegated the authority. And there were other questions. Should Washington try to raise troops in Canada? Was the payment of the detached companies Washington's responsibility? Might he re-enlist the free black soldiers? (He had already done it, to keep them from joining the British Army.) Would the Congress please raise the pay of engineers and chaplains so that he could recruit some? And, finally, should there not be some uniform plan for binding loyalists of all provinces by oath not to help Britain?[8] This bill of particulars reads more like a special message from President to Congress than an inquiry from a military theater commander. It was the shadow of things to come.

While doing all of these things that only the agents of independent nations do, the Congress received the King's Proclamation of Rebellion. Swollen with moral indignation, the Congress denied the charge. "What allegiance is it that we forget? Allegiance to Parliament? We never owed—we never owned it. Allegiance to our King? Our words have ever avowed it,—our conduct has ever been consistent with it." But they could not resist lecturing the King on law. "Rebellion" was not a legal term. If his Proclamation was going to be wrong on the facts, it should at least state the law of the matter properly.[9]

II

The Americans lived as a long, thin splinter of a people along a saw-toothed coastline. Such folk took to seafaring. For the same reason, every army of occupation, including the British garrison of Boston, could only be supplied by ships. George Washington's Virginia house overlooked the shipping route between the Atlantic and the port of Alexandria, and when he went to Cambridge he grasped the supply situation of the British easily. With permission of the Congress he commissioned about eight little men-of-war in New England ports to harass the British oceanic lifeline to Boston. In 1775 his ships intercepted twenty-three prizes of great benefit to the besieging Continentals, and in 1776 and 1777, before the Congress took them into the Continental Navy, they had cut out thirty-two more and made a name for their boldest captain, John Manley. The naval operations in Massachusetts Bay, under Army auspices, were a credit to Washington's judgment.

Many members of the Congress went down to the sea in ships and did business in great waters, or hired men to do it for them. It was only a matter of time until someone suggested maintaining a regular Continental Navy. The first to offer the suggestion were Rhode Islanders, but the Congress did not unanimously applaud the proposal for there were some who were suspicious of Yankee notions. Pennsylvanians, Marylanders, and Virginians claimed to fear that a regular

Navy would lure British blockaders to strangle the trade of the Delaware and Chesapeake Bays. Others argued that a Navy would be useful to protect the trade of New England but not of the South, since there were few Southern merchant ships and most Southern produce moved in British bottoms.[10] Any belief that the British would refrain from blockading fleetless resisters seems overoptimistic, but it shows that some still anticipated very limited British operations.

Nevertheless, without much forethought, the Congress in early October had already taken the first steps toward the founding of a Continental Navy by appointing John Adams, John Langdon of New Hampshire, and Silas Deane of Connecticut as a committee to buy vessels to serve against the British. The committee immediately purchased several, but later realized that the use of merchant vessels as men-of-war was only a makeshift solution. It was then that the Rhode Islanders introduced the idea of building regular fighting ships. By this time the Congress, through its ship-buying committee, owned two ships, six brigs, three schooners, and five sloops. Washington had four other vessels at sea by now to vex the Bostonian British, and Colonel Benedict Arnold had become the self-made commodore of a sloop and two schooners on blue Lake Champlain. Almost absentmindedly the Congress had also acquired some smaller craft to serve as despatch-carrying packets. The Congress was sliding sideways into becoming a microscopic naval power, without having examined naval policy as a whole.[11]

The munitions-hungry delegates thought much about the possibility of intercepting British vessels, especially those carrying valued military stores. Early in October word came to Philadelphia that two such vessels were being sent from Britain to Canada. Result: a committee on how to catch them. The plan resolved upon was to fit out two ships of ten guns each for a bitter-cold North Atlantic cruise of three months to try to intercept those lush British store-ships and any others they could handle. To vote ships was easy and gratifying, so the Congress exuberantly increased the number of ships and their armament, to four ships of ten, fourteen, twenty, and twenty-six guns respectively.[12] By such small practical attacks on specific problems the Congress was habitually to fall into great general policies—in this case the ultimate founding of the Continental Navy. No strategic board paused to calculate seriously whether naval warfare was to the best interest of the cause.

Next the Congress decided to raise seagoing infantry, voting on November 10, 1775, to establish the first and second battalions of American marines. They were to be good seamen who could fight on land or sea, as occasion demanded. Despite possible pain to the present Corps, candor compels the admission that the Congress regarded them as part of the Continental Army,[13] for, though ships had been acquired, the Congress had not yet formally voted to establish a navy of which the marines could be part.

By this time a continental navy, but not a Continental Navy, was in being as a scattered and decentralized mixture of fresh- and saltwater vessels, and paper resolutions to buy more vessels. The Army operated those that were actually afloat. This fragmented waterborne and paper-authorized force was not an organized Navy because of lack of congressional action to establish and govern a Navy. The earlier Adams-Langdon-Deane committee, which had been charged with the duty of buying vessels, had completed that work and at the moment concerned itself only with writing a set of naval regulations. Thus no committee of the Congress had responsibility for carrying out the whole congressional commitment to naval operations. The Congress sensed the vacuum in mid-December and rushed to fill it, but not before happily and gloriously adding to the paper strength. It enlarged the force still more (on paper) by acceding to the Rhode Island proposition to build authentic frigates. Five were to have thirty-two guns, five were to have twenty-eight, and three were to have twenty-four. Thus the Continental Navy may properly be dated from these actions of December 13 and 14, 1775, for to manage the multitude of details of seaborne warfare the delegates established the Marine Committee, which drew a member from each of the united colonies.[14] The policy was charted, the course was laid, the Continental Navy lived. The Congress then named a corps of officers on December 22, headed by "Ezek" Hopkins of Rhode Island, "Commander-in-Chief of the Fleet," equal in status (but in no other way) to Washington. He was supported by four captains and thirteen lieutenants, who were graded as first, second, and third lieutenants.[15] Of all these officers only one impressed himself on the national imagination, First Lieutenant John Paul Jones. (Although Washington referred to Hopkins as the "Admiral," no American held that rank for almost a century to come.)

It was clear from the proceedings of these busy days that the mission of the little naval force was, in the main, to do what it could to interfere with the supplying of the British forces in America. No other defensible reason could be put forward for this puny effort to meet the world's foremost seapower in its own element. If seapower was necessary to defend the American coastal plain from complete British reconquest, it would have been better to surrender immediately or try to run on the crest of the Appalachians and eat squirrel meat, rather than to bare colonial skins to Britannia's trident.

Before thirteen frigates could be built, somebody had to design them. The design of the Continental Navy is one of the most obscure aspects of the War for Independence. Humiliating as it is, we must admit that much of what we know about the design of the ships of the Continental Navy has been learned from drawings made in British shipyards after the Royal Navy captured the American vessels. It is not certain who designed any of them. Most likely the plans were made in Philadelphia for the approval of the Marine Committee, which then sent copies to the selected builders. These drawings were quite large and were difficult to convey from Philadelphia to the builders. The delay of the couriers is alone almost enough to explain why not one frigate was afloat at the time intended, March 1776. The first frigates launched may well have been built from local plans or rules of thumb, by men bored with waiting for drawings to come from Philadelphia. (At least five of the frigates varied widely from the specifications approved by the Marine Committee.) These vessels ordered in 1775 for delivery in 1776 were definitely not copies of any other ships then in any naval service. Their designs seem to have been derived from the American experience of developing small, swift sailing vessels, for the Americans placed a high value on their own opinions of how to lay down the lines of fast ships with good seakeeping qualities. They had good clean lines, but their admittedly good speed owed something to the fact that they were more lightly built than their British equivalents. The only similarity of building practices with those of any foreign yards was that each American fighting class was slightly larger in dimensions than the British counterpart, a practice also followed by French naval builders. There is no reason to believe that American builders looked to France for an ideal. Their own acute observation of sailing qualities would be enough to account for the differences from the British. They were right, too. All things considered, it was a good idea to build each

class slightly larger than its British opposite number, an idea followed with great success in building the United States Navy twenty
years later, that tiny armada which so humbled the Royal Navy in
single-ship duels in the War of 1812.[16]

Just as the designing of the Continental Navy was one of the most
obscure operations of the War, so the first administration of it was
one of the war's most fatuous programs. After the Rhode Island
motion passed, the Marine Committee distributed building contracts
to those colonies with the most political leverage, rather than selecting
sites noted for the production of fine ships. The several Congressmen
from the state in which a ship was to be built then picked the builder
of the ship. This was an early form of national spoils-politics, but not
necessarily the worst method of choosing builders, since political
agreement would be an essential quality of a builder under such
circumstances. One serious but natural error usually made, as the
Congress later learned with pain, was to have the ships built in the
most important ports most likely to be occupied or at least blockaded
by the British. After letting a contract for a ship, the local artisans
could have slices of the cake by subcontracting parts of the work,
though no two building sites used precisely the same system. The
effect of legislating for a Continental Navy was to repeat a part of
the history of British public naval finance—the attraction of businessmen to an instant heavy industry and the creation of a primordial
military-industrial complex.

Nothing in the history of the Congress so effectively proved the
need for an executive as the witless schedule of production adopted
by the Marine Committee. Whatever the Americans had so far done
well had been the result of brilliant, barely credible improvisation.
Now the Marine Committee poured molasses into the rickety machinery of rebellion. In a land where communications hardly existed,
it tried to systematize and centralize control over the building of the
Navy. Most of the members of the Marine Committee had been
schooled by the sea, yet when brought to collective action they made
decisions which they could not sanely have made as successful shipowners working in their own interest. How could they *not* have
known the impossibility of getting these ships into action by March
1776? Yet that was the date written into their resolution. On the
day the Congress voted the resolution, there remained 108 days in
which to do the job. It took thirty-one days to draw the designs and
twenty days to copy the first set of drawings. Fifty-seven days re-

mained, of which ten were used to scour Philadelphia and environs for messengers willing to take paper dollars to ride hundreds of miles on horseback in the dead of winter in order to carry the bulky bundles of drawings to the builders' yards, and then a few days of travel time. Probably seventy of the 108 days passed before any master shipwright could begin to frown and move his lips as he read off the dimensions on the huge sheets sent from the Congress. No wonder a few builders had gone ahead by rule of thumb or local plans. As well have orders to turn water into wine or raise the dead as to be told to build a fighting frigate in fewer than forty days after receiving the plans. To be sure, something like it was done later in 1814, when men in weeks built smaller craft of green timbers on the fresh waters of Lake Champlain; but the miniature fleet of 1814 was expendable, intended to fight but once, and never expected to be much beyond swimming distance from a shore.

The Marine Committee had no such jerry-built improvisations in mind in 1775. Most of them felt entirely competent to pass on the most minute specifications in exact dimensions, and they intended to obtain uniformity in their little fleet by agreement among themselves before working up the drawings. The program was more worthy of Laputa than of Philadelphia. The only cheerful note in the whole of the 1775–1776 naval program was that the colors of the ships were to be chosen by the builders or captains. They could choose from white lead, yellow ochre, black oil paint, Spanish brown, or red iron oxide. When the ships went to sea (as some ultimately did) they were gay against the blue sky, ultramarine water, and whitecaps of the oceans, in white, red, blue, and yellow paint, with contrasting colors to pick out the carved work. The topsides were usually yellow with black stripes, or black with red, white, and yellow stripes in very narrow bands—brave colors for brave men.

Even before the December renewal of their hereditary allegiance to their King, the Congress of the united colonies entered the field of international law and spent several days making regulations for the governance of their naval force. Washington's seagoing armed force first posed the legal problem. Massachusetts had passed an act for fitting out provincial privateers and for a court to rule on prize cases. Washington sent it to the Congress, observing that it took care of the local situation—captures made by provincial vessels manned by local crews—but that he had no authority to deal with cases arising from captures by the armed vessels fitted out at the expense of the Congress. He asked for the establishment of a prize court because "I cannot spare Time from Military Affairs,"[17] which was surely the truth. In response the Congress, almost seven and a half months before making any formal claim to independence, plunged into the making of international law by accepting in the same month a report on the legality of the seizure of British ships and cargos: all British vessels captured by the colonists after having been used against the colonies were forfeit. Three weeks later the Congress resolved that *any* transports in the service of the King were good prizes on capture, whether owned in America or in Great Britain. In order to adjudicate questions arising out of such captures, the Congress urged all provinces to establish prize courts,[18] which certainly showed approval of the initiative of Massachusetts in putting such captures under the color of law.

During these same weeks the Congress also adopted a set of articles for governing the Continental Navy—the kind of regulations used in the public fleets of sovereign nations everywhere.[19] They were produced by that first committee composed of John Adams, Langdon, and Deane. Adams is generally credited with the authorship.

From the Massachusetts enactment that provided for prize courts it is obvious that private men-of-war had already gone to sea against British naval vessels, or vessels chartered for the service of the Royal Navy in 1775; but the question became continental when Parliament's Restraining Act of December 23 arrived in America late in February 1776. The act closed the colonies to all commerce, and indignation flared like a flame under a bellows. The act was to be effective on March 1, so the notice was short. Angry shipowners itched for reprisals. The traditional kind of reprisal for any high seas damage was to license private warships to prey upon the commerce of the alleged aggressor, a practice called privateering. The huge British merchant fleet was quite vulnerable to such profit-seeking rovers. The Congress resolved on March 19 to approve privateering, thus again meeting a specific problem with a generalized policy that was to have far-reaching consequences.

In these ways thirteen colonies, while professing loyalty to King George III and denying the authority of King-in-Parliament, had founded a Navy, provided for a prize court system, and tacitly approved of provincial navies, provincial privateering, and provincial prize courts. They wrote a system of discipline and doctrine for their

Navy; they authorized private warships to rove the seas carrying congressional letters of marque and reprisal (the legal name for privateer licenses).

But the Congress was leading from weakness against the Royal Navy which, on paper, had all the trumps in this life and death game. There was no colonial fleet, of course, except the lightly framed merchant vessels. The independent exertions of the several provinces were dissipations of what were, from the beginning, limited amounts of resources and manpower. Privateering by its nature could not be decisive, but it offered a much more attractive way of life to adventurous men than any navy could offer, since it was safer and had the excitement of gambling for huge profits, if luck allowed. Specific operations with limited objectives—such as Washington's harassment of the British supply service to Boston, and Arnold's seizure of the naval control of Lake Champlain—were probably as much as should have been attempted. Generally throughout the naval war to come, the Continental ships were poorly armed, poorly manned, and poorly commanded. Their best service was as commerce raiders which augmented the munitions and supplies of the Army. Most Continental ships saw no decisive action but spent their time carrying despatches, diplomatists, and congressional freight. This hints that what the Congress needed was not a regular Navy but a fast, sleek packet service fit for blockade running. As for the fighting ships ordered in 1775, those that were actually finished had to get to sea by stealth, if indeed they ever got to sea at all. Yet they were more powerful and more costly ships than the Congress needed for privateers or for packets. And once at sea they had no bases in the western hemisphere and could replenish their stores only by capturing supplies, or salable cargos to sell in neutral ports. It is a real question whether the Continental Congress or any single colony should have attempted systematic offensive operations on the high seas.

III

Prolonged rebellion in any country where fertile soil abounded would not pass unnoticed in the foreign offices of the world powers. And America was not just any country. For three centuries it had been the stakes of European diplomacy, and even France gave up for a time its policy of dominating continental Europe in order to seek the kind of treasure Spain had found. The French adventure ended in the gross humiliation of the Great War for Empire, 1754–1763. For Britain the result of that war had been a triumph almost beyond the dreams of glory, for British arms eliminated France from the New World and humbled French pride everywhere. French leaders did not find this humiliation a source of spiritual graces; they privately resolved not to endure it, and watched Britain's every move in hope that the lion would pull up lame. Perhaps Spain would help restore French pride, since the nations were partners in the blood-kin formal alliance of the two branches of the House of Bourbon which ruled France and Spain, called the Family Compact; but Spain really had much to lose and little to gain by change. "Procrastination" might well have been the Spanish royal device. Portugal feared overly protective Spain and clung to Britain to protect its independence, that *liberdade* gained so bloodily in the previous century. The idealized balance of power teetered on bayonet point. Diplomacy was corrupt and irrationally competitive in any age in which decadent feudal scions had no excuse for existence except to lead troops in battle. But it was this diplomacy of powdered wigs over lousy heads, of stilettos neatly stowed in silk stockings, this rivalry by corruption, perfidy, and murder within the forms of courtly etiquette, that made American independence possible.[20]

Everyone understood that another war between Britain and France was probable. Many powerful Frenchmen were eager for war, and foreign minister Étienne-François, Duc de Choiseul, positively thirsted for it until he left office in 1770.

From the time the Congress began practicing *de facto* independence in the summer of 1775, it always acted as if foreign help would come. Perhaps in their hearts the members doubted it, but they enjoyed the stimulation of hinting at it; they soon had visible and audible encouragement. Julien Archard, Chevalier de Bonvouloir, a Norman whose family supported him in the West Indies on condition that he stay away from Normandy, found the turbulences of British North America intriguing. He went to Philadelphia in 1775 with the conscious intention of contriving a connection between France and America. He found a useful intermediary in the person of Francis Daymon, a widely acquainted bookseller who also served as librarian of the local subscription library. Through him Bonvouloir met and talked with several Congressmen, after which he traveled in the colonies to study public opinion and feeling. That same summer he went to France and put himself at the service of the foreign minister, Charles Gravier, Comte de Vergennes, who listened and then sent him back to America in September. Bonvouloir encouraged the Congress by saying that the French court would receive an American delegation as friends. Thus in America he told the Americans what they wished to hear, and, in France, Vergennes was inclined to believe Bonvouloir's somewhat exaggerated reports of the ability and the will to war of the disaffected colonists. The exchange had a strong influence on the thinking of the French government.

In the minds of a few members of the Congress, one of the several reasons for an interest in foreign help was the possibility of private profit which might be made out of foreign aid. Amicable gestures from France opened this possibility because it was a common practice of the age for government buyers to receive a commission on the money they spent, that is, a few cents of each dollar spent on behalf of the government went to reward the purchasing agent for his work—5 per cent was common. This was a tempting way to wealth, for where war is waged, there money is spent. For example, long before a deal was made with France, the Congress had heard rumors that Congressman Robert Morris of the Philadelphia mercantile firm of Willing and Morris stood to share a profit of his firm in the sum of twelve thousand pounds sterling from an Army gunpowder deal. True or not, the story stirred annoyance which boiled to a fierce intra-congressional quarrel in later years. As early as 1774 an element of the Congress smelled money in military operations, and this faction waxed rather than waned. Congressman Silas Deane of Connecticut, brushing against great riches for the first time, interceded with General Schuyler in 1775 to use more Connecticut men as Army supply contractors. At the same time one Army officer offered to resign his commission so as not to alienate those to whom he wished to continue to be a contractor for Army supplies.[21]

Quite apart from these earthy considerations, the Congress decided to exploit the opening into continental European politics. On November 29 it appointed a five-man Committee of Correspondence. Two weeks later it gave the committee a small sum for the expense of agents abroad, whereupon the committee wrote, on December 12, to Arthur Lee, the agent of Massachusetts in London, asking him to learn the attitude of the great powers toward America. Bonvouloir then addressed the Congress, unofficially promising a hearty welcome to American ships in French ports and hinting that something more tangible than good fellowship might be available from France to help prosecute the war.

Almost simultaneously the governor of Virginia, John Murray, Earl of Dunmore, outraged Virginia rebels with the kind of warfare they would least tolerate. He had only two hundred regulars, some Scots loyalists, and a few blacks. Being plainly short of manpower, he promised freedom to any contract laborer or slave who joined him as a soldier, and then retreated to ships from which he waged counter-insurgency, firing plantations, confiscating tobacco, and burning Norfolk. He also tried to incite Indians, and the whites accused him of plotting to poison wells. Dunmore had long reflected on his emancipation proclamation, and, like a later emancipator, he issued it only for military ends. It drew eight hundred black soldiers into "Lord Dunmore's Ethiopian Regiment," raising his armed strength to eleven hundred. They operated as marines, fighting ashore and on shipboard. Practically all had joined him in stolen boats because they could escape only by water, and they made good pilots. Dunmore's operation, for lack of a good base, accomplished little, and his men rapidly died of disease in overcrowded ships; but Dunmore became a secret hero to American blacks and a monstrous beast in the minds of American whites.[22] Dunmore probably made more rebels by raising the phantom of race war. The liberty Dunmore promised to black men was not what white men had in mind at all.

The Boston Port Act and its associated coercive statutes had united the colonies. The Lexington-Concord bloodshed caused the colonies to arm themselves and begin undeclared self-government. The great slaughter on Breed's Hill meant that the only possible solution of the quarrel would be a military solution. The winter of 1775–1776 marked the arrival of American political affairs at a point where there could be only two resolutions of the tension: either the British would inflict disastrous and humiliating defeat on the Americans and reduce them to prostrate submission, or the united colonies would become a nation. From the reconvening of the second session of the Congress of 1775, there was a growing impatience with the pretense of opposing only evil advisers and bad legislators while remaining loyal to a legitimate king. By January 1776 the contest had changed from a constitutional storm to a revolution. During the tumults from 1764 to 1774 earlier governors had professed to see tendencies toward independence, but they did not qualify as detached political commentators. What most strengthened the cause of independence was the painful mental impact of the Prohibitory Act, which was as important to independence as the Boston Port Act had been to contumacy. Such an excommunication technically banned colonial trade entirely, and closed off North America like a hermit kingdom.

At first the American opponents of imperial policy had been much encouraged by the vocal support of the small parliamentary group that followed the Earl of Chatham, William Pitt. For example, Pitt rejoiced publicly at news of Lexington and Concord. But the steadiness of Frederick Lord North's majorities showed that confidence in the opposition was misplaced; the opposition never came close to crippling a Ministry bill aimed at America. The Americans were ignorant of the true structure of British politics. To place their hope in Pitt showed how wrong they were, for their best friends were the faction of Rockingham Whigs who could not get along with Pitt—though it made little difference, since no coalition of opposition factions would have been strong enough even to upset the good temper of North, much less to hamper his program.

But the transition from constitutional turbulence to a revolution was not merely American reaction to British action. There was also a revolution of the American mind; ideas triumphed that were incompatible with the standing order. The American attitude toward the organization of the Empire went through a radical transformation (although radical about little else), as American Whigs painfully talked and thought their way through their problems until they came to believe in the need for a change in the essential relationship of the parts of the Empire.[23] In the process of arriving at a revolutionary rationale, the Congress of 1775 had created a revolutionary junta. It was ill-informed, groping, and shapeless, and its turnover was rapid. A few strong minds, in the Congress, the provincial governments, and the military, did all of its acting and thinking. Nevertheless, the presence of delegates from all the colonies, so much in agreement about the disadvantages of British policy, gave it a *de facto* representative quality, and the Crown might have given legitimacy. Wise Britons could have dealt with the Continental Congress as a political group apart from Parliament but nominally under the Crown. Alas, such wisdom was not to be expected of the eighteenth century. It was psychologically impossible for the rulers of Great Britain to surrender to what they could only see as the most egregious kind of insolence.[24]

The Congress *was* an effective body despite some grave weaknesses. Embodied in the Congress the united colonies existed and functioned for twenty-two months before a single true state government was organized. It enacted a uniform commercial law (the Association), founded the Continental Army and Navy, commissioned officers, printed money,* made military and naval regulations, entered the thorny scrub-forest of diplomacy, and defined certain crimes against the union of colonies, and capital crimes within the jurisdiction of the armed forces (and hanged one of its own soldiers for conspiracy, before the Declaration of Independence). For all this it could claim authority only from the people of the united colonies as a group. It is a persuasive conclusion that final authority in English-speaking North America rested not with King-in-Parliament, nor in the admittedly temporary authorities of the revolted colonies, but in the whole people, joined together through the Congress in what Washington in 1775 hopefully called an "indissoluble union." It is difficult to make a profession of faith in the proposition that the union came from the states; the reverse is better history.[25]

Politically the Congress reached the point of no return in January of 1776. Through 1775 it was possible to be loyal to King George and also to favor prosecuting the war against his malevolent servants. Since talk had led nowhere, so the argument ran, it was necessary to win by arms, in order to persuade the British to negotiate for a restoration of the old conditions. There was less of this kind of talk in New England than elsewhere, but there were many elsewhere who thought the Yankees overzealous. The crest of militant but loyal opposition as a powerful force in the Congress subsided in January 1776, when James Wilson brought in a motion, supported by middle states Congressmen, that the Congress express its opinion on independence. If it came to a vote, Wilson and his friends believed and hoped the delegates would back away from the idea of independence.[26] To the pleasure of some zealous Yankees, the Congress rejected the mo-

---

* The very complicated currency problems of the Congress have been postponed for later discussion.

tion. Never again would the Congress come close to denying that independence was a thinkable proposition. From this point the drift was toward institutionalizing their practical independence by a legal, juridical announcement.

C H A P T E R

6

———————

Means and Ends

Lacking reliable figures, we can only estimate that the population of Britain outnumbered the two and a half million white Americans about five to two. Perhaps 70 per cent of the white Americans were of English, Welsh, and Scottish ancestry, and those strains dominated in all colonies except Pennsylvania which was two-thirds German and Scots-Irish, and New Jersey where slightly less than half were English and Welsh.[1] The white American society was stable. Few people were very rich, and only one in twenty whites was hopelessly mired in poverty. Americans were a class-conscious people and deferential to their betters, but the social ladder had rungs instead of barriers to getting ahead. A majority of Americans owned property, and each could reasonably hope to own more. Farmers, merchants, and lawyers ran this fluid little society.[2] With astonishing cockiness they intended to keep right on running it, and saw the British rearrangements of the Empire as foreign threats to their own standing. To repel the threats they contrived a positive program, organized more efficiently than their opponents, and showed respectable skill at propaganda. The loyalists had no counter-program, no continental organization, and not many useful propaganda outlets. The rebels were firmly united only in opposition to novel British legislation. Flexible lines divided them on many issues. Few of the rebels were democrats.

Means and Ends

Who were the rebels? Let us look first at those north of the Mason-Dixon line, and then at the Southerners. Northern college alumni were overwhelmingly rebellious and provided about a third of the signers of the Declaration of Independence. Perhaps they learned from ancient history to sniff tyranny in every tainted breeze; perhaps an American education reinforced provincialism, or, more likely, infected them with incipient nationalism. A squirearchy ruled inland New England and joined with seaboard rebels only when British coercion threatened the independence of their judiciary. The Northern seaport merchants, alarmed by violent disorders, steadily fell away from the resistance movement from 1765 through the 1770's, but many able businessmen stayed and were able to direct the public opposition to British policy.[3] In a few places they were even more radical than the artisans—for example, in Newburyport, Massachusetts—but this was exceptional. Those who rebelled were usually fighting to hold their places as local leaders.[4] Lesser businessmen were discontented because of reverses, and despaired of redress. Town workmen had an ancient grudge. The Navy ignored the "Sixth of Anne"—the statute prohibiting naval impressment in America—and workers frequently rioted against press gangs. Thus it was relatively easy to organize violence against enforcement of novel statutes.[5] Loyalists, of course, classified most rebels as rogues, ignorant riffraff, or demagogues. General Gage grossly underestimated their determination and perseverance.

The South was relatively more populous then than now. Because of Thomas Jefferson's fuming about his unmanageable debts, some have charged Southern leaders with rebelling to avoid payment. Southern farmers did owe millions of pounds to British merchants, and parliamentary prohibition of paper money made it harder to pay up,[6] but debt was not monopolized by deadbeat grandees. Most Maryland debts to Glasgow merchants (a good sample) were less than ten pounds, and many men complained of the irresistible temptations of the lax credit practices of Scottish factors.[7] Law was the intellectual distinction of the South, and its study made men conscious of claims to rights. The annoyance of Southern leaders was grounded on social and political pride. Local magnates, experienced and talented in government, tolerated little interference from below and would not accept interference from above. As great men at home, they felt British intervention in colonial affairs to be an intolerable snubbing.[8]

Contrary to tradition, North Carolina had too few democrats to staff a revolution; its democracy was an invention of nineteenth-century thinkers to explain Jefferson's later popularity.[9] The artisans of Charleston, the only important group of Southern white workmen, leaped into the Revolution to get some political leverage for themselves. They had no pretense of democratic virtue but worked hard, risked much, and stayed out of the Army. White Georgians really had very little reason to complain. The province of Georgia needed British protection against the Spaniards and Indians of Florida. On the other hand, Georgia was hardly necessary to the other colonies, but came into the War for Independence under influence of a kind of psychological epidemic.[10] (Error-prone Gage had predicted that fear of Indians and slaves would keep the South quiet.)

The Congress spread the psychological contagion by acting as a fountain of propaganda publications appealing to every level of intelligence.[11] In the churches, preaching was often propagandizing. Religious rebels abounded, which was important in an age when the pulpit was a respected source of belief. Revolution was preached as a defense of religion. Anger at the King reminded Americans that he headed both state and church. Although royal officials did not really wish to decentralize authority, whether profane or sacred, a decade of speculating about the possibility of creating an Anglican diocese in America had alarmed everybody, even the Anglicans, for a vigorous bishop could harass all dissenters and could also recover control of his own church from the lay vestrymen. Even the locally suspect Pennsylvania Germans were nine-tenths Calvinist and Lutheran, not inclined to pacifism, and dubious of English controls.[12] As for New England, an admittedly incomplete list names seventy clergymen who rebelled by deeds; many more spoke sedition.[13] The Reverend Jonathan Mayhew, perhaps the hottest clerical rebel, asked whether the Americans would be "consumed by the flames, or deluged in a flood, of Episcopacy?"[14] Such propaganda may have owed some of its success to the heterogeneity of the population. Many could not rightly call Britain "home."

II

Many native-born Americans put on scarlet coats and died by violence for King and Country, but history is written by the winners, and the loyalists of the War for Independence are in the shadows, not well understood, and ignored if not forgotten. This is unfortunate, if only because we could know more about the division of the Empire if we knew more about the Americans who opposed the separation and why they took their stand.[15]

Loyalists were a miscellany. Every class, condition, creed, and color provided enough loyalists to be noticed. Most conspicuous were the Crown bureaucrats and executives who were practically all loyalist. Many of them were Treasury employees and beholden to Lord North and associates. Some high Crown officers lost a good thing; for example, in seventeen years the attorney general of New York had risen by land-sharkery from a condition of debt to a fortune of eighty thousand pounds, but lost 90 per cent by the Revolution.[16] For several reasons, and with notable exceptions, most Scots were loyal to George III, especially the Scottish merchant-factors of the South, who suffered from a contrived anti-Scots defamation in the press.[17] There were also groups of loyalists in the chief ports—some newly rich from war profits, some fresh from Britain, mostly Anglicans—who could expect to receive more status from royalty than from rebels. Some middle- and lower-class loyalists were fairly recent immigrants who had markedly improved their circumstances and feared economic reverse.[18] Generally loyalists were scattered, leaderless, of mixed origin, and lacking any profound political philosophy. They produced no national leader.[19]

Religion made loyalists. The few dedicated Anglicans, some New England nonconformists who disliked Congregationalism, a scattering of obedientist sectaries (mostly Germans), and the pacifist Quakers produced theologically motivated loyalists. Some Quakers were said to have spied for Britain.[20] The few hundred Methodists were suspect because their leader John Wesley condemned the Revolution.

Virginia and Massachusetts had the fewest loyalists, while the Floridas and Nova Scotia, neither of which rebelled, had the highest ratios of loyalism. In the original thirteen states one can guess that loyalists were majorities in each of several pockets of population in Georgia, the Carolinas, Maryland,[21] Pennsylvania's southeast quarter, New Jersey, and New York, though the New York estimate is certainly debatable.

It is hard to say how many loyalists there were. The surviving list of rich loyalists who filed claims for damages is not much help because they were not typical. A better way to count loyalists might be to study British Army enlistments in America. We have reason to think 15 per cent of loyalist males joined the King's forces, and there were nineteen thousand separate American enlistments. By methods known to statisticians and demographers, more easily summarized than explained, an adjustment of the figures to allow for females and for politically apathetic people permits a rough estimate that about half a million unorganized white loyalists stayed true to their King, although outnumbered by one and a half million organized white rebels.[22]

North Carolina loyalism presents a special case. The most important cause of cleavage was the belief that the colony's eastern assemblymen were oligarchs. Westerners were discontented with the assembly's hard-money policy and with the eastern-dominated judicial system. In 1771 malcontents said, "There should be no Lawyers in the Province, they damned themselves if there should."[23] There were also many settlers from Scotland, newly oath-bound to the King who had given them land and tax privileges which might be lost by disloyalty. When the provincial government seemed intolerable, frontiersmen organized as "Regulators,"[24] but Governor William Tryon and the militia crushed them at the Battle of the Alamance in 1771. Thereafter the westerners hated the assembly, and when the assembly plumped for revolution, ex-Regulators (and the Scots) became loyalists. A nasty civil war followed, with the loyalists behaving rather less atrociously than their enemies.[25]

The case of New York proves that loyalists were conspicuous where protected, while rebels were silent where intimidated. Early attempts to get signatures for the "Association" boycott showed loyalists to be a majority in various places, numerous enough to prevent some local elections and to interfere with Continental Army supply.[26] After New York became the British headquarters, loyalist numbers increased, though some estimates of their number have been arithmetically impossible.[27] Nearby rebel officials were importuned for passes to visit New York. Governor William Livingston of New Jersey finally denied passes to everybody, including his wife.[28]

Two other centers of loyalism have been closely studied. In Bergen County, New Jersey, every social stratum provided loyalists, but most were landowners of Dutch ancestry and Calvinist leanings.[29] In Delaware half seem to have been loyalist, and a fifth indifferent; the Revolution there was obviously the work of a militant minority.

Means and Ends

It is hard to study loyalist thinking because only the most fervent recorded their philosophy. Benjamin Franklin's son William, the loyal governor of New Jersey, settled his conscience with the principle of legitimate government.[30] The most articulate loyalists were clergymen who offered no very interesting arguments. The Reverend Jonathan Boucher tried to formulate a conservative theory from the never-accepted philosophy of Sir Robert Filmer, the early seventeenth-century Stuart apologist, but made no converts.[31]

Why did people choose either revolution or loyalism, one over the other? As group action, the loyalists' choice was often the choice of self-conscious minorities who felt weak and insecure, and who feared their fellow Americans more than they feared the Crown. Minorities, with some justice, are suspicious of political arrangements for the common good if the common good is defined by the majority alone.[32] As a private internal decision of the solitary conscience, the choice between revolution and loyalism may have depended much on temperament. This is an area of pure hypothesis, which as yet cannot be tested by any known psychologico-historical method. Nevertheless, if left entirely free to choose, the man who placed abstract virtue, duty, and the common good above all other considerations, even above the obligations of family and friendship, would seem the potential rebel. If equally free to choose, his neighbor of the same social position whose moral code was personal and clannish, who placed the highest value on the preservation of his family and the protection of his friends, would fit better into the enlarged tribe which is a monarchy, and would seem to be the potential loyalist.[33] But of course the choice was never made in a vacuum. Pressures operated, up to the point of blows, tar, and feathers.

III

Congressional finance cannot be understood piecemeal, if it can be understood at all, and must be described straightaway through 1780. By adopting the Army the Congress assumed great expense and embraced fiscal improvisations. Taxation? Taxation was a very touchy topic. On June 22, 1775, the Congress committed itself to $2 million in "bills of Credit"[34]—the birthday of the dollar. George Washington could soon correctly tell the Congress that its cost estimate was preposterously low.[35] The Congress hired two treasurers, but the money was committed before they could sign the bills. No one was shocked; the colonials were used to relying on paper money.[36] When the Congress went broke in December it authorized another $3 million.

In the printing press the Congress seemed to discover perpetual motion. Usually the delegates underestimated the cost of foreseeable operations and printed part of the needed money immediately, but when they came to print the next installment inflation had worsened and they had to increase the quantity. The more they printed, the more they needed. Annual emissions tell the story: 1775, $5 million; 1776, $19 million; 1777, $31 million; 1778, $63.5 million. Public confidence began to fail in 1777 (Pennsylvania proclaimed punishment for refusing to accept Continental dollars).[37] The Congress studied the problem diligently late in 1778 and decided to try to withdraw $41.5 million from circulation, trusting the states to meet quotas in the next eighteen years which would extinguish all commitments. If they had won the war at that moment, the plan might have worked, but, out of stark necessity, the 1779 emission was $140 million and the printers worked all year. The paper dollar was worth a fourth of a cent in gold in March 1780.[38]

The Congress printed $242 million in all. The states further weakened the medium by printing $210 million (half by Virginia). There was no way to prevent state emissions. Together they were too much to bear.

Inflation followed this flood of fiat money, but people did not know whether to blame paper money or a conspiracy against liberty by speculators and monopolists. States adopted price controls which proved to be ineffective, and the Congress decided in 1778 that price control was bad policy. Congressman John Jay wrote an essay in 1779 promising that the Congress would honor the dollar, but it had no effect. There were state meetings to discuss controls in late 1779, this time encouraged by the Congress, but if price regulation could ever have worked it was now too late. Loyalists thought the currency chaos proved them right, but the chief sufferers were the soldiers.

Inflation hurt the Army. For example, General James Varnum resigned in 1778 because he could not live on his paper salary.[39] Washington reluctantly approved paper currency, but changed his mind when it failed (he blamed "stock jobbing" and speculation).[40] Officers at Pittsburgh threatened to fix prices themselves.[41] By late 1779 the Congress could not make military plans.

There were three alternatives: to confiscate property, to repudiate the currency, to surrender. If the war was just, repudiation seemed the best choice.[42] In desperation the Congress devalued the dollar to one-fortieth in March 1780, promising to replace it with bills bearing 5 per cent interest. State laws then fixed depreciation rates for settling old private debts according to dates incurred.[43] But the new bills sank quicker than the old, and in April stood at 135 to 1. By 1781 only an occasional speculator would take Continental dollars—at 500 to 1 or 1000 to 1.

The Congress always expected the states to help with money, but every state seemed keen to avoid outdoing any other. The Congress put out state taxation hints in 1778, firmly asked them to pay up shares of $10 million already requested, and then asked for another $60 million in 1779. If the states had taxed themselves heavily it could have been done, but as of October they had paid in a trivial $3 million. The Congress then switched to requisitions of materials, an impossible plan because transport was unavailable.[44] (This failure precipitated the devaluation of 1780.)[45] A system of sight drafts on state treasuries in 1781 also failed. Altogether the states gave the Congress material support worth in specie about $5.8 million.[46]

As we have seen, the Congress began with fiat money, but when the presses were working well it decided to try also to borrow. At first, bonds moved sluggishly, but when the Congress actually began to *pay* interest (with borrowed French gold) the market improved. In specie value this paper brought in something under $8 million, even though the flowing fiat money eroded the foundations of credit.[47] The most effective medium of exchange in these dark years was the certificate of impressment, by which, on Washington's initiative, the suppliers of the hungry Army of a well-fed country gave negotiable receipts for impressed supplies.[48] From late 1779 the Army survived by this technique in lieu of plundering. Most of the people whose property was impressed received fair prices.[49] The total real value of the certificates can be estimated at about $16.7 million.

Financially this was a war of fits and starts. If all of the money and manpower had been clenched into a fist, so to speak, and struck at once, victory might have come swiftly; but the Americans spent their energy and resources in small annual spurts, dragging things on and on. Nevertheless, that generation paid more than half the cost of its war, something not done by Americans since the War of 1812. The collapse of the currency was also a weakening of the Congress, because it showed a bankruptcy of ideas in the minds of the most incendiary rebels, who now had to accept the leadership of cooler businessmen to patch the leaks in the ship of state.[50] As James Madison later said, the United States had survived by pumping all the time instead of patching the leaks.

IV

The final shape of the Army was visible in about two years.[51] In organizing it the Congress uncertainly proposed and Washington tried to dispose, but as time passed the policy process worked like this: Washington learned hard truths in the field and passed suggestions to the Congress, which either wrote them into policies or ratified what he had done of necessity. Thus Washington served as war minister of the Congress as well as its commanding general. Congressional thinking naturally tended to be provincial, and committees were overworked; the Congress had to have the kind of information only Washington could supply.[52]

The form adopted (September 1776) was a Continental Army of eighty-eight regiments, with money and land bounties to be offered for enlistment, the Congress to pay the money and the states to find the land.[53] Officers' commissions would be Continental, not state. To meet quotas the states ultimately resorted to conscription, which had been universal in the colonies. Although the goal was something over seventy thousand men, the peak strength under this policy was 34,000 in 1777. (With a despotic government and adequate supply, the United States could have raised a hundred thousand.) But paper armies had the advantage that they *might* become flesh and blood, and the British had to remember that dangerous possibility.

Washington had originally taken command of a chaotic, individualistic Yankee army, and he did not like Yankees much.[54] He thought they needed stricter discipline and complete reorganization.[55] The Congress responded by revising military law in line with British practice, though it denied Washington's request for five hundred

Means and Ends

lashes as an intermediate penalty between a hundred stripes and the gallows.[56] Fervor declined steadily after the first flame of anti-British indignation[57]—perhaps cooled by inflation. By trial and error, states arrived at conscription systems which usually provided that groups of eligibles each produce a soldier on demand in any way the group could, whether by lot, by hire, or otherwise.[58] Through the war the Army became steadily more professional, less idealistic, more cosmopolitan, and occasionally villainous. The men would suffer agony when necessary, but they poorly tolerated unnecessary hardship. The Continental Army had twenty-eight mutinies from 1777 to 1783, involving groups from squad size up to a regiment.[59] Of course, without this refractory spirit the War for Independence would not have started; an easily regimented people would not have risen.

One military innovation of the Congress was to narrow the gulf between officers and men by keeping the officers poor. The gulf certainly shrank; Washington found the officers unable to keep discipline.[60] American officers received about half the pay of the British, but John Adams thought their scale might be thought "extravagant"[61] and he blamed complaints about the parsimonious treatment of the officers on Southerners' distaste for egalitarianism. Congressmen, recalling Cromwell's career, feared the officers, and not without reason for there were some who later meditated a caesarian *coup*. Actually, as Washington observed, the original pay was so low that serving as an officer could be regarded as conferring a favor.[62] The concept of the gentleman was presupposed, gentlemen were wanted for officers, and, in the end, most officers received justice. Another difficulty was the insistence of states on appointing officers, but Washington, after 1776, was able to reserve the right of promoting them—excepting generals, whose promotions had to be equalized geographically.

A flood of foreign officers, mostly French, inundated the Congress, wishing to improve their service records during a period of European peace. Some were invaluable, others were nuisances. What the Army needed in the way of foreign officers were drillmasters, engineers, and generous millionaires. They got them, including the well-connected, brave, rich, young idealist Gilbert du Motier, Marquis de Lafayette. The Congress also received too many who could not speak English, a few of whom were more interested in winning heiresses than battles. Many arrived with agents' contracts promising high rank, to the anger of native American generals. An engineer volunteer, Thaddeus Kosciusko, was able and became a useful Continental colonel. By 1777 Washington lost patience with the many who reported to him with dubious credentials and no English.[63] In the same week rich Robert Morris, who spoke no French, complained that the commission-hunters adopted him as father.[64] The Congress resolved that no more be sent who spoke no English,[65] and in September celebrated what might be called Foreign Officers Day by voting to ship back unassigned foreigners, their passage to be paid by drafts on the Americans in Paris who had sent them.[66] Wisely retained were Casimir Pulaski and Johann de Kalb,[67] whose commissions turned out to be death warrants. The net gain included Lafayette, a Prussian Captain Steube (self-ennobled to Baron von Steuben), Kosciusko, de Kalb, and Count Pulaski. Their merits outweighed the annoyances of the rejects and troublemakers.

Lafayette was the most valuable, because he was intelligent, paid his way, was influential in France, spent lavishly, and was "anxious to risque his life in our cause."[68] Captain Steube, calling himself a baron and a lieutenant general, enjoyed his American career and helped to regularize infantry tactics.[69] Charles Lee was one of those British officers, like Horatio Gates and Richard Montgomery, who resigned their British commissions when they saw promotion unlikely. Lee carefully cultivated an eccentric personality, but Washington, who knew him, advised that he rank number three in the Army. Gates had been a British major, but immigrated to Virginia. Washington knew him and wished to have his military experience available, so he became adjutant general. Johann de Kalb, of peasant origin, styled himself a baron in order to get ahead in the French Army, became a Continental general, and died bravely at Camden in 1780.

Of native officers, Nathanael Greene was next in ability after Washington. He began with no reputation; Congressman Roger Sherman listed the new brigadiers of 1775, closing with "and one Green of Rhode Island."[70] Greene learned war from books but lacked personal magnetism. Perhaps he modeled himself so consciously on Washington that his men sensed an artificial quality in him.

Black men served on both sides in the war. Their chief reward was personal freedom, not because people thought it right but out of necessity. The initial British shortage of troops led the British commanders to promise freedom to slaves who enlisted, and American legislators, excepting those of the Carolinas and Georgia, matched the offer. In mixed units the blacks were equal to white troops in combat, and in some ways were superior because, having slight attachment to home, they accepted enlistment for the duration. Furthermore, it did not occur to them to expect comfort, hence they endured hardship with less complaint. The use of black troops weakens the theory of the war as a class war against the British aristocracy, because this most depressed class first fought on the British side. (The Carolinas and Georgia would probably have preferred to be Crown colonies rather than accept the abolition of slavery.) General Thomas Sumter paid his Southern freedom fighters with slaves plundered from loyalist plantations, and, though the Swamp Fox guerrilla general Francis Marion called it inhumane, the ex-Quaker Greene cautiously approved. By the end of the war the Continental regiments averaged about fifty blacks each,[71] some serving as substitutes for drafted whites.

Although a few friendly New England Indians appeared in the first armed flockings around Boston, to Washington's slight embarrassment, [72] the only step the Congress took with regard to the Indians was to begin to organize three Indian superintendencies in the hope of keeping the frontier Indians neutral.[73] On balance, many more Indians helped the British than helped the white Americans.

The jerry-built Continental Army had grave weaknesses of supply and communications. Its staff functions were performed through a dozen poorly coordinated offices, but, after all, the general staff as an institution arrived at perfection more than a century later. Outside the Army there was little sacrifice because sacrifice could not be compelled; but the Army was a projection of the insurgent society that created it, and it won the war without resort to the autocracy which could have made it a better fighting machine.[74] Military despotism would have made the Army something other than the spear point of a recalcitrant republic.

V

The size of the Continental Army fluctuated wildly. It was never up to paper strength yet got results far out of proportion to its size. It began as 16,000 disorganized men around Boston. In 1776 the total whose names had been on muster rolls, however briefly, was 89,651; but in Washington's camp in March 1777, after inspiriting victories at Trenton and Princeton, there were but 981 Continental regulars though the *paper* strength of the whole Army was 76,000. Numbers rose to 34,000 in the summer, but Washington, preparing to leave Valley Forge in May 1778, could think himself lucky to have 11,800 regulars. This mercurial force received an infusion of 7,500 steady French regulars after 1778, yet Greene waged his decisive campaign of 1781 in the South with a force built around 1,651 Continentals. Temporary absence without leave must have been among those unalienable rights with which these young men were endowed by their Creator. But true desertion was a crime, and at least a third of the regulars deserted permanently, sometimes as the only alternative to starvation. Detection of deserters was difficult, penalties in practice were light, and pardons were frequent.[75]

Colonial militia—the troops of local governments—augmented the Continental Army. Before the end of the seventeenth century compulsory militia service was an established American tradition. Militia quality varied in direct proportion to density of population, New England having the strongest and the South the weakest. Professional soldiers valued the militia little, mostly because those used in earlier Anglo-French wars had been locally conscripted vagabonds and scapegraces put in uniform and sent away to improve their neighborhoods. It was quite a different breed that loaded muskets in 1775. They have had a bad press, but a second look at their record shows that militia disasters happened when the militia were ordered to fight like regulars. When used in ambush, for sniping, for waylaying red-coated couriers, and for harassing supply detachments, they helped greatly. Late in the war the proper battle formula evolved: the use of militia as skirmishers backed by massed Continentals. Despite excessive turnover, lax discipline, and an urge to question why, they were essential to victory.[76]

The hardships of the Army proved that the country was grossly unprepared. With roads lacking and wagons scarce, the only abundant supplies were water, firewood, and corn meal mush. Local governments competed for materiel. Soldiers had never enough clothes to be free of lice. Washington's troops in Massachusetts seized eighty thousand pounds of gunpowder from the British, and shot it off in nine months. Less resolute at the beginning than later, Washington thought at first "the Army must absolutely break up."[77] Its suffering may have testified to patriotism, but it also proved unreadiness.[78]

For a supply service the colonials copied the dimly understood system of the British Army, which was itself really too decentralized. A blurred American copy, lacking any central authority, was hardly a "system." The Congress overorganized by setting up departments according to the kind of supply each was to procure and distribute, all to be supervised by the distracted Congress. Supply officer succeeded frustrated supply officer, each one of them financially responsible for subordinates' acts, however far away. Supply duty was never sharply defined nor well performed. The Congress may have felt negligent, inasmuch as it found reason to abandon an inquiry it voted in 1778 to decide whether Quartermaster General Thomas Mifflin should be tried by court martial. Such an inquiry could inculpate the Congress. When paper money became as fog on a warming day, it was noticed that purchasing agents were working on commission, which discouraged economy because the more they spent the more they made. Unlike inflation, this was a problem the Congress could solve by putting the agent-officers on salary.[79] (How to make the salaries worth anything was another question.) The history of supply is the almost endless story of such petty reforms, and of numerous failures. The story could lead to the belief that the Congress thought complexity and red tape were marks of good policy. But the "system" hampered able men and gave incompetents their excuses for failure. An intelligent despot could have run a better war, but the war was fought to prevent the rise of such a man.

Merchants acted as wholesale agents of the Congress while remaining in private trade. Undoubtedly interests conflicted, but it seemed necessary because only the merchants understood large business. These men saw no need to separate public and private business, and occasionally bought for the public from their own partners, to the scandal of sturdy agrarians. Congressional attempts to investigate supply in 1778 foundered because the accounting was impenetrable. Military officers receiving from congressional purchasers looked on accountancy requirements as reflections on their honor. Public argument about supply provoked more irascibility than reform. Washington was not directly involved, but he dimly connected shortage of supplies with large business operations and fumed in the language of medieval ethics about "those murderers of our cause (the monopolizers, forestallers, and engrossers)" and urged that they be hanged.[80] After all, this mismanagement penalized the common soldier for his fidelity. Finally, in 1780 the Congress adopted the European system of contracts to supply rations at a price per ration, and supply improved slightly.

The ration story is one of bare survival between crises. Only crumbs from a rich table reached the Army through obstacles of red tape and fading currency. The men were best fed in 1775–1776 when each colony fed its own. Thereafter they had better cooking equipment than food supply. In 1777 a bitter officer remarked that "The new method of supplying the Army is by showers of Manna from Heaven."[81] The chief reform before 1780 was the prevention of competition between Army purchasers scrambling for supplies. The prescribed ration[82] was adequate when available, but malnutrition was apparent when Continentals fainted from hunger at a moment of victory. Salt—necessary to preserve meat—was always short, and to keep live beef cattle with the troops for daily slaughter was rarely possible.

As for the handsome blue and buff uniforms, more have appeared in paintings than on battlefields. The Army looked as if dressed at rummage sales. Uniforms came in driblets of disparate items: bales of hose wore out before shoes arrived, and so on. It was not for lack of administrators—clothiers general were everywhere.[83] In the battle of Eutaw Springs in South Carolina, September 8, 1781, many on the rebel side were naked except for pads of swamp moss to prevent muskets and cartridge boxes from galling. Always the suppliers hoped the current set of rags would last until the expected early peace.

Because the country could not produce enough weapons and ammunition, the Congress relaxed the "Association" in order to import foreign munitions. Fortunately Virginia could supply the whole South with domestic lead in 1780 and 1781.[84] Since the Royal Navy commanded the coastal waters, land transport had to be impressed from unhappy farmers. Like soldiers, the horses were underfed. The teamsters were poorly paid civilians, and many quit to go into private hauling, leaving purchased supplies to rot beyond the Army's grasp. Small units could win fights under these handicaps, but not large armies.

Means and Ends

Despite administrative difficulties, Washington, with European help, made an army on the European pattern. Humiliated by frequent retreat, shamefaced at continuous entrenchment, nevertheless, when logistics and terrain permitted, its fighting won approval from disinterested professionals. Washington adapted tactics to the chronic shortage of artillery and developed excellent, fast-moving light infantry. There was neither feed nor horses enough for large cavalry units. Under foreign engineers, the engineering was satisfactory. Experimentation with a rifle brigade proved the musket more useful. The men felt inferior to the British regulars but believed (erroneously) they were superior marksmen, which gave them heart to carry on. In every engagement there was a large proportion of panic-prone recruits, but the zeal of good junior officers checked panic and kept up morale. There were many acts of great courage[85] and some brilliant field expedients. The occasional panics were brief, and the perseverance of the Continental Army, all things considered, commands the highest admiration.

VI

In recent great wars nations have regulated their civilian manpower as intently as their military. Not so eighteenth-century America. Neither the Congress nor the states had a manpower policy. They hesitated to impress men or property, though they ultimately did—and took property more freely than men. The Army used many kinds of artisans, often drawing musketeers from the ranks and setting them at their civilian trades. Local authorities also set up factories. Officials learned how important labor was, but acted in sporadic fashion, habitually tailoring specific solutions to specific problems.[86]

Outside Washington's staff there was no security of information, except that so much fable blended with fact in public gossip that it was hard to sift the truth. Washington found it so difficult to get acceptance of official announcements as authentic that he requested (but failed to get) a press for printing communiqués. Newspapers printed military news without restraint. Postal service posed lesser problems. The New York postmaster became Postmaster General and had to follow the Army on foot. There was a false alarm of loyalist infiltration of the Post Office,[87] but most argument was on whether to scrimp on postal service or promote convenience.

When the Congress took over the Army in 1775 it left medical affairs to Massachusetts, partly for economy and partly on the theory that the war would be brief.[88] In July, after the battle of Bunker Hill, the Congress set up a ridiculously small medical service called the "Hospital." Two years later the delegates reformed the service to allow for expansion, though the medical men did not get equivalent military rank until 1780. Medical care had all the characteristics of the American war effort—the chronic shortages, the awkward administrative structure—but the personality quirks and passionate antagonisms of successive directors enlivened its story. The senior physician of 1775 was Benjamin Church, physician, author, and traitor. The next, John Morgan, lost his place through the intrigues of the politician-physician William Shippen, who, as Morgan's successor, showed a fine talent for making enemies. The last director was John Cochrane, appointed in 1780. Morgan exulted in print at Shippen's departure in 1780 as the "merited disgrace" of one whose cardinal qualities were "indolence, love of pleasure and dissipation. . . ."[89] Benjamin Rush had earlier blamed Shippen's incompetence and neglect for the fact that "many hundreds of our brave countrymen died in the hospitals whose lives might have been saved. . . ."[90] Considering the medical record, a wounded man may have been better off if not treated. In winter camps the "hospitals" were log huts, knee deep in straw for warmth. They were more for dying than healing. In the field, medical care was rough—septic first aid, crude amputation, strong purgatives, bone setting, and little else. Sporadically there were mass inoculations against smallpox.

The question of prisoners of war was a legal and emotional tangle. The Americans followed international usage, but the British had to decide whether their captives were traitors. They temporized by suspending the writ of habeas corpus, incarcerating without trial, and thus avoiding bloody retaliations. The situation remained chaotic until Elias Boudinot became Commissary of Prisoners in 1777. He spent $40,000 of his own money (and became a Congressman to press his claim). Sir William Howe preferred dealing with Washington rather than the Congress, though the British exasperated Washington by sending him Continental dollars for the support of British prisoners while insisting on hard money for the support of Americans in captivity. Eventually the contestants established regular exchanges except for Americans taken at sea. The British put the sailors in the Royal Navy and held the others on charges of treason or piracy until 1782. The tradition is that Americans in British hands suffered atrociously. Some did, but in general the British were guilty only of excessive legalism.[91]

Both sides had far-flung but primitive spy nets extending from the wilderness to the European courts, but spent most of their money and energy around New York and Philadelphia. Even by special courier, intelligence could not possibly travel overland much more than a hundred miles a day, and the opposing commands usually had to rely on newspapers, rumors, deserters, and casual observers. Really good spies cost *hard* money, and the Congress, of course, rarely had gold. Even so, Washington was too stingy with his espionage money, in order to avoid embarrassing the Congress. A most interesting Continental spy was James Rivington, the vituperative quasi-loyalist editor from New York, who may have spied from the first and certainly worked for Washington by 1781. He ran a coffee house much frequented by British officers, and on one occasion acquired the British naval signals. Despite personal unpopularity because of his loyalist cover, he lived on in New York after the war.[92]

On the American side the administration of the war might be called a travesty except that it was the effort of men strong in good intentions and weak only in experience. Sometimes inefficient at the top, always inefficient at bottom, it suffered because the small pool of talent was drained to make top appointments. Supply, a paramount function of command, was worst managed. In detail its story is the tedious tale of endless trials all leading to error. The pervasive evil was the grasp of the Congress on all reins. Only by 1780 was it clear that execution was work for executives, a truth reached six years after the Congress took over the Army. The Department of War came into existence by authority of an act of February 1781, too late to get credit for the decisive victory of that year.[93]

The Continental Army surely had a morale problem. The high rate of desertion was evidence that Americans would not universally submit to unnecessary hardship. They had courage, good will, and patriotism, but not enough to eat. Those who stayed were held together by the things that moved their minds and emotions: political philosophy, atrocity stories, flags, sermons, and the examples set by steadfast officers. The Army was a mishmash of quite different institutions and activities untidily bound together by a common purpose. One may speculate that it had two strengths unavailable to the British: its officer corps opened a career to the talents of otherwise obscure white men, and rank could be forgotten in bivouac discussions of the issues which had brought on the war.

VII

The ramshackle Continental Army would seem to be no match for any professional army, but the British also had grave problems. Scattered in many fixed posts, the British Army could detach only a fraction of the number needed in America. Recruiting in England and Scotland netted only fifteen thousand men by 1778. The corrupt Irish Parliament was persuaded to part with troops, but violent Ireland could not be left wholly unpoliced, and Ireland met but a part of the deficit. The government decided that renting foreign troops would be cheaper than making army life more attractive to Englishmen. German princelings rented out Braunschweigers and Hessians at prices that pained King George. Nevertheless, in money they were the cheapest effective soldiers for use against an alien foe, though they were no political bargain, for their use against Americans made conciliation practically impossible. (Even German intellectuals decried the practice.) Thirty thousand German lads, mostly unwilling conscripts,[94] were present in America in an average strength of never less than eleven thousand, and they suffered 2,200 casualties in twenty engagements. Americans encouraged their desertion, and perhaps ten thousand succumbed to the temptation to become Americans.

The only wholly acceptable excuse for prodigious efforts to suppress the American insurrection would be that the loyalists were both numerous and competent. In 1781 Germain said his motive had always been to win back the loyalists. If he wrote truth, it explains much of his otherwise curious conduct of the war. At first British officials believed the loyalists could restore order after British victories. Later the British wished to arm them, and operated where loyalists supposedly abounded; but loyalists were put off by the Army's brutal discipline and caste system. Thus the British first overestimated the loyalists, then motivated them poorly. Caste may have been the key. In British eyes the loyalists seemed provincial squires at best and peasants at worst. From the loyalist point of view, open support of the Crown could be hazardous, because British protectors moved about, leaving known loyalists exposed to the anger of rebel neighbors. And the violently un-British behavior of the Indian auxiliaries cooled some loyalists. Despite all difficulties the British used many armed loyalists, including several very capable regiments. Loyalist troops aroused pure hatred. In any fight solely between Americans, both sides inclined to take no prisoners and occasionally slaughtered the wounded. By 1778 there were about 7,500 loyalist soldiers (Washington had no larger force), and perhaps thirty thousand served at one time or another. These numbers encouraged the British to persevere by giving the illusion that a majority of Americans supported their King. Both sides hoped to use Indians—if only to deprive the enemy—but the British got most, though their value was variable.[95] Black America remained a relatively untapped pool of manpower.

The British regular enlisted man came from the dregs of society. Under severe discipline he became a professional soldier who fought like an automaton. The British public saw him as a necessary evil. He traded liberty and social opportunity for an animal security, since his enlistment was for life while his food, clothing, and shelter were better than that available to the free English unskilled worker. The Army was a collection of regiments—six elite royal household regiments and near a hundred line regiments, each with a paper strength, rarely realized, of five hundred. It served a social function for a fermenting society by providing a receptacle for aristocratic froth at the top and human sediment at the bottom.[96] Each regiment had a lieutenant colonel commanding, because the salaried rank of colonel went to generals who were paid, as generals, *per diem* only while fighting. Commissions were bought and sold—from four hundred pounds for a line ensign to seven thousand for a household colonel. Thus only the rich could be officers. Ludicrous as this system may seem, in a caste-ridden society it produced a harmonious and generally capable officer corps, because if a regiment disgraced itself, no pedigreed sprig would wish to buy into it. Aristocratic vanity operated to military advantage.

British military problems differed from the Americans'. Although they moved men and supplies freely in coastal waters guarded by the Royal Navy, and could tax and spend, their stubborn, energetic, but unimaginative civilian leadership was really attempting the impossible. To be sure, if taxing, borrowing, and spending could win, victory would have been won. Frugality was forgotten, and Britain's national debt rose from 130 million pounds to more than 200 million. Although public finance was mismanaged, the money was there, but British power was weakened by the distance at which it had to be exerted. Everything had to be ferried across the Atlantic, to an inhospitable land of great summer heats, bitter winters, endemic malaria, and scattered population. British coasters carried supplies to Cork whence they went to some conquered American port. Generals habitually ordered a third more than needed, as assurance against corruption, but arrivals were unpredictable, which led to many anxious moments and a few real but temporary shortages. Inland from the sea, supply and health posed persistent problems, yet a troubled general might not hear from home in four months. A reasonable man could believe the Americans capable of surviving without foreign help.[97]

If war were athletics, bound by rigid rules of scoring, the British team would have won. The machinelike British infantryman, in scarlet, white, and black, used his flintlock musket for crushing volley fire and for bayonet charges, and he was mindlessly brave. He could not be supported by heavy artillery in roadless country, nor cavalry where short of forage, but he was better trained, equipped, and supplied than the Continental soldier. For cavalry the British relied mainly on a few loyalist units. Gunners of field artillery and siege mortars excited American admiration for their competence.[98] British engineers were good and produced excellent maps. Medical care could be had, such as it was; the best surgeons were those who came for clinical experience.

British troops fought in line abreast, several ranks deep. They marched to pipes, fifes, and drums in precise formation at sixty steps a minute to within a hundred yards of the enemy, fixed bayonets, dressed ranks, marched closer, fired one or more volleys, and (if still alive) closed with the bayonet. Since all men were in the open, panic was contagious—hence the unending drill to make the tactics habitual. With thought forbidden and feeling suppressed, they took very heavy casualties without cracking. The goal was to disorganize rather than kill, because out of his formation the infantryman could not fight and usually ran or surrendered. But at the flanks were men who were encouraged to think: tall grenadiers on the right and short light infantry on the left, both of them taught to skirmish. Light infantry was the soldiery of the future. (The Germans had similar units, called *Jägers*.) The stiff, formal tactics imposed on the other troops had to be relaxed on the rough terrain of America as time passed, and the relaxation may have loosened up later European tactics.

In the last year of war the somewhat padded British Army payroll listed nearly 200,000 men, but most were penned in garrisons at home and abroad, or fighting a war in the West Indies. In North America there were usually about 35,000 regular troops, including loyalists and Germans. Howe, who brought out more men than Wellington had at Waterloo, could quarter 17,000 in and around Philadelphia in 1777 and 1778, but none of his successors could ever assemble that many in one place. This dispersed force marched about, usually with impunity, but it could not conquer the United States. As Pitt said, the soldiers in America were too many for peace and too few for war.

The British in North America at any given moment had nearly twice as many regular troops as the Continentals. In ships they outgunned the Americans a hundred to one. Britain was rich, had good credit, and a taxing machinery. The Royal Navy, if more wisely administered, could have ruled the waves. But vast distances, official corruption, an unlighted and badly charted coastline, the absence of a clear military objective, and a rigorous climate all operated against the British, whose European command experience was of little use in the New World. The Americans had poor credit, neither the machinery nor the inclination to collect taxes, a poorly trained and equipped militia, neglected fortifications, a shortage of weapons and ammunition, and a general tendency in the white majority to do as they pleased. But they were politically motivated, were fighting at home, had little official corruption, and were used to their terrain and climate. There was no military key to America; if a state were overrun the Americans could farm, recruit, and regroup elsewhere. They were self-sufficient except in weapons and gold. Their military leaders were naturally talented and eager to learn.

7

Toward Independence, 1776

Independence had become privately thinkable by January 1776. In that month it also became speakable. The reason was the appearance on January 9 of the pamphlet signed *Common Sense*, by Thomas Paine, a rather unpersonable and obscure English ex-Quaker corset-maker, who had been shrewdly sent to the American rebels by Benjamin Franklin. Paine, like Socrates, brought political philosophy to the marketplace. The pamphlet's theory, style, and language made it one of the most effective brief writings ever. It was an argument for independence, a defamation of the British constitution, and a promotion of a simple continental union. Its novelty was that it denounced the heretofore sacred British constitution as grossly defective, and drew the conclusion that self-government was a natural right of the Americans. The war needed an object. Reconciliation could come only as a grace of Parliament, revocable at will. To win the contest some foreign armada must come rolling and creaking across the chill blue Atlantic—the French, of course—but no foreign nation would lend a navy only to reconcile America and Britain. After appealing to settled convictions by citing Magna Carta and natural law, Paine urged something new and shocking—republicanism. Those Americans who blamed only Parliament were blind to the royal brutality of their King. For the price they were paying in blood and treasure they should get something of value, specifically, an independent republic. Thomas Paine was not an unreserved democrat before the 1790's, but he was a leveler who believed in the republican principle that all free males should vote.

The pamphlet sold more than a hundred thousand copies. As in all good polemics its readers felt the author had written their unspoken thoughts. The appearance of *Common Sense* coincided with news of the burning of Norfolk by Governor Lord Dunmore, and together the two events probably stiffened the Virginia rebels so needed by the cause.

It was not known at first who wrote *Common Sense*, and it was attributed to Franklin or one of the Adamses. John Adams said its republican argument was a "tolerable summary" of what Adams had been urging in the Congress for nine months, and that all its points had been made in the Congress.[1] But Paine was not trying to cash in on an intellectual fad. He showed his sincerity by giving his share of the first printing's profits to buy mittens for the chilly soldiers in Canada. His printer, less altruistic, was slow to pay, and also printed a second edition with unauthorized revisions for his own profit.

Paine's one brilliant and complete success was this striking pamphlet, which dared to present for all to read what a majority was thinking privately. Events and the printed word had coincided in time to make discussion of independence open, respectable, and necessary.

II

While Americans were talking independence and Howe's cramped army lazed in besieged Boston, the British sought to get some good from the reputed loyalism of the Carolinas, hoping to limit rebellion to ten colonies. North Carolina's former Regulators, for instance, might wish to avenge themselves and their King's honor. The Scottish leaders of the North Carolina backlands corresponded with the new governor to concert an action with a British army coming from Ireland. In February 1776, according to plan, the Highland Tories

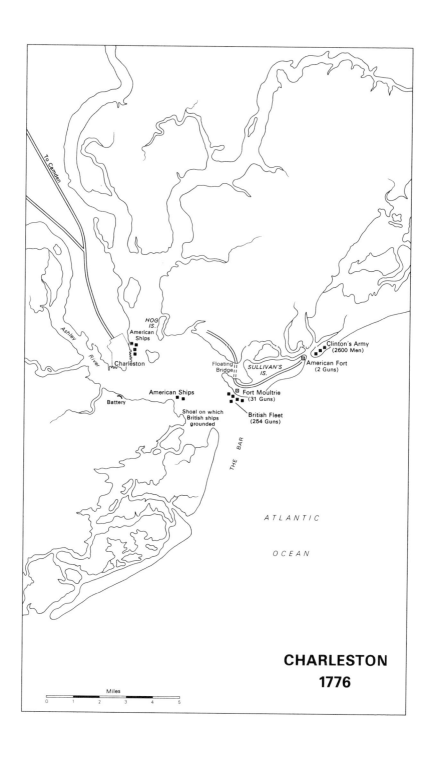

To Camden

Ashley River

HOG IS.
American Ships

Charleston

Floating Bridge

SULLIVAN'S IS.

Clinton's Army
(2600 Men)

American Fort
(2 Guns)

American Ships

Battery

Fort Moultrie
(31 Guns)

Shoal on which
British ships
grounded

British Fleet
(254 Guns)

THE BAR

ATLANTIC

OCEAN

**CHARLESTON
1776**

Miles
0   1   2   3   4   5

came to Cross Creek to battle for King and Country. Thousands gathered, but when they noticed that the British regulars had not arrived all but sixteen hundred prudently retired across the sandy pine barrens to their homes. The dauntless remainder headed for Wilmington, but the rebels intercepted them at Moore's Creek Bridge on February 27, and killed, captured, or dispersed them all. This was a decisive battle of the war, for, if the rebels had lost the deep South early in 1776 a declaration of independence could hardly have passed the Congress. The new American tactic of rural risings worked in North Carolina as in Massachusetts.

But a British army was on the way and had yet to be fought. The Congress sent the eccentric, slovenly, and popular Major General Charles Lee, "given up to the Southern Colonies as the most exposed, with great Reluctance,"[2] to defend the South. General Sir Henry Clinton, who was to command the fresh force from Britain, went south by water at the same speed Lee went by land.[3] They met at Fort Moultrie, the bastion of Charleston.

Charles Lord Cornwallis brought the British force to Cape Fear directly from Ireland. In the War Office there had been intelligent doubts about this operation, but rashness prevailed. When the transports hove-to off the North Carolina coast there were, of course, no loyalist troops to cheer them, so they steered for Charleston. Although open to the sea, Charleston had the protection of shoals, and its entrance channels converged near Sullivan's Island where the Americans built a crude but sturdy and well-armed large battery named Fort Moultrie after their local militia leader. Clinton, with the help of his naval colleague Admiral Sir Peter Parker, put his men ashore on the next island north. On June 28 Parker's ships shelled Fort Moultrie while the mosquito-tortured redcoats tried unsuccessfully to wade across a channel to attack, but the ships suffered more than the fort and the infantry found no footing. Clinton re-embarked and asked Parker—who had lost a ship and the seat of his pants—to set sail for New York. In almost all such operations there was a light two-way traffic of deserters, but not a single American deserted in this campaign.

When Virginia's Governor Dunmore learned that Clinton's force had passed without offering to help him, he despaired of reconquering the colony and left Virginia. Since Howe had meanwhile left Boston for Halifax, the King's men, early in July 1776, controlled no land of the united colonies.

III

Through the months from June 1775 to March 1776 a British garrison of about eleven thousand, including several surplus major generals, idled in Boston. Major General Thomas Gage had delayed reporting the battle of Bunker Hill, perhaps hoping to be able to report that he had taken Dorchester Heights as well, but soon abandoned the idea of another offensive because of the risks. He civilly proposed to the selectmen of Boston that the inhabitants be disarmed, and they as politely declined. An Englishman in Boston wrote that if Gage sallied again, "we shall have it on both sides of our Ears they being at least 3000 strong in Town, with Arms in their possession; a pretty pass we are come to. . . ."⁴ Although physically cramped, the British garrison behaved fairly well, taking special care not to harm the property of John Hancock, president of the Continental Congress, as if Gage still hoped for reconciliation. Gage actually was a decent, dutiful man, and as good at his job as any successor before 1782, but, while avoiding blunders, he won no successes. Caught between political forces eager to hurt each other, his career ended in oblivion as Howe succeeded to command.

Across the lines the word "powder" burned itself into George Washington's brain. He might have been able to carry out some kind of operation before spring 1776 if he had not been required to see every grain of powder as practically sacred. He called four councils of war to consider assaulting Boston and each voted "no" unanimously. In the early fall of 1775 there was political reason to delay, because the leaders were awaiting replies to the congressional resolutions sent to Britain. There was also reluctance to destroy Boston by bombardment, but before the end of October the Congress resolved that the town be destroyed if necessary, and this policy was urged even by Hancock who had the most to lose. While the ground was bare the Army lacked both big guns and powder for assault, but early in 1776 the powder scavenging of the Congress and the sledding of captured guns from Ticonderoga made up the deficiencies.

Apart from training good soldiers and cashiering bad officers, the only military profit of this period was the exposure of the highly placed British agent, the previously mentioned Dr. Benjamin Church, senior Army surgeon and former heated revolutionary. His girl stupidly gave incriminating documents to the wrong man, who turned them over to the American command. After four hours of interrogation she blew Church's cover. The Army took him into custody, and he later died at sea.

Came spring and Washington decided to attack. Howe, like Gage, had done nothing to secure Dorchester Heights, which commanded Boston from the south. Generals William Heath and John Thomas went to work fortifying the Heights, the racket of construction drowned by heavy gunfire from the pieces that Henry Knox, the bibliophile-artillerist, had sledded from Ticonderoga as soon as the winter snows permitted. The diggers put barrels of stones on the crest to roll down and break the formations of any advancing attackers, and crowned the Heights with stout redoubts.

A charade followed. Howe told Bostonians he would leave Boston intact if he could go quietly, which was duly reported to Washington. Five hours after Howe's final decision not to tackle Dorchester Heights, the British infantry put out in small boats in foul weather, as if to attack, and then rowed back to Boston to make it appear that only the weather thwarted them.

The garrison and the thousand most apprehensive loyalists embarked in transports which sailed away on March 17. Some respected emigrants went directly to England; the others went to Halifax with Howe. Howe would have liked to go to New York, but his shipping was not sound enough to weather Cape Cod in the heavy seas that often run on the coast in March. Because of a rumor of smallpox in Boston, Washington selected an occupying party of pockmarked soldiers. There were no more decisive operations in New England because the terrain promised no strategic profit. Beyond each defensible hill was another, and the valleys led only to wilderness.

The evacuation of Boston seems to have been long preconcerted. Philadelphia had rumors as early as March 5 or 6, and positive assurance of evacuation on March 15.[5] News that it happened came on March 25. Not only had the British gone; they had left a bounty of guns, ball, shells, hay, wheat, coal, salt, rugs, blankets, wagons, caissons, and other supplies to please a beggarly conqueror. The Congress was properly grateful, voting Washington a medal and formal thanks. While Howe was puzzling over his own new problems in Halifax, the Harvard Corporation translated Major General Washington into George Washington, LL.D. Perhaps he would have traded his honorary diploma for authentic intelligence of Howe's next move.

IV

The relations of the united colonies and France became a serious association in the first half of 1776, rather than the somewhat gingerly and tentative courtship it had been in late 1775. There is no reason to think any Frenchman really understood the Anglo-American quarrel, but many Frenchmen thought they did, and such inner conviction, not reality, governs human behavior. The atmosphere of French life was right for the Americans. France had sunk so low in international esteem after the humiliations of the Great War for Empire that it had not even been consulted about the dissection of Poland. The popular intellectuals of France could always find in the image of America some feature to support their prejudices, whether the absence of feudalism and priesthood or the presence of noble savages and an agriculture to please the most discerning physiocratic eye. Even Robert Turgot, Baron de l'Aulne, the prudent Minister of Finance who was one of the two men fully informed of the fiscal shakiness of France, coined the phrase "America, the hope of the world!"—which turned out to be, for France, an enormously expensive slogan. The French radicals differed from the Americans in defining liberty, but they knew what freedom of the seas meant, and blamed its suppression on the modern Carthage, London. French conservatives thought British parliamentary government turbulent and factious, and undeserving of American loyalty. And the French West Indian nabobs absolutely needed North American trade, a connection which would later make it easy for French materials to reach American soldiers.[6] King Louis XVI was coolest on America. He was pressing for frugality and knew war was the enemy of economical government.

The French government decided quite early to help the American rebels. French ministers thirsted for revenge against Britain, and the American uprising gave them an opening. Charles Gravier, Comte de Vergennes, Foreign Minister from 1774, found in his files a memorandum by a predecessor, Étienne-François, Duc de Choiseul, urging the reduction of Britain's international weight. It convinced Vergennes, but he had to learn whether the Americans were in earnest and would persevere, hence his use of the remittance man Julien Archard, Chevalier de Bonvouloir, in America in 1775. After Bonvouloir's first optimistic report, Vergennes had sent him back to Philadelphia where representative Congressmen convinced him they were in earnest. A French businessman in America also told the Congress his firm (Pliarne, Penet, et Cie.), if asked, could supply arms at going prices, and hinted that shipping would be untrammeled.[7] Pliarne's company sent the first real aid—fifteen thousand French Army muskets from the King's stock (to be replaced in royal arsenals by the firm); this help alone was enough to keep the war going for awhile.

Bonvouloir's reassurance convinced Vergennes that no mere reshuffle of British cabinet portfolios would satisfy the Congress. Vergennes then either wrote or prompted the writing of *Réflexions* (April 1776) for Louis XVI, urging secret aid to the Congress on the ground of French self-interest. The argument was that a reconciliation of Britain and America would strengthen Britain militarily, and that France should therefore encourage friction because Britain's policy was Down with France. The King could understand that a reunited Anglo-American empire might seize his rich West Indian sugar islands. Only Minister Turgot disagreed; he correctly thought intervention dangerously expensive. On May 2 a million royal *livres* capitalized a dummy trading company, Roderigue Hortalez et Cie., which was directed by the sprightly, fantastic Caron de Beaumarchais. The King of Spain matched the sum. No American agent had yet arrived in France. The program was a Franco-Spanish project to harass Britain.[8]

The presence of Caron de Beaumarchais in this tableau is a pleasant flash of color, but his importance should not be overstated. He was useful, but Vergennes chose him, not vice versa. He is hardly important enough to deserve the analysis which uses Freud's magic to explain him as suffering from an oedipal condition,[9] but he *was* engaging. Despite lowly origins as a watchmaker, he succeeded by business, by the theater, and by profitable marriages in getting rich enough to buy an office which admitted him to fun-loving court circles where social graces carried him forward. He succeeded in a counter-espionage task for Louis XV's government, and was thereafter regarded as an available agent. He ran procurement and shipping for his American military aid cover company efficiently (even buying English marine insurance and textiles), but his accountancy was wretched, mixing private and public money inextricably. His prices and freight charges show he intended to profit from all transactions, and he finally (in tears) told the Americans they owed him 3.3 million *livres*. (The United States paid his heirs about ten cents on the dollar in 1835, a fairly realistic figure if it was proper to exclude interest compounded from 1783.)

The American Congress continued to be active. Late in 1775 it began to stir itself to create an opening to the non-British world. Characteristically it complicated its work by dividing foreign politics and foreign commerce, having a committee for each, with overlapping membership, so that it is sometimes hard to tell which did what.

When the King excommunicated his continental colonies in 1775, the Congress sent a circular letter to colonial merchants, retailing British atrocities, and then set up a committee to correspond with friends abroad, provided that the letters were open to congressional inspection. For expenses the committee received three thousand of the novel paper dollars.[10] The first members were Benjamin Harrison, Benjamin Franklin, Thomas Johnson, John Dickinson, and John Jay. Robert Morris joined them in January 1776, at which time the group was named the Committee of Secret Correspondence. In 1777 it became the Committee for Foreign Affairs. The other group of economic managers, appointed a few weeks earlier, was simply named the Secret Committee and assigned to export American produce and import munitions. It was renamed the Committee of Commerce in 1777. Of the two, the Committee of Commerce was the more successfully clandestine.

Owing to a harsh characterization by John Adams, the Plutarch on whom writers have drawn for generations, fat Benjamin Harrison, fifth of that name, has been underrated. Apparently the sharp-witted and talkative Adams had a low regard for slow thought and speech. Nevertheless, Washington valued Harrison highly, and when Harrison spoke he usually said something intelligent. On the other hand, Robert Morris may have been overrated by posterity, partly because of high praise by John Adams. There is no doubt of his persuasiveness, boldness, and popularity, but a faint harmonic tone of avarice echoes through his life, and his boldness became a reckless overreaching which later put him in debtors' prison. By the conflict-of-interest standard (never of much interest as a standard applicable to Congress-men), all of the economic administrators—of whom Morris was the chief—were suspect except Franklin. All but Franklin were mer-chants, and all, including Franklin, were land speculators with a sharp eye on the public wilderness.

While these committees were beginning to work at making friends abroad, the Congress as a whole frequently discussed the advantages and disadvantages of trying to trade abroad in 1775 and early 1776, talked of what might be hoped from France and Spain, and ques-tioned whether it would be both prudent and possible to make formal commercial arrangements with them. Some delegates seemed to think such trade and such covenants were essential to victory, but that in-dependence was a prerequisite to foreign contracts and trade.[11] Inde-pendence talk was private until the reception of *Common Sense* showed that discussion of independence was publicly acceptable. To win, it really was necessary to violate the ancient British mercantile laws by opening the ports to all comers, but it was emotionally diffi-cult to accept.

The Committee of Secret Correspondence quickly decided to have some representation overseas. There was one colonial agent yet re-maining in London, the irascible Arthur Lee, one of the least diplo-matic Americans of his generation. On December 12, 1775, the Com-mittee wrote to Lee to ask that he try to learn the attitudes of the great powers toward the American cause. Lee, a Fellow of the Royal Society, a Doctor of Medicine and a barrister, a friend of that noisiest of English radicals John Wilkes, was a man who trusted only him-self. He even doubted the political reliability of Franklin. His sus-picions of all mankind were warmly reciprocated, and had he not been the brother of Virginia's Congressman Richard Henry Lee—and thus, through his brother, allied with the most zealous delegates from New England—he might well have been fired and forgotten. But he stayed abroad in the embryonic foreign service until 1781, and then returned to serve in the Congress where he saw most of his motions go down to defeat. The Committee of Secret Correspondence also retained the services of Charles W. F. Dumas, an old friend of Franklin, to run a kind of listening post at The Hague, an excellent place for that sort of quiet operation.

Silas Deane, a tarnished figurine of the Revolution, deserves the credit for first knitting together the French and American skeins. In importance the listening posts in London and at The Hague ranked well below Deane's overtures to France in the spring of 1776. The Committee of Secret Correspondence sent him to Paris to speak of the possibility of a treaty, and to work for the Secret Committee of munitions buyers. This mission followed a suggestion by Bonvouloir that the Congress ask Vergennes for what it wanted. With Vergennes, Deane was to use the argument that France might well inherit the British economic advantages of North America. He was supposed to be a secret agent covered by an appointment as a traveling representative of Morris, Willing, and Company, but his purpose was not impenetrable, especially since he had to idle around Philadelphia a month after his scheduled departure date (he got away on April 3). As Joseph Reed wrote, "His errand may be guessed, though little is said about it."[12]

Deane *was* conspicuous. He was an ex-Congressman more highly valued in Philadelphia than by his Connecticut constituency which failed to re-elect him in October 1775. In the Congress he had served on more than forty committees, including the munition-buying group. He very soon saw opportunities in purchasing, and generously offered to share them with a few Connecticut business friends, "as it would be in my power to help them, and in theirs to serve their Country. This hi[nt is a]ll I can give on this head, and if you will come down, the sooner the better."[13] There were to be greater opportunities in a business way for a man in Paris who both represented the Continental Congress and shared in the profits of Morris, Willing, and Company. It is well known that Robert Morris financed the American Revolution, but it is also true that the American Revolution financed Robert Morris. Of course Morris had the help of businessmen such as Haym Salomon and William Bingham.

In the anguish of their supply problems the rebels faced a real maritime and legal dilemma. The British Navigation Acts, the royal proclamation of cloture, the Prohibitory Act, and their self-boycott, called the Association, closed American ports to foreigners. To carry on the war it began to seem necessary to swallow the revulsion against dealing with latinate nations which had been traditional enemies for generations and which were still stained with popery. When Anglo-American reconciliation on decent terms seemed hopeless, the Congress found it possible to reflect not only on trade but on formal written treaties with France and Spain. To trade freely and to negotiate with foreign nations would in fact be acts of independence, but it was pretty late to boggle at that legalism. Three days after Silas Deane was afloat, on April 6, 1776, after a fierce debate, the Continental Congress put on yet another piece of national regalia and opened North American ports to the ships of all nations but Great Britain.[14] This was a most grave decision. From that moment nothing but a quick and crushing British victory could prevent a declaration of independence.

When Deane came to France his hosts greeted him with cordiality easily understood, because they learned that he came to buy what they had intended to give. Deane wished to pay, since he got a percentage of what he spent. Contracts were easily drawn, and French ships began to carry materials to the West Indies, guarded by the Navy when necessary. Should the United States have paid? The question is now moot, but, after all, the Americans beat Burgoyne's army in 1777 with gunpowder shipped by Beaumarchais. The buyers kept the amount of French aid secret, perhaps for security, perhaps to make it hard to guess what profit the buyers made. As of October 10, 1776, Hortalez et Compagnie had spent 5.6 million *livres* and had received only the 2 million *livres* from the French and Spanish royal treasuries.

Because the aid was mostly in supplies procured in Europe, loaned partly from public and partly from private stocks, and purchased in several currencies, the accounting cannot be precise. But the French did far more than the Spanish. Converting the approximate totals of the whole war into eighteenth-century gold-value dollars, the total of outright subsidies was about $2.4 million (a sixth Spanish), and the total of loans, all repaid after 1789, was about $6.6 million (Spanish about $250,000 of the whole). When supplies and pay for American ships and crews in European waters are added, the grand total would be about $9.3 million. In today's purchasing power, for American independence the French spent roughly $2.5 billion and the Americans $1 billion. To put it another way, the French gave about 2.3 per cent of their gross national product. The French help was necessary to win. In the fall of 1776 General Sir William Howe put it correctly: "If that door were shut by any means and it were publicly known here, it would in my opinion put a stop to the rebellion upon the arrival of the reinforcements in the spring."[15] It was more than a matter of morale. The Continental Army would have been out of powder.

V

Political philosophy, fears, international politics, and resentment combined to pull the American rebels toward a declaration of independence after the spring of 1775. It is harder to reconstitute the atmosphere of a past age than to write its history from the records of its most intelligent communicative minds. To understand how contemporaries saw reality we must remember the world of feeling that is reflected in the symbols used by the winning propagandists. The drift toward independence in 1775 and 1776 was accompanied by a fear of British and loyalist conspirators who were thought to be working to corrupt an American Eden. Evidence of genuine conspiracy is scant, but opposing conspiracy theories energized Philadelphia. For example, some people expected the Pennsylvania assembly to ally itself with the Crown to put down its opponents under the fraudulent pretense of protecting the liberties guaranteed by the seventeenth-century Penn charter, even if its loyalism started civil war.[16] Such fancies need mention only to protect us against seeing the Revolution as a war of philosophers. The American Revolution must be remembered as a drama played against a backdrop of obsessive fears and passions.

The swing to independence was not a mass or class movement. It occurred among laborers of Charleston, tobacco aristocrats, Hudson Valley landlords, seamen and longshoremen in all ports, Northern merchant princes and professors, and lawyers everywhere. The strongest support came from small businessmen and artisans who felt their upward mobility was slowed after 1763. Their understanding of the reasons was obscure, but they believed the Whig polemics. In the Continental Congress after Lexington and Concord—to use anachronistic terms—there were a left, a center, and a right. Militants believed Britain would not soon budge, and they expected and accepted the probability of a long war. A larger group voted alternately for force and conciliation in the hope of changing British hearts and achieving a satisfactory settlement. A few conciliationists voted reluctantly for resistance, with the cloudy hope that firmness would somehow bring a return to the golden age before 1763.

Toward Independence, 1776

A sample of leaders for independence illustrates their motives and the support they drew. Charles Carroll of Carrollton, owner of nearly a thousand blacks, a very early supporter of independence, had years before thought of moving to Spanish Louisiana to get away from the unenforced but degrading anti-Catholic penal laws. Brigadier Nathanael Greene of Rhode Island, a lapsed pacifist, wrote the first strong plea for independence on October 23, 1775. Franklin, fresh from English humiliations, told Ezra Stiles on November 10 that the continent was ripening toward independence. In December Congressman Samuel Ward of Rhode Island, his local political career disrupted, recorded his willingness to die for some very important unnamed object—probably independence. In February 1776, Christopher Gadsden, a man popular with the Charleston white mechanics, tried to persuade his provincial congress to declare independence; failing that, he returned to the Congress to press harder. Francis Dana, a Massachusetts lawyer, went to England in 1774 to investigate British policy; he returned in April 1776 convinced that conciliation was impossible. By that time independence was the goal of his circle, and John Adams, who claimed he was for independence in 1775, wrote to James Warren on April 22: "If you are so unanimous in the measure of independency, and wish for a declaration of it, now is the proper time to instruct your delegates to that effect. . . . The Colonies are all at this moment turning their eyes that way."[17] New Jersey sent dour, studious Abraham Clark to the Congress on June 22; he was for independence before he arrived.

As the leaders inclined toward independence, the rebel provincial congresses showed the same shift. From early 1776 the pattern was for the local rebel constituent body to permit its Continental Congressmen to favor independence if the subject came up. In chronological order of permissions: Massachusetts, January; South Carolina, March; North Carolina, April—when Cornwallis and Parker appeared off the coast. Virginia, on May 15, was the first to *mandate* its delegates. Support from New England could be assumed, but the five middle colonies were silent.

In the days May 10–15 the Congress went ahead to tell the colonies to become states. John Adams correctly believed this the most important decision ever taken in America. Specifically, the Congress asked the people to suppress royal government. Like most events in politics, it was a response to a particular situation, in this case the

Pennsylvania assembly's absolute refusal to consider the subject of independence. James Duane of Pennsylvania grumbled to John Adams that the resolution was "a machine for the fabrication of independence," and Adams happily agreed.[18] Independence was now a fact of public life. Seven weeks later, by resolutions of June 24, the Congress demanded allegiance from all Americans, defined treason, and declared George III a public enemy. The Congress obviously thought itself a national government. This audacity was stimulated by the arrival of a New Jersey delegation pledged to independence; it replaced an earlier delegation of waverers alarmed at the ease with which New Jersey could be invaded. The firmest of the men from New Jersey were the poet Francis Hopkinson, the brooding leveler Abraham Clark, and Princeton's Scottish president John Witherspoon. Numerically, independence had a sure majority now, but Maryland, Pennsylvania, Delaware, and New York needed nudging.

In a related episode in North Carolina, a mass meeting in Mecklenburg County adopted some remarkable resolutions (May 1776), sometimes since called the Mecklenburg County Declaration of Independence. It was not quite that strong a statement, but it did call for complete disobedience to royal authority unless "the General Congress of this Province . . . shall provide otherwise, or the legislative body of *Great-Britain* resign its unjust and arbitrary Pretensions with Respect to America."[19] This action was unrelated to affairs in Philadelphia, unless it was prompted by two agitators sent by the Congress in November 1775 to stir up the Carolinas.

If all these brave words had been unaccompanied by deeds, the rebels would have been in the familiar position of indignant Americans who gather to draft and adopt magical incantations called resolutions, and then disperse with hopes that evil will disappear. But strongly defiant acts matched their seditious utterances. In November 1775 the Congress got down to detail in the matter of local governments, advising popular representation in the bodies that reorganized the several provinces. At the same time it began to act on the report of its committee that visited the Army, voting to enlarge the Army and to strengthen its regulations while trying to improve military organization and maintenance. In December the Congress began to build a Southern fighting force which it hoped would reach a strength of sixteen regiments by the following spring.[20]

Local governments were equally fervent. Already the New York

Toward Independence, 1776

Committee of Public Safety had suppressed the royal post office in New York and substituted a courier service to ride between New England, the seat of action, and New York. At the other end of the country royal government was collapsing in Georgia. In July 1775 Georgians pirated royal powder from an inbound ship. From August to December, when the rebels took over the provincial judiciary, the polity of Georgia was the polity of terror. The governor, arrested in January 1776, fled the jurisdiction in February. In May 1776 the Rhode Island assembly refused to swear allegiance to King George and instead voted to strike his name from every public legal document.

In the first six months of 1776 the Congress was interested in the question of independence but preoccupied primarily with the war it was waging—raising troops and searching for artillery, small arms, clothes, and rations. So successful were these attempts that by May 1776 the Congress had about half the military strength it had voted in the previous twelve months—not bad for an untaxed country operating on fiat money. Six months before declaring independence the Congress had completed its continentalization of the postal system, without which the Revolution could hardly have moved at all. Its Surveyor of the General Post Office of the United Colonies, William Goddard, held the office described by one newspaper as having previously been an office "under Ministerial and Parliamentary authority."[21] Privateering became completely an arm of the war service by a resolution of May 23, 1776, which authorized colonists to take any British ships and goods as lawful prizes. That both the Congress and the Army thought themselves to be independent of outside courts before July 4, 1776, was sadly shown by the hanging of Private Thomas Hickey, Continental Army, on June 28, after conviction of plotting to assassinate Washington. That was a continental crime, punished by the continent.

From April 1775 to July 1776 no important measure of the British government or its agents was truly conciliatory. The quarantine of the colonies by act of Parliament, which closed the colonies to all commerce and is usually called the Prohibitory or Restraining Act (December 22, 1775), was known in America late in February 1776. This act was little short of a process of outlawry and could be interpreted as Parliament's declaration of American independence. The British burned Portland (then "Falmouth"), in the Maine District of

Massachusetts, on October 18, 1775, after local men obstructed the loading of naval stores. Governor Dunmore initiated the destruction of Norfolk, Virginia, on January 1 when he burned many warehouses and about fifty houses. (The neighboring rebels regarded Norfolk as a loyalist center, so they burned another nine hundred dwellings). Both burnings kindled fierce anger. American troops in Canada suffered severely that winter, and the news of the full extent of the Canadian disaster coincided exactly with news from Europe that the King was hiring German troops to use in America. German recruiting had an inflammatory effect on the Congress, which called them "foreign mercenaries."[22] "Myrmidons from abroad," Samuel Adams labeled them.[23] The American leaders expected about seventeen thousand Germans, in addition to fifteen redcoated regiments already afloat in transports sailing to America. This meant the British might have thirty thousand men in America by June. If the prospect of fifteen British regiments was chilling, the intrusion of German troops was infuriating enough to overcome fear. No other decision of the North Ministry could have so stiffened the backs of the American insurgents as the decision to use German soldiers against them. The use of Germans made Paine's argument for a foreign alliance a clincher. The weight of the German forces had upset the Anglo-American balance. The Congress would have to call on the old world to redress the balance of the new. But first the united colonies must say they were independent.

Virginia, the most populous colony, was ready. Archibald Cary reported and Edmund Pendleton moved a committee resolution in the Virginia convention on May 15, instructing the Virginia Congressmen "to declare the United Colonies free and independent states, absolved from all allegiance to or dependence upon the Crown or Parliament of Great Britain."[24] It passed unanimously.

Richard Henry Lee, masterly brother of the insecure Arthur, represented Virginia in the Congress. To him the German recruit contracts were the final injury. He feared Americans would be beaten to their knees unless they could get foreign help (from France, of course), and only a statement of independence would tempt a foreign prince to intervene. After independence "a proper confederation" would follow. France could not harm America.[25] On June 7 Lee offered his famous resolution: "That these United Colonies are, and of right ought to be, free and independent States, that they are absolved from all allegiance to the British Crown, and that all political connection between them and the State of Great Britain is, and ought to be, totally dissolved." The following two paragraphs called for "foreign Alliances" and "a plan of confederation. . . ."[26] The order of ideas shows that independence was a means to foreign help and domestic union.

After discussing Lee's resolution for three days, the Congress postponed action until July 1, "and that no time be lost, in case the Congress agree thereto," the delegates at the same time appointed a committee to write an elaboration of the independence paragraph of the resolution.[27] Lee's motion could probably have passed on June 10, but the Congress delayed to get unanimity, because if any colony repudiated the vote of the Congress the rebel cause would suffer incalculable damage. John Adams and Thomas Jefferson each recorded the opposing arguments, and their memoranda show that many honest men wished to postpone the stark decision as long as possible.[28] Adams summarized his own debate points. To declare independence would help to unite Americans, to ease treaty negotiations, to encourage formation of state governments, to depress loyalism, to stimulate the states to support the war, to motivate privateersmen, to tempt foreign vendors, and, perhaps, to weaken the unity of Britain. His feeling of the need for a list shows there was a real debate. The most influential opponent was John Dickinson, whose reluctance and moderating influence had probably served his country, but now his work was finished. And so was he, for a time, because he lost much stature in the public view and reappeared as a national figure only with the drafting of the federal Constitution in 1787.

The chief fear was that New York would not come along. The difficulty was that New York's three most militant rebels, John Lamb, Isaac Sears, and Alexander McDougall, were distracted by other circumstances and were not at home to lead their faction. The question of independence became merely one of many issues dividing the rebel Livingston group, which had an absorbing provincial revolution to attend to, hence it failed to get undivided attention.[29] The Congress could only hope that New York would glance away from local affairs to look at the problems of the continent.

The start of congressional action on declaring independence was not the beginning of independence. For a year the country had been independent in fact, and had committed many acts not usually done except by sovereign nations. Most of the time and energy of Congress in the first half of 1776 had been soaked up by military and fiscal trivia, and only the seemingly urgent need for strong friends abroad forced the matter of declaring independence onto the calendar. Hence the Declaration of Independence is an episode in diplomatic history: to make itself respectable enough to suitor for an alliance, the young and functioning republic prepared to write itself a certificate of legitimacy.

VI

The committee to write the certificate (appointed June 11) consisted of Franklin, John Adams, Robert Livingston, Roger Sherman, and Thomas Jefferson. They handed in a draft which suited them on June 28. Although Adams and Franklin helped to improve it, the paper was chiefly the work of Thomas Jefferson.

Jefferson was then thirty-three years old. He had much practical experience in politics as a member of the House of Burgesses. He had also practiced law successfully in most of Virginia's fifty-seven counties, but he was more interested in making than in practicing law. From his mother he inherited the Randolph genetic strain which has produced more public-spirited Americans than any other. When Jefferson arrived at the Continental Congress he was assured of being well received because of his admired revolutionary pamphleteering. His natural amiability did the rest. Already he showed why he was to become one of the two or three ablest politicians in American history—combining shrewdness, tact, and a hatred of personally bitter contentiousness. He constantly exercised his broad but not very original mind. In person he was physically vigorous, tall, loosely jointed, sandy-haired, and gray eyed. Almost everyone found his conversation interesting and persuasive.

He had formed his political philosophy from the history of law and jurisprudence, more to reinforce his predilections than to search for new ideas. As a revolutionary he wished to reform, not to innovate. He saw North America as an excellent site for an experiment in republicanism. As for monarchy he believed all kings could degenerate to Stuart kings. In short, his practical politics was precursory of the nineteenth century, while his legal and political philosophy was derived from the seventeenth. He did not embroider his committee's report of June 28 with these details, but found in commonly accepted precepts of natural law what they needed to justify the certificate of congressional legitimacy. Apart from this paper, for which Jefferson is most famous, he preached no grand system of natural law. To him and his fellows the complimentary term for a revolutionist was Whig.[30] Regarding British rule, he calculated that 160,000 British voters chose the Parliament which made laws for four million Americans, and he regarded their claim as unacceptable. His high regard for the document he and his committee presented led him in old age to order its title carved on his tombstone. He had blind spots and inconsistencies, but if he had died on June 29, 1776, he would yet be remembered.

8

Independent, Invaded, Intractable

Before Jefferson sat on the congressional committee to write a declaration of independence if it were wanted, he had previously written his "first ideas" on the Virginia convention as a draft preamble to the proposed constitution of Virginia. These "first ideas," much revised, served as his guide to that part of the Declaration which is an execration of King George III,[1] but the rest he did from memory. He consulted nothing in print, but drew on useful ethical aphorisms about resistance to tyranny, all of which had been intellectual currency since before 1492. In late June 1776, when he presented his text to his fellow committeemen, Benjamin Franklin, John Adams, Robert Livingston, and Roger Sherman, it was handed over as a draft to be revised. For example, Jefferson had laboriously pointed out that the British and Americans together could have become a great and free people, but the British were too proud to collaborate, hence the Americans would go that road alone, out of regrettable necessity. As polemic, this was a penetrating glimpse of the obvious and disappeared in revision. Franklin interjected his scientific turn of thought by changing Jefferson's "sacred and undeniable" principles to "self-evident" truths, an eighteenth-century scientist's phrase for axioms, and a rather happier wording. When the committee finished its revisions the full Congress also changed the document for the better. The purely verbal changes uniformly improved the paper.[2]

One substantive change was *not* an improvement. The Congress, in October 1774, promised that the states would abolish the maritime slave trade after December 1, and reaffirmed the promise in its act of April 6, 1776, which opened the ports of North America to all except British ships, and, in the same act, barred the importation of human chattels. Jefferson had written a condemnation of George III for not allowing the abolition of the slave trade, but his words failed of inclusion because neither Georgia nor South Carolina had any thought of such a policy, and the New England delegates had uneasy consciences since some of their best friends had been large operators in the maritime slave trade. This ought to have aroused a certain embarrassment in the hearts of those who voted to approve the phrase "all men are created equal." It has troubled some of their posterity.

The final draft of the Declaration of Independence was a work of high literary art. It not only drew on an acceptable political philosophy and summarized it felicitously, but the authors organized the piece according to the currently acceptable principles of logic and rhetoric. This was no accident. Jefferson wrote it in conscious harmony with the most important theory of persuasive writing to meet the standards expected by the best contemporary minds when dealing with proofs which were intended to convince the reason. Unlike grim and narrow-eyed vituperators of a later age, who call forth cheers by pointing with pride and groans as they view with alarm, while preaching to the converted and angering the infidel, Jefferson and his fellows combined logic, brevity, and taste with persuasion. Effective pleaders then knew that prolixity insulted the intelligent.[3]

Until July 2 it was not absolutely certain that the Congress would declare independence. Delaware was absent. New York had denied its congressional delegation the authority to vote for independence. The internal tension of Pennsylvania politics handicapped the Congress—for example, some members from Pennsylvania, including Robert Morris and Thomas Willing of the Philadelphia mercantile firm which had much of the business of supplying the Army, abstained from voting on the final passage of the resolution to declare independence. The arrival of the New Jersey delegation, elected on June 22, made independence probable, but only the coming of Caesar Rodney of Delaware clinched the vote. The ballot, on July 2, by states, was 12 to 0, as New York delegates watched with approval though abstaining. The precise chronology is this: The committee that wrote the draft reported out the Declaration on June 28. The Congress resolved to declare independence on July 2. The text of the Declaration of Independence received approval by the delegates on July 4.* A Philadelphia newspaper printed it on July 6, and the local Committee of Public Safety in Philadelphia was first to proclaim independence, on July 8. The text uses the word "unanimous," but this did not come true until the New York Provincial Congress approved of independence on July 9, when it accepted the Declaration because, it said, the reasoning was "cogent and conclusive."[4] The New York Congressmen declared their vote on July 15, which finally made the lineup "unanimous."

Caesar Rodney and some forgotten, lathered horses ought to get special credit. Rodney was a tall, thin, pallid man of whom John Adams said, "His face is not bigger than a large apple."[5] He sweated eighty miles on horseback to arrive on July 2 to put Delaware on record. This brave, practical, clear-minded man then went out and bore arms in the Delaware militia before returning to the Congress in 1777. President John Witherspoon of Princeton, a Presbyterian minister who entered politics reluctantly and became the leading token Scot of a rebel cause that was rather short of Scottish rebels, came to Philadelphia in time to exhort waverers effectively, and stayed to serve on more than a hundred committees, wherein he bore witness to the natural and Christian virtues of fortitude, prudence, resignation, and hope. The local pressure on such men to support independence seems, on balance, not so much the force of political philosophy as an earthy concern to lay hands on French gunpowder and muskets. France would send more munitions to an independent country fighting Britain than to rebellious British provinces. Mere

---

* The last two survivors of the committee that reported out this document —Adams and Jefferson—died within a few hours of each other on the fiftieth anniversary of its official date. It has been said by those who claim to know that the odds against this coincidence are one billion, two hundred million to one.

rebellion might end in reconciliation, which would be no advantage to France.

Fifteen days after approving the text of the Declaration of Independence, the Congress resolved to give it its title and to have it engrossed on parchment and signed by every member.[6] In time all signed except John Dickinson, who hid out for awhile in Delaware to escape the hurt looks of his colleagues and the I-told-you-so's of some loyalist in-laws. From the viewpoint of every King's counsel and most judges of English common-law courts, the list of signatories was a tally of traitors, hence their names were secret until January 18, 1777, when the Congress sent authenticated copies to all the states for their archives. Folklore says that scholarly William Ellery of Rhode Island (a man fond of reading Cicero, even on his deathbed), watched the expressions on the faces of the signers as they took quill in hand, for, after all, they might be signing their own death warrant. He reported, it is said, that all signers showed "undaunted resolution."[7] This is a regrettably impossible tale, because the signing went on for several months.

The Declaration of Independence is such a familar piece of American political furniture that we tend to forget that the idea of independence was seriously debated among the rebels. Practically all of the arguments against declaring independence were rational, except one lunatic notion that Britain might allow Spain and France to join in putting down the rebellion in return for a three-way partition of North America. The chief opponents of independence, as named by Jefferson, were James Wilson and John Dickinson of Pennsylvania, Robert R. Livingston of New York, and Edward Rutledge of South Carolina. (Jefferson did not identify the victim of partition panic.)[8] On the day after Lee's motion for independence, Rutledge gave his views at length to John Jay, perhaps hoping to influence the New York convention's attitude toward independence. Rutledge said he believed it correct to plan a treaty to be sent to France for negotiation, and correct to form a confederation, but it would be a tactical blunder to declare independence. Such a declaration would narrow the range of choices in future negotiations, and would tip off the British before the Americans had accomplished very much in America. It would put the rebels in the position of asking a foreign power to unite with them before they had united themselves. To

Rutledge, every colony seemed to be near anarchy, and as long as they remained disunited it would be folly to think they could negotiate a treaty. The only reason the supporters had for pushing the idea of independence at this time was "the reason of every Madman, a shew of our spirit."[9] A reasonable man could hold Rutledge's opinion, and, indeed, it was the strongest argument against declaring independence to come from the rebel side. But if the Congress had delayed until it could properly confederate the states, the delay would probably have been permanent. It was long after the Declaration that the free white American people made a union that satisfied most of them.

Americans have chosen July 4 as their Independence Day. They could as well have chosen July 2 or 8. The choice of the day on which the Congress merely authenticated the phraseology of its statement is less logical than the choice of the day on which the Congress voted independence or the choice of the day it officially proclaimed independence. John Adams wrote to his Abigail that July 2 would be "the most memorable" American anniversary. In the next generation people doctored his dating for partisan and hagiographical reasons, so that some have been confused about what happened on July 4.[10] What did the Congress do on July 4? The Congress voted that the text of the Declaration be authenticated. It did not order the clerks to have it engrossed until July 19. Thus the only deeds of July 4 were that President John Hancock bravely affixed his bold signature and Secretary Charles Thomson added his name to attest to the correctness of the text. Then why is July 4 Independence Day? On that day the document lay untitled; moreover it was not yet engrossed on parchment, nor did any signer after Hancock and Thomson put his name to it before August 2. In fact, some of the signers were not even members of the Congress at the time the Congress approved the Declaration, and some who were members and later signed it had voted "no." Matthew Thornton of New Hampshire did not take his seat until November 4, whereupon he signed the Declaration, no doubt with "undaunted resolution." The reason Americans celebrate the Fourth of July is that the Declaration of Independence appears in the *Journals* of the Continental Congress under the date July 4, complete with title and list of signers. The format has given posterity reason to believe the job was all done on that one day.

Independent, Invaded, Intractable

The Declaration of Independence opens with a two-paragraph epitome of the natural law of revolution, follows with a list of King George's "repeated injuries and usurpations" by which he intended to establish "an absolute tyranny over these States," and goes on to observe that humble petitions had achieved nothing. It regrets that "our British brethren" have ignored warnings, reminders, and appeals. Then, drawing on the words of Richard Henry Lee's original motion, which in turn had been a mirror image of the Declaratory Act of 1766 (which declared that the colonies were and rightly ought to be dependent on the Crown and Parliament), the Declaration of Independence announced the existence of a new nation. In literary form it combined the structure of a statute, a common-law indictment of George III for tyranny (on twenty-seven counts), and a contract binding its signers to compliance to the point of death.

The two paragraphs on natural law together make one preamble, as in a statute. Today this part is the remembered part, but it owes its fame to the democratic meditations of the next century, beginning at about the time of the Missouri Compromise of 1820. Contemporaries paid the least attention to this philosophical introduction. Even loyalists failed to attack it, and Jefferson never made much of this bit of natural law. It is a mistake to believe the preamble was the soul of the Revolution, that the bloody footprints of ragged Continentals pressed into Jersey snows because those tense and shivering young musketeers were philosophers of natural law. The independence paragraph was the enlivening paragraph, so far as words inspired the lads who fought the War for Independence.

After the preamble come the twenty-seven counts of indictment for tyranny, none of which refers to Parliament or the Navigation Acts. It is the King they are renouncing. (So strong is the rejection of George III that there is a claim to see the American Revolution as the symbolic killing of a father.) According to the Declaration, the King was very hard on American colonial assemblies, moving their meeting places maliciously, dissolving them, nullifying their acts, frustrating their hope of making naturalization easier. He also impeded the administration of justice. The description of his tyrannies will not always stand detached historical analysis, but some deed or other, of King or royal agent, was at bottom of every count of the indictment.

Why the King? In the late 1760's the vexed colonials had a trust in sweet reason and believed a simple presentation of the facts would cause the ministers to redress their grievances. When successive ministries failed to crumble under the bombardment of American syllogisms, the colonials looked to the King to protect them against the oligarchs (which, incidentally, is good Tory theory). When the King also failed them, the deadlock convinced the colonials that the King headed a royal and ministerial plot against liberty. In truth, British policies and attitudes were not rational enough for us to accept the pattern as that of a cool conspiracy to destroy representative institutions. In Britain's colonial policy much was narrow snobbish ignorance and arrogance, but nothing was Machiavellian.

And thus a King, warmly acclaimed by Americans who fired salutes and lit bonfires at his accession, declined in popularity until one of the best-known documents of new-world history devoted two-thirds of its space to his alleged villainies. The shift was not rapid. Thomas Paine's *Common Sense* was but the climactic episode in what could be called a long train of abuse. A precedent for every harsh American word written about the King in the years 1774–1776 can be found in the Virginia press alone during 1766–1774, in its commentary on the treatment of America *and* the treatment of the radical opposition in England.[11]

George III was no tyrant as defined in the ancient language of political philosophy, because the word "tyrant" meant usurper, and the King's title was flawless. If he were as described he would have been a "despot," a lawful ruler who rules lawlessly. Actually he was no innovator, and he never aimed at absolutism. He tried to be the head of the strongest faction in British politics in order to win back traditional powers yielded by the Crown. He went into party politics to try to beat his opponents at their own game by the use of patronage. He succeeded. After the election of 1775, seventy peers held salaried public offices, and 170 of the Commons had either public jobs or government contracts. All this makes him seem more like "Boss Guelf" (the family surname) than a royal brute. But the Declaration of Independence gave him an American reputation for despotism which lasted more than a century after 1776.

Even if contemporaries found the preamble of the Declaration of Independence relatively unimpressive, we cannot dismiss it, because later generations accepted it as the chief moral heritage from the Revolution. One might infer from it that Americans invented the right of revolution, but they did not. Such a right had been agitated since before philosophers learned to write. Those who first wrote it were Greeks, and it seeped into their creative literature, as when Antigone told King Creon:

> I dared.
> It was not God's proclamation. That final Justice
> That rules the world below makes no such laws.
>
> Your edict, King, was strong,
> But all your strength is weakness itself against
> The immortal unrecorded laws of God.
> They are not merely now: they were, and shall be,
> Operative for ever, beyond man utterly.[12]

Because of the long prevalence of latinate dictatorships ruled by nominal Catholics, one might mistakenly believe that the handful of active Catholic leaders of the American Revolution were anomalous, but they had medieval theological authorities to cite had it occurred to them. Christian morality did not allow them to subvert legitimate authority, but they could invoke the principle of self-defense against injury by a ruling despot. They could either refuse to obey unjust laws, or, as a last resort, actively resist to protect the common good against an excessive or habitual abuse of power which endangered public order—provided the resistance did not bring on evils greater than the evils they tried to cure. Granted the case against George III, their position was in line with their moral theology.

The Congress could lean on John Locke—at least for the right to rebel. He had justified the Glorious Revolution of 1688, and his language entered the Declaration of Independence, slightly amended. John Locke lives more kindly in memory if one knows only that his writing was a source for the political language of the Declaration. On closer examination he becomes steadily less attractive. His authorship of an empiric psychology, *An Essay Concerning Human Understanding*, which he set about in 1671 and which saw print in 1690, introduces him humanly enough, since he began to write it while working as baby-sitter for the grandson of Anthony Ashley Cooper, Earl of Shaftesbury. The child was the result of a match made for the Coopers by Locke, and both match and child pleased the family. But the book which contributed something to the American Revolution was his *Second Treatise of Government*, which distilled practically all earlier theories of the right of revolution. It was written in such generalities as to allow his readers to color their own interpretations of its doctrine with the folklore and history of England's Great Rebellion, and with later American experience. Here was the phrase "life, liberty, and property" which Jefferson changed to "life, liberty, and the pursuit of happiness." Here also was the idea that rebellion was proper after a "long train of abuses" made other relief seem hopeless. Locke wrote his political essays before the Glorious Revolution and published them after the event to justify that revolution. The *Second Treatise* has the tone of sturdy traditional Whiggery opposing the novel encroachments of the Crown, and thus appears conservative. Locke himself may not have been all that conservative, but, being a bit of a careerist, let his philosophy appear with at least the veneer of moderation.

It has been fashionable to derive Locke's intellectual pedigree from a time at least as early as the thirteenth century. St. Thomas Aquinas influenced the orthodox Anglican divine Thomas Hooker (1554?–1600), and Locke quoted Hooker much. But Locke's most recent analysts think his frequent references to Hooker and to the more remote past was really a kind of scholarly filigree to distract from Locke's repudiation of the essence of the Higher Law tradition running back through Hooker, St. Thomas, Cicero, and the thinkers of the ancient Near East, Aristotle, Samuel, Moses, and even some earlier obscure Mesopotamians. These interesting speculations need no further exploration as far as they concern the American Revolution, because they never crossed the minds of those educated leaders who found it useful to crib phrases from Locke's *Second Treatise*. Locke was a respectable authority and that was enough.

Nevertheless, Locke wrote enough anti-democracy to give us an idea of how much anti-democracy his American disciples would swallow. If liberty is a navigating star for generations of Americans since the Revolution, Locke is not a wholly satisfactory pilot. He believed in toleration—except for atheists and Catholics. He advanced the right of revolution—but only for majorities. He defended public generosity—but not to the "idle poor."

Locke's real radicalism was his application of scientific empiricism to moral questions, which in the long run had a destructive effect on public morality. But his position was modish. Politics did not seem to fit the pattern of the natural laws of material nature as did the laws governing the movement of, say, planets and comets. Perhaps men could discover the natural laws of polity just as they had discovered unchanging laws ruling in astronomy and mathematics. (Perhaps there was a Law of Empire to match the Law of Gravitation?) In any event, to men who speculated along such lines Locke seemed to point the way to learning how to harmonize the politics of men with the universal natural order. Such ideas were in the air. Locke's age was also the generation of Newton, and Kepler died just sixty years before the appearance of the *Second Treatise*. As early as the 1720's and 1730's American assemblymen boldly speculated about the effectiveness, in politics, of applying principles of natural law in disputes about parliamentary privileges and constitutional usages.[13] Were they continuing the dialogue of King Creon and the defiant Antigone? Not at all. They were thinking of what were later called scientific laws, not the Higher Law of God as cited by Antigone and the nineteenth-century abolitionists.

There is little in Locke to match the aspirations of a modern liberal democrat. Locke believed the state must be supreme over the individual in the emerging capitalist society for which he wrote. He thought its rulers should be those men who agreed that the greatest possible increase of national wealth was the greatest possible public good. Among men who believed this aphorism, the majority should rule. To be sure, all rational beings were free, but rational beings made up less than half the population of Great Britain. Liberty, to Locke, was freedom from dependence, and man was free enough if he had liberty to dispose of his property and his person. This was the political philosophy of grasping individualism, and would produce at best what a writer called "a limited liability state."[14] It could have been the grandfather of the classical liberal state as it existed in the imaginations of liberal economists of the nineteenth century, except that it provided for much government regulation. Toward the poor it was merciless. A reasonable man may suspect that if Locke could also have soaked up Darwin he would have invented Social Darwinism.

Not all of these ideas were in the philosophical baggage of the American Revolution, of course. The American rebels took what was respectable and persuasive of their case, and ignored the rest.

But Locke, in conventional wisdom, has been an intellectual hero of the Revolution and deserves rather more attention than he usually gets.

To return to the Declaration, it is worth noticing that there is almost nothing of economic grievance in it except that one of the twenty-seven counts of the indictment of George III for tyranny is a complaint that the Americans had no voice in the levying of taxes imposed in Britain to be collected in America. The omission of the word "property" from the Lockean phrase modified by Jefferson may not have been a matter of taste only. Thirty-seven years later Jefferson said he doubted whether property was a natural right. (Jefferson, of course, often changed his mind.) "The pursuit of happiness," the phrase substituted for Locke's word "property," probably did not mean a chase after happiness. The word "pursuit" then meant an occupation, as when a man took up the pursuit of a profession. That is the only way the word was used in the polemic writings of the rebels during the controversies with Britain. No American spokesman seemed to think happiness was a holy grail for free men to seek; all seemed to think it was theirs by right.[15]

The Americans later described their independence as the inevitable result of the destruction of their contract of government with the King, and they pointed to the Declaration as the act which dissolved the old government. The new state constitutions were contracts to form new governments. Such emphasis on the contract theory of government—which could be studied in the plausible but unhistorical works of Locke, Thomas Hobbes, and others—shows the Revolution as a backward-looking event, at least in original intention. If the rebels had been forward-looking they would have offered a new table of organization for the Empire. But Americans had no theory of empire, except for a few vague pamphleteering hints of what was later clarified as "dominion status" (a theory of empire which is itself now *passé*).

Those who now read the Declaration as a radical document are tracing their intellectual ancestry through Thomas Paine to the theorists of the seventeenth-century Great Rebellion, rather than to Locke. In the history of political philosophy this is a defensible position, grounded on a radical tradition of English political dissent extending back to the late middle ages. In the eighteenth century such dissent was a very weak intellectual force in Great Britain, but, just

Independent, Invaded, Intractable

as the notion of limited government survived among the parchments in the dusty pigeonholes of Tudor lawyers, to be brought out and brushed off for fresh use against the Stuarts, so the radicalism of the Stuart and Commonwealth generation, like the roots of a desert plant, lay dormant while awaiting the rains of some revolutionary April. The minority leaders (some of them incredibly republican) were powerless in British politics, but they preserved the old claims to resist tyranny, to govern only with the consent of the governed, and to allow freedom of conscience. They won nothing in eighteenth-century Britain, but they kept the sparks glowing for posterity to use to set fires. Their libertarianism was but an episode in the history of liberty.

Across the Atlantic they were more influential. In the American circumstances the struggles for national independence and personal liberty were parallel. Those Americans who were top dogs in their neighborhoods rejected the intervention of any external political authority. At the same time individuals tried to draw limits around their private lives into which external authority could not trespass. In the end the nation became a sovereign without a superior, and individuals, more tardily, have ever since been trying to prove that all men are equal, and to define the limits of public interference in a man's private life. Thus, first came national independence, then came the setting of the limits of the state. The setting of the states' limits was the constitutional movement, from the late 1770's to the early 1790's.

Although it is obvious that in July 1776 all Americans were not equal—even if the word "equal" meant only equal before the law—to interpret the Revolution as nothing but a change of masters will not explain all that happened. There was more to it than the expulsion of scarlet coats and the tearing down of symbolic crowns. Whether they intended it or not, the framers of the Declaration of Independence by their choice of words assured that later American history would be made by quarrels over natural rights. The eighteenth-century idea of natural rights included the equal protection of the laws (though certainly not equality of talent, property, or social status). As a corollary it included the practice of happiness, which in due time was to be explained as covering personal liberty, subject only to limits fixed by the people themselves in their governments. The seven-year struggle for independence overlapped some ambitious campaigns for social reform, few of which succeeded then, but all of which set goals for future generations. The War for Independence was not the whole of the American Revolution.[16] That war was won by late 1781. The Declaration by which Americans legitimized their nationality was for the export trade of the moment. Its authors had no intention of dissolving their deferential society, which was a good society for free white males, but in which women, blacks, Indians, and white bondsmen had no say. Americans have not yet been able to bring themselves to organize society to fit the flaming preamble of the Declaration of Independence, but the equality clause still serves as the official guide to the common good, in spite of the sluggishness of movement in that direction during two centuries. If time allows, the people may get the equality clause into their hands and mark it as their own, making the words "all men are created equal" ring true.

II

On the day the Congress received the first draft of the Declaration of Independence from its committee, June 28, 1776, there were no British troops in the united colonies. On the day the Congress voted Independence, July 2, the soldiers of the King were pouring ashore by the thousands on undefended Staten Island. One who saw the armada which brought the British Army wrote in his diary, "I declare that I thought London was afloat."[17] General William Howe, soon to be knighted "of the Bath" in a ceremonial bathtub in New York, had returned to the land where he was assigned to command.

While Howe's force had been receiving a great infusion of strength in Halifax, the Ministry at home appointed his brother Admiral Richard, Earl Howe, to collaborate with him in reducing the Americans to obedience. The brothers Howe were armed with a wisp of hay and a cattle prod. They were authorized to give absolution to penitent rebels in the hope of dissolving the rebellion, or, failing the necessary repentance, were to crush them with overwhelming force. To combine a conciliatory mission and a staggeringly powerful military command in the same persons was at least an interesting experiment in colonialism. The swarthy sailor-brother, called "Black Dick" by his seamen, held his appointment, in a sense, by accident. The government promised him a sinecure to keep him out of opposition, since he was a Member of Parliament unsympathetic to the war, but absentmindedly gave the job to another. Then, to soothe him, they appointed him to extend amnesties to insurgent Americans and gave him a large part of what they thought was the world's best navy to use if his conciliatory mission failed. Black Dick did not thirst for American blood, but he seemed to feel that a vast flotilla would be trumps in hand for his diplomatic game. The government did not intend that he should deliberately restrain his naval operations in favor of amicable politicking to make friends. Brother William's intentions were to dominate New England, add the large Canadian garrison to his command, bring the troops to decisive battle, and thereby make peace.[18] The Howes failed, but it is unfair to think, as some have suspected, that their political sentiments made them military shirkers.

General Howe, it will be recalled, had gone from Boston to Halifax. If he could have steered for New York in March 1776 he might have been able to seize enough land to feed an army, but he came too late. On arriving in New York in July he had 32,000 professional soldiers, fully armed and provisioned, supported by his brother's ten thousand seamen in ten ships of the line, twenty frigates, and hundreds of transports. Great Britain spent 850,000 pounds to outfit this expeditionary force, the largest sent from the British Isles to that time. New Yorkers could not see all the men, but they could see a forest of about fifteen hundred masts. The behavior of the troops on Staten Island required British courts martial to sit daily to try cases of crimes against civilians, a bad start for a conciliatory mission.

Why New York? The British troops in New York had been shipped to Boston in 1775, but whoever held New York held a naval base, could navigate many miles inland up the Hudson River, and held the southern end of the natural military route from Canada. Any British force in New York was also a threat to New England, the hornet's nest which contributed so much vigor to the American cause and so much inflammation to King George's temper. Although New York was then small in population, New York City's twenty thousand people made it the country's second city. New York's reputation for loyalism, and its known reluctance to declare independence, probably made it seem a good base from which to launch peace feelers. We cannot be sure, of course, but if Howe had come in March

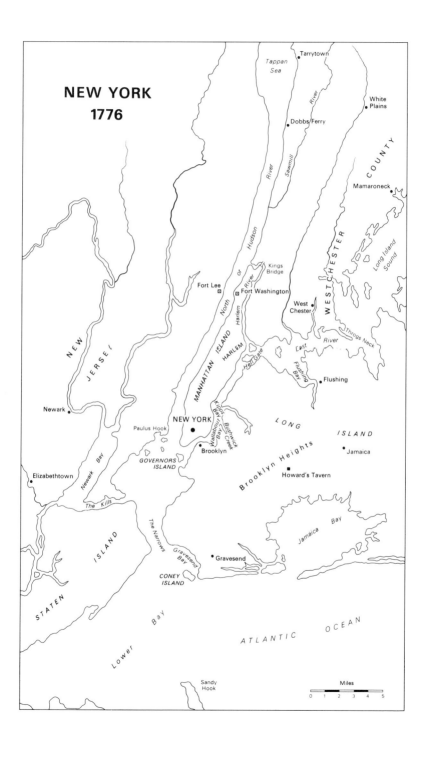

NEW YORK
1776

Tappan
Sea

Tarrytown

White
Plains

River

Sawmill

Dobbs Ferry

WESTCHESTER

COUNTY

Mamaroneck

River

Hudson

Long Island Sound

Kings
Bridge

Fort Lee

NORTH

Fort Washington

RIVER

Harlem

West
Chester

Throgs Neck

River

East

NEW

JERSEY

MANHATTAN ISLAND

HARLEM

Hell Gate

Flushing
Bay

Flushing

Newark

NEW YORK

LONG

ISLAND

Paulus Hook

Wallabout Bay

Kidd's Bay

Bushwick Creek

Brooklyn

Jamaica

GOVERNORS
ISLAND

Brooklyn Heights

Howard's Tavern

Elizabethtown

Newark Bay

The Kills

STATEN

ISLAND

The Narrows

Gravesend
Bay

Jamaica Bay

Gravesend

CONEY
ISLAND

Lower

Bay

ATLANTIC

OCEAN

Sandy
Hook

Miles

0 1 2 3 4 5

it seems unlikely that the Congress could have declared independence.

When Howe left Boston, the Congress and Washington could only wait anxiously for his reappearance. Washington and Charles Lee had earlier told the Congress that New York might attract Howe. Washington was not sure his command included New York, but Lee (with John Adams seconding) argued that Washington's conduct would have to inspire the Congress rather than wait upon congressional feeling. Giving in, Washington sent Lee, even before the evacuation of Boston, to begin fortifying the outskirts of New York City. Lee correctly told the Congress that the city itself was fit only for a battlefield and could not be defended against a combined Army and Navy attack; but he believed the enemy could be kept off Manhattan proper. His optimism encouraged the Congress to vote a garrison of eight thousand for New York and Long Island. The Congress told the uneasy Washington to hold New York if at all possible. Since Washington then had but six thousand men, he asked New York for a couple of thousand militia, and sent to Connecticut and New Jersey for help.

Washington knew he had too few men, and lacked arms enough for even that meager force. Both men and weapons were hard to get. New York complicated the politics of the situation by appointing a commissary to supply the troops, even though Washington had his own Commissary Joseph Trumbull who fed the troops more economically (this problem Washington passed to the Congress).[19]

The American tactical decision was to hold a line against invasion at Brooklyn Heights, because enemy artillery on that eminence could easily flatten New York City. East of Brooklyn the farmers had several hundred thousand head of beeves and sheep which could not be moved to the mainland easily, but nobody seems to have suggested meeting the British on the beaches. Charles Lee chose Brooklyn Heights, and Washington approved. Sir Henry Clinton, neurotic but no fool, thought Washington disposed his forces "absurdly," and believed the British landing could have been opposed[20] at that vulnerable moment of every amphibious operation when infantrymen are being converted from apprehensive passengers to warriors. Washington *was* confused. He had marched his sorefooted men hither and thither until he could not make a strength report on the eve of battle. He lamely wrote, ". . . . I believe our Strength is much the same, that it was when the last was made. . . ." He gloomily added news of the Army's bad health.[21]

Perhaps the potentially most promising defensive effort was an attempt to subvert the Germans who had been posted at the Amboy ferry, opposite a large body of Continentals. But the distribution of promises of rewards for deserting was badly done, the British officers told the Germans they would hang if captured, and the smashing British victory followed immediately, so it came to nothing.[22] In the following years desertion weakened the German units more than combat; a careful psychological offensive to seduce land-hungry German plowboys could not have been less profitable than the attempt to defend indefensible New York.

Washington put a large proportion of his men on Long Island, even though the East River would hamper any withdrawal. Nathanael Greene fell ill, and field command devolved on John Sullivan and Israel Putnam, who showed little competence. Howe, on August 26, landed on the south shore of Long Island, just as did those who took Nieuw Amsterdam 112 years before. His tactics were skillful. He pinned down the American center and right, where he inflicted dreadful slaughter among the best Continental troops—who stood firmly. Then a strong body rounded the American left end. The road at that place was patrolled by five young militia officers—actually hired watchmen—who surrendered without resistance when surrounded, and told the British the way to the American rear lay open. Howe then put troops across the American left end to veil his movements there, and easily marched on behind the Americans to capture almost all of Sullivan's left-flank troops, including Sullivan himself. With total victory at hand, Howe paused before Brooklyn Heights to wait for naval help from his brother's ships sailing into the East River to trap the American force. But both wind and tide were against the ships, and they could not get into the river. Helped by a regiment of Massachusetts fishermen, Colonel John Glover's Webfoot Regiment, the imperiled Continentals crossed to Manhattan in small boats. The last crossings were made in fog and rain, a meteorological circumstance which encouraged some earlier chroniclers to see the hand of the God of Battles. It should be noticed that Howe tried to capture, not kill, the force on Long Island.

Sullivan claimed he ordered that fatally open road to be guarded, but we have his word only. The human loss totaled eleven hundred men, including two generals, but there was no panicky flight. The Americans on the front fought gallantly, especially the Marylanders. The orderly withdrawal was itself somehow regarded as a victory.

As a military matter, considered in a vacuum, the best thing for the Americans to have done was to burn New York City, fortify the Highlands up the Hudson, and place the Army at Morristown, New Jersey. Both places were hard to attack but close enough to New York to make the British cautious about security. Colonel Joseph Reed, later president of the Congress, urged burning New York to deprive the invaders of quarters, and was critical of Fort Washington as a bastion for keeping a foothold in the New York area. (He was certainly right about the fort.) Washington had qualms about fleeing New York City because morale was already low after the Long Island defeat. In any event, political considerations prevailed. To surrender New York City now would have a bad psychological effect in the Congress (which had been willing to destroy Boston). Washington received orders not to burn New York. The general was still confused, but his solid, slow mind was groping for answers; he had certainly not distinguished himself, but he was beginning to grasp the scope of large operations.[23]

Sir Henry Clinton, who planned the tactics of August 26 for Howe, wished the attack had been pushed home completely, but General Howe was satisfied. The reluctance to annihilate the enemy was related to brother Richard's appointment as pardoner. The Howes intended, apparently, to use no more force than necessary to promote reconciliation. Merciless warfare won battles but did not revive loyalties.

At that period New York City occupied only the lower tip of Manhattan Island. The British had the town by September 15, though the Continentals were not chased out of the vicinity for many weeks. Unofficial arsonists set the town afire simultaneously in three places as soon as the redcoats settled in. The firemen had disbanded, their pumps were out of order, and the church bells had been taken by the Americans for casting field guns. The fires destroyed a third of the town and banished hopes of having pleasant winter quarters. Throughout the war New York was the British North American headquarters. It was overcrowded and stank. The housing shortage hurt loyalists the most, because they flocked to New York for protection but had no claim to lodgings.[24] When Rivington's vituperatively loyalist *Royal Gazette* resumed publication in 1777, its advertisements reflected garrison life: light reading, wines, military apparel, and pills to cure "a certain disease."

Washington never looked worse than in the Long Island affair. It was his worst defeat. A commander may properly risk a few companies as expendable, but Washington had risked the Continental Army, the war, and even independence as though they were expendable. And a week later he believed he was not at fault. New York, he wrote ungenerously, could be defended "if the men would do their duty."[25] His leading biographer attributes his bad showing to exhaustion, but that only proves inability to delegate authority. Furthermore, no first-rate general officer in history could confidently promise to defend New York in the existing state of the military arts. The extenuating fact is, Long Island was Washington's first conventional battle with a full army under his command. He showed hesitance and indecision, and divided his forces for fear an attack would come where he was unready. The loss of New York weighed heavily on his mind for the next six years. He had an almost compulsive obsession to try to recover the place. Since he never had a naval force of his own strong enough for the job, his preoccupation with the reconquest of New York somewhat weakens his reputation for naval wisdom. The loss of New York was a blow to the United States. The best port in the country was under the Union Jack, and its adjacent counties were a kind of No Man's Land. New York State became a headless torso. The state was perpetually in money trouble and unable to keep promises to the Congress. For the remainder of the war, the feeling between the Congress and New York was reciprocal impatience.

III

The Howe conciliatory mission was not the first attempt to harmonize the differences between Britain and the colonies by talks in America. James Drummond, a Scot who had lived for some years in the colonies, tried to reconcile Britain and America. He said he had started in November 1774, at the request of several Congressmen. He proposed three steps: to calculate each colony's contributions to defense, to levy that amount by taxation through its own legislature, and to surrender the claim of Parliament to tax. He discussed his plan in London early in 1775, and he had some influential listeners in America, including members of the Congress. He failed in London, because the military men wished to try to prove America's vulnerability.

Another attempt was that of General John Burgoyne who tried to arrange a conference with Charles Lee on Boston Neck in July 1775. Lee left it up to the Massachusetts Provincial Congress, which received the idea frigidly and advised a preliminary council of war in the Army. Lee dropped the idea.

Some time before the autumn of 1775 there was talk in England of appointing a viceroy with full powers to run an American war because it was so distant and so dispersed. The Spanish or the Portuguese might have been temperamentally able to take such a step in like circumstances, but it would be most un-British, and, worse, it could exalt the Congress by giving the colonists the impression they could negotiate as a group with an equal but opposing power.

Lord North steered a different tack. In October the government persuaded Parliament to approve a conciliatory commission. Probably most of the members who voted for it believed the commission was merely to accept surrenders of towns and colonies, and then go on to reorganize America. Admiral Lord Howe needed placating, and his family was popular in America, so he got the job. He was a most inarticulate man, and his silences gave the impression of serenity and quiet courage, while his speech was filled with *non sequiturs* which, to his bumbling peers, may have made him seem wisely delphic. Exactly what could he and his brother offer as a final settlement? Just this: the colonials would contribute to defense the sum of 5 or 10 per cent of the amount voted annually by Parliament for the armed forces, in return for which Parliament would forgo taxing. But Lord Howe was not to mention these terms until the colonists knelt in contrition.

What a splendid idea for, say, 1764. Of the Ministry one may say, this was their blindest hour. Once the Congress was practicing *de facto* independence, there could be no more foolish notion than the idea that the newly united colonies would accept a status something like Ireland's. Certainly the government gave the Howes much better firepower than pacification powers.

Lord Howe arrived in America about a week after the Declaration of Independence. He was disappointed not to have come before, but, even so, thought his peacemaking would take about ten days. Twice he sent officers to Washington, first to deliver a letter to "Mr. Washington," and next to "George Washington, Esquire, etc., etc.," but the only Washington known to the Continental Army was a "Major General George Washington," so the mail was undeliverable. A British general, piqued at this punctilio, said that "Esquire" was "a customary mode of address even to foreign ambassadors," and that in public remarks Lord Howe often gave Washington the title "Excellency."[26]

Unable to get in touch with Washington (who had no authority in the matter anyway), Lord Howe sent personal letters to his own friends, and from other Englishmen to *their* friends, urging reconciliation. Many of these found their way to the Congress, which learned from studying the documents that His Lordship could only absolve penitents, though he hinted at rewards to any who helped to restore peace. The Congress thought Howe's offer derisory—if a little dangerous (that matter of the rewards)—and ordered the papers published. Franklin, in a friendly manner, sent to Howe to tell him the offer amounted to little, as though offering pardon to France because the kings of England had once been kings of France.

So the great invading force of the brothers Howe moved inexorably toward the fight with the Continental Army on Long Island, with results we have seen. The only benefit of Lord Howe's try at making peace before shooting was to prolong the lives of those who might have died earlier in the conquest of New York.

One of the fruits of the British victory on Long Island was that the Howes had a real live Continental general as a prisoner—John Sullivan of New Hampshire. Sullivan's military distinction was to be achieved years later, but he was a skilled politician and was noted for bravery, quick temper, and generosity. What mattered more to his captors was that he combined general rank with status as an ex-Congressman. Lord Howe decided to send him to the Congress which, of course, received him and listened to him attentively. In Lord Howe's characteristically disordered conversations Sullivan thought he had detected a hint that Parliament would agree to the repeal of the obnoxious acts which so vexed Americans. Howe later said Sullivan misunderstood him. Whatever he may have said, all Lord Howe really intended was to talk with some members of the

Congress as private persons. His government would not permit him to recognize them as public officials.

On the days September 2–5 there was much argument in the Congress. The question was not one of principle but of practical politics. Some were for bluntly rejecting Howe's invitation to talk; others favored acceptance. John Adams wished the Congress to ignore Howe. President Witherspoon feared the Congress would somehow disgrace itself and thereby encourage the loyalists. It was an annoying dilemma. Nobody expected peace to come from a conference with the admiral, but Howe's invitation might provoke rumors that he came to America with concrete propositions. If the Congress declined even to listen to him, it might seem rather bloody-minded.[27] The upshot was the choice of a committee to see Howe and to try to learn whether he could treat with persons who represented the whole United States, and, if so, what his authority and propositions were. The committeemen chosen were Franklin, John Adams, and Edward Rutledge—no bad choice.[28] The committee was a much more capable group than the one it was to meet.

Despite or perhaps because of the message Sullivan brought, there was skepticism in the Congress about the possibility of serious *official* conversations with Lord Howe. Just in case Howe did not treat them with the respect due to a committee of the United States, the members of the committee were to inquire into the state of the Continental Army in New York, so that the trip would not be time wholly wasted if they were not received.[29] The attitudes of the members of the Congress were cynicism or doubt rather than anger or defiance. So, with little dissent, the three emissaries of a declared republic went pessimistically to Staten Island to confer with the senior British officers who had come to pacify or crush them.

The British received their American visitors amicably. Going somewhat beyond the demands of military courtesy, they drew up troops to give the delegates the musket salute with fixed bayonets, an honor usually reserved to legally commissioned military men, but which John Adams grumpily said the Americans neither understood nor heeded. The house in which they met had been temporarily a guardhouse and was very dirty, but the hosts had cleaned one room handsomely, carpeting it with moss and decorating it with foliage. Lord Howe sat his callers down to lunch on claret, bread, and cold ham, tongue, and mutton.[30]

Then to the talk. The admiral said he could not deal with a congress but could discuss the situation with influential gentlemen. The influential gentlemen said they would listen. Lord Howe's only specific proposal was that the Americans return to allegiance and obedience, and expect kindness in return. The congressional delegation replied that the British government had treated them with contempt, and the Congress had not declared independence until Parliament ostracized the colonies by statute. Since that time every state had set up its own government, and the delegates, apart from the Congress, could hardly speak for them. They told Lord Howe he could get power to treat with the United States quicker than the Congress could get power to bind the states into submission separately. But it had become clear that Howe had authority only to forgive sins and could do nothing else. With his usual diffuseness of speech, he gave some uncertain affirmations of the repeal of the statutes which so offended the Americans.[31] Inasmuch as the Congress had in fact been functioning as a sovereign legislature for about seventeen months, Howe's invitation to repent was almost offensively naive, and certainly unacceptable.

The diary of Lord Howe's secretary, Ambrose Serle, anticipated the failure of the fanciful mission. Before the Staten Island conference he wrote that the Congress had published Howe's writings with its own adverse appendices, and continued, "Their Leaders seem resolved to run all Lengths, and to draw the poor miserable People after them. No Resource remains for Britain but her Sword, which she has often drawn in the Defence & Protection of these ungrateful Regions."[32]

News of the rejection of absolution reached England shortly after news of the Declaration of Independence. When Parliament met in November, opposition leader William Petty, Earl of Shelburne, used the American deadlock to mock the King's Speech from the Throne. He said the government offered friendship so tardily that the Declaration of Independence was justifiable in self-defense. If the colonists were traitors, so were the Whigs of 1688. More seriously, Shelburne predicted war with France. The King's Speech said "that no people ever enjoyed more happiness under a milder government," which was proved, Shelburne retorted, by taxation without consent and stripping them of their charters. The Speech explained the government's aim: "to restore to them the blessings of law and liberty, equally enjoyed by every subject," to which Shelburne added—by sending to America an army of foreign mercenaries.[33] In any legislative body assuredly commanded by a cohesive majority, this kind of forensic fireworks is usually set off by the minority for amusement, but Shelburne had exploded one true bomb, the real possibility of a French war.

What the government thought was what counted, and the government thought what Lord George Germain thought on this question. He now hungered to wage war thoroughly, and he was disenchanted with the brothers Howe because their mixture of politics and war was a "sentimental manner of making war."[34] The answer to the outspoken Declaration of Independence was to be a silent determination of serious war.

CHAPTER

9

Diplomatic Dawn
and Military Dusk

The first political act of American nationality had been the boycott of Britain by the agreement called the "Association" (1774). When the fighting started, the economic isolation hurt the rebels, and, as seen, the Continental Congress moved step by step until in April 1776 it permitted everybody to enter American ports except Britain. By then, French aid was coming through pretended merchants. Ships from Bilbao, Nantes, and Rotterdam brought war materials priceless to a raggle-taggle army. Some American produce moved to Europe in partial payment, most to the French tobacco monopoly. Arthur Lee, brother of Richard Henry Lee, handled Spanish supplies with Don Diego de Gardoquí; Silas Deane, representing Morris, Willing, and Company, Philadelphia merchants, dealt with Caron de Beaumarchais for French supplies. The British knew about this trafficking but pretended official ignorance to keep the war from spreading.

The congressional faction which revolved around the Lees and the Adamses looked on foreign aid and saw that it was good. But it might be short-lived. Suppose Britain, France, and Spain decided their interests were better served by friendship? Something should be done

162

to keep amity from breaking out in Europe. Perhaps an offer of some American advantage could encourage discord? The Committee of Secret Correspondence, as it later wrote, had suspected Britain of wishing to conciliate America mostly to deflect the interest of continental Europeans: "Prospects of accommodation, it is well known, would effectually prevent foreign interference. . . ."[1]

The original motion for independence by Richard Henry Lee on June 7, 1776, contemplated alliances and confederation as well. On June 12 the Congress appointed a committee to plan treaties, its members being John Dickinson, Benjamin Harrison, Robert Morris, John Adams, and Benjamin Franklin.[2] With the Declaration of Independence out of the way, the committee on treaties reported a complete "Plan of Treaties" (July 18). The first draft was tailored for King "Lewis" of France by name, but the plan as printed two days later omitted names of nations and kings. For ideas the committee had relied on conventional practice. Franklin gave Adams a printed collection of treaties, with exemplary passages marked, and Adams assembled these passages (and others) in one plan. It resembled the later Treaty of Amity and Commerce as negotiated with France in 1778, and remained the model for most American treaties signed before 1800.

It was to be a commercial treaty, not an alliance. At the time John Adams saw no need for more than a formalized commercial relationship with France. The Congress voted its approval on September 17, as a plan to be proposed to "His Most Christian Majesty" the King of France. (It has ever since been known by the catchphrase, "The Plan of 1776.") The model treaty ran to thirty articles and two annexed forms of passports for shipping governed by such a treaty.[3]

A week later the Congress adopted a set of instructions for the negotiators who were to go to Europe with this proposal. At first there was thought of promising not to make a separate peace, but the Congress immediately recoiled and limited the guarantee to an assurance that the United States would not rejoin the British Empire and would accept a reciprocal agreement in writing that neither party to an American treaty would come to terms with Britain without six months' notice to the other. The negotiators were to ask for an immediate supply of war materials, good engineers, and eight completely manned and fitted ships of the line. The United States had little to offer on its side except the continued annoyance of King

George, so the Congress added something for King Louis to think about by saying that France probably did not wish the United States to fail, but might overestimate the ability of the country to carry on alone. Therefore it should be understood that the Americans needed help immediately, and could also use a sympathetic declaration by France, since "a reunion with Great Britain may be the consequence of a delay."[4]

To soothe and interest the King of Spain, the Americans were to tell him not to fear any interference with his Latin American empire by the United States. Inasmuch as the United States had just proved its inability to defend its best port, the assurance fell just short of levity. Indeed, if the United States had lost the war, this diplomatic offensive of 1776 would now seem pathetic. There was at the time no evidence that the Congress was a very fit body to carry on a war and to bring the efforts of thirteen rebellious provinces to a common focus. The Congress and the state political leaders had to learn empirically from successive defeats. Their difficulties stemmed from inexperience and from the ramshackle structure of the central authority as embodied in the Congress.

Having armed the negotiators with a plan and some dark hints, the Congress had to name the men. On September 26, 1776, the choices were Silas Deane, Benjamin Franklin, and Thomas Jefferson, appointed to go to Europe to contract with great powers to promote a distant rebellion. Deane was already in France, working for the "Secret Committee" for purchasing (later the Committee of Commerce). Jefferson declined election, so Arthur Lee, also in Europe, received the appointment. The three, Deane, Franklin, and Lee, were to talk with any ambassadors in Paris and to try to persuade their governments to recognize American independence. If possible they should negotiate treaties of commerce as equals, if the terms of such treaties were not repugnant to any treaty which might be made with France. If they could do no more, they should at least try to keep the other European princes out of the war on King George's side. But it must also be clear that the United States could not undertake to help them in any of *their* wars.[5] Deane, of course, knew little of all this. Never a shrinking, shy man, he had drafted his own model treaty with France, which he submitted to Conrad Gérard on November 23 with the caution that it was entirely his own idea. Nothing came of it. A month later he learned of his appointment to the mission.[6]

Diplomatic Dawn and Military Dusk

The Congress, so bravely dealing with mighty potentates by correspondence and agents, had by Christmas fled from Philadelphia to cramped Baltimore, as Sir William Howe's scarlet-and-green-clad soldiery advanced unchecked toward Philadelphia. Nothing daunted, the Congress raised the ante in its foreign gamble, and authorized the American mission to borrow up to two million pounds sterling in Paris on the credit of the United States, repayable in not less than ten years at a rate of interest not to exceed 6 per cent (lower if possible). With this instruction went the commonsensical suggestion that the creditor might accept American produce in payment.[7] This was bold, but in their hearts the Americans were not quite that assured. They had begun to suspect they would not get massive aid from France on the optimistic terms imagined in the summer of 1776. If they had known the facts of French fiscal life they would have been even less hopeful. France was a very rich country, but its public finance was starved by the folly of letting out tax collection to farmers general who paid fees in advance for the contracts to collect specific taxes, and who were allowed to keep any surpluses. France would not spend as freely as the Americans wished, except to support military allies. The American negotiators lacked powers to make such an arrangement, but at the end of 1776 the Congress despondently authorized a military alliance. It was dangerous to make a military connection with a Catholic despotism, and some thought it would be worse than the old degrading subordination to Britain.

In this moment of darkness the Congress conceived a plan of militia diplomacy. Commissioners were to go to Vienna, Madrid, Berlin, and Florence. Together they should try to bring France, Prussia, and Austria to join in preventing Britain from shipping continental troops to America. If France could be persuaded to attack Hanover, or any other part of King George's dominions, that would do the job. To tempt France into a more active part in the war, the commissioners were to suggest a partition of maritime Canada and a sharing of the Newfoundland fisheries, and to offer as many British West Indies as the French could conquer. Spain was to be lured by offers of Pensacola and help in a war against Portugal. The value of a Florentine connection to either party is not apparent.[8]

The Congress gave credentials to the negotiators,[9] guaranteed their expenses, and told them to live in Paris at the level they thought necessary in order to be respected. The Secret Committee was to export produce or bills of credit in the sum of ten thousand pounds sterling for their expenses in Paris.[10] The new mission was to be secret until announced by the Congress, which shows a serious intention of operating covertly until an announcement would have propaganda value; after all, every act of the Congress was supposed to be secret, hence this was something special. But the secret was not kept. A fortnight later a Philadelphia businessman casually asked whether Franklin and others were really going as ambassadors to France. Franklin and Morris irascibly noted in a memorandum, "The Congress consists of too many members to keep secrets."[11]

The mission to Florence remains a puzzle. There is no clue in the *Journals*. The only Tuscan connection at the moment was Philip Mazzei, a Florentine and a friend of Jefferson, who was living in Virginia and trying to build a wine industry. He had translated the Declaration of Independence and sent a copy to the Grand Duke.[12] But he would not have had time to get a reaction from Italy, so the blank in the story remains unfilled. No American official went to Florence anyway.

To anticipate for the moment, Franklin was to take care of both French and Spanish affairs, but the Congress sensibly gave Lee responsibility for Spain on May 1, 1777. Ralph Izard was the man who did not go to Florence, although appointed to the task on May 7. The Congress, on May 9, asked William Lee, the third brother of the Lee trio and a sometime sheriff and alderman of London, to represent the United States at both Berlin and Vienna. These men spent much time snugly in Paris at the expense of the United States, volunteering unsolicited advice and expecting to be kept *au courant* of Franco-American relations.

Franklin was past seventy when he accepted the Paris assignment, and had supported himself since age ten. He had spent sixteen years as a colonial agent in London, which was good preparation for the task ahead. Thoroughly read in the literature of the time, he never lost the earthy touch. His wit and humor lacked brilliance and malice, though he had a touch of cynicism. His mind had as many facets as Jefferson's, but he was more concerned with matter and behavior than with ideas and principles. Perhaps that is why he never bothered to marry the woman known as his wife. Nearly always he held something of himself back, as though playing life like a game of whist. Only when digging into sciences was he wholly open and unreserved.

Diplomatic Dawn and Military Dusk

In other matters he seemed a spectator—bland, friendly, but detached. With Jefferson and John Adams his was one of the best three American minds of that generation. He enjoyed the fruits of material success, liked to wear a uniform, had a black page boy and other household slaves (and is remembered as an early abolitionist), yet presented himself before the King of France in Quaker dress as a way of creating distinction in a place where men dressed as brightly as peacocks and drew only passing glances.

Franklin arrived in Paris on December 21, 1776, and was an instant sensation. John Adams, who came to Paris fifteen months later, left us a note on Franklin's celebrity.[13]

His reputation was more universal than that of Leibnitz or Newton, Frederick or Voltaire, and his character more beloved or esteemed than any or all of them. . . . His name was familiar to government and people, to foreign countries, nobility, clergy, and philosophers, as well as plebeians, to such a degree that there was scarcely a peasant or a citizen, a valet de chambre, coachman or footman, a lady's chambermaid or a scullion in a kitchen, who was not familiar with it, and who did not consider him a friend to human-kind. . . .

And this was written by a man who did not like Franklin very much. Hero worship was shown in the diary of a young visitor, so carried away that he even admired Franklin's paunch:[14] "His silver hair and his large front assured him reverence and Esteem. Persuasion and Goodness sat on his lips, and the benignity of his whole Aspect was admirable. He spoke little and chiefly on [sciences], was dressed in a plain suit of grey and white silk stockings. . . ." In later years John Adams thought him a tremendously overrated man,[15] but he was the right man in the right place at the right moment of history.

On the whole the diplomatic militia was a less successful corps than the musketeer militia of eastern Massachusetts. Madrid, Berlin, and Vienna refused official acknowledgment of the existence of Arthur and William Lee. Ralph Izard waited vainly for any hint that he would be welcome to live in Tuscany. Later on, Francis Dana spent some time in St. Petersburg, but with little profit. In future years John Adams learned how to manipulate the levers of power and borrowed money at The Hague. Excepting Franklin and Adams, these men approached their work as clear-eyed upright reformers, proud of their ignorance of diplomatic protocol, impatient with courtly forms, hoping to substitute the image of the virtuous, rustic plaindealer for the suave courtier tending to the interests of his prince. They went about Europe trying to get autographs on commercial treaties, bypassing first secretaries and gray eminences, hoping to substitute logic for etiquette, and accomplishing exactly nothing. Only gradually did they come around to the thinking of history-minded John Adams, who concluded that the traditional ways of transacting diplomatic business, built up over long millennia, must have some utility. Another besetting difficulty was the rivalry of state agents who scoured Europe for money and materials in competition with the agents of the Continental Congress. The representatives of the states, by and large, were an unpromising lot, rarely did well, and in some cases were swindlers of their home assemblies. Finally, life in the Paris center—the only place where much was accomplished from the beginning—was complicated by the fact that Arthur Lee, Franklin, and Deane were temperamentally incompatible. Of course Lee got along with no one, but the fact that he and Franklin found Deane hard to take is to their credit.

The news of the Canadian fiasco arrived in Philadelphia in May 1776, and General John Thomas went to command the sick and shivering Continental Army. John Hancock said there was no money available, but "There are still laurels to be acquired in Canada. . . ."[16] The only real hope was to slow Sir Guy Carleton's chase. Benedict Arnold built a Lake Champlain squadron, so Carleton had to build one, at great cost in time.[17] These naval forces came to battle at Valcour Bay on October 11, where Arnold substantially delayed Carleton. When the pursuer was finally able to move forward, he said the season was late and returned to Canada. Howe's advance across New Jersey eclipsed the great importance of Arnold's delaying action, because the Congress heard of it while packing to get out of Philadelphia. But Arnold was in high spirits; he counted his force at nine thousand and added, "Our people are daily growing more healthy."[18]

The Canadian expedition cost much money and about five thousand soldiers. Its failure brought a cloud of gloom. Strategically it was a disaster, because the British reopened their military route westward, strengthened their influence over the northern Indians, and made it impossible for the Congress either to supply or protect potential Indian allies. The Old Northwest became indefensible, in the sense that later American victories there could not be permanent conquests.

Naturally there were attempts to fix the blame. John Adams angrily blamed both the want of hard money and the incompetence of the officers. On the contrary, the officers did what was possible. What was not plain to Americans was that the Canadians did not welcome paper money or liberation. George Washington's proclamation to them at the start of the campaign showed no understanding of Canadian circumstances and said nothing that might incite Canadian rebellion. General Philip Schuyler of New York was the nominal theater commander, and there was an attempt to assassinate his reputation by accusing him, among other things, of pocketing the money intended for the campaign. The New York Congressmen spent much energy in his defense. The Congress investigated the campaign and wisely accepted the correct report of its committee: the invasion failed because of the policy of calendar-year enlistments, lack of gold, and the ravages of smallpox.

Ignoring the human suffering, one can see the Canadian invasion as immediately advantageous to the United States in some respects. The entry of armed rebels into Canada stirred London to divert the first large shipment of reinforcements to Canada, which delayed Howe's movement to New York. It also convinced the Ministry that Carleton should stay to protect Canada. Thus Howe, not Carleton, succeeded Gage in the colonies, although Carleton seems to have been much the better soldier. If such a large reinforcement had not gone to Canada, the British campaigns farther south would necessarily have followed a different course.

The Congress still hoped to win Canada. It instantly resolved to try another invasion, but the misfortunes near the Hudson River were too painfully distracting. There was another Canadian plan in 1778, and in that year a Philadelphia paper printed a rumor of the arrival of a set of Canadian congressmen.[19]

A handsome logical structure of proof has exalted Arnold's role: the entrance of foreign navies assured American victory. The foreign navies came in because the Americans defeated General John Burgoyne in 1777. The Americans could defeat Burgoyne because the invasion from the north was postponed a year. The invasion was postponed because Arnold commanded Lake Champlain for four weeks in 1776.[20] There is a variable omitted from this theorem, but it is partly true.

Once New York City was British, the invaders under Sir William Howe methodically cleared the American rebels out of the vicinity by a war of threatening moves which resembled play at chess. There were fights at Harlem Heights and White Plains, but the key turned out to be Fort Washington, the capture of which was a German military triumph. The fort was the Continentals' last stand on Manhattan Island. It was merely a pentagonal earthwork, with no interior buildings except a wooden magazine and some offices. It had no water supply, no fuel, nor any conventional defensive outworks. There seems to be no reason to think it could be held, but Washington tried, even after Black Dick Howe's ships had gotten past the fort and upstream of it. When it was practically certain to fall, the attacking commanders—who had thirteen thousand men—summoned it to surrender, but the much smaller garrison was defiant. Perhaps they did not know that this defiance forfeited all claim to mercy, and that international law would allow their conquerors to cut the losers' throats. The attackers overran the place on November 16, 1776, taking 2,818 prisoners and a vast, priceless quantity of Continental military materials of all kinds. Howe was still bent on conciliation and treated his captives as prisoners of war, though their defense, irrational by eighteenth-century military standards, cost the attackers 458 killed and wounded.

As in the Canadian reverse, the question of responsibility arose. The Congress has often received the blame, but it had given Washington full discretion by resolution of October 11. Washington obliquely hinted that it was Nathanael Greene's fault,[21] but Washington would have received credit for any victory, and congressional dissatisfaction with his exercise of command began to appear privately. Two days after the fall of Fort Washington, Charles, Lord Cornwallis, with 4,500 men crossed the Hudson and took Fort Lee. General Greene's men in Fort Lee escaped with little of their equipment, and set off toward Hackensack to join Washington. Grumbled Massachusetts Congressman Elbridge Gerry about these two setbacks, "I wish they may be forgot, as there appeared to me a Want of Generalship."[22]

Washington was in low spirits. He reported that the Army was breaking up—actually, almost half of it had been captured in ill-chosen positions—and that he had on his own authority asked New England to send militia. Not a single Continental recruiting officer was as yet commissioned, and it was "essential . . . to keep up some shew of force and shadow of an army." He correctly predicted that Howe would invade New Jersey.[23] Howe did, and Washington fell back before him, abandoning the neighborhood of New York port.

Diplomatic Dawn and Military Dusk

For the next five years the counties immediately adjacent to Manhattan, especially between New York City and the fortified Hudson Highlands at West Point, were a neutral ground between the lines. A few stalwart Dutch farmers refused to leave their farms, but in general the region was a dangerous place and provided cover for daredevils, avengers, thieves, and a few glory hunters.

II

Washington, with his miserably depressed and dwindling force, retreated across New Jersey followed by Howe's army, which seemed to enjoy the march. As a pursuer wrote, it was "the finest Weather for the Season ever known, and such a Fall as no Man can recollect; the Weather has been as favourable for our Operations since we took the field as it possibly could be."[24] But Howe moved sluggishly, partly because he was carrying olive branches in one hand, and partly because he had some difficulties with supply and with inefficient juniors. Furthermore, his was a professional army, with winter just weeks away, and no eighteenth-century professional armies fought winter campaigns if they could avoid them. Howe has also been suspected of slowing his army's advances in favor of speeding his own advances to Mrs. Joshua Loring, wife of his commissary.

At any rate, Washington safely reached and crossed the Delaware River. Being an experienced Potomac riverman, he left no boats for Howe on the Jersey side. Howe remained undisturbed. It was now December and time for wintering indoors. After all, Washington's force had dwindled from many thousands to a remnant, and he could be expected to surrender "as any temperate, rational European would have done."[25]

Civilian life in New Jersey between Philadelphia and New York was tense and distressing. The German troops looked on New Jersey as a conquered province and looted without distinguishing friend from foe. The state had been rather evenly divided in its loyalties to begin with, and when the militia rallied in rebellion they were rough on their loyalist neighbors. Then Howe's men marched through in triumph and the loyalists got their own back. The alternating dominance of requited hates promoted lasting bitterness. Once the reasserted Crown authority seemed firm, New Jersey quieted and gave the appearance of yielding. The mixed population had no provincial pride and no uniformly educated leadership such as the Harvard alumni provided in Massachusetts (Princeton was but thirty years old). Howe offered pardon to all who would sign pledges of allegiance, and got so many takers that he ran out of printed forms. One signer of the Declaration of Independence, Richard Stockton, a man who seems to have taken short views, signed a submission to the King. In all, probably five thousand people scrawled signatures on loyalty pledges. Unfortunately, the German soldiers could not read and continued to show the frivolous attitude toward the rights of portable property first called to public attention by Cornelius Tacitus.

The Congress mistakenly thought it a disaster when the British captured Major General Charles Lee. His flashy eccentricity dazzled the Americans into thinking him the very model of an eighteenth-century major general and led them to pay his five-figure debts so he would be free to serve in the Army. In December, tired of bivouac life, he lodged himself in an inn between the lines where he was picked up by a British patrol on a tip from a local loyalist. As a newspaper said of the informer, "Our people are greatly exasperated. . . ."[26] The downcast Congress voted money for his comfort and asked Washington to inquire whether he was being treated well. (He was.)

The sparkling stream of successes, from April 1775 to May 1776 (when the Canadian failure became known) had cast a brilliant light. Now the dark news from Canada, New York, and New Jersey made it seem that twilight was falling. As Thomas Paine wrote in December, these were the times "that try men's souls," when the "summer soldier and sunshine patriot" shrink from duty. (Less well remembered was Paine's blame of those who had done too little in the previous winter and delayed the Declaration of Independence after December 1775.[27]) The Massachusetts leader James Warren ascribed the decline of fighting spirit to the "Indecition" of the Congress, its procrastination, its laxity toward loyalists.[28] And Pennsylvania was a paralyzing distraction. Its deadlocked government was so near stagnation that some Congressmen threatened to govern it directly, to present a united front of thirteen states instead of twelve states and an anarchy.

With enemy advance parties drawing close to Philadelphia, the Congress behaved like a band of panicky bureaucrats afraid of damaging its public image, the manner of which can best be seen by simple chronology: *December 9*: Resolved that if the Congress had to leave Philadelphia it would go to Baltimore. *December 10*: Published a proclamation pointing to past American military successes and the freedom of most states from British intruders, affirming that the war was by no means lost, calling on all to rally to save Philadelphia; ordered Washington to patrol the New Jersey roads from north of Trenton to Philadelphia and to report regularly. *December 11*: Denied the "malicious" and "scandalous" rumors that the Congress would leave Philadelphia; asked Washington to contradict such gossip. (They later struck this denial from the *Journals*.) *December 12*: Departed from Philadelphia to go to Baltimore.[29] President John Hancock and family were among the last to arrive in Baltimore, bringing an elaborate household and a newborn Hancock.

The move to Baltimore was no disorganized flight and was probably a good thing for efficiency in the long run, since the delegates showed a marked increase in the tempo of their achievements in the next several months. As anyone who has lived through a big war knows, there is apparently nothing like a feeling of crisis to unite people at work on a common task. The accountancy showed that the move was orderly, all very matter-of-fact in the records; for example: an order of December 21 to pay the cost of hauling the Congress's money by wagon to Baltimore under armed guard. The cost was 142 1/11^d.[30]

While in Baltimore John Adams found no fault in it except its high prices. He also remarked on the continuous turnover since the First Continental Congress, with new faces from ten states. "The rest," he wrote, "are dead, resigned, deserted or cut up into Governors, etc., at home." Singling out John Witherspoon and Benjamin Rush especially, he thought some of the new men were very able.[31] Undoubtedly the move to Baltimore was seen by some people as contemptible flight, for Robert Morris felt called upon to explain that it was not from "pannic" for the personal safety of the delegates but for the preservation of the Congress as an institution.[32]

The commanding general was feeling low. As he wrote on December 18 to John Augustine Washington, ". . . *If every nerve is not strain'd* to recruit the New Army with all possible expedition, *I think the game is pretty near up*."[33] Two days later he told the Congress of his unauthorized acts and of his great needs: he had set up an artillery corps under Henry Knox, he needed more engineers soon, he had raised the pay of the gunners on his own initiative, he needed a commissary of prisoners and new generals to help his overworked generals. Reliance on the militia and on short enlistments was pernicious. He needed more power, not for his own sake but to hold the Army together.[34]

The manpower situation *was* desperate. All but fourteen hundred men would be eligible for discharge on December 31, while the enemy had twelve thousand men in New Jersey. In taking unauthorized steps Washington had risked character, personal assets, and even personal liberty. Now it was up to the Congress to ratify his acts and empower him to meet emergencies.

When the Congress left Philadelphia it made a general statement that Washington had all power necessary to direct the war. When it reconvened in Baltimore, having found the place it sought for "quiet and uninterrupted attention to the public business . . . ," it defined the general's power in precise language and for a period of not more than six months. On December 27 Washington received specific authority to raise troops, to enforce acceptance of Continental currency, and to commandeer supplies.[35] The delegates generally approved this romanesque dictatorship, though Samuel Adams rather pointedly noted that it was "for a *limitted* time."[36] If disaster followed, Washington knew at whom the finger would point, so he quickly shared with the Congress his hope that any failure would "be imputed to the true cause, the peculiarly distressed situation of our Affairs, and the difficulties I have to combat. . . ."[37] But Washington's dictatorship was neither an attempt by the Congress to stand clear of responsibility nor a propaganda trick. It was an absolute necessity in the state of the union as of the last week of 1776.

III

Having overrun New Jersey, the British held a chain of posts from the Hudson to the Delaware. Clinton went to London, and Cornwallis planned to take leave soon. Howe admitted on December 20 that his line was "too extensive," but he trusted the inhabitants and the strength of the advanced bodies. Thus "the troops will be in perfect security."[38] He was wrong. George Washington was now

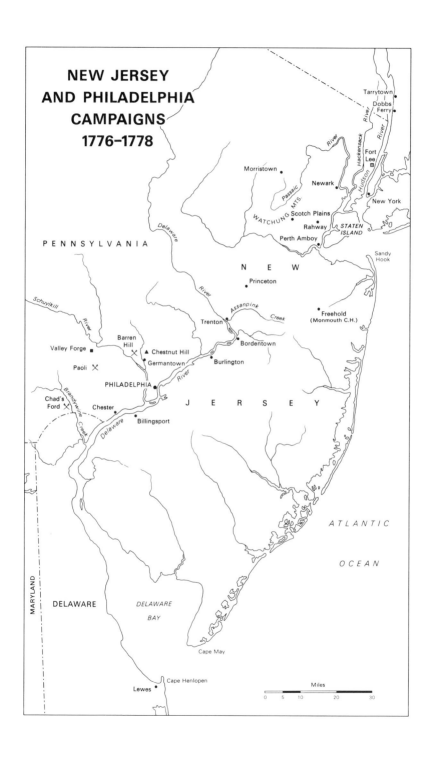

NEW JERSEY
AND PHILADELPHIA
CAMPAIGNS
1776–1778

PENNSYLVANIA

Tarrytown

Dobbs
Ferry

Hackensack River

Hudson River

Morristown

Passaic River

Newark

Fort
Lee

Delaware River

WATCHUNG MTS.

Scotch Plains

Rahway

Perth Amboy

STATEN
ISLAND

New York

N E W

Sandy
Hook

Princeton

River

Assanpink Creek

Freehold
(Monmouth C.H.)

Schuylkill River

Trenton

Bordentown

Valley Forge

Barren
Hill

Chestnut Hill

Germantown

Burlington

Paoli

PHILADELPHIA

River

J E R S E Y

Chad's
Ford

Chester

Billingsport

Brandywine Creek

Delaware

ATLANTIC

OCEAN

MARYLAND

DELAWARE

DELAWARE
BAY

Cape May

Cape Henlopen

Lewes

Miles

0   5   10   20   30

his own master, not merely a kind of executive secretary. Actually the Congress all along thought he could manage. With everything in hazard he struck an eleventh-hour blow.

There were German garrisons at Trenton and Bordentown. The Continentals kept German corporals busy frustrating American chicken stealing until the Germans were used to trivial alarms. Colonel Johann Rall, commander at Trenton, contented himself with patrolling the roads near town and keeping a battalion alerted. Washington planned a triple crossing of the Delaware, but only the Trenton thrust succeeded. (A spy had warned the defenders, who paid no heed.) On Christmas, 1776, Washington's force crossed upstream, split in two columns under Greene and Sullivan, and marched ill-shod through sleet and falling snow on roads paralleling the river, with the artillery rumbling along. Both columns met pickets a mile from Trenton and ran into town on their heels. Surprise was complete. A few German foot soldiers and some British horsemen escaped to the south, but Colonel Rall's men, trying to retreat to Princeton, came under fire from Greene's field guns. When Rall fell fatally wounded, with the disregarded warning note crumpled in his pocket, his troops, numbering 909 men who were probably well-thawed with Christmas *schnapps*, surrendered. Washington immediately recrossed to Pennsylvania where the sight of the prisoners proved his success and was enormously cheering.[39]

Cornwallis, then embarking for England, received orders to take more men to Trenton and repel the Americans or at least save the Germans, hence Washington faced superior strength when he crossed back to New Jersey. He tricked the enemy in Trenton by having men noisily fell trees and pass repeatedly before fires to give an impression of numbers. Meanwhile the Continentals stole quietly around Trenton toward Princeton where several British regiments, marching to join Cornwallis at Trenton, met the American van. Thinking the rebels an isolated party, the British attacked and lost a fierce fight (Princeton, January 3, 1777). Washington then marched to Morristown in northwest New Jersey. Howe could only pull back his "too extensive" chain and stay closer to New York, while the Continentals suffered the winter at Morristown, the privates yearning for more salt pork and the general yearning for more privates.

When the Congress moved to Baltimore it had left a committee of three in Philadelphia. Thus they were the first delegates to get the good news of Washington's resurgence. They urged Washington not to exchange the Germans but to settle them in central Pennsylvania to learn how Germans there could prosper. They also sent a slightly garbled report of the Princeton affair:[40]

He decamped in the middle of that night, made a forced march and met Mr. Howe . . . gave him battle, put him to the rout and took 500 to 700 prisoners, pushed forward took possession of Prince Town and 8 ps. of canon, with a number of officers of the 20th Regiment and this morning we are told he is still pursuing. . . .

The aide who brought the good news of Trenton received a horse and a recommendation to a regimental command. By New Year's Eve the Congress had the pleasure of doing business in a room ornamented by a captured silken German battle standard. At the moment no one wished to forget Trenton and Princeton because of an apparent "Want of Generalship."

Washington's stroke was so well planned that when two of the three elements failed to carry out their missions he was still able to win with half-clad troops in foul weather. And these were troops who had been on the run for four months. Germain analyzed the affair like a chess critic. Because Carleton failed to keep the pressure on the Americans in upstate New York, the rebels were able to rebound along the Delaware. But, as we see it, credit goes to the Continental enlisted man who showed recuperative power enough to match the resourcefulness of his senior general. With a foot-dragging force, no plan would have worked. With these willing men, any one of several generals then in the field could have pulled off the double stroke. The Trenton and Princeton series should not be exaggerated in importance; as military matters they were only episodes of outposts. But in the gathering dark they lit a lamp which burned all that winter.

Once in Morristown, the survival of the Continentals depended on the British conviction that it would be too costly and uncomfortable to dig them out. In fact, the Army was still pitiably weak, and Washington overcame his repugnance to militia to plead that the Congress get him all the militia possible from Pennsylvania and Maryland. The British thought he was stronger than he was, and he hoped to let them linger in ignorance, hence "Militia must be our dependance. . . ."[41] As for its part, the Congress was chafing to get back to Philadelphia. Attendance had fallen off because of the cramped and remote location of then tiny Baltimore. Little could be done to help Washington while the Congress was in a backwater where the members saw only each other. Finally, on February 27, the Congress adjourned to meet in Philadelphia on March 4, and managed to assemble a quorum on March 12.

Luckily Howe left Morristown alone, mostly because wintertime was not wartime. Instead of practicing his profession of warring, he seems to have spent the winter professing the attraction of Mrs. Loring.

10

The Year the British Might Have Won—1777

The Congress stayed in Philadelphia from March 1777 until late in the summer, when it left again to avoid capture or scattering by the army of Sir William Howe. Among the acts of this session, one has had an omnipresent effect ever since: the adoption of a national flag. On June 14, 1777, among thirteen formal resolutions and three legislative orders, was one which read, "*Resolved*, That the flag of the thirteen United States be thirteen stripes, alternate red and white: that the union be thirteen stars, white in a blue field, representing a new constellation."[1] It was an act of much greater psychological importance than its framers could have known. In the kind of republic which the United States became in the next two centuries—a nation of heterogeneous population not deeply rooted in ancestral land—the flag has assumed the same kind of place in the national consciousness that a royal family or a concept of *patrie* or *Vaterland* has occupied in the feelings of other peoples. Probably no modern civilized nation has venerated its national emblem as much as Americans. To them it has assumed a moral value transcending the mundane purposes of national identification. As a tribal totem it satisfies the real and almost universal hunger for a public symbol of spiritual kinship above and invulnerable to the contentions and changes of politics—and for which no other totem is available to the United States.

II

The British and the loyalists expected 1777 to be their year. Loyalists, hoping vengeance would be theirs, called it the year of the three gallows—referring to the three sevens in the date.

British leaders, both officers and civilians, were rather less bloody-minded than loyalists, who gloated over the prospect of using gallows, but they certainly intended 1777 to be the decisive year. The Canadian situation shaped their strategy. The American attempt of 1775 to add Canada as a fourteenth rebellious colony had diverted many thousands of British troops to that province to defend it against what turned out to be unheard American propaganda and futile American military operations. Once the beaten Americans fled and the Canadians continued in their glum detachment from both rebellion and legitimacy, the problem remained: how to use that large army in Canada against the insurgents farther south.

A plan evolved in the winter of 1776–1777, usually credited to General John Burgoyne, though some think it was the idea of Lord George Germain, the Colonial Secretary. The senior officer in Canada was General Sir Guy Carleton, governor general and feudal *seigneur* since 1775. This competent Irish-born soldier had come out to Canada with General James Wolfe in 1759, ostensibly as quartermaster general but actually was Wolfe's confidante and engineer, which is a measure of his ability since Wolfe was no man to tolerate mediocrities. There was no reason for Carleton to smile at the arrival of Burgoyne, who had spent the winter lobbying for his own glory in England.

In Canada Burgoyne ranked second to Carleton. Nicknamed "Gentleman Johnny," he was a man of talents. He had gained some military renown for bravery under fire in Spain in the Seven Years' War, married a daughter of the Norman-conquest family of Stanley which produced the interminable line of Earls of Derby, entered the House

The Year the British Might Have Won—1777

of Commons, wrote a play which Garrick produced in 1775 (and another play for the bored British garrison of besieged Boston), and used all his talents and charm to advance himself. He was rich and a favorite of King George, and he showed a certain Byzantine political acumen by managing to get into a violent policy disagreement with poor General Thomas Gage, governor of Massachusetts, just as Gage was passing offstage to oblivion. Burgoyne arrived in Canada in the spring of 1777 with his (or Germain's) plan to make some use of the sedentary army there.

The men were to join Howe, and to be under Burgoyne's command in the process. A wiser colonial secretary would have let Carleton take them, leaving Burgoyne to command the Canadian garrison. But the relations of Carleton and Germain were sour for reasons unknown, though reason might be suspected in Germain's disgraceful record as a soldier. In addition to this civil-military frost, there was also the fact that the two Howes had political leverage even more powerful than Burgoyne's, and if Carleton were to set foot in William Howe's theater of operations he would instantly outrank Howe and would be honor-bound to claim command.

To place the men under Howe's control could be done by sea or by land. If they moved by sea their departure would leave the Champlain corridor unlocked and open to another invasion. If they went by land up the Champlain trough and down the Hudson Valley, they would, in their march, block the entrance to Canada. So by land it was. Germain explained the operation to Carleton in a letter in which he also mentioned his chagrin at Carleton's withdrawal from New York late in 1776, because it relieved pressure on the Continentals and freed them to win their successes at Trenton and Princeton.

Carleton was to keep three or four thousand men for the security of Canada, and send the rest south under Burgoyne and Colonel Barry St. Leger. St. Leger was to strike east from Lake Ontario along the water-level route of the Mohawk Valley to link a small force with Burgoyne's main body at the head of the Hudson River.

A copy of this letter went to Howe, who received it late in May 1777, weeks before Burgoyne was in motion. That Howe was fully informed in advance is an especially important fact, because Burgoyne understood that he was going to join Howe, or at least to occupy the Hudson Valley and thus contain United States troops in

New York State, so that Howe could move against a proportionately weakened Washington. The correspondence does not show that the conquest of the Hudson line was a permanent objective. The mission was to bring massive reinforcement to Howe.

To Carleton, Germain's letter was as a snakebite. The restriction of his command was unpleasant enough, but it was the sort of thing an officer accepts dutifully. It was the blame for the Trenton-Princeton follies that was an empurpling outrage. Carleton had been wounded under Wolfe in the same war during which Germain had been kicked out of the Army for disobedience and incompetence. But Carleton stifled his anger and promised all possible help to Burgoyne (Burgoyne later told Parliament that Carleton kept his word). Burgoyne received the troops as ordered, and Carleton told him to act on his own judgment if Howe remained silent, while remembering that the mission was to join Howe.

The expedition had 6,840 foot soldiers (including 3,116 Braunschweigers) and 357 artillerymen. St. Leger was to have 675 redcoats and any Indians he could recruit for his frontier foray from blue Ontario's shore. They mounted the operation with reasonable speed, except for the tardy arrival of a final shipment of recruits. Carleton hired as much transport as he could for the artillery, and levied a *corvée* of five hundred Canadian laborers, but Canada could not supply adequate vehicles for all purposes, and draft animals were rare. It took some time to get the *habitants*, the carts, wagons, and horses where they were wanted. Burgoyne's sergeants could shout "Forrr-rd Harrch!" on June 17, 1777.

British security was not very tight. Arthur Lee, traveling in France, was able to write from Bordeaux on February 20 that Burgoyne was to attack Boston, Howe to attack Philadelphia, and Carleton to attack the back settlements. As will be seen, Burgoyne had only the vaguest notion of how to get from the outlet of Lake Champlain to Boston, and actually reflected on the possibility of marching in that direction. Carleton was not himself to attack in the west, but he was to provide a force to operate in the forests. Lee's information was close to the mark. His letter was in the hands of the Congress before May 1.[2]

The Congress tried to sidestep responsibility for appointing a commander to block Burgoyne. Inasmuch as New England and New York delegates were each very keen to frustrate the other's claim to what is now Vermont, and the senior officer in the north was the

The Year the British Might Have Won—1777

New Yorker Philip Schuyler, the Congress tried to avoid getting involved in that real estate rivalry and asked Washington to appoint a general. He prudently begged off on the ground that it was a "delicate and critical" matter. He not only declined that honor but also refused to estimate the number of militia needed in the north, leaving that decision to the Congress.[3]

Meanwhile, what of General Howe? There is an old legend that he moved against Philadelphia as Burgoyne came south, because General Charles Lee, during his winter of comfortable captivity, had persuaded him to capture the congressional seat. That story may be dismissed.

By late 1776 Howe had a beachhead in Rhode Island. He proposed to attack Boston from Rhode Island, and to move simultaneously both north and south from New York. If Germain could bring the force up to 35,000 men, Howe might be able to succeed in all three directions, perhaps even to recover Virginia, inasmuch as he thought Pennsylvania was peaceably inclined (he was correct about southeastern Pennsylvania). But Germain had no surplus of soldiers, so Howe cut back his plans for 1777 to this: the Boston operation was scrubbed; a force would act defensively on the lower Hudson to cover New Jersey and ease the advance from the north, while the main body took Philadelphia. The last word Howe received from Germain before leaving New York was that the King (still hating Massachusetts) believed good results would follow from a diversion against Massachusetts and New Hampshire. There was not one hint that Howe was to think his own operations of less importance than the invasion from Canada.

Howe had the full story of the Burgoyne project in May 1777, in a letter which crossed his own letter of April 2 in which he told Germain he planned to invade Pennsylvania by sea, and thus temporarily abandon New Jersey. He said he would leave only enough men in New York and Rhode Island to hold them, although enlisted loyalists under Governor William Tryon would be available for raids up the Hudson or against the shores of Connecticut. To Carleton, with a copy to Germain, Howe wrote that he could not send a strong force up the Hudson, but he would try to open a ship lane past West Point. Germain approved Howe's plan, adding only that he trusted Howe to finish his work in time to cooperate with the force from Canada. Howe received this on August 16, on shipboard in Chesapeake Bay, rather too late to reverse himself to help the column laboring south under Burgoyne.

It has been believed that Howe and Germain, together or separately, neglected Burgoyne. They did not. They gave Burgoyne's problem their routine attention and they bungled.

III

When the ground dried in the month of May 1777, and troops could move freely, Howe sent probing columns in various directions. None of these marching bodies pushed home a serious attack. Washington was frankly baffled, and nervously shifted his scant forces from place to place to meet threats that came to nothing. The Philadelphia press became quite impatient with Howe and thought he ought to fight like a man instead of being "a sleepy sculking General" playing "this bopeep kind of game."[4] Meanwhile, the summer soldiers and sunshine patriots were beginning to return to the Continental Army, which slowly grew in strength. As spring ended, Howe withdrew his counter-marchers from northern New Jersey to New York.

Howe had not been playing peek-a-boo. His moves had been reconnaissances in force to test whether an advance toward Philadelphia by land would be a better choice than by sea. Apparently the quick reactions of the Continentals convinced him that it would be cheaper in blood to go by sea, for he began to load his men on board transports on July 5. Washington was still puzzled. "The amazing advantage the Enemy derive from their Ships and the Command of the Water, keeps us in a State of constant perplexity and the most anxious conjecture."[5] Howe's unlucky troops sweated eighteen windless days in New York harbor before they sailed away. Washington was frantic to know their destination. New England? That would have pleased the King, but Howe regarded Philadelphia, the seat of the Congress, as the enemy capital. He thought its taking would be a worthwhile feat of arms. The only question left for Howe was whether to land his men by way of Delaware Bay or Chesapeake Bay. He had no qualms about Burgoyne's operation. A week before Howe left New York he learned that Burgoyne had taken Fort Ticonderoga without meeting solid opposition.

Washington too learned of the loss of Ticonderoga, but his job was to oppose Howe. He stayed where he was, though he sent General Daniel Morgan with an excellent body of men to reinforce the Americans in the north. Meanwhile, he waited anxiously for word of a sighting of Howe's floating army. It was seen off the entrance of Delaware Bay, tarried awhile, then disappeared again. (The naval officer in tactical command off Delaware Bay advised General Howe against approaching Philadelphia that way.) After another nerve-wracking three weeks, Washington learned that Howe had entered Chesapeake Bay, and it appeared he would land at Elkton, Maryland, seventeen miles from Newcastle, Delaware. Washington immediately set out to intercept the invader, as fast as possible.

The two armies met at Chad's Ford of Brandywine Creek, in the engagement we call the battle of the Brandywine, on September 11. The battle was a duplicate of the battle of Long Island. Howe outflanked the Americans in the same way, but this time he went around the Americans' right flank instead of their left flank. One circumstance was identical: John Sullivan was the flank commander who was beguiled, as on Long Island. Although the British were not entirely rested from their cramped passage by ship, and the Americans were relatively numerous, the British success was complete in all respects except that Washington extricated most of his force to fight another day. This ability to take defeat without being destroyed was to become the distinctive quality of Washington and the Continental Army.

It was obvious that the Union Jack might soon ripple over Philadelphia. The Congress for a second time voted Washington dictatorial power over materials of war, authorizing him to seize all he could get and to give congressional promises-to-pay at prices written by his officers on the faces of the certificates. The purpose was to corner the market in the public interest before the British captured the supplies, or before the profiteers cornered the market in their own interest.[6]

After a surprise attack cut up General Anthony Wayne's American detachment at Paoli (September 20), General Howe's army marched into the streets of Philadelphia from the south on September 26. The Continentals and their militia auxiliaries were still a useful force, and Washington, on October 4, counter-attacked at Germantown, where an unwillingness to bypass a strong point, and a foggy drizzle which obscured vision (causing Americans to fire on each other), upset the timing of the attack and forced the Americans to withdraw.

To one who thought in European terms, the British had captured the enemy capital and great results should follow. The conquerors relaxed to await the results and seem to have fallen into a doze. Americans had no concept of a national capital. What Howe had won was a set of winter quarters much more comfortable than charred and smelly New York. The heady wine of victory put him to sleep.

In the wake of these lost battles, Washington had explanations. His intelligence before the engagement at Brandywine Creek was "uncertain and contradictory," though he had taken "all pains to get the best."[7] Lacking adequate information, he could not deploy his men properly. John Adams, a native of the country which sprang to arms in April 1775, attentively noticed that the route of Howe's march lay through a land of convinced Quaker pacifists.[8] The Continental Army had two weaknesses of equipment: the men had to make their own cartridge boxes (for measured charges of gunpowder, twisted in cartridge paper in preparation for action) and were unable to make them proof against damp. Hence a sudden downpour at Germantown had wetted perhaps ten thousand cartridges. And about a thousand Continentals were fighting on their bare feet; after powder, ball, and musket, the shoe was the infantryman's least expendable possession.

As for Howe, once he had his men quartered in Philadelphia there was but one major discomfort. Below Philadelphia, Americans held out in the well-designed river forts until the end of November, so that supplies for the British troops upstream had to be offloaded below Philadelphia and hauled up the west bank of the Delaware by wagon train, constantly harassed by defiant American patrols.

Howe's opposite number had plenty of his own administrative and strategic troubles. Washington called the attention of the Congress to a shortage of generals. He needed thirteen brigadiers and had but eleven. One of the brigadiers, Francis Nash of North Carolina, wounded in the battle of Germantown, was at the point of death. He needed six major generals and had but four. He did not wish to appoint colonels as temporary brigadiers because they tended to be less zealous and less likely to command obedience.[9] Only the Congress could commission permanent general officers. Washington also had militia trouble. As long as the river forts held out he needed New Jersey militia (who, in southern Jersey, were a species as elusive as Cape May warblers). At the moment New Jersey lacked a governor, and what militia it had were up north to fend off any possible invasion from New York. There being few Jerseymen available, Washington had to send both Continental soldiers and sailors into the forts on the river. This weakened the Army by sixteen hundred men, in order to do a job a state ought to do for itself.[10] He wished to gather all his men in one place to defend a winter post.

Thus Washington, vexed and beaten, prepared to go into Valley Forge. Howe seems to have been materially better off, as Francis Hopkinson later wrote:

> Sir William he, snug as a flea,
>   Lay all this time a snoring,
> Nor dream'd of harm, as he lay warm,
>   In bed with Mrs. L - - - - - g.[11]

There was less to Howe's victory than met the eye of the loyalist press in New York, which erroneously reported that the Congress had fled north to Bethlehem and that part of the victorious British forces were within a few miles of "rebel army and Congress."[12] In London the ministers were elated at news of the occupation of Philadelphia, and thought things might come to a happy end as Burgoyne struck the final blow.

The failure to destroy Washington's army in the thirteen months before the repulse at Germantown assured American victory in the long run. Never again would the British be able to spare sufficient strength to do the job. One young Englishman who was acquainted with Washington began to see the chief virtue of the senior American general (and some vice in his own senior) even before Brandywine:[13]

He certainly deserves some merit as a General, that he with his Banditti, can keep General Howe dancing from one town to another for two years together, with such an Army as he has. Confound the great Chucclehead, he will not unmuzzle the mastiffs, or they would eat him and his ragged crew in a little time were they properly conducted with a man of resolution and spirit. Washington, my Enemy as he is, I should be sorry if he should be brought to an ignominious death.

Although "the great Chucclehead" had shown "resolution and spirit" in earlier years, Howe was never to understand the peculiar American circumstances he faced.

The Congress had a poor attendance in the summer of 1777, so sparse that it resolved on July 17 to recall the absentees to their seats (an order which it could not possibly enforce).

Three days after the British victory at Chad's Ford, the delegates realized they might have to decamp to avoid capture or dispersal. Accordingly they resolved on September 17 to go to Lancaster, Pennsylvania, if they had to leave Philadelphia.[14] It is said that this was the suggestion of Alexander Hamilton, who had temporarily left his paperwork job at headquarters and was in the field in command of a body of foragers and scouts, and thus knew rather more about British troop movements than most people. On September 19, between midnight and dawn, each Congressman caucused with his own heart in the stilly night, and by daybreak they were streaming westward toward Lancaster. There were enough of them in Lancaster for a quorum by September 27, but, after transacting some minor business, they found Lancaster unsuitable and adjourned to "York-Town," where they met on September 30, passed a motion to recess until October 1, reconvened the next day, and stayed in York until it was safe to return to Philadelphia.[15] Thus, in a conventional if unrealistic sense of the word, York, Pennsylvania, was the capital of the United States through the winter of 1777–1778. York was not really much better for the purposes of the Congress than Lancaster was. One may speculate that its most noticeable advantages over Lancaster were that it was a little farther from British Army headquarters, and lay beyond one more river.

Along with its records and delegates the Congress took the name of its favorite Philadelphia newspaper, the *Pennsylvania Gazette*, and soon began to publish a newspaper at York under that name as its principal medium of communication with the people of the United States.

The York session drew a scant attendance, was quarrelsome, and accomplished little. The delegates obviously were suffering from what has been called cabin fever, a detestation of companions with whom one is isolated. In October 1777 they frequently numbered as many as seventeen to twenty-one members, but by February they had, on one roll call, a mere nine, each from a different state. These survivors of a York winter were naturally somewhat annoyed at absent delegates who wrote to complain of decisions taken, and some sharp answers suggested that the critics might well come to York and help in the deliberations. It is noticeable that attendance improved in direct proportion to the improvement of the weather in the spring of 1778.

The little interior Pennsylvania-Dutch town of York was comparatively inaccessible to American civilians, though it might have fallen to more aggressive British military men. The people of York were not terribly hospitable, and the comforts, amenities, and diversions of the place fell far short of those available in Philadelphia. Living quarters were cramped, rents were high. The drinking water was so hard that one member complained of its hyper-laxative qualities. All in all, the members of the Congress had a relatively hard winter, and one might be inclined to pity them except that this was also the bitter winter of Valley Forge.

I V

Burgoyne's army had begun its advance south on June 17, 1777. By July 7 it had taken Fort Ticonderoga, because the American General Arthur St. Clair neglected to include inside his perimeter a hill fourteen hundred yards away. When the British capped the hill with a battery which commanded Ticonderoga, the American garrison departed eastward the same night (July 6) across a floating bridge illuminated by a burning building. After moving into the fort, the British pursued the Americans, who fought a brisk rear-guard action at Hubbardton (July 7) with no sign of demoralization. The loss of Ticonderoga seemed disproportionately catastrophic to the Congress. Fumed John Adams, "I think we shall never defend a post until we shoot a general."[16] But the Americans were unintentionally drawing Burgoyne to a real catastrophe.

From Ticonderoga Burgoyne had intended to move up shimmering Lake George and then to cross overland to Fort Edward on the Hudson River, which would have required a mere sixteen miles of foot-slogging through easier country. The chase of the Ticonderoga garrison lured the British along the relatively difficult overland route from Ticonderoga to Fort Edward, which Burgoyne reached on July 29. This route became the supply and communication line, though it was exposed to disruption from the east. The use of an axe-hewn road instead of smooth Lake George quadrupled the overland distance. A year of idleness in Canada had much increased the baggage, as always happens with sedentary troops. Burgoyne himself needed thirty carts for comforts. The column also included senior officers' wives, children, and servants. The chopping and digging for the

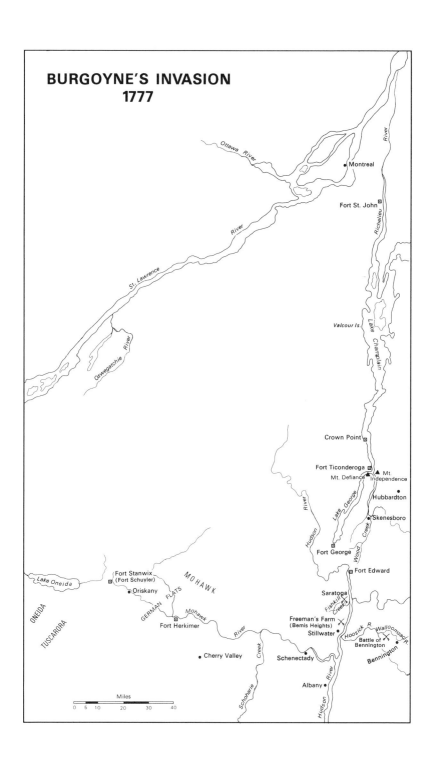

BURGOYNE'S INVASION
1777

Ottawa River

Montreal

St. Lawrence River

Fort St. John

Richelieu River

Oswegatchie River

Valcour Is.

Lake Champlain

Crown Point

Fort Ticonderoga
Mt. Defiance
Mt. Independence

Hubbardton

Skenesboro

Lake George

Hudson River

Wood Creek

Fort George

Fort Edward

Fort Stanwix
(Fort Schuyler)

Oriskany

Lake Oneida

MOHAWK

GERMAN FLATS

Fort Herkimer

Mohawk River

ONEIDA

TUSCARORA

Cherry Valley

Schoharie Creek

Schenectady

Saratoga

Fishkill Creek

Freeman's Farm
(Bemis Heights)
Stillwater

Hoosick R.

Walloomsac R.

Battle of
Bennington

Bennington

Albany

Hudson River

Miles
0 5 10   20   30   40

movement overland overstrained the feudal loyalty of the Canadians who had been pressed into manual labor, and they deserted by the dozens. The force then waited a fatal month at Fort Edward to accumulate supplies for the next month. (If Ticonderoga had fallen in 1776, it could have been a magazine for 1777.) Soldiers, camp followers, Indians, and Canadian civilians numbered about six thousand at the moment, all expecting to eat and drink regularly. They had too few horses; overburdened carts kept breaking down; hay had to be brought over hills and through mud all the way from Canada; and enlisted men had to manhandle wheeled vehicles and artillery.

Getting to Fort Edward had been fairly easy. Staying there was difficult. Advancing was harder. But Burgoyne's servants could always rummage through his thirty carts and come up with champagne for dinner.

On the other side of the lines, the Americans—as they so often did —enlarged their problem by injecting provincialist rivalries. Until August of the 1777 campaign, except for a two-month hiatus, the senior American officer in the north was Schuyler of New York. He had a good and liberally educated mind by eighteenth-century standards, and had served in the French and Indian War. In politics he occupied a rather lonely place in opposition both to royalism and to the populism of the New York Sons of Liberty. Loyalists thought him a troublemaker; rebels thought him a loyalist. He was tall and erect, a glass of fashion in dress, and his correct but austere manners repelled equalitarians.

Schuyler set to work to organize resistance by assigning General Benjamin Lincoln of Massachusetts to run a kind of bosky reception center for militia, though they were almost invincibly disorganized. And they were few. Schuyler was very unpopular with New Englanders who saw him as an aristocrat who must despise the yeoman, and as a Yorker who must oppose the Yankee. Schuyler found himself hampered by innuendos of disloyalty and dishonesty. Failures in his theater made them credible. Samuel Adams thought he might be a good civilian politician but certainly a poor soldier. The virus of this distemper was the suspicion of all New England leaders that all New York leaders lusted to annex Vermont by foul means.[17] (The feeling was reciprocal among New Yorkers who believed the Connecticut River was the western boundary of New Hampshire and Vermont rightfully a part of New York.)

Horatio Gates had commanded at Ticonderoga when Carleton turned back in 1776. The Congress offered Gates the same command in 1777, but he declined to serve under Schuyler. (Conventionally, commands were offered to major generals, not thrust upon them.) In the face of hardened Yankee hostility to Schuyler, the Congress replaced him with Gates in March, reversed itself in May, and reversed itself again on August 4. Gates assumed command on August 19, with Lincoln, Benedict Arnold, and Daniel Morgan as his chief subordinates. A stolid general had replaced a melancholy man, whose gloom had been contagious. There is a touch of self-pity in Schuyler's comment, "If Job had been a general in my situation his memory had not been so famous for patience."[18] The Congress feared that he was prone to defeatism, and the abandonment of Ticonderoga had made him seem unwilling to fight. But to blame Schuyler for the loss of Ticonderoga was most unfair. Even St. Clair, who left Ticonderoga so hurriedly, defended Schuyler in a published letter which said that Schuyler knew nothing of the evacuation of the fort until it had been lost.[19]

Gates received almost dictatorial powers in the Northern Department. At the moment he took over, things were looking up, partly owing to Schuyler's administrative ability. But a good military administrator is worthless without soldiers to administer, and Schuyler's presence had inhibited the recruiting of New Englanders. New England leaders became more cheerful when Gates took charge. A Connecticut delegate wrote to his governor that New England should now drive Burgoyne into the lakes without waiting for the Congress to act, for "surely we can eat them up at a meal."[20] The mails from Philadelphia carried many other northbound letters of the same spirit.

Until the middle of the twentieth century Gates stood low in the eyes of writers, because they needed a contrast to Washington's heroism. Actually, though Gates fell short of greatness, the Congress genuinely liked and trusted him, because he was an adequate officer who did an adequate job until his cataclysmic defeat at Camden in 1780. But Washington disliked Gates and criticized him adversely in writing, and that has created the necessary Lucifer as a foil to the Archangel Michael. One may safely believe that the Congress posted Gates to command against Burgoyne for what seemed sufficient military and political reasons, not to set up a rival to Washington out of sheer malevolence.[21]

Having settled their internal political problems, the Americans could now pay better attention to their military peril. It was not the Congress nor the Continental Army which countered Burgoyne, but a rising like the one that humiliated General Thomas Gage's troops in April 1775. Burgoyne's delay at Fort Edward gave the rebels a month to rally. Washington stiffened Gates's force with a cadre of two brigades of regulars from the lower Hudson and asked the New England governors to summon their militia.

The response was vigorous. In six weeks Gates commanded twenty thousand men, a very temporary soldiery, self-armed and self-supplied, but truculent. They enveloped the far outnumbered British in front, on the flanks, and in the rear. Burgoyne's Indians hurt him, for they killed and scalped a girl traveling to Burgoyne's encampment to marry her loyalist fiancé. Such a tale brought out even more angry men. British generals at first estimated these rustics as much like Jerseymen; better to have classed them in the genus *Concordiensis*. An example of their effective use was a raid which scaled two tall hills overlooking Ticonderoga, found the fort too hard to crack, but returned with 293 scarlet-coated prisoners taken from the Fifty-third Regiment. Burgoyne was in deep trouble. "Wherever the King's forces point," he wrote, "militia, to the amount of three or four thousand, assemble in twenty-four hours. . . ."[22]

The invading army seemed more like a besieged garrison than a striking force. The supply service was so slow that Burgoyne listened with interest to proposals to raid into southeastern Vermont for carts, grain, beef, and recruits, reported to be in Bennington. He decided to try the experiment with seven hundred Braunschweigers under Lieutenant Colonel Friedrich Baum. The Germans occupied the left flank of the line of battle as listed in the table of organization, and it would dishonor them if another force were used on the left. Baum (who could speak no English) was to get loyalist recruits, beef cattle, carts, and thirteen hundred horses for his men, who were dismounted dragoons forced to march stiffly in high riding boots. He should levy on the towns for supplies, after taking hostages, and arrest any persons acting under authority from the Continental Congress.

General John Starke, with a New Hampshire commission, raised 2,600 men and set out to resist the raiders. When they met at Bennington, August 16, the rebels tricked Baum into thinking they might be loyalists, and killed or captured nearly every one. Baum, who died of wounds, had earlier asked for reinforcements. Burgoyne sent Lieutenant Colonel Heinrich Breymann with 650 more Germans. Starke's force, now strengthened by Colonel Seth Warner's four hundred Massachusetts veterans, surprised Breymann, who barely escaped with about two-thirds of his men. Burgoyne had spent near eight hundred men for nothing.

Within a week of Bennington, British arms proved inept on the other flank. Colonel Barry St. Leger, with six hundred European soldiers, many Indians, and some provincials, came east from Lake Ontario to take Fort Schuyler and press on to the Hudson. Lacking artillery, St. Leger could only try to starve the 750-man garrison under rebel Colonel Peter Gansevoort. Eight hundred German settlers of the Mohawk Valley rose like Yankees, left their green and gold fields, followed their local New York General Nicholas Herkimer to relieve Fort Schuyler, and walked into an ambush (August 6) at Oriskany, prepared by Mohawk Chief Joseph Brant and the besiegers of Fort Schuyler. Herkimer's tough farmers fought on even terms until a thunderstorm wetted everyone's powder. When the ambuscaders returned to their siege lines they learned that the garrison had sallied and plundered their camp. Herkimer, badly wounded, withdrew eastward, having lost half his men. Colonel Gansevoort sent Marinus Willett sneaking through the Anglo-Indian siege lines for help. Willett met Brigadier Benedict Arnold coming with a thousand volunteers sent by Schuyler who still commanded that area, and at Arnold's approach the Indians deserted. St. Leger, helpless without Indians, broke camp and set out for Canada via Oswego on August 22.

General Herkimer died on or about August 20. The Congress had been trying to think of a reward for him to show its pleasure at the news that for the first time since the defense of Fort Moultrie someone had energetically tried to save a fixed American post.[23] The British first learned of St. Leger's failure on October 28, in news from France. Thus the French knew Burgoyne's operation was not going smoothly before London heard.

If Burgoyne's army was to advance, the main body had to move down the west bank of the Hudson, because the east bank was hilly and slashed with ravines. But across Burgoyne's path lay high ground, called Bemis Heights. On this elevation Gates dug in, probably content to let Burgoyne try to take it the way Howe had taken Bunker Hill. Gates's well-engineered lines ran all the way to a bridge of boats on his right.

Crossing from the east bank on September 13, Burgoyne moved southward a few miles daily toward Gates, passing through Saratoga (now Schuylerville). On the 19th he launched an attack in three columns, the westernmost of which was to try to outflank Bemis Heights from the side farthest from the river. This column erupted into open fields at Freeman's Farm, where a fire-fight developed against Americans unofficially commanded by Benedict Arnold. The British lost almost six hundred men. They held the field, but the victory was pyrrhic, and no free redcoat ever got any farther. Burgoyne had no clear answers to four essential questions: Where were the Americans? How strong were they? Where was Howe? Where was Clinton? He could have retired to Fort Edward or Ticonderoga without disgrace, but on September 21 a courier from Clinton stole through the lines with news that Sir Henry would try to force the Hudson River forts from the south. For this or less rational motives, Burgoyne stayed put, even though his rear was constantly harassed.

Clinton's diversion from the south had as its theme Safety First, the worst of principles on which to base amphibious operations. He waited until he had some new men from Europe to secure New York City, then sailed up the Hudson early in October, methodically knocking out Continental fortifications and worrying about somebody taking New York behind his back. His advance party got as far as Kingston, which they burned, and then scuttled back to Manhattan Island, satisfied that such a minor distraction fulfilled their obligations to poor bogged-down Burgoyne. Clinton had gone no farther upstream than he could go without the slightest risk to New York City.

On the day Clinton started his circumspect operation, Burgoyne cut his army's daily ration by a third. On October 7 he decided to try again to break through on his right. Gates sent a strong force of defenders who converted themselves into attackers. They fought the second battle of Freeman's Farm, and did it very well. British losses were heavy, and, since Burgoyne could afford no losses, this was the fatal engagement.

Burgoyne pulled back to Saratoga on October 8. Actually, his only way out was a rapid retreat, abandoning everything too heavy to carry. Ticonderoga itself was in danger, rebels were sailing on Lake George as free as yacht racers, and the east bank of the Hudson was crowded with Yankees anxious to get at the British. In this crisis the British commander was strangely languorous. The desertion and surrender rate went up and up, bombardment was continuous, but only Burgoyne's champagne corks popped in reply, from his lavish private mess. He had started with near seven thousand men, plus Indians and

Canadian provincials, plus about three hundred women, children, and servants. The garrison at Ticonderoga was a thousand strong; about eight hundred had been lost at Bennington, and perhaps that many on the bloody pastures of Freeman's Farm. With a maximum strength of 5,500 underfed men, Burgoyne could no longer hope to cut his way southward through the well-entrenched Americans, who now outnumbered him almost four to one. Von Riedesel, the senior German, volunteered to force an exit to the north and back to Canada, but Burgoyne declined. Perhaps Burgoyne was in shock because of Clinton's failure to do more with his curtailed New York garrison.

The chief reason for Burgoyne's entrapment was Howe's campaign to take Philadelphia, which in retrospect appears fatuous. Burgoyne himself was full of confidence until the Bennington drubbing. It seems unjust to accuse the British strategic planners of frivolity if another plausible explanation can be found. They were most ignorant of American geography. Burgoyne on a map moved more easily—in anticipation—than Burgoyne on the ground.

Burgoyne made two serious tactical mistakes, one in what we now call psychological warfare and one in the field. He published three proclamations denouncing the rebels for setting up the most atrocious tyranny in history, asking his Indians to go easy on old men, women, children, and wounded soldiers, and telling his British soldiers their German comrades had come to fight for George III and the British constitution. Most of what he said was merely derisory, but the implicit emphasis on the scalping knife was infuriating to white people. His battlefield error was the decision to move to the Hudson River overland from Ticonderoga. In this he unknowingly committed himself to the defensive, to keep his supply line open. To remind white Americans of what red Americans might do to them called out a host of angry young enemies. To change a well-working war plan in mid-campaign was a stupid snap-judgment.

V

For five days, like some great animal mired in a bog, Burgoyne's army lay inert. Baroness von Riedesel thought they could yet have escaped except that their general "liked having a jolly time and spending half the night singing and drinking and amusing himself in the company of the wife of a commissary, who was his mistress and, like him, loved champagne."[24]

Burgoyne finally regained common sense and opened talks on October 13 which led to surrender four days later, under terms known as the Convention of Saratoga. The 5,700 British and Germans were to surrender their weapons, march to Boston, and embark for Europe under pledge not to fight again in America. Gates allowed these lenient terms because he feared that Clinton might yet save Burgoyne's force. A stronger man might have driven a harder bargain, but Gates wished to get the arms while he could. The victory certainly gratified Gates's friends. And a letter attributed to Washington says he was satisfied that the threat of Clinton would not allow Gates "to insist upon a more perfect Surrender."[25]

Most Americans were quite pleased. At Cambridge, Massachusetts, town and gown combined for a party on the Common, drinking the usual thirteen public toasts.[26] The Congress, which usually received its best news while in exile from Philadelphia, had the word unofficially at York on October 20. All of York's bells clanged, and Washington, when he heard, had his gunners fire thirteen rounds. Eleven more days of uncertainty passed before Gates's despatch arrived in confirmation. The delay was owing to the torpid travel of James Wilkinson who carried the papers, but who received a brigadier's commission as reward, nevertheless. Folklore claims that Sam Adams wished to vote him a pair of spurs instead.

The Convention of Saratoga would permit the use of Burgoyne's men at home to replace other troops who could be sent to America, or, if France came into the war, they might be used on the continent. Most of them arrived safely in Cambridge; some Germans had already fallen out to seek their fortunes in rural America.

Although the rebels widely celebrated the frustration of the invasion, some began to question the terms of the surrender because it did not weaken British manpower. But the Congress could not repudiate the Convention flatly without disgracing itself and repudiating Gates. What *could* be done without disgrace was to stall and to delay, so that, at the least, British replacements would not be available for the spring of 1778. Lord Howe unconsciously helped. For his own naval convenience he suggested embarking the Convention Army at Newport rather than at Boston. Congress seized this opportunity for the prolonged discussion at which all such assemblies are so skilled. Meanwhile, the captured troops were eating regularly and expensively, so the Congress asked the British command to defray the cost of the rations. And if they were to be released on promise of not serving again in America, it would be necessary to identify them if they broke the promise and were caught in America. Hence the Congress requested a descriptive list of all enlisted men. The request outraged Burgoyne, who replied ". . . The public faith is broke."[27] The Congress, though angered at this reflection on its character, declined to be so rude as to contradict a British officer, and pretended to believe Burgoyne no longer felt himself bound by the agreement. Now the Congress could try to rise to a higher level of negotiation. It asked that the Ministry in England either ratify or reject the Convention. Until then the Congress would keep the captives.

This was all diplomatic tactics—an effort to squeeze recognition by Britain. As soon as the Congress had received a copy of the Convention of Saratoga, it had sent out for books on international law, and studied Vattell, Pufendorf, and Grotius.[28] Readers found what was wanted. If His Majesty's government acted on the Convention in a public, formal way it would be granting *de facto* recognition of the Congress as a lawful government.

While awaiting word from Britain, the Congress ordered General William Heath, commandant in Boston, to make sure that all transports were properly supplied, and to insist that all accounts be settled in silver or gold. Heath was to prevent actual embarkation until further notice from the Congress. The Congress waited. But the British Ministry was silent.

The rationale of the congressional maneuver was that Burgoyne no longer felt any obligation, that all military gear had not been delivered as the Convention required (which was true of cartridge boxes, flags, and drums), and that the conquered general refused to make up the descriptive list of men in his command.

The English-speaking world of the eighteenth century was morally more callous than we are in most ways, but superior to us in at least two: the middle class did not publicly imitate the private vices of the aristocracy, and public warfare was as decently conducted as such nasty business can be. Therefore it is fair to notice the ethical question here. The Congress has been damned for violating a pledge. Admirers of Washington have taken this tone, because, they claimed, he was indignant about the behavior of the Congress; actually he accepted it placidly. The Congress followed the letter of the international law of the time, which is all that a warring power can be asked to do. And we know now what the Congress could not know, that General Howe planned to bring the Convention Army to New York, retain the men for battle in America, and, according to the military custom of the time, to release an equal number of American prisoners in exchange, on the ground that the Convention was dead.[29] If guilt there was, it was shared equally.

While politicos played diplomatic chess, the captured enlisted men had time for reflection. Probably many felt as Baroness von Riedesel had felt when she was safely in custody: "I was content."[30] By mid-November, only a month after the signing of the Convention, eighteen hundred men of Burgoyne's army, both German and English, had deserted and melted into the population. Gates correctly predicted the Convention Army would never return to England.[31] Burgoyne and his senior officers also left, to go to England with the permission of the Congress, on condition that they would return if asked. The dwindling captured corps remained near Boston for a year until the British Army refused to pay for its rations. It would be cheaper to feed the prisoners inland, and it would also put them out of reach of rescue operations. The Americans had no ships free to move along the coast, so Washington requested each state to provide militia as guards of the column of prisoners,[32] who marched from Massachusetts to Charlottesville, Virginia, and then in smaller groups to prison camps as far north as Lancaster, Pennsylvania. In time the opposing armies exchanged most of the officers and many of the enlisted men. Others, especially Germans, escaped with the tacit and passive permission of their guards, probably attracted by the hope of someday owning some of the richest loams of the world. A few men remained as prisoners until 1783.

Certainly in the calendar year 1777 the brothers Howe had earned no Roman triumph. Their conduct of the war did not suit Lord George Germain at all. When it was plain that Burgoyne's men were irretrievably lost, Germain moved to get rid of the Howes as well. This brought on some sharp Byzantine politicking in England, where the Howes still had political leverage in the House of Commons. But when Lord North was faced with a choice between General Howe and Germain, he sacrificed Howe and kept Germain.[33] Germain himself was not blameless. He had given Howe more discretion than Howe could be trusted with, and the Burgoyne operation was not one in which the planners calculated the risks very carefully. But Howe knew the situation and estimated it badly, as shown by the fact that his mighty army was uselessly polishing brass in Philadelphia when most needed. Decades ago, writers assumed Howe was kept in the dark, perhaps by accident, but we now know he was informed of Burgoyne's mission. He was not ordered to help Burgoyne, but he received discretionary power which he exercised by sailing off to Philadelphia.

The year 1777 was the last year in which the British could have won the war by plain military conquest—if there ever was such a time. They failed because of contempt for the rebels, because of divided commands, poor communications, and blunders and waverings in strategy. Their senior soldier in America was slow, simultaneously reckless in strategy and cautious in tactics, unimaginative, and irresolute on small points while making the big mistakes with poise and assurance. The British Ministry at home underestimated the need for speed and skill, deprecated the rebel strength, was blind-ignorant of American geography, and never solved the problem of occupying conquered territory while going on to conquer more—if indeed they knew it was a problem.

After 1777 things were going to be harder for the British. Part of the preparation for a dark future was to substitute the neurotic Sir Henry Clinton for the sluggish Sir William Howe (May 1778). The profit margin on this transaction is still invisible.

||

Hard Words and
Cold Comfort, 1777–1778

With Howe invincibly lodged in Philadelphia late in 1777, it was necessary somehow to preserve the Continental Army. The men had been in the field six months and thrice suffered defeat. The real problem was to keep the underclad, underfed soldiers alive, which might have been done by marching them to a warmer place—except for lack of shoes. But departure would be giving all of Pennsylvania to Howe.

At the moment the Army was in a Roman-legion kind of camp which seemed very strong British scouts from Philadelphia. Should they settle in one place or keep moving? The decision was to winter at Valley Forge, about twenty miles northwest of Philadelphia. From here it was theoretically possible to protect both New Jersey and Pennsylvania. Much earlier the Congress had proclaimed that December 19 would be a national day of thanksgiving. By ironic coincidence, on that day the Army marched to Valley Forge. At least it would not be exposing a "considerable tract of fertile Country to ravage and ruin."[1]

Military supply had become unmanageable. Joseph Trumbull, the commissary general, resigned because of exhaustion. His place remained empty while the soldiers shivered and hungered, suffering .cruel and unnecessary hardship in a rich country. With barrels and salt scarce, meat could not be stored very long but required continuous and rapid delivery. But the inadequate wagon trains of the summer of 1777 practically disappeared that winter. Farmers had cut back meat production in the spring of 1777, and the result was shortage so serious that it would have taken every surplus animal of the middle states to meet the Army's needs in January 1778. Meanwhile, the states began to enact price controls, causing farmers to hold meat off the market or to sell covertly to the British. One could list about ten reasons for the Army's misery, but they come down to the failure of inexperienced officers to make a badly framed "system" work. The weakest link in the supply chain was transport.

It was all unnecessary. Only the slave population was worse clad, fed, and housed than the Army. There was plenty of food in the country, but not for soldiers. The white American civilians of the towns were enjoying an inflationary binge of spending, and, near Philadelphia, the clinking of British coins drowned the rustle of Continental paper dollars. Sterner rebels would have confiscated what they needed, but the Congress and Washington still feared to alienate friends and to encourage soldiers to "licentiousness, plunder, and Robbery. . . ."[2]

Immediately before the Army went into camp, a dispirited Yankee regimental surgeon noted its decline in health because of exhaustion and exposure.[3] A fortnight later Washington told the governors of New England that the sufferings of his troops were barely credible. He had 2,898 men unfit for duty because they were barefoot "and otherwise naked."[4] (A Rhode Island unit was called "The Naked Regiment.") Men buried themselves in hospital straw or slept in private houses to keep warm. The clothiers knew where clothes could be had, but wagons were not available for hauling. The men who did have clothes wore captured uniforms, homespun, and rags. Washington had to add the onerous discipline of frequent roll calls and bedchecks to inhibit the men from wandering in the vicinity to loot. The winter temperatures were lower than in the year before. The next two winters were to be successively colder, but the men luckily could not know the future. Meanwhile, they survived only because they had unlimited firewood, drinking water, and fried mush.

Hard Words and Cold Comfort, 1777–1778

The British in Philadelphia were short of firewood, bedding, and hay.[5] They imported most supplies, but by Valley Forge standards they lived high. Their wagon supply route required three thousand guards, and for this or other reasons Howe did not molest the Continentals. To live in Philadelphia kept him on the defensive.

As for Washington, he was as close to despair as he had been in December 1776. He resented criticism of his inability to threaten Howe, and he was bitter that promised food and clothes had not arrived.[6] The Army's friends came closer to breaking its spirit than did its enemies. Desertion was so easy that Joseph Galloway, civilian governor of Philadelphia, said 2,300 Continental deserters asked his help (of whom only a fourth were native Americans). But Valley Forge became the school of the Army, not its grave. Convinced men stayed and, with the help of General Friedrich von Steuben, learned a uniform system of tactics which made them one army rather than an association of regiments. But while these enlisted men learned to fight by the numbers, the officers became restless as they watched their pay shrink in purchasing power.[7]

Officers began to resign at a rate that alarmed Washington. He recommended that the Congress vote them half-pay for life. (A pay raise would be too inflationary.) Opponents said patriotism should be sufficient motive. A paid army could be as tyrannical as George III, and the Congress could not bind posterity. Friends of the officers' position suggested it would be wise to give them a permanent value in their commissions. As for binding posterity, what about the growing war debt? Finally, the unanimously voted compromise was to give half-pay for seven years after the war. And the Congress remembered the enlisted men. Each man who persevered for the duration would get a bonus of $80.

One major administrative reform came out of this bitter season. Nathanael Greene had accepted the post of quartermaster general, and received full responsibility and full control over his hitherto independent juniors.

Since the Army survived its worst trial, it now remained for Washington and the Congress to plan for 1778. Try to recover Philadelphia? Move nearer New York? Make the Valley Forge enclave impregnable and await a British attack?[8]

II

While all ranks shuddered through the winter of Valley Forge, the higher officers and the Congress had their nerves rasped by differences of opinion about each other's talents and methods.

From the beginning of Washington's tenure of command, he and the Congress adopted a kind of rhythmic approach to grand strategy. They started each fall to plan the next year's operations, but they rarely completed preparations as early as they intended. Nevertheless, the planning routine was that Washington would write to the Congress in the fall, posing next year's problems and opportunities, and the Congress would debate and resolve all winter. Because the Congress could rarely do everything necessary, the story of the War for Independence has sometimes seemed the story of how the Congress frustrated its commanding general. Some narratives of the Revolution, with Washington as heroic protagonist, imply that the Congress was more a hindrance than a help in winning independence. Some assume that an important faction was jealous of military popularity and power, and that Washington's detractors believed he blundered at Germantown in tarnished contrast to Horatio Gates's authentic victory in the north. This faction, it has been thought, was cohesive enough to be called a cabal. To that word it prefixed the name of an Irish officer of the French Army, Thomas Conway, who had come to join the Continental Army. Hence it was "the Conway Cabal."[9]

What follows is a narrative of the events through which the thread of a plot against Washington is supposed to run, the plot being the alleged "Conway Cabal." If one were not predisposed to find a conspiracy in the sequence, it seems improbable that the gossamer "evidence" would carry conviction. But the reader may judge for himself.

Some members of the Congress, confined in York, sneered at Washington after the battle of Germantown, and he knew of their grumbling. He chose to respond with a well-founded critique of the supply weakness, about which the lowliest hungry musketeer was well informed. The Congress replied by admitting a concern for making the supply service more workable, but added, gratuitously, that the general was too finicky about the use of his authority to feed and clothe his men. Washington, we may safely suppose, took firm grip of his temper. Very little, he replied, was available within his reach. It would be better for the states to supply the Army by use of civil power than for him to use bayonets. The situation was desperate, he continued; the Army might dissolve, and the supply officers had done nothing. (It was not the officers' fault. The supply system framed by the Congress early in 1777 was unbelievably complicated and demanded simplification.)

To meet this most pressing of needs, Washington asked for a committee of Congressmen or several members of the newly formed Board of War to visit his camp to discuss strengthening the supply service. The Congress accepted the invitation on January 10, 1778, and appointed a committee of six members.

The Congress had not previously neglected the subject of army administration. Six months before the Declaration of Independence, the delegates discussed the subject of setting up a "war office," and in June 1776 the Congress formally accepted a proposal for a board of war and ordnance to undertake most of those things civilian authorities do to maintain an army in being. It was to have five members of Congress and a paid secretary, plus clerks—the whole group to be sworn to secrecy.[10] After Howe took New York it was plain that the board of war and ordnance was more of a game than a reality, that Washington held the Army together by sheer nerve. The board was so heavily committed to preventing the rise of a Caesar or Cromwell that it had made the military almost too weak to fight. By trial and error the Congress learned it must reform or lose the war. A new Board of War, comprising three members who were not members of the Congress, received approval in October 1777. It had all the duties of its predecessor plus the obligation to make estimates of the future. Its chief merit was that it brought soldiers into the top administration of the Army. This was not a matter of philosophy. The Congress simply did not have time for the details of the daily life of the armed forces.[11]

The new board was only a month old when the Army moved to Valley Forge. In the coming months the board revealed some defects, most particularly that it became a repository for tired officers and irascible Congressmen. To conspiracy sniffers it has seemed odd that Gates became a member as did the exhausted Joseph Trumbull and the reputation-clouded ex-Quartermaster General Thomas Mifflin (never convicted of any misbehavior). The fact that Gates was on a board, by order of the Congress, which was in a position to influence the conduct of the war by Washington, has seemed sinister. It may be noted that Gates and Mifflin, appointed to visit Washington's camp, found reasons for not going. If this were melodrama one could believe they were ashamed to face the noble man they were persecuting, but, as it worked out, within a year it was found very hard to get anybody to serve on the Board of War.[12] It was the creature of the Congress, and if the Congress had no actual power the board necessarily had no power.

The only witness who left a deposition that there was a true cabal against Washington was George Washington.[13] In the first year of command he was deferential to the Congress and the provincial assemblies, though quite outspoken in criticizing blunders, selfishness, and injustices. By this combination of firm but respectful correspondence, and by his solid unwavering devotion to duty, he was well established as the leader of the war effort by the middle of 1776. He was sometimes impatient of the tardiness of the Congress and of its inadequacies of judgment. As could be expected, the Congress always had some mediocrities, and its average level of intelligence seems to have declined during the war as the sharper members received more demanding assignments outside of the Congress. But the Congress had its troubles too. It had one great and overriding problem which touched Washington not at all, the problem of affairs in Europe. Even a wise delegate might be excused if he became a little snappish on domestic questions, when required to deal with the benevolences and malevolences of great states abroad. Washington's thinly veiled contempt for the judgment of the Congress on supply problems late in 1777 and early in 1778 might stir consciences but would make no friends.[14]

The Congress in November adopted a resolution praising Gates for his services, continued his rank as major general in the Army, and asked him to serve as president of the newly forming Board of War.[15] It has been believed that immediately after Burgoyne's capitulation, Gates denied Washington the troops Washington had loaned to him. Fact: by November 7 Gates had sent back four of Washington's five brigades of regulars. It has been said the return of the troops was done tardily, thus contributing to the defeat at Brandywine Creek. Fact: Washington did not ask for their return until after the battle of the Brandywine. Nothing in Gates's record to this point showed him as a man scheming for Washington's downfall.

The work of the Board of War was usually the kind of paperwork the Congress had previously done. It now gave such work to the board simply because the delegates were too busy to attend to so much detail. The board originated but one important military plan, an attempt to make real the hope of conquering Canada, which had not died after the failure of 1775–1776.

The novelty of the board's plan was to give command to Gilbert du Motier, Marquis de Lafayette. Perhaps the French *habitants* would welcome an army commanded by a Frenchman. Accordingly, on January 22, 1778, the board proposed an invasion of Canada under Lafayette's command, and with Thomas Conway as second in command. The board showed a certain insensibility, for Lafayette would not accept Conway, and Conway, once named, would not voluntarily step aside. Lafayette threatened to go home with his officers, but in the end the Congress pacified Lafayette by firing Conway and substituting General Johann de Kalb. The Marquis then went to Albany to see his force and found chaos. He felt publicly humiliated.

The corps assembled at Albany was pretty sorry. The return showed 1,437 men "fit for duty," but a cautionary memorandum added that the number included a brigade of 611 "some being twelve, & some sixty years old, unable to perform a long & quick march." And they would sleep cold too, for they were short 303 blankets. There was another regiment, not yet mustered, of which the report promised "we'l [*sic*] find a large number of little boys and old men."[16]

This was the American manpower of a visionary design for simultaneous attacks on Detroit, Niagara, Oswego, and Montreal, synchronized with a French army to come by sea to storm Quebec. Even if it were successful militarily, it might have been a diplomatic disaster. How do you persuade a victorious French army to give up Quebec?

To believe that the Canadian Dream was a scheme to discredit Washington requires belief that malice was all-pervasive,[17] and that stupidity had no place. But it was a wretchedly conceived operation, and its witlessness argues that the Board of War was poor at strategic thinking. To send cub scouts and senior citizens against British professionals would seem rather obtuse than malicious. What could be malicious in it? Only that Washington was bypassed in the planning, and that an independent command would divide Washington and Lafayette. The hypothesis that it aimed to separate Washington and Lafayette depends upon a rather self-centered account by Lafayette in later life, the kind of evidence least to be accepted.

The officer for whom this nebulous "conspiracy" was named, Colonel Thomas Conway of the French Army, requires attention. He had come from France, recommended by Silas Deane. In America he was pushy, because as a soldier of fortune he needed higher rank to raise his status in French eyes.[18] To the pain of Washington, who found him unimpressive, the Congress promoted Conway to brigadier and then to major general and inspector general late in 1777, as part of a reorganizing plan to professionalize the Army in the European fashion.[19] After the Canadian bubble burst in 1778, Conway (along with Lafayette) was unemployed and wrote rudely to Washington, demanding a divisional command. About this time Washington learned that Conway had written a deprecatory private critique of Washington's abilities as shown in 1777, which hardened Washington's dislike of him. The letter was to Gates, which has been enough in some minds to implicate Gates in a conspiracy against Washington. Simultaneously, Lafayette was a problem to the Congress. He also wished an independent command, and he wished to see the last of Conway. Conway's position as a war-surplus general had become increasingly uncomfortable, so he adopted a tactic he had used before—he offered his resignation. To his surprise the Congress accepted. Conway was shot in a duel with Brigadier John Cadwalader, thought he was dying, apologized in writing to Washington, returned to France, and later made good as governor of French India.

On balance Conway was an average professional officer, but impertinent, socially indiscreet, and inclined to try to elbow his way through life. Because Washington and Lafayette disliked him, and for no other probative reason, he has become a minor villain of the War for Independence. A court could find him guilty only of bad manners.

Certainly there were influential Americans who thought Washington was overrated. One was James Lovell, an ex-schoolmaster and former rebel spy who represented Massachusetts in the Congress for more than five years without even a leave to visit his family. As one who knew the French language, Lovell received an appointment to the Committee for Foreign Affairs and gave it all his energy. He admired Gates and wrote of Washington with sarcasm. The Frenchman who dealt with him most, respected him, finding only that he was ignorant of European affairs. Lovell was also an intense partisan of the alliance between New England and Virginia zealots. He once received a letter which said Washington had been guilty of mistakes "as might have disgraced a soldier of three months' standing,"[20] which proves only that the sender thought the remark would not offend Lovell. Lovell may well have wished that Gates would succeed Washington, for he wrote to Gates, "We want you in different places, but most of all in a third which you are not called to ballance about. We want you most near Germantown."[21] What of Lovell's own record? Without any doubt he was as devoted to the cause as Washington, and worked as hard in his own job. He likely expended more foot-pounds of energy on behalf of American independence than any other member of the Continental Congress. His vice was that he was not equally devoted to the person of George Washington.

Another nominee for the "Conway Cabal" was Dr. Benjamin Rush, the same who had written a letter extravagantly praising Washington in 1775, with the intention of having it intercepted by the British for its political effect in England.[22] Rush appears to have changed his mind about the senior general when, no longer a member of the Congress, he had passed through the British lines after the battle of the Brandywine to attend the captured American wounded. The contrast between the order and discipline of the British Army and the tatterdemalion appearance of the Continental Army appalled him. From October 1, 1777, through the following January he wrote a series of letters most uncomplimentary to Washington, comparing him unfavorably with practically all other generals, describing the Continental Army as a mob, and so on, at great length. This was the strongest indictment of Washington that has survived in military literature. Rush's intensity leaves no doubt: he was out to displace Washington. If there could be a one-man cabal, Rush was it (but it had nothing to do with the abrasive Conway).[23] One of these letters came to Patrick Henry, who passed it on to Washington. Washington, quick to respond to this sort of thing, immediately recorded his knowledge of "the intrigues of a faction, which I know was formed against me."[24] This phrase—"the intrigues of a faction"—was accepted at face value for the next century and a half.

To understand the feelings of whole-souled rebels like Lovell and Rush, one must remember that Washington had won pitched battles only at Trenton and Princeton, and had lost New York and Philadelphia. Meanwhile, Charles Lee had commanded the repulse of the British assault on Charleston, and Gates had taken Burgoyne prisoner. We can see today that Washington was much the best of the three, but at the time people obviously could not foresee the disasters awaiting Gates and Lee, and the ultimate success (with French help) of Washington's strength-conserving strategy. Not only did he have a short tally of field victories, but there were members of the Congress who thought him backward in supply matters, slack in preventing desertion, unintelligent in security matters, lax in regulation and discipline.[25] The Congress was equally at fault in these things, if fault there was under such circumstances.

There is no proof of a plot to disgrace a hero. Some leaders were adversely critical, but if they lacked confidence in their general it was their duty to speak. Only Washington named them a "faction." Only Rush tried to get him unstuck. If Lovell wished to displace the commanding officer, it is quite likely that Samuel Adams and Richard Henry Lee thought the same, but the matter was never mentioned on the floor of the Congress.

Thomas Conway cannot be linked with any of the hard evidence of political dissatisfaction. He was on the make and on his own. To have both Washington and Lafayette opposed to his advancement frustrated him completely. It may be added that John Laurens, son of the president of the Congress, and Nathanael Greene also objected to Conway's elevation. Greene, with some reason, was perennially jealous of the favors shown to officers who came swanking from abroad for no purpose but to achieve a rank that would command some attention at home. The Congress has been damned for promoting Conway to major general in December 1777 over Washington's opposition, as if it were done to annoy Washington. This ignores the facts that the delegates also wished to win the war. To honor a French Army colonel might help in cultivating the good will of the French Court, and Conway was a qualified professional soldier. The

Hard Words and Cold Comfort, 1777–1778

Congress did not know of Washington's distaste for him until after the promotion.

The Board of War has been seen as the creation of the "faction," but Washington himself had appealed for an improvement in the administration of military affairs. As recently as 1951 a respected scholar saw the work of Gates in its presidency as an affront to Washington: "Gates . . . proceeded to embarrass Washington by directing the Board of War in such a way as to ignore or minimize the authority of the commander in chief."[26] The long line of demoted commanders of the Army of the Potomac might smile sardonically at that comment, as might the shade of Douglas MacArthur. The board was not the staff of Washington, it was an agency of the Congress, and a tenderness for the feelings of sensitive generals in conflicts over public policy is not contemplated in the civil tradition of the English-speaking peoples. The ineptness of the board while Gates was its president teaches us more of his incapacity as a strategist than of his skill as a caballer.

But the concept of the Conway Cabal will be with us for awhile. At least fourteen articles in the *Dictionary of American Biography* take it for granted. The historian of the Continental Congress believed in it devoutly, and gave most of a chapter to it, describing the caballers as a "bunch of schemers."[27] But at no point in any account of the Conway Cabal is there mention of a meeting of the plotters, nor of any circular letter to all. By definition a cabal is a collective effort. This "cabal" had none.

There was some discontent. It was the kind that focuses on every leading personality when things go badly, and things had been going badly in the winter of 1777–1778. On balance, Washington was well treated by the Congress. The relationship was officially honest and courteous, and most delegates were on good terms with him. Where lines of authority were not clear there were necessarily some frictions. If Washington had never run for office and thus gained an empathy with politicians, he would probably have been a bit imperious, and there would have been more heat generated. But he deferred to the Congress, and the Congress usually trusted him, as shown by the grant of a dictatorship in December 1776. That its trust continued is plain from the grant of another dictatorship over military matters in the Philadelphia district in April 1778, to renew that which had been given when Howe first threatened Philadelphia. This one ran to August 10, 1778. Perhaps the muttering and grumbling against Washington while the Congress wintered at York were but symptoms of the confinement and isolation the Congress undoubtedly felt. This murmuring had no apparent effect on the course of the war. The popularity and esteem of Washington increased steadily through the war, and the prestige of the Congress fell at about the same rate, though for quite different reasons.[28]

III

The Congress had much more to do in the winter of 1777–1778 than grapple with the problems of its military establishment, and with the irritabilities of civilian and military leaders. While suffering the silence of its mission in France, from which came not a word all winter, it had the unfinished business of Richard Henry Lee's successful motion of June 7, 1776, which had already led to the Declaration of Independence but which had provided further that the Congress draft a plan of confederation.

Most conventional narratives of the Revolution treat the Articles of Confederation as only the weak precursor of the Constitution, but the Articles should be seen as part of the Revolution. The Confederation's framers were trying to solve concrete problems. The most pressing problem was to unite against Britain by unifying policy among factions of the Congress. To understand the winning of independence it is necessary to understand the writing, provisions, and reception of the Articles of Confederation.[29]

Framing a contract to bind these differing states was psychologically difficult. The pervasive localism may be seen in the instructions to the delegates from Georgia, elected in July 1775. The Georgia Provincial Congress agreed to be bound only by the decisions of the Continental Congress that were acceptable to the delegates from Georgia. If every state took that view, it would require the votes of all states to make any effective decision. The early Congresses were more nationalistic than *that*, but in the summer of 1776 nationalism was waning because the rebels controlled every colony except places actually garrisoned by redcoats. Thereafter the local leaders wished only for a limited league of mutual defense and an interstate committee for foreign affairs, possessing merely such authority and manpower as the states chose to give.

Even before the Burgoyne threat had evaporated, a polemicist claimed to fear the establishment of a central authority as the innovation of a quasi-royal court before which the people must be prostrate, and he advised postponing confederation. In answer, another writer replied that the rebels were not fighting for a form of government but for rights and liberties; direct government by all the people was impossible, and some central direction seemed necessary.[30] The exchange showed how gingerly both sides approached the question.

The Congress revealed no feeling of urgency. The summer and fall campaigns of 1776 were distracting, as was the flight to Baltimore. After returning to Philadelphia the Congress went on the road again in 1777, settling in York where the delegates finally began to give the matter their continued attention. The problems posed by writing the Articles during the war were not new, and their composition was literally a papering over of long-standing provincialisms. The chief difference was that the hand of King George was not felt, and Americans were free to think for themselves. They did not feel very national. The United States was probably referred to as "they" more often than not.[31] There was no unanimity about the nature of the proposed union, for which eighteenth-century man cannot be blamed since universal agreement on the subject remains to be achieved.

There were also intellectual difficulties. They had no experience of government except local government. They had to practice thinking continentally and constructively, since most of their reflections had been more anti-British than pro-American. The fear of the rise of a glittering court was not atypical; many believed the Congress could become just as dangerous to them as any King-in-Parliament.

The idea of a continental confederation was old. There had been seventeenth-century suggestions along that line, and the Albany Congress of 1754 produced a sophisticated plan, partly by Benjamin Franklin, which failed of support. In 1775 Franklin was ready again with a plan in his pocket. He showed it to Thomas Jefferson, but they reluctantly concluded they lacked the votes. They then gave it to the Congress on July 21, 1775, off the record, but copies got out and fell into British hands. The New Jersey Convention rejected it as not opportune, and North Carolina said it could only be a last resort.

Franklin's difficulty was that his plan presupposed independence, and the summer of 1775 was a bit early for that assumption. The plan came before the Congress again in January 1776, but independence was still premature.

Outside of the Congress the first proposal seems to have come from the Provincial Congress of New York, antedating the Franklin-Jefferson calculation, but after the Lexington-Concord raid. New York's cautious scheme looked more toward conciliation, for it proposed a union presided over by a viceroy. It would have *internal* legislative power subject to royal veto, and it demanded nothing for the colonies except repeal of the "Intolerable Acts." Whether New York's plan should be pressed in the Continental Congress was left to the discretion of New York's delegates. They saw in it no merit.

Then came the resolution for independence, with its commitment to confederation. The Congress did not doubt that it was the agency for the work; there was no move to call a constituent assembly. Even if the notion of a convention had come up, the physical difficulties of convening the assemblage would have been discouragingly great. The Congress put John Dickinson to polishing a plan of his own which the members discussed through June. On its goal there was agreement, on its means divergence—based on dislike of centralization.

After an intermission to approve, declare, and promulgate independence, the Congress settled down to confederation in earnest on July 12, 1776. Debate reached high heat by July 22, disappointing those who hoped to do the job quickly. The difficulties were serious. First, how should the vote be distributed? Four colonies had a combined population greater than the other nine and could jointly govern all. The smaller states said their weight was less but their risks were total, therefore they plumped for equal votes. Second, how to measure quotas of contributions? By population? By wealth? And if by population, were blacks people? Third, who owned the western wilderness? If the vast claims of a few states stood, the small states might become obscure appendages. The states with western claims replied that it was absurd to say that rights were no rights because they were large rights. By August 20 the Congress was deadlocked. Six months of silence followed, made more somber by news of the operations of the brothers Howe with their immense firepower.

Hard Words and Cold Comfort, 1777–1778

Outside the Congress the press noticed the King's intransigence. One satirist wrote the speech the King *ought* to give, but since George III did not deliver it the writer concluded that the Americans should lay "a permanent foundation of civil government, which shall secure to us the enjoyment of our just rights and privileges, both civil and sacred, to the latest posterity."[32] But there was slight public pressure for confederation.

The Dickinson draft differed somewhat from Franklin's. Dickinson called for a meeting of the states at Philadelphia, the delegates to be elected annually, and their number left to the discretion of the electing state. Franklin wished a peripatetic Congress moving annually from state to state and composed of representatives in a ratio of one for each five thousand males aged sixteen to sixty. Dickinson proposed the one-state, one-vote formula, with most questions requiring seven "ayes" to pass, and a few requiring nine votes; Dickinson's proposed delegates could not sit more than three years in any six. Franklin thought each delegate should have one vote (and would allow proxies) and that half the members be a quorum; he opposed any limit on length of service in the Congress.

Franklin's draft stated powers broadly and generally. For example, it provided that land purchases from the Indians be made by the Congress for the common advantage. This makes Franklin seem philosophically nationalist until we remember that he was a speculator in western lands. Land speculators had more hope of getting something from the Congress than from the provincial assemblies, hence congressional control of western land buying was a requirement for the gigantic real estate operations planned by Franklin and many other eminent revolutionaries.

Actually, Dickinson far outstripped Franklin in nationalism. Not only did he list particular powers of the Congress which would have diminished the provincial assemblies, but he went much beyond. Dickinson proposed the following specific powers for the Congress: war and peace, the laws of military and naval captures, maritime prize law, privateer commissions, admiralty courts, prize-case appeals courts, embassies, treaties and alliances, intercolonial boundary disputes, currency, Indian relations, the western boundaries of the "colonies," boundaries of new colonies, "Disposing of all such Lands for the general Benefit of all the United Colonies—" (the most fiercely controverted of the whole list of powers), postal service, commissions

215

of generals and some other Army officers, naval officer commissions, Army and Navy regulations, appointment of a council of state, choice of its own president, secretary, and time of adjournment, assignment of quotas of men and money raised by local authorities, borrowing money, naval force, weights and measures.

The list is imposing, but a crushing negation followed immediately: "But the United States assembled shall never impose or levy any Taxes or Duties, except in managing the Post-Office. . . ." To amend this (or any other part) required the consent "of every Colony."

Thus far the draft projected a government of delegated powers, but in an earlier article (Dickinson's third), dealing with what we now call the reserved powers of the states, it was affirmed that "Each Colony" retained complete power over its "internal police, *in all matters that shall not interfere with the Articles of Confederation*" (emphasis added). This was a great leap toward centralization which would have barred each colony from passing any law which hampered the operation of the Articles. The country was not willing to go that far, and the clause disappeared in the process of revision, leaving the Confederation as an agency with delegated powers only.

The proposed council of state would have one member from each colony to conduct the business of the Confederation between sessions of the Congress. The projected union, described as perpetual, would have authority to admit but one new member, Canada (Franklin would have taken any British new-world colony, and even Ireland).

Financing, the rock on which this rowboat of state eventually shattered, did not produce much difference in the drafts. Both provided that expenses be paid from a common treasury accumulated from taxes levied by the local assemblies severally. On the amounts to be paid there were some differences. Dickinson wished contributions in proportion to total populations, excluding Indians and slaves; he also wished a triennial census for the purpose. Franklin wished to distribute the burden according to the total of males in each colony, aged sixteen to sixty.[33]

The proposal in Dickinson's draft to admit Canada as a state (which became Article XI of the Articles of Confederation) was written when Canada still seemed a threatening base for British operations. As this threat was found to be illusory, interest in Canada receded in the minds of the writers.[34]

Hard Words and Cold Comfort, 1777–1778

On balance, Dickinson's draft was quite nationalist when compared to Franklin's, and its much advertised provincialism rests more on a contrast with the federal Constitution of 1787 than on a comparison with anything that came before.

Although many clauses aroused heat and provoked argument, three main issues were points of difference: Should votes in the Congress be equal or in proportion to population? What should be the basis for determining contributions of money to the common fund? Who should own the western wilderness? Now free of British political interference, the delegates had the problem of reconciling their state governments and a central authority of their own creation. There were two opinions on this. One opinion favored a true central authority. The opposing opinion was that no legislature could be superior to a state legislature. Men who held this latter opinon dominated the Congress in 1776 and 1777, but declined in power thereafter. The nature of the American union was quite as important as the question of independence, and, with notable exceptions, those most zealous for independence were most zealous to keep the central authority weak.

Although it was not immediately clear, Dickinson *had* planned a central government that left the states only their own internal affairs. Proceedings toward adoption began swiftly, then steadily slowed to a crawl as men began to read the implications of the document. The delegates accepted the name and general purpose by April 1777, and then fell to arguing (briefly) about reservation or delegation of power by the states. The notion that every state should keep all power not explicitly delegated to the Congress was brought forward without full realization of its colossal importance, and only Virginia (for reasons still obscure) voted "no" on the proposition which later became an issue of such gravity. Articles I, II, and III of the final draft (name, reserved powers, purpose) received approval by early May, but then the wrangle became earnest, and no decisions could be reached through May and into June. In fact, nothing confederative happened during the rest of the summer, partly because of disagreement, partly because of a multitude of military, fiscal, and diplomatic distractions. The Congress had become the repository of "jealousy, ill-natured remarks, recriminations, and soured tempers."[35]

Then came the flight to York, when Howe took Philadelphia, and the shocked delegates realized they must unite or the cause would perish. From October 7, 1777, they began to work as though agreement was necessary—which it was. They soon settled a most crucial issue: the proportion of representation. The solution (Virginia alone voting "no") was that each state have one vote. No question in the *writing* was so troublesome, though the land question was the more formidable in the *ratification*. Virginia had not surrendered the point without a parliamentary battle. First, an amendment to give the three smallest states one vote each and the others one for each fifty thousand white inhabitants failed 2 to 9. Next, an amendment to give one vote for each thirty thousand white inhabitants failed 1 to 11. Finally, Virginia tried to arrange representation according to money contributed and lost 1 to 10. (On each roll call* there were twenty "nays" and six or seven "ayes.")[36]

Once the Congress climbed over the obstacle of representation, things moved more easily. The delegates decided to assess state quotas of money on the basis of the value of land plus improvements, by the close vote of 5 to 4, all Southern states voting for it, all New England against, New Jersey for, Pennsylvania and New York divided. They also decided that state delegations should number not less than two nor more than seven. (Thereafter no state could vote unless two of its delegates were present.) Finally, no delegate could serve more than three years in any six. As the historian of the Continental Congress said, "By this measure Congress effectively inoculated itself with the germ of pernicious anemia."[37]

A matter concerning all future generations of Americans came up in a motion to amend Article IV, which provided that citizens of each state have all privileges and immunities of the other states. Ominously, South Carolina and Georgia tried to exclude free blacks from this guarantee. No other state agreed at the moment, but the attempt was part of a movement which steadily narrowed the liberty of free blacks in the next eighty-five years.

The western lands aroused more immediate interest. On October 15 eight states voted against giving the Congress power to limit the western boundaries of states. A counter-proposal to allow the creation of new states in the West received the support only of its maker, Maryland. This eight-state decision was not to stand as the last word, and the whole question was later to endanger the ratification of the

---

* The recording of yeas and nays by name appears to have begun late in 1777. Thereafter it was not invariably the practice.

Articles. This question had irked Marylanders for some time, beginning with the voting of lands as bounties for enlistments in the Continental Army. Maryland would have to buy from states with claims to the West. As early in 1776, "Her View then was to have these Lands declared a common Stock as being purchased (if ever purchased) by the joint Blood and Treasure of the Confederacy or find no Land to her Ruin."[38] And there was more to it than finding land for bounties, as we shall see.

At length, in 1777 the delegates finished "Certain Articles of Confederation and Perpetual Union," a league of sovereignties at best. They seem to have frozen the British constitution of about 1760 as they wished to believe it had been, with the Congress holding the weak position they had polemically assigned to Parliament. This analogy cannot be systematic, but it seems a useful standard by which to judge. The requisitions of money and men were identical with older parliamentary practice (and worked no better). The Congress provided a kind of continental court where conflicts of local interest could be adjudicated but not enforced. And, like the circumstances of the League of Nations and the United Nations in the twentieth century, important new questions were quite often taken up outside the designated chamber. In sum, the Confederation could give advice and hope to be supported by public opinion; it could not amend itself except by unanimous consent, and it could not *make* anybody (except the military) do anything. (The soldiers could be flogged and hanged for violations of rules adopted by the Congress.)

After settling the land question—as they thought—all had gone so smoothly that the Articles were complete by November 15, 1777. We may suppose the delegates exhaled with relief and hoped the states would ratify quickly. The ratification procedure was by reference to state legislatures which would authorize their delegates in the Congress to sign in the names of the states. Then, when all states had ratified, the Congress would proclaim the Articles in effect. The delegates ordered three hundred copies of the Articles printed for distribution. The president of the Congress had them in hand on November 28 and gave eighteen copies to each state delegation, reserving the remainder for himself.[39]

In sum, the Articles proposed that the Congress was to control embassies, treaties, the armed forces (even in peace), interstate agreements, making war and peace, joint disbursements on behalf of all states, the alloy and value of coin, weights and measures, relations with Indians outside the states, commissioning of general officers, privateering, and borrowing money. All other powers were reserved to the states. This coincides remarkably with what the pamphleteers and agitators had claimed were the only powers of the King-in-Parliament. What the Articles denied to the Congress was what rebels had denied to Britain. The added check to prevent abuse of power was the provision that to amend the Articles required a unanimous vote.

In later years, when defending the proposed federal Constitution, John Dickinson dismissed the Articles of Confederation as a makeshift arrangement, compared it with the loose alliances of ancient Greek city-states, and added that the Congress dared not use its complete power in any crisis.[40] One might suggest, in reply, that if implied powers could be found in the United States Constitution they could be found in the Articles of Confederation. But the lack of a coercive power over persons, and the absence of power to regulate interstate and foreign commerce, would be hard to repair by the most zealous interpretation. Above all, the missing connection in the circuit of power was the taxing power. Generations which so closely interleaved liberty and property would necessarily boggle at an implied power to tax, though in emergencies they found in the war power sufficient justification to quiet their consciences about the impressment of property to keep the Army alive.

When the Congress was able to move back to Philadelphia in the summer of 1778, after the British evacuation, the delegates expected ratification to be rapid. The impeccably groomed Dr. Josiah Bartlett, who seems to have been the most popular civilian in New Hampshire, an intelligent and learned man easily tired by the garrulity of his fellow delegates, had been first to vote for the Declaration of Independence and first to vote for the Articles of Confederation. Now New Hampshire became the first state to have an official signature on the Articles as a ratification (July 9, 1777). Seven other state ratifications followed on the same day. Two followed soon, but recalcitrance showed in the Maryland, New Jersey, and Delaware delegations. The common quality of these three states was that none had any western land. And thus, at 10 to 3, ratification halted.[41] Years would pass before the score became 13 to 0.

The delay pained those who had ratified, because by this time they knew of an alliance with France. They expected soon to see a real living minister of France in Philadelphia, perhaps escorted by a formidable army under the white and gold French flag. Could France take seriously an alliance with thirteen unconfederated and discordant ex-colonies?

Although the Articles were dormant, they were not dead. The actual drafting of them gave a lift to the delegates' spirits which probably helped to continue the war. When the Articles became effective by unanimous ratification in 1781, the document gave a legal footing to the *de facto* power the Congress had tried so long to exercise. It helped white Americans to think of themselves as one nation, and John Marshall later said it kept alive the idea of union until the people could adopt a more workable system. Any British theorist who reflected on the Articles might have seen an irony: if King George had not used force against his American subjects, there is no reason to think they could have united until Britain took the lead in forming the union.

12

Foreign Entanglements and Embraces, 1778

Although Europe's international affairs in the 1770's could not be controlled by the American rebels, the magnetic fields and lines of force of European diplomacy accidentally favored the War for Independence. For fifteen years the French government had aimed to dull the glitter of British glory. Britain's American troubles offered the opportunity, and the Continental Congress knew what to do. The first step had been to get arms from France. Next came the use of French ports for American privateers. But France held back from open warfare, awaiting a favorable moment to hurt Britain. A war against Britain required the help of the Spanish, who were willing to aid the Americans covertly but reluctant to promote openly such a bad example for the Spanish colonies overseas.

Practically every war fought in America from the late seventeenth century through the War for Independence was fought to preserve or to disturb the balance of power in Europe. From 1700 on, America weighed heavily in that balance, and its weight, in the minds of theorists, seemed to increase steadily. A separation of America from Britain would reduce the relative weight of Britain. Étienne-François, Duc de Choiseul, Foreign Minister of France, was eager to get on with the good work. When he retired in 1770 he left a memorandum in his files on how to reduce England to the position it "ought to occupy in the Balance of Europe."[1] Among his suggestions was the notion of promoting the independence of the American colonies. Thus when Charles Gravier, Comte de Vergennes, succeeded to Choiseul's old office in 1774, the uproars in America seemed to offer an attractive opportunity. While reorganizing his files, Vergennes discovered Choiseul's thoughts on the "Balance of Europe" and asked himself two questions: Would the colonies revolt? If they revolted, would they persevere?

Simple revenge was not the French motive. What weakened Britain strengthened France, and France's strength (including the security of the rich French West Indies) was Vergennes' responsibility. The glory of the reigning house of France demanded a restoration of French primacy in European politics. The French showed no desire to recover their lost American empire. It was dominance in Europe for which Frenchmen yearned.

In August 1776, Vergennes might have been willing to go to war, but then came news of the fall of New York; again in the summer of 1777 the French inched to the brink but recoiled at news of Burgoyne's initial success. This continual poising to pounce would itself probably have led to war because of the constant generation of heat by friction in the West Indies. As insurance against the loss of these wonderfully profitable islands in any future contingency, the French readied an expedition in August 1777, the force to comprise about four thousand men and half a dozen ships. The plan was no secret, and the British, foreseeing the possibility of an "incident," tried unsuccessfully to dissuade the French. Upon failing to talk the French out of the operation, Frederick Lord North's government resignedly wrote orders for six ships of their own to go out to the Caribbean to redress the balance. We may suppose a collision was thereafter inevitable. Although the British regularly kept a squadron on station in the West Indies, the French sent only what we call task forces. Therefore a French expedition could only raise British suspicions to a very nervous level.

It is clear why the French helped the Americans, but it is not so clear why they made an alliance. The answer is that the French were self-serving. A formal alliance would lessen the possibility of reconciling an Empire which, thus strengthened, would seize the French

West Indies. This threat of Anglo-American aggression probably originated in the Congress; it appears in the *Journals* as early as December 1776.[2] The question of the timing of the alliance is also of moment. The news of Burgoyne's surrender and the battle of Germantown reached Paris simultaneously. Germantown seemed no American defeat, and the Continental Army had survived. In November King Louis sent word of his interest in American independence.[3]

In a sense, the War for American Independence had thrown the profits of the Great War for Empire once more on the gaming table. The French did not play their cards for the benefit of the United States. At bottom there was an incompatibility in the Franco-American relationship, deeper than the superficial paradox of alliance between Protestant republic and Catholic monarchy. The Americans had quasi-imperial views of their own importance which would make them too strong, in French opinion, and the French privately figured that everything beyond the crest of the Appalachian divide was now part of the stakes of the game.

The British easily penetrated Franco-American attempts to disguise their relations. Because the war was a civil war, it was easy for loyalists to act as rebels when they were really agents in place, and William Eden, Under Secretary of State, could recruit plausible adventurers more interested in money than politics. He even had one who thought spying was the best avenue to a professorship at King's College. Lord George Germain, Colonial Secretary, had three thousand pounds a year for spies, but he never accounted for its use. He used a Moravian acquaintance of Benjamin Franklin, named James Hutton, to keep up with Franco-American negotiations in Paris. An English rake, George Lupton, posed as an American, and kept his ears quivering in the presence of Silas Deane whenever possible. Joseph Hynson, a Maryland sea captain, met the British ambassador's secretary weekly in Paris; once he was able to give him an entire batch of despatches on American progress in Paris.

An American, Paul Wentworth, was the chief runner of British agents in Paris. His best operator was the American physician Edward Bancroft, Franklin's secretary, who sent data in invisible ink, signed "Edward Edwards," in sealed bottles hidden weekly in a hollow tree on a Tuileries terrace. It was Silas Deane who had invited Bancroft to come over to Paris from London to aid the cause, which

Bancroft did very promptly indeed. Bancroft served himself best and kept his espionage secret: it was not known until sixty years after his death. Deane was rather stand-offish, and Bancroft became his only intimate, learning all his secrets and joining all his complicated and sometimes dubious moneymaking schemes. Thus the British government learned of Franco-American relations before the Congress did, at a profit of five hundred pounds a year for Bancroft. He was not worth it. The King discounted Bancroft's information because he did not trust him, and Franklin, knowing there was a leak somewhere, offered occasional falsehoods. After all, the sooner an Anglo-French war the better, so Franklin did not mind the British knowing of increasing French help to America.

The irascible Arthur Lee suspected Edward Bancroft but misplaced his confidence in his own secretary. Bancroft, perhaps to rid himself of a competitor or to cover himself with the cloak of American patriotism, betrayed Lee's secretary with proof that he had been speculating on the London Exchange on the basis of inside information on the progress of American affairs.[4] Bancroft may also have poisoned Silas Deane on the eve of Deane's return to America in 1789. Only Bancroft was present at Deane's death, which, in his medical capacity, Bancroft certified as suicide. Deane knew things about Bancroft which could be embarrassing. Bancroft was skilled in tropical poisons after residence in South America.[5] He had once arranged his own arrest on an allegedly covert mission to England and then arranged his "escape." A full-blown three-dimensional character was this Springfield, Massachusetts, physician, novelist, speculator, and spy—who had once been a pupil of Silas Deane, schoolmaster.

On the French side, Vergennes was a bumbler compared to Wentworth, but that was because French spies lacked patriotic motivation and were usually mercenaries, or criminals, or psychotics. French espionage was informal, unsystematic, and inefficient.

The only secret intelligence of much value to the Americans in Paris was naval intelligence. Franklin gathered that kind of information, usually in French (unsigned), from friends and agents in continental seaports. Its value was variable.[6]

The importance of all these espionage tricks and systems can easily be exaggerated. The most valuable information floated freely among merchants and politicians. Actually, what was important could be deduced from plain public facts, as Germain deduced in August 1777 that war with France and Spain was practically certain if the American fighting continued long.

II

After the bad news of Burgoyne's surrender, the North Ministry rushed conciliating agents to Paris to make some vague overtures before a French treaty was signed, but both Deane and Franklin said the recognition of independence must come first. Vergennes knew of the British approach, and it stimulated him to offer an alliance even though France had to go ahead without Spain for fear the United States might make a separate peace. Franklin helped to bring Vergennes to this point by letting him think Britain's proposal was interesting. No spy could get inside Franklin's mind, so Vergennes could but fear the worst, and act.

The Franco-American military treaty did not require France to go to war, but a military alliance would be in effect if there were an Anglo-French war—which there was sure to be. The terms were generous.[7] France recognized American independence and renounced French ambitions on the continent of North America (but not the West Indies). Neither party would make a separate peace with Britain. The treaty required the United States only to guarantee the French West Indies in return. The British ambassador sent the gist of the agreement to London on the day of signing (February 6, 1778), and four copies of the text—via Bancroft—in forty-two hours, but the government pretended ignorance, in order to postpone war, and meanwhile was organizing a peace mission to the Congress.

All these months the Congress had only rumors and conjectures from private commercial and familiar correspondence—rumors of a treaty, hints of important despatches coming, something about an obscurely described proposal to come from Britain, advice to do nothing hasty. Then, almost twelve months after the date of the last letter received by the Congress from Paris, while still at York, the winter of their almost intolerable discontent thawed: on May 2 came news of the alliance with France. It being a Saturday, the Congress was in recess until Monday when Silas Deane's brother Simeon brought the despatches. Quickly the delegates reconvened, opened the packet, and found a Treaty of Alliance and a Treaty of Amity and Commerce.[8] On Monday, after a recess until three in the afternoon, the Congress ratified the treaties unanimously and adopted a resolution of gratitude for the "truly magnanimous conduct" of the King of France.[9]

No one was happier than Gilbert du Motier, Marquis de Lafayette, who wrote: "Houra, . . . now the affair is over, and a very good treaty will assure our noble independence. . . . I hope a grand, noisy *feu de joy* will be ordered, it will give high spirits to our soldiers, it will run through the whole continent, it schall reach the ears of our good friends in philadelphia."[10]

This was written on Sunday, and many members wrote letters in all directions in the same spirit that day. Boston had the news ten days before it reached the Congress, and celebrated with illuminations and the usual thirteen toasts, now including one to "Lewis the 16th, of France."[11] The congressional clerks went to work as a propaganda ministry, sending texts to sea captains and editors. There was a proclamation to the whole people to be read to congregations by the clergy. The treaties and the proclamation were rich lodes of aphorisms for 1778's Fourth of July orations. The Congress also let out a letter from William Bingham, its agent in Martinique, pseudonymously predicting an Anglo-French war. The loyalist Joseph Galloway, also pseudonymously, deprecated the prediction of war as a perennial idle rumor,[12] but an English gambler was willing to buy an insurance policy against war, "to pay ten guineas a day, to receive a thousand when war is declared against France," that is, a bet that war would break out in fewer than a hundred days.[13] He made 910 guineas, for war came nine days after his June 8 bet.*

The Treaty of Amity and Commerce, which accompanied the alliance, was almost identical with the congressional Plan of 1776. It included the revolutionary notion that free ships make free goods,[14] and would allow each signatory to trade with the enemy of the other except in contraband of war. The list of contraband stores was carefully narrowed and restricted. Each signer received "most favored nation" treatment. Since 1775 the Americans had been trying to broaden their trade, hence the Plan of 1776. But only the French

---

* The alliance and the Anglo-French war did not affect the operations of Caron de Beaumarchais through his dummy supply firm called Hortalez et Compagnie, which functioned well until the end of fighting.

accepted it during the war. Because the treaty violated the canons of mercantilism by admitting foreigners to the trade of France, it was at once the first paragraph of the obituary of mercantilism and the preamble to the system of reciprocal trade treaties.[15] France was nominally mercantilist, but philosophy went overboard when there came a practical chance to hurt Britain. Perhaps some Frenchman thought of writing the equivalent of the British Navigation Acts into an American treaty, so that France could replace Britain in the American economy, but such a policy, even if acceptable to America, would have turned other European nations away from any idea of joining the battle.

The French also sent the name of their minister to the United States, Conrad Alexandre Gérard, appointed on January 20, promoted to be a petty noble in March, and received in Philadelphia on July 12. He was experienced in foreign politics since the days of Louis XV. From his arrival in 1778 until the departure of his successor in 1784, the lines of power in the United States formed a triangle, with the apexes being the Congress, the French minister, and George Washington. In the land of fried mush, Gérard knew what to do. As Congressman Samuel Holten wrote of Gérard's generous table: "The dinner was grand and elegant and in the French taste."[16] It was Gérard's job to overcome anti-French tradition and to keep the Americans on their toes. He also had to check American expectations which went beyond the letter of the alliance. After all, he was obliged to do what he could for Spain, the old dynastic partner, even if Spain's hopes clashed with American dreams of the West. For reasons of health he returned to France in October 1779, having done well; his successor was to be the Chevalier Anne de la Luzerne.

A joint commission of Benjamin Franklin, Arthur Lee, and Silas Deane had handled American affairs in France since late in 1776. The Congress sent John Adams to replace Deane in 1778, but Adams arrived after the treaties had been arranged. Because France sent a single minister, the Congress thought the United States should have but one in Paris, and in September settled on Franklin as the man.[17] Only Pennsylvania objected; its objection to Franklin was that he used his grandson as secretary, and his grandson was the son of the firmly loyal royal governor of New Jersey, Sir William Franklin. Lee stayed on as commissioner to Spain, which post he had held since May 1, 1777.

The Congress wrote a set of rather dreamlike instructions for Franklin, which require no notice except of the governing principle that he should not commit the United States to anything without the consent of the Congress.

The success of the mission to Paris caused exultation in the Congress, which sent new and broader instructions to its threadbare corps of militia diplomatists, commissioners to Berlin, Vienna, and Tuscany, all living in Paris. And perhaps commissioners would be appointed next to Lisbon, The Hague, Stockholm, Copenhagen, and St. Petersburg; had they been named, they too could have lived in Paris, where the assemblage of unacceptable commissioners received permission to live up to their new national dignity by drawing bills of exchange on the French treasury. The next diplomatic event was a somewhat comic anti-climax in the form of an unsolicited "recognition" of the United States by the "Emperor" of Morocco, if the letter to the Congress of a self-styled consul of all nations without consuls in Morocco may be believed.[18] Perhaps it was an attempt at a shakedown; if so, the writer was working a barren orchard.

Despite—or perhaps because of—the difficulties of transatlantic communication, Franklin was a success as Minister to France, where he was respected by diplomatists as a competent peer. He conducted foreign policy and acted as merchant, banker, judge of admiralty, and consul general. He supervised public and private warships and once even tranquilized a mutinous naval crew by persuasion. Conscious of his limitations, he moved in these matters slowly but surely.

III

In the arguments about the Articles of Confederation, with exceptions of course, it was noticeable that those who were hottest for independence were coolest toward the organizing of a workable central authority, and those who were inclined to go slow on independence were the firmest in favor of a true confederation. Inasmuch as they were all rebels together, that is about as far as factionalism went. But this factionalism spilled over into a ferocious personality clash revolving around the works and person of Silas Deane, coinciding in time and interest with the French alliance.

The root of the trouble was that many members of the Congress were even less concerned about legislative conflict-of-interest than they are now. Some of them were public contractors, collecting commissions for what they bought for the United States through agents. (Cost-plus contracts are now routine, but not if made with public officials.) These operators were a conspicuous and tactically useful element of the revolutionary force, but their insensitivity about public funds contrasts curiously to the nobility of character claimed in their own propaganda. In their favor it may be said they financed the war on their own credit. On the other hand, the war financed them by creating a sellers' market.

Most notable among them were Congressman Robert Morris, partner of Morris, Willing, and Company, and ex-Congressman Silas Deane, partner of Robert Morris. In Paris, Deane represented both the United States and the Philadelphia mercantile firm, getting 5 per cent commission on public purchases and a share in the firm's profits, which were often marked up 400 per cent over French costs. He also got his accounts into a Gordian snarl.

The ever-suspicious Arthur Lee suspected Deane of dishonesty, specifically of buying things for sake of the 5 per cent commission which the French intended to give. Lee demanded a congressional investigation. He made one other charge he could not substantiate at the time, but which turns out to have been true: that Deane, Edward Bancroft, and Samuel Wharton, the Philadelphia merchant and land speculator, had leaked the news of the French alliance in order to make a killing on the London Stock Exchange. Samuel Adams later wrote his opinion that Deane and friends hoped for a monopoly of American foreign trade rather than for American independence. It was their only object, "the Cake which they hope shortly to slice and share among themselves."[19]

Arthur Lee's antipathy toward Deane had early beginnings. Beaumarchais may have given Lee some general ideas about French help, but Lee learned no details. His pride was hurt when he arrived in Paris and found himself an outsider. He blamed Deane, on the theory that Deane was concealing graft. Actually the French opposed Lee's participation, knowing him a liar, thinking him a spy, and doubting the prudence of dealing with a man whose brother William was alderman for the city of London. Vergennes had caught him in a lie early in 1776, when Lee said agents of the Congress had received encouragement from Spain, a falsehood which Vergennes could easily discredit by consulting the Spanish.[20]

Gérard arrived in Philadelphia on July 12, 1778, with a French naval squadron and Silas Deane shining in reflected glory. As a mark of esteem, Deane carried a diamond-studded snuff box with a portrait of Louis XVI on the cover. Before the Congress he had things pretty much his own way at the beginning, for he counter-attacked two men who were in France, and Richard Henry Lee who was in Virginia. He should have won early, but he handled his case poorly.[21] A motion that Deane defend himself in writing failed, but encouraged recrimination and the revival of old grudges. For example, a warning by Arthur Lee in 1776 that Joseph Reed would bear watching, surfaced and helped to crystallize the disjointed opposition to Lee and his friends.

The zealots were by now identifiable as the two Adamses, all Lees, James Lovell, William Whipple of New Hampshire, Ralph Izard of South Carolina (the unemployed commissioner to Florence), Henry Laurens of South Carolina, Elbridge Gerry of Massachusetts, and lesser-known men. They had in common an opposition to increasing congressional power and a fear of foreign alliances. On the other side were Robert Morris, John Hancock, William Henry Drayton of South Carolina, and most of the Virginians except the Lees. There was an interesting coincidence of the Puritan Ethic in the temperaments of most of the anti-Deane men, and somewhat sybaritic inclinations in Deane's supporters.[22]

The public approval of Deane by the French government seemed such a strong point in his favor that Thomas Paine took to print to say that the French public aid to the American rebels before the alliance was a gift. Gérard, embarrassed, demanded that the Congress deny Paine's assertion, thus precipitating much ill feeling but eliciting a congressional lie that the French government did not supply the rebels before the alliance. Paine was not blameless. His newspaper article used information he could only know as hired secretary of a congressional committee, and he was sworn to secrecy. After Gérard's demand for repudiation, Paine had to resign.

Meanwhile, Deane took to the press to appeal beyond the Congress to the people, defending himself and blackguarding Arthur Lee. The Congress became so turbulent that Henry Laurens resigned the presidency on the public ground that congressional behavior was intolerably graceless. When John Adams read Deane's defense he exploded to the wily Edward Bancroft, speaking of Deane's "vile Passions," "Arrogance and Presumption," which left no choice but to ruin the United States or Deane, who, like a wild boar, should be "hunted down for the Benefit of Mankind."[23]

Robert Morris defended Deane, so to speak, by saying in print that a Congressman had every right to make a business partnership with Deane; if Deane misbehaved, Deane should be called to account.[24] An anonymous essayist of Massachusetts suggested that the ventilation of Deane's affairs should encourage every state to look into the conduct of its delegates who may have had business relations with Deane—starting with the Pennsylvania delegation. A curious amount of "fury" had been roused by daring to question the man (Deane) whose friends now gave him the ridiculous title of savior of the country.[25] Loyalists, of course, enjoyed all this, and even fabricated an aphorism for attribution to the Chevalier de la Luzerne, Gérard's successor, who was said to have urged the Congress to "Press your people hard with taxes, the more beggars, the more soldiers."[26]

Perhaps the heat of the Deane-Lee quarrel can be understood better if one remembers that there was an opposition to a French alliance in principle. It seems never to have been permanently popular in New England, perhaps on religious grounds. And perhaps the Americans could have won the war alone. But they won it with the use of French resources which would not have been available outside of an alliance, since it was not to the French interest to support the war in any other way. A number of farsighted men, who happened to be on the anti-Deane side, foresaw that difficulties might later arise from this entanglement in the affairs of Europe. Shorter-sighted men predicted contamination of utopian America by decadent France, even to the flooding of the United States by Popery. None, of course, exactly foresaw the puzzles which came out of the Anglo-French wars after 1789.

When the Congress recalled Deane, the French government feared it was the work of an anti-French faction, and thought it politic to tell the Americans that Deane suited France very well. Once the treaties were signed the French were determined to see the venture through. The recall of Deane seemed to show a certain wavering of the American spirit. The French were *au courant* with events of the Revolution but never understood the American character; they found the vacillation and instability of the Congress inscrutable, when actually it was just the American Way. Naturally the zealot-politicians, who despised Deane, would look at every proposal of his French admirers as though studying a dubious bank note. To Gérard this was plain obstructionism, and most unbecoming to a loose league of rebels warring against the world's foremost empire while weakly supporting a small army commanded by backwoods generals. From annoyance it was a short step to a suspicion that the anti-Deane element was a faction that might suddenly choose reconciliation with Britain. That was about as great an error of judgment as Gérard could have made.

Thus Gérard felt compelled to enter into the factionalism of the Congress to keep the United States firmly allied with France. He even hired Paine as a French propagandist but could not get along with him. When the Anglo-French war finally started, Gérard successfully lobbied to get the Congress to declare the binding nature of the Franco-American alliance, and in the process further alienated those who looked to Samuel Adams for leadership. All in all, American politics was full of surprises for the French, who had no experience of the working of a representative assembly for many centuries past. It is not surprising that Vergennes began to process Gérard's recall, ostensibly for reasons of health. He had not failed, but a new face might be useful. His relief was the Chevalier Anne de la Luzerne.

Luzerne used honey where Gérard had failed with vinegar. He kept open house for the delegates (with a good cuisine), acted as party whip over those who would follow French leads, and continued the practice of hiring American writers in the French interest, though some of them were ideologically motivated to do it free. He got results. He brought the Congress around to a more vigorous defense of independence, united them more strongly among themselves, and attached them more firmly to France despite political and theological aversions. The interference of France in the affairs of the United States could be labeled as domineering, but it must be remembered that France had not taken advantage of American difficulties. Instead the government of "Lewis 16th" had promoted the new country to equality among nations.

The Deane controversy and the falling into line of anti-Deane and pro-Deane factions brought the first jelling of a conservative congressional group, at least as well coordinated as the heated rebels had been. The leader of this element was Robert Morris, whose influence increased steadily thereafter. It is worth noting that the closest friends of Morris had not been in the vanguard to declare independence, but were foremost in the scramble for supply contracts. They were not evil men. As John Jay, who was one of them, put it, the country could probably get more advantage from the "enterprise, activity and industry of private adventurers, than from the lukewarmness of assemblies."[27] (Adventurer then was synonymous with investor.)

The Continental Congress was not a projection of national politics, since there was no national politics. It was not a national legislature, nor even a national forum, but a convention of state legislatures. Hence it was not necessary or possible to appeal to and to mobilize a national body of voters with a national viewpoint, since there was no nation. The result—which so misled Gérard—was a kind of whirling confusion of interests, issues, leaders, opinions, shifting factions, and temporary political alliances, all dyed with provincialism and localism.

The Deane affair simultaneously strengthened the merchant-delegates in the Congress by driving them to work together in future disputes, and somewhat weakened public confidence in the probity of the Congress. It also ruined Deane. Unvindicated, his accounts unsettled, claiming much back salary, humiliated, broke, he changed his mind about the American Revolution. It was his hard luck that he had been sent to pioneer in international relations and manage politico-economic affairs for which neither he nor his employers had much competence. What reputation he had left was tattered by the publication of eleven letters to eminent Americans, intercepted by the British, in which he said the Revolution had been a mistake. The letters had no political effect, because they did not begin to appear until the day Cornwallis surrendered, but they destroyed his credibility in the United States. He died in 1789. The Congress voted in 1842 to accept his accounting.

IV

While wrestling with the affairs of Silas Deane, the Congress had to consider a peace proposal from Britain, usually called North's Conciliation of 1778. It might better be named King's Pawn Gambit Declined.

The winter of 1777–1778 would have been a good season for Frederick Lord North to have resigned (which he attempted in March 1778), but the King had lately paid North's unmanageable debts, and the chubby, good-humored First Lord of the Treasury stayed because of gratitude. As early as November 18, 1777, ministerial leaders knew that John Burgoyne's operation was falling apart, but North did not announce it to Parliament until December 3, when it provoked growls and rumblings in the opposition. On December 11 North arranged the recess of Parliament for the customary long holiday until February. If he had moved faster and publicly North might yet have saved something, but he chose to operate by stealth. He told Parliament he would offer a peace plan after the recess.

British agents appeared in Paris in mid-December. They offered Deane and Franklin safe conduct to London, an immediate armistice, and high rank in a proposed colonial peerage. Franklin answered with stories of British atrocities in America. The King was willing to create up to two hundred American peers, including Franklin, Washington, John Adams, and Hancock. Adams thought it fantastic folly to dream that American republicanism could be thus reversed.[28] This interview speeded Vergennes to make the treaty with the United States, certainly the result furthest from North's hopes. The English public, as usual, was inspired to unity by bad news.

When Parliament reconvened, North was ready with a set of bills. Several of the offensive laws were repealed: the Tea Tax of 1767, the Massachusetts Government Act, and the Prohibitory Act of 1775 (which had excommunicated Americans from the Empire); left on the books were the Boston Port Act, the Administration of Justice Act, and the Quartering Act. Parliament also renounced all authority to tax except in regulation of trade, and the King was to appoint commissioners to treat with the Continental Congress as a lawful body. In a few days came news of the Franco-American alliance with its gloomy assurance of an Anglo-French war. An opposition leader, William Petty, Earl of Shelburne, proposed a federal union with America, and the mischievous John Wilkes in the Commons ironically compared the unanimous loyalty of the Americans in the 1760's with their apparently unanimous congressional disloyalty in 1778.[29] North had an estimate of the situation from the economist Adam Smith, retired Glasglow professor and at the moment a commissioner of customs, which may account for the government's misreading of the omens. Smith thought the Americans would be pliable "when they compare the mildness of their old government with the violence of that which they have established in its stead," and made (for an economist) the truly astonishing statement that the Netherlands were "a much richer and more fertile country than any part of America."[30] (Smith's nonsense excites the suspicion that North's personal finances were so deranged because Adam Smith may have been his investment counselor.)

The commissioners appointed to make peace were Frederick Howard, Earl of Carlisle, William Eden of the Board of Trade, George Johnstone, ex-governor of Florida, General Sir William Howe, and Admiral Richard Lord Howe. They had authority to negotiate with the Congress, other rebel bodies, and Washington. They had no authority to acknowledge American independence nor to promise the withdrawal of British forces. Any commitment they made must receive the approval of Parliament.

The instructions to the commissioners were a half-surrender by Britain, since, if the gambit succeeded, Britain would retain only the powers to regulate trade and to tax colonial imports from foreign countries. (Of course, the Americans would be giving up their Army and Navy, their provincial commissioning powers, and their currency.) The British had receded quite a way from their position of 1774, because France was now the important enemy. The honesty of the British proposal, however, is open to doubt. The Emperor Joseph II said in 1781 that he was told the British did not intend to keep any agreement reached by the Carlisle Commission. This is slender evidence, except for the self-evident fact that almost all diplomacy of that generation was stained by deceit.[31]

After wasting time trying to promote an armistice through agents in Paris, North made haste by sending the texts of his conciliatory bills to America even before Parliament voted them, hoping to forestall ratification of the French alliance. Printed copies reached General Washington first, from Philadelphia. Although unauthenticated, and perhaps a fraud perpetrated in Philadelphia, the general told the Congress he thought they were genuine. The Congress agreed because Howe had made feeble gestures of the same kind before. The proposals had an advantage for the British military because they might slow the war-weary Americans' preparations for the next campaign, discourage foreign friends while inspiriting the loyalists, weaken the constancy of some rebels, and, strategically speaking, allow a detachment of force for defending the British West Indies. If a treaty with France were made, the offers could tempt the Conress to reject the alliance. After four days of speculation the Congress settled down to act on the proposals as if they were authentic. A committee comprising Gouverneur Morris of New York, William Henry Drayton of South Carolina, and Francis Dana of Massachusetts drafted a reply, mostly by Morris.

They said the proposals were a sign of weakness, because Britain receded from previously obnoxious and allegedly immovable positions. Then they argued the wicked insincerity of the enemy: either the British now admitted they had sacrificed men in unjust warfare, or, more likely, they were laying a line of traps for the unwary Americans. They concluded that the British overtures were intended to divide Americans. There should be no conference with the commissioners unless the British withdrew their forces *or* acknowledged the independence of the United States. Finally, any persons who negotiated with the British "ought to be considered and treated as open and avowed enemies of these United States." The report received unanimous approval, and the Congress ordered it published.[32] This firm stand was bravely taken ten days before the Congress knew there was a French alliance, and when the delegates had been almost a year without news from Paris.

The Congress could not be certain of British sincerity. Perhaps the overture was a ruse, but they could not be sure of *that*. President Henry Laurens thought more citizens than those in the Congress should be involved if they actually sat down to negotiate peace with the British, and certainly no one state should enter such talks by itself. Washington agreed. The view of Laurens and Washington implied the need for some kind of national convention to consider British proposals. *If* Lord North had conceded independence, he probably could have arranged a peace conference before the Americans learned of the French treaties, but independence was the essential ingredient, probably held more firmly in 1778 than in July 1776. A false rumor of the arrival of British commissioners in Philadelphia on April 30, eight days after the adoption of the reply, was rather nerve-wracking until discredited, but the Congress remained faithful to the ideal of independence. It was never really shaken. The only question was whether they could make it good. Then, to the great relief of all, came Simeon Deane on May 2 with the happily received texts of the French treaties. The month of May and the first week of June passed with no official word from any responsible Briton, but plenty of unofficial words from irresponsible Britons.

One prudent ex-Congressman, Christopher Gadsden of South Carolina, saw a possible danger in the congressional counter-proposal to talk if either the British forces were withdrawn or independence were recognized. If the British forces left before the King accepted American independence, the United States would have to keep its Army intact indefinitely, the Royal Navy could harass the coast indefinitely, and the British could propagandize the American people indefinitely,[33] all of which would be very uncomfortable—indefinitely.

Although North knew about the French alliance before his peace-makers left Britain, he sent them anyway. At the very least, the conciliatory gesture would make it harder for the opposition to support the American rebellion. But North also ordered the evacuation of Philadelphia weeks before Lord Carlisle and his retinue had sailed, without telling the commissioners. They had a nasty shock when they first learned it on arriving at New York, and they were quite angry with their own Ministry. Eden let his anger be known to the government in a letter accusing the ministers of deliberately contriving to make the commissioners appear ridiculous. Carlisle pointed out sarcastically that an army in Philadelphia would have been an inconvenience to the Americans if the conciliation failed. The commission had to hole up in New York.

Whether unnerved by the news of a British reduction in force, or just congenitally stupid, from this time the commissioners and their agents acted more like stage Englishmen in a nineteenth-century American farce than like suave diplomatists. First they publicly deprecated the French alliance as unauthorized by any state delegation of powers to the Congress.[34] Then they sent an agent, John Berkenhout, to Philadelphia under the cover of a physician looking for a place to set up practice (he could have been hanged). He was to cajole and if possible bribe American leaders, but he chose to talk with Richard Henry Lee and Samuel Adams, two zealous and perspicacious men who had him locked up and shipped back to New York. Sir John Temple also visited Philadelphia seeking whom he might corrupt, but left after some inconclusive conversations.

Most egregious of attempts upon American honor was the try at bribing Joseph Reed of Pennsylvania, an ex-Continental officer who had declined command of the cavalry and also the office of chief justice of Pennsylvania in order to enter the Congress. Reed was high in Washington's confidence. He had influential friends in Britain and was groundlessly believed to be pessimistic of the success of the War for Independence. Reed and ex-Governor George Johnstone, one of the commissioners, had a mutual friend in England. Johnstone sent a female loyalist to Reed with an offer of ten thousand pounds sterling and any American office within the King's gift if he could help reunion. Reed promptly opened the matter to the Congress, where the prevailing attitude switched from suspicion to rage. A resolution declaring Johnstone *persona non grata* passed immediately. An amendment to refuse to deal with *any* of the commissioners failed 3 to 7 (the roll call was 8 to 18).[35]

There was real embarrassment for Reed in this episode, since Johnstone brought a letter from Reed's brother-in-law, Dennis De Berdt, to Thomas McKean of Pennsylvania, written in most flattering terms, which could make it seem that Reed just might somehow be involved with Johnstone.[36] (This may be the origin of the sour my-wife's-no-good-brother joke in American lore.) De Berdt's concrete proposal was that the Americans elect a new Congress; then, if the people still wished independence after considering the terms of the Carlisle Commission, the King would concede independence. The only reason to think Reed was approachable might be found in a letter from Reed to Morris, July 18, 1776, on the Howes' earlier attempt at conciliation, in which he had said that if the Howes had authority to give "the two great cardinal points of exemption from British taxation and charge of internal government," the whole American resistance would have been worthwhile even if the states returned to being colonies of Britain.[37] But how could the British know he once was reconcilable? Perhaps Mrs. Reed mentioned it to Dennis.

The commissioners pressed on to make pen pals. They brought and wrote letters to many Americans, offering practically everything except independence. President Laurens said of Johnstone: "he has honoured me with a Letter much too polite to be sincere."[38] Thomas

McKean observed that the letter writers worked under a serious handicap, "it being treason to correspond with Enemies by the laws of Pennsylvania."[39] Congressional anger lived unabated, perhaps subsisting on the cramping effects of life in York, Pennsylvania. A resolution that by order of the Congress all letters to delegates from or brought by the Carlisle Commissioners were to be laid on the table failed to pass, but many were turned in, and some appeared thereafter in the press, notably those written to Francis Dana, Joseph Reed, and Robert Morris.[40] The general technique of the writers was to appeal to the natural nobility of the recipients while offering dignities (and more crass rewards) for cooperation. The failure to adopt the resolution to turn in all such letters was probably owing to the question of personal liberty it raised, not to fear of revelations. It mattered little. The Carlisle Commission was awkward, raw, and foolish.

Having failed with permeable cloaks and dull daggers, the Carlisle Commission fell back to negotiation as its last resort. Lord Howe and Sir Henry Clinton, who had succeeded Sir William Howe as commanding general and peace commissioner, asked Washington for a passport for Professor Adam Ferguson, a revolutionary theorist of the University of Glasgow whose works had once been high in American favor. Ferguson was the secretary of the commission and would take despatches to the Congress. Washington said he could not act without congressional instructions. In character, the commission then sent attested copies of the proposals by mail before the Congress could frame an answer for Washington to Clinton. As a concession to the amenities, for the first time, the senior British officers in America humbled themselves to address Laurens as the president of the Congress and noticed the Army's commander.[41] The clerk began to read the message, but on the second page the inept emissaries of His Britannic Majesty had inserted an insulting reference to King Louis XVI, which provoked uproar in the Congress and brought a successful motion to read no further. After a three-day cooling-off period the Congress took up the diplomatic note again. Upon reading it, little deliberation seemed necessary, and an answer was approved, by states 12 to 0, by roll call 31 to 0, offering the policy approved in April: to make a treaty of amity and commerce with Britain (consistent with existing treaties) if the British pulled out their armed forces or acknowledged the independence of the United States. The delegates added that they had read the insulting letter only in the hope of stemming the flow of blood, but had discovered from its language that the King still clung to his invalid belief in the dependence of Americans upon the King-in-Parliament.[42]

The French, of course, had a stake in this game. Once the Congress was re-established in Philadelphia the Carlisle Commission wished to move there but could not get congressional permission, probably owing to the influence of Gérard who believed their appearance in the same city with the Congress would make it appear that a true negotiation was under way. A delicate triangular balance existed among France, Britain, and the United States. The British were rather defensive about France, and inclined to fear the French rather than to resent their intervention. The French alliance came as no surprise to the British after the good espionage of Paul Wentworth and Edward Bancroft in Paris. The French feared an accommodation between Britain and America, and the Americans, particularly Franklin, exploited this fear well. The best the British could do was to insinuate that such an accommodation was forever possible. To French royal servants, the shortest way to such a conciliation would seem to be by way of corruption, and Vergennes was shaken to hear that Carlisle had taken half a million guineas to America for the purpose (actually, Carlisle took only ten thousand guineas and could find no one to give them to).

One concrete point which the Carlisle Commission and the French concentrated upon was the matter of Burgoyne's captive army. The commission wished for literal compliance with the Convention of Saratoga in order that the British could use the troops in the broadened war abroad. It was Gérard who gave the Congress its final exit from the agreement, suggesting that the King might not feel bound if the Ministry accepted the Convention, hence the King must himself ratify. Because this would have been a kind of recognition of the United States, it was outside the limits of practical politics at the moment, and, anyway, the Carlisle Commission never had such wide authority as to be able to promise the King's autograph. They did not even have power to commit Parliament or the Ministry to anything.

The only intelligence shown by the Carlisle Commissioners was their decision in October 1778 to quit. They announced their imminent departure ceremoniously in manifesto and proclamation, which they circulated by violating the international conventions on the uses of flags of truce. The Congress was quite annoyed at white-flag bearers distributing British propaganda, and resolved on October 16 that the states should arrest anyone caught distributing handbills for the commission. The manifesto of the commissioners threatened the rebels with the kind of war usually reserved for such lesser breeds as Frenchmen and Spaniards, and promised to lay waste to the country systematically. Americans replied that it was always possible to massacre Burgoyne's men in reprisal. The Congress published its own counter-proclamation (October 30), observing, among many other things, that Britain had failed to conquer free men and had then "meanly assailed the representatives of America with bribes, with deceit, and the servility of adulation."[43]

The rejection of the Carlisle Commission advances seems to have given general satisfaction in America, where the most interested people suspected the offer to be a clumsily disguised attempt to divide and conquer. Both private letters and the press reflect the American attitude. Too much blood had been spent to buy less than independence, and the Continental Congress was more valuable than a bench full of Americans in either Commons or Lords. Every state had proved itself quite as capable of choosing a governor as the Crown had been. The offer came too late.

Probably the loyalists also felt some relief at the failure of the North Conciliation of 1778, because a stern reconquest, not a friendly reunion, was to the best interest of famous or infamous loyalists. In Britain most of the returned commissioners reported the bad news that most Americans now hated the self-styled homeland. This was bad news because policy had been based on the theory that there was a very large number of American loyalists. Unwisely, the Ministry did not hear what it did not wish to hear, and went on in the same manner as before. Anger probably governed. Professor Adam Ferguson had been chosen to be secretary of the commission mainly because he had publicly doubted the wisdom of British policy, and therefore might be personally acceptable in America. When he returned he was not so moderate. By 1779 he had talked himself into believing that Britain would probably win in America, and solemnly wrote the nonsense that half the American population favored the royal cause. An anonymous British writer, signing himself Marcus Brutus, came nearer to the point of the episode when he wrote that the rejection of the conciliatory propositions in America really meant that the United States did not recognize Great Britain as a nation.[44] There were later schemes for reconciliation cooked up by the government, but none of them proposed to admit the independence of the United States until military defeat was conclusive. The continent of North America was just too large a parcel of real estate to surrender until compelled by force.

Later conciliatory proposals followed the lines of the 1778 approach and aimed to prevent complete separation and complete independence. They always suggested first an armistice, then negotiations. In the backs of their minds British ministers always thought they could trump an American ace by approaching individual state governments. As for the offers of 1778, a cynic could say that Lord North proposed to give up what he could not get anyway—tax revenue—and that he tried to keep the pearl of real value, the regulalation of American commercial life. In private it may well have been the case that North knew the Congress would not listen to any peace proposals except propositions that his King and colleagues would not swallow. North did try to resign in favor of William Pitt, Earl of Chatham, early in 1778. We can only speculate on what Pitt might have done, but Shelburne and Eden seem to have thought he would have withdrawn all troops from the interior, held a few strong coastal enclaves, concentrated most force against France, repealed all controverted legislation, and then let nature, leavened by the British tradition of cultural, economic, and legal ties, take its course. But it is most unlikely that Pitt would have yielded the Navigation Acts, and it is just as unlikely that republicanism in America would have died a natural death after 1775.

The Congress could not honorably accept the Carlisle offers after it learned of the French alliance, unless it negotiated jointly with the French. If North had moved quickly and publicly in, say, November 1777, it is faintly possible that he might have gotten in ahead of the French and kept America in the Empire by repealing the odious acts added to the statute books since 1767. Why were the British outplayed by the French? Surely it was part indolence—that long parliamentary recess from early December 1777 into February 1778 —but it may also have been a consciousness of British naval weakness coupled with a hope for some unforeseen good fortune. Then again, it may have been indecision.

CHAPTER

13

A Maritime Dimension
Added, 1778-1779

With the entry of France, the war became a contest of fleets as well as armies. Great slow gaudy ships of the line, carrying up to 120 guns, and other ships ranging down to stubby bomb ketches, could now play decisive parts.

Warships changed little from 1700 to 1850. They had large crews because they had to work the sails as well as the guns. Handling the guns was tiring. The guns themselves, which threw balls up to forty pounds, might carry three miles, but they were not accurate beyond six hundred yards. There was much arcane speculation about tactics in the rival fleets, but the differences boiled down to one essential: the British tended to fire at the ship, while the French liked to disable the enemy's rigging in hope of capturing her.

The United States had several navies: the Continental Navy, the privateer fleet, and some state navies. All hoped to support themselves by captured loot, but when the French came in the Congress let its naval effort slacken. We cannot list the Continental warships accurately because so many small vessels were bought and chartered; a chartered vessel, however briefly in service, appeared on the list as public. Similarly, the Congress acquired foreign vessels.[1] About a dozen ships were ordered to be built in the last months of 1776, of which one seventy-four-gun ship achieved flotation in 1782, and became a gift to the French, who never praised her. A thirty-six-gun vessel, *Confederacy*, got afloat in 1778 and fell into the hands of British captors in 1781. Two frigates of this hatch were finished, but only one, *Alliance*, in time to see action. The Navy was almost valueless until 1781, when Robert Morris became Superintendent of Finance and used the few remaining ships as packets to carry money and diplomatists in hazardous waters.[2] Actually, the Congress had exhausted itself financially by its naval program of 1775 and never caught up again, not even with record-keeping.

Ordnance and rigging posed problems almost beyond the industrial competence of the American people. The guns differed according to place of manufacture, and so did the powder. Inaccuracy of fire was therefore the prime distinction of this fleet. Luckily, Virginia could produce all of the hemp needed for cordage, though it was never more than a sideline of Virginia agriculture.

The chief maritime skill in America was ship design, and the surviving records are plans for fast, heavily armed vessels which could be called super-frigates. There seem to have been designers in every major port. If there had been supply service to match, this would have been a superior Navy.

By hindsight we can see that shortages of money and materials prevented the Continental Navy from amounting to much, and that the Congress should not have bothered. The fleet was short of leadership too. Even before independence, John Hancock wrote of "the shameful Inactivity of our Fleet . . . the frequent neglect or disobedience of Orders. . . ."[3] By July 1777 the Marine Committee gave up, and received permission from the Congress to stop building and to resume again only when it was in the country's interest.[4]

American nationalism, reluctant to gloss over the naval failures of the War for Independence, has done what it could to glorify this fleet in which all officers were amateurs, and which lost all but one ship. The glory hunters have concentrated on biography, for there were at least three captains who performed very well. Generally the ships were better than their captains, but courage and intelligence marked three commanders: John Barry, Joshua Barney, and John Paul Jones.

Barry was senior captain, served well in every capacity, and had command of the sole uncaptured ship at the end of the war.

Joshua Barney, a seaman at thirteen, commanded an Atlantic passage at fifteen, became a continental officer at sixteen, and was three times a prisoner of war, making a spectacular escape from Mill Prison, Plymouth, England. At twenty-two, as commander of the Pennsylvania State ship *Hyder Ali*, he took HMS *General Monk*.

But John Paul Jones is the man remembered. Born John Paul in Scotland in 1747, he went to the West Indies from whence he fled the law to Virginia, adding the name Jones as a precaution. Legend surrounds him, and it is well to deny at once that he ever had a scorching romance with a Russian princess. The truth is barely credible. He used Brest as a base from which to harass Britain, even landing a raiding party in Scotland. His strongest force comprised a leaky old East Indiaman, several other wormy hulks, and crews drawn from seventeen nationalities. This remarkable man humiliated the Royal Navy by taking HMS *Serapis* (September 23, 1779), a larger ship than his own *Bonhomme Richard*, within sight of English soil. Thus Jones became an American hero, though not American by birth or sentiment. Immediately after the war he became an admiral of Russia and never returned to America while alive. He has been overidolized, for he was a colossal egotist interested only in Jones. Nevertheless he was great as tactician, policy molder, seaman, and leader of men.[5]

Privateers were privately owned warships licensed to prey on enemy shipping as reprisal. There may have been as many as two thousand American privateers altogether. If one in three made a successful voyage, the investors made money. Investors need not go to sea to profit, but could buy shares in several ships to distribute their risks. They were frankly business ventures, with shares or "lays" conveyable speculatively in advance of operations. Agents, who served much like securities brokers, seem to have made the most money.

Privateers were active against royal supply ships and transports in 1775, but were not unleashed against commerce until the spring of 1776. Congressional resolutions which authorized all-out privateering explicitly said it was in reprisal for the damage done by Great Britain after the Proclamation of Rebellion in late 1775.[6] When the Congress got around to its diplomatic offensive late in 1776, it intended to try "to war upon British property" from French ports if the French government did not disapprove.[7] Until Burgoyne's defeat, the French government was reluctant to have the Americans use French bases, but Benjamin Franklin kept the French in a nervous state by talking of possible reconciliation with Britain, in the hearing of French agents.

Privateersmen, if they failed to capture British loot, often seized anything else of value, thus qualifying as pirates. They also engaged in collusive trade with the enemy by faking captures. No American political agency was really strong enough to discipline them until the erection of the federal judiciary in 1789. But they did a deal of good for the rebel cause. The figures are not wholly reliable, but the most careful calculation possible shows a net loss of merchant vessels by the British of 1,108. Privateering is believed to have driven up the price of food in the West Indies, to have provoked a great rise in marine insurance rates, and to have depressed West Indian exports, cutting the profits of West Indian trade by perhaps as much as two-thirds. The black pawns of imperialism proved valuable prizes: about five thousand blacks, the property of British slavers, are said to have been taken and sold in the West Indies. Some British merchants, putting first things first, used French ships to carry their Atlantic cargos.

Privateersmen had it better than soldiers or regular sailors except in one respect: if captured in armed ships they were held as traitors or pirates, rather than prisoners of war; if taken in unarmed vessels they found themselves quickly impressed into the Royal Navy. Not until 1782 did they get lawful status. Most prisoners spent the duration miserably in Kinsale, Ireland, aided only by local charity which the United States never recompensed. In an effort to get prisoners to exchange for the wretched rebels, Benjamin Franklin commissioned a fleet of privateers to go out and capture men for swapping, but his captains were too much interested in booty to achieve his end, though very successful at taking ships near England.

The privateers, of course, did nothing to preserve the American merchant fleet, which was dead by 1780. The Royal Navy finally put the privateers out of business too in 1781, when only one in seven managed to slip home safely.

Opposed to the patchwork American sea force was the reputed ruler of the waves. Actually, Britannia's seafaring sovereignty was shaky. It was lucky for the Americans that the war came between Pitts. No very capable First Sea Lord managed naval affairs from 1763 to 1783; in the Admiralty there was gross corruption; and the

King, more interested in the Army, economized on the Navy. The government paid six million pounds of the national debt in the years 1763–1775, mostly by naval economies. The First Sea Lord during the War for Independence was Edward Montagu, Earl of Sandwich, of whom few kind words have been written. He had an able permanent secretary to whom he should have listened more attentively.

British naval architecture was on the downgrade too, while the French were improving their ships of war. British designers seem to have been so very satisfied with their improvements of rigging that they let their underwater hull lines degenerate to the lines of bath tubs, much inferior to some of their seventeenth-century lines.[8] From the moment the French entered the war, the past neglect of the Navy was noticeable and painful. The Royal Navy counted 131 ships of sixty or more guns, but actually found it hard to keep seventy at sea at once, while the French had fifty-eight. If Spain came in, the Royal Navy would be outgunned on the water, though not on Sandwich's desk-top lists. Despite the omens of 1774, Parliament appropriated less money and authorized fewer men for the Navy in 1775 than in 1774, and really did not strain itself until the naval budget had risen sluggishly to 150 per cent of 1774's, in the year 1782.

Manning was harder than funding. In the years 1774–1780 the British paid for 176,000 men, lost 1,243 by combat, and noted 42,069 deserters (increased to 79,000 deserters by 1783). Impressment of seamen, brutal discipline, and a generally hard life encouraged desertion. Crews were almost always in poor physical condition. Desertion was not political, for the rate was about the same after France came into the war as before. Why stay? The reward for doing well under degrading conditions was a chance to do more of the same under the same conditions.

The Navy's quality can be measured statistically by the index of single-ship actions. In one-to-one fights in the French and Indian War, the Royal Navy won seventeen, lost none, and four were indecisive. In the War for American Independence, Britain won thirteen, lost six, and eleven reached no decision. There is no use trying to make a case for the Royal Navy in this war. Its only glory was that in single-ship fights the French never actually captured a British man-of-war. But British strategy was defective, Admiralty decisions were unwise, and, despite Britain's claim to rule the seas, the French were able to move freely when opportunity offered them a chance to win the war—which they eventually did.

II

Spain could help to tip the naval balance against Britain. Luxuriating in a brief renaissance as a world power, Spain, having acquired everything west of the Mississippi in 1763, went on to found Los Angeles and discover San Francisco Bay. St. Louis sprang up in 1764 and became a trading post of consequence. Only in Texas, where tough Indians defied Spanish efforts, did Spain fail in this generation. It was the hard luck of the United States to have to deal with Charles III, the last really competent King of Spain. Although France asked only the humiliation of Britain, Spain wished some concrete profit, preferably real estate. The Spanish foreign ministry sent Juan de Miralles, a Cuban merchant, to look after its interests in Philadelphia; he arrived even before Conrad Gérard, the French minister.

Early in 1779 there were interesting rumors of a Spanish alliance in Philadelphia. These proved false. What did happen was that the Spanish sent an ultimatum to Britain (April 3) and nine days later (before the ultimatum expired) made the secret Treaty of Aranjuez with France, after which Spain declared war on Britain (June 21), ignoring the United States in the whole business. Spain had been trying to finesse Gibraltar from Britain as the price of mediating the war, which might have been a good bargain for the British. After a year of frustrating approaches to Britain came the ultimatum: each side to hold what it had, an armistice, a Spanish mediation. Great Britain contemptuously ignored this unsolicited intervention. Then Spain took the plunge, probably tempted by Britain's apparent naval weakness.

The treaty with France provided that the Franco-Spanish war against Great Britain would continue until Gibraltar and Minorca were Spanish again. (The French also secretly dealt the Spaniards into the Newfoundland fisheries, a crucial matter for New England.) News of the entrance of Spain into the war reached the Congress early in August,[9] stimulating hopes of more generous terms from

Britain.[10] As a delegate wrote, "Many tories wish to be thought converts. . . ."[11]

Vergennes knew of the Spanish play for Gibraltar in 1778, so he had Gérard suggest to the Congress the advisability of being ready to deal with Spain just in case the Spanish successfully mediated the war. Gérard optimistically addressed the Committee of the Whole (February 15), but his confidence was misplaced, for all he did was precipitate a seven-months' wrangle in the Congress in which the Adams-Lee group fought to have their own men abroad instead of more of Deane's kind. The prize was not worth the finagling, since Franklin could talk with the Spanish ambassador in Paris, while Arthur Lee, commissioned to Spain, was barred from the country. When the mission to Paris was reduced to Franklin's one-man job, the unemployed John Adams had returned home. Now it was decided to send a minister to Spain. After rough debate in the Congress, the compromise was that John Jay would go to Madrid, John Adams would return to Europe to be on hand to negotiate a peace if and when, and Arthur Lee would come home.

Jay's mission was hopeless, since his instructions required him to insist that the boundaries of the United States included everything east of the Mississippi River, and he was to insist also on the right to navigate the river. Spain would never accept such a description of reality. William Carmichael later put it precisely when he wrote that Spain wished to bar "every other nation from the navigation of the Mississippi and indeed of the Gulf of Mexico."[12]

But Jay, tough-minded spouse of a Livingston, energetic but rather vain, went to Spain to live in almost permanent embarrassment. Even before he could open the foreign ministry door the Congress rained due bills on him, which he was forced to dishonor. The Spanish government suggested that its King would pay forty thousand pounds for some ships laden with American produce. Later they changed the proposition to an offer to purchase four frigates and some lesser warships for a hundred thousand pounds. But at this point came news of the devaluation of the Continental dollar, and the United States seemed too poor a risk to bother with. In desperation Jay asked for the loan of the hundred thousand pounds, the American ships to be a gift. He finally got the loan of a third of it ($150,000) and absolute silence on the subject of a treaty with the United States, which is what he had come for primarily.

A Maritime Dimension Added, 1778–1779

He also learned some lessons: first, repudiation of paper money earned contempt, and second, even such a country as Spain had to pay 30 to 40 per cent on borrowed money; this last was owing to slanders about Spanish solvency spread by the French treasury, but neither Jay nor the Spanish knew that. After studying whimsical monarchy, Jay became incurably addicted to republicanism.

The conflicting ambitions of Spain and the United States with regard to the Trans-Appalachian West made a true rapprochement impossible. Not only did Spain think American republicanism a scandalous example to Spanish colonies, but the Spanish feared an advance of Americans westward. On Gibraltar and Minorca, Spain could deal with France; on the Old Southwest, Spain could not deal with the Congress. As a French minister said, no doubt with a shrug, "The Spanish, like little children, are to be attracted only by shining objects."[13] Spain genuinely feared that a result of the War for Independence would be American control of the Mississippi. The French tried to deprecate the threat by saying that under the Articles of Confederation the Americans would find it hard enough to defend themselves, let alone conquer a continent. The Spanish opinion—told to Gérard by Miralles—was that Spain needed the insurance to be gained by Spanish conquest of the area between the Appalachians and the great river. France, said Miralles generously, could take Canada. Gérard dismissed any thought of Canada, but became a convert to the Spanish position on the West. Gérard then suggested to Congressman William Henry Drayton of South Carolina that the Congress might be wise to agree to Spanish hopes for the West in return for a Spanish subsidy to be banked in Paris.

When the Chevalier Anne de la Luzerne succeeded Gérard in Philadelphia, he consistently supported Spain's western ambitions because the Congress needed Spain more than Spain needed the United States, and France needed both to humiliate Britain. The technique was to alarm the Americans about talk of an armistice, with each side to settle for the territory it occupied. This just might scare the Americans enough to make the necessary guarantees to Spain. Vergennes strengthened the argument by injecting the thought that Americans were inconsistent in claiming the western rights of a King whose authority they were trying to reject. But the Congress, for the moment, was unshakable. In the dark days to come in 1780, however, the Congress would have been willing to make the deal; Spain missed the chance by an indolence which provoked lasting American resentment. The ideal Spanish solution was for the Congress to renounce Florida, the Mississippi River, and the whole Trans-Appalachian West. It would have suited France well, because of inability to deliver Gibraltar and Minorca. But it was not to happen.

Spain did not withhold direct help. For example, salt, the basic necessity of the army ration, came mostly from Spain and the Spanish colonies. The governor of Louisiana took Pensacola and the Floridas in one of the best-executed operations of the whole war (1781). The Spaniards occupied the bluffs of present-day Memphis, and took and burned Fort St. Joseph at present Niles, Michigan. American privateers used New Orleans as a base, and, when most needed, the Spanish Army garrisoned Saint Domingue for the French, and once met the French Army payroll in America. The Congress, in June 1777, appointed Oliver Pollock its agent in New Orleans to buy blankets and other military supplies for the Continental Army, promising to ship flour down inland rivers to cover the costs of purchases he was to make. But the western Indians prevented the flour shipments. Poor Pollock made the mistake of being the only man in the world who accepted Continental dollars for gold at face value. His bankruptcy coincided pathetically with the preliminary treaty of peace in 1782.[14]

The important fact about the entrance of Spain into the war was that the naval balance changed. To the improved French sea force, which for once was equal in its own element to the French Army on land, Spain added a fleet which was slightly larger, if less efficient. The two together outnumbered the Royal Navy by a narrow margin on paper and by a wider margin in combat-worthy ships. From now on the British Admiralty had many worries.

In the beginning the British had two strategic options. They could block the American coast and use the Army as naval infantry to make life miserable for the rebels while negotiating, or they could conquer territory enough to crush the Continentals. In practice they temporized, then tried for a quick territorial conquest, bungled it, and lost Burgoyne's army. Next came the Franco-American alliance with its threat to the West Indies (a threat enhanced by the entrance of Spain the following year). It seemed advisable to the British to evacuate Philadelphia in 1778 in order to be able to send troops to the richer, riskier Caribbean.

In one sense the large British armies in North America were an encumbrance because their survival depended upon British control of the sea, and the necessity to assure control of the sea routes to North America diverted warships from the critical area of the West Indies.

Before France came into the war, the rebels waged a naval micro-war of their own, occasionally with good results. John Manley (an Englishman who used the *nom de guerre* John Russell) sailed the converted schooner *Lee* out of Gloucester in November 1775 and caught the royal ordnance brig *Nancy*, crammed with munitions. American sea raiders twice captured New Providence (now Nassau) in the Bahamas, and once dropped into the harbor of Prince Edward Island and took the governor prisoner. An attempt to free American prisoners who were being worked as coal miners on Cape Breton Island failed early in 1777 only because the liberation flotilla captured so many freighters on the way that it was too burdened with captives to go on to Cape Breton to fight.[15] The Army's heroic naval stand at Valcour Island under Benedict Arnold had delayed Carleton's invasion from Canada in 1776. That was about the sum of public naval success before the French alliance. A great many American merchant seamen were taken by the British, meanwhile, but few defected despite severe pressure to serve in the Royal Navy. American businessmen went into blockade running—with particular interest in salt and gunpowder—in which the risks were great and the rewards greater, quadrupling the wages of the seamen engaged and, as with privateering, making good profits if a third of the runners returned safely.

On its side, the Royal Navy did not effectively blockade the coast of North America. It has been doubted that it could have been done, but the British did a fair job of it in the War of 1812. Admiral Lord Howe was generous in allowing fishing for food and in sparing coastal towns the havoc the King wished to see. The British had enough advance information to have prevented any Continental warship from getting to sea, but did not try very hard, probably because the Congress made it easy for the Royal Navy by having so many ships in the Delaware River and at Charleston where they could be captured when the war spilled into those regions. The Royal Navy went for the necks of the bottles, instead of the vineyards, by successively corking the Hudson, the Delaware, and Chesapeake Bay, thus capturing two finished ships, destroying four which were being built, and taking many of the smaller purchased craft. They also captured more than a thousand merchant ships, to the great profit of navy men and admiralty judges.

Then came the French, and the revelation of British ineptitude in high places. In the previous war with France the British had denied France the use of the Atlantic Ocean. In 1778 they did not even try. For once it was not Germain's fault. He urged that Sandwich send a force to intercept any French fleet trying to pass Gibraltar, but Sandwich thought Britain too weak to try. Next Germain asked for a squadron to match any increase in French naval strength in America. The Admiralty accepted this proposal but carried it out sluggishly.[16] Because the French could move freely on the North Atlantic, British operations were always hazardous thereafter. Every land campaign was risky because the French might cut a waterborne supply line. Any naval campaign could lose a base. Any attempt at a territorial conquest could cost an army. And in all of history Britain had never yet defeated France singlehanded (a generalization still true). The Carlisle Commission was the closest approach to a good response, and that episode fell somewhat short of statesmanship.[17]

In April 1778, Comte Jean d'Estaing, an amphibious soldier-sailor, took twelve ships of the line out of Toulon, past Gibraltar, and on to Philadelphia. His military principle was that "promptness is the first of arms," but he took plenty of time to drill his men before they arrived in Philadelphia in July, bringing Minister Gérard and Silas Deane. The Congress, of course, was pleased to see and to help the fleet.[18] There was a flurry of overoptimistic plans, including a revival of the Canadian conquest scheme, but cool hands managed to kill the Canadian idea in six months of diligent cold-water-pouring.

The fact of d'Estaing's presence was a British failure; the Ministry had not chosen the wrong policy but had failed to agree on any policy. Despite ninety days' notice of d'Estaing's departure from Toulon, the British had lost the initiative and could only hope the French were not coming with Spanish helpers to land in England itself. Five months after the correct prediction of French operations, the British learned d'Estaing was steering west, and sent Admiral "Foul Weather Jack" Byron (grandfather of the poet) chasing after with thirteen ships which had been dangerously subtracted from the home fleet.

Having deposited Gérard safely, d'Estaing steered north, shadowed by Lord Howe's frigates. Since Byron had not yet come, the British were wholly on the defensive. Was the Frenchman going to try New York or the British post at Newport? The French squadron hung off New York harbor for eleven days, before d'Estaing decided the entrance was too shallow to risk his ships, which drew twenty-three feet of water (at highest tides, with a northeast wind, the entrance was but thirty feet deep). Washington agreed,[19] and d'Estaing resolved to try his luck at Newport.

The French force arrived at Newport on July 29 (provoking loyalist announcement that Rhode Island was to be held as hostage for carrying out the alliance[20]). It intended to cooperate with a land offensive under General John Sullivan. Unfortunately, Sullivan was not ready until August 9, when the attack began very promisingly. Lord Howe, though outgunned, bravely came along shore and dropped anchor while waiting for an opportunity to do something constructive. The French came out and began chessboard maneuvers for thirty-six hours, as preliminary to giving battle, only to be interrupted by the tail of a hurricane which badly damaged both forces. Howe returned to New York and refitted in remarkably fast time, but d'Estaing, knowing of Byron's imminent approach and having no local facilities for repairs, sailed to Boston, leaving Sullivan to extricate himself as he could. Luckily for the soldiers, Howe chased d'Estaing, and Sullivan got to the mainland, furious at d'Estaing's apparent desertion.

The affair could have led to recriminations between the new allies, but the Congress rejected a temptation to investigate and instead voted its thanks to all concerned. The fact is, all the naval stores at the disposal of the Congress had earlier been shipped to Boston, so d'Estaing had no place else to go.[21] Sam Adams, no Francophile, asked his Boston friends to cool any anti-French talk there.[22] And Washington took it on himself to tell political friends in New England that harmony was necessary while he tried personally to tranquilize Sullivan.

The French naval excursion had not been fruitless. It lacked dash but had important results. The French had proved themselves in earnest. Equally important, British resources were severely strained. An advantage also accrued to the Americans because British troops had to be detached to defend the West Indies. Later the British decided that Newport had become a shaky bastion, and gave it up. Thus American privateers could use Long Island Sound more freely. George Washington also saw for himself the indirect but real benefits of the mere presence of a powerful naval force.

Before the French entered the war, American warships in European waters had been flying the white ensign of France, which provoked the Royal Navy to board almost any ship under that flag, even in French territorial waters. But such close British surveillance did not continue after the Franco-American alliance. Instead the Admiralty waited for news of French naval departures and then tried to guess the destinations. The British decision not to blockade France was the gravest and most calamitous policy decision made by Britain in the whole war. Sandwich told the British public the home fleet equaled the Spanish and French navies, which was a politically useful lie. His figures included *everything* that would float, plus some ships being built. The true ratio was four to three against Britain.

The first fleet action between Britain and France was the indecisive battle of Ushant, 1778, when the British squadron under the Whig Admiral Augustus Keppel could not bring the French to close. The French were correct in fighting as if playing chess, because if they had lost on this occasion they could not have continued helping the United States. Keppel was court-martialed on a charge of not trying hard enough, but acquitted. A delighted mob sacked the house of his accuser and broke North's windows, but the opposition could not get Sandwich fired. Thereafter Sandwich relied on superannuated but politically docile admirals who were brought out of retirement one after another to die of fatigue or at least break down physically. Ushant marked the end of the war as the American War. From now on it was a world war.

In early 1778, John Paul Jones was becoming the phantom of the Irish Sea (his *Serapis* capture occurred in 1779). Perhaps in reprisal for the British burning of six American coastal towns, Jones laid about him freely in British waters, although with no such calculated terror-ism. The Marine Committee of the Congress later hoped Jones or someone might burn London, Bristol, Liverpool, Edinburgh, or Glasgow.[23] What Jones did was to land at Whitehaven, and at St. Mary's Island, Scotland, April 23, 1778. It was a gallant operation with a tiny force and no really valuable material results, but it alarmed the British into ungenerous and rather un-British accusations of mercenary motives. Jones was pretty upset "by the dirty insinuations of the Enemy —that my Enterprize at Whitehaven was *in consequence of a capital sum paid me in hand by the Court of France*."[24] Off the coast of Ulster, Jones also took the British sloop-of-war *Drake* after an hour's fight, and carried it to Brest.

The French and Spanish mounted an expedition to invade England in 1779. The notion was not hopeless, but the attack was not well planned. Of the four responsible officers, the junior was a stripling of seventy-one and the senior a more mature seventy-nine. The massed soldiery on the Channel coast suffered from dysentery, while the combined squadrons felt the ravages of smallpox. The British response was so indecisive that disease decided the outcome. Physiologically incapable of attacking, the invaders melted away, though they had shown more spirit than the British. The affair confirmed Vergennes in his belief that the war should be won overseas, and he now resolved to despatch a large army to North America.

From this time on, the big show in Europe was at Gibraltar, which the Spanish had begun to besiege as soon as they came into the war. A vast amount of force was absorbed in its siege and defense. The French had to help in order to keep Spain happy. The policy now was to besiege Gibraltar and to take the offensive in America. Gibraltar survived, but its siege kept Britain on the defensive in Europe after 1779, and let French fleets come and go at will. The French might have secured an American base immediately and have used it against the British supply line in such a way as to starve British armies out of America, but the Gibraltar distraction, and the magnetic attraction of the West Indies—to defend French islands and to conquer British islands—barred that strategy. Hence the British too used the North Atlantic as a highway.

The French Navy had shown itself methodical and well drilled, even if it lacked dash and pugnacity. The British Navy was the victim of neglect and of partisanship among its civilian directors, and its tactics had become fossilized. It was not able to win decisively against an enemy willing to stand up and slug it out.

III

Although cramped for space and fuel, the British Army in Philadelphia got through the winter of 1777–1778 well enough. In the spring came a change of commanding generals, orders to evacuate Philadelphia, and orders to send eight thousand men to the West Indies. With France now in the war, it was clear that British generals in America could expect no further reinforcements.

The new commander was Sir Henry Clinton. Sir William Howe offered his resignation after Burgoyne's surrender, at no pain to the King, and irascible Clinton succeeded him, mostly because he was nearby. There really was little choice. Jeffrey Lord Amherst declined to serve, and Charles Lord Cornwallis was on leave. Clinton was thought good enough for what would be a secondary theater of operations, though he was not keen on getting the promotion. Clinton was energetic and well schooled in his trade, but he shunned high responsibility and could never be called brilliant. His orders were to move his force to New York by sea, but he feared it might take so long that the unleashed Washington would dash into New York ahead of him. He was also burdened with three thousand refugees for whom he lacked transport if the troops also went by sea. With a bit of good luck on the French side, d'Estaing might have trapped a seaborne British force as it left the Delaware, but Clinton did not know that d'Estaing was near. The troops had to go to the West Indies by way of New York, because that was where the ships were gathering. So off the redcoats marched into Jersey, on June 18, 1778, encumbered with a twelve-mile baggage train.

The Congress returned to Philadelphia in time to celebrate the Fourth of July with "an elegant entertainment, and a fine band of musick."[25] The city was in good condition except that the British had made an open pit in front of the State House, which they used as a combination cesspool, pit for dead animals, and revolting charnel for the bodies of dead soldiers.[26]

Quartermaster General Nathanael Greene had the Continental Army ready to move, and as soon as Washington knew which way Clinton was marching he began pursuit. The British made only three miles a day, and the Americans caught up with them on the sweltering 28th of June near Monmouth Court House. Charles Lee had returned from captivity and insisted, by rank, on commanding the van. The battle went well for the Americans at first. Then, as a British general noted, Lee's men "were soon repulsed & driven back with little or no loss on our part."[27] More Americans died of heat and fatigue than from combat. Washington galloped onto the field, put

A Maritime Dimension Added, 1778–1779

Lee under arrest, and assumed command himself, but it was too late, and Clinton got away. Washington's account of Lee's withdrawal was detached,[28] but he is said to have blued the air with his language at the time. Who won the battle of Monmouth? The British buried a few of their casualties, but the Continentals buried 249 redcoats left on the field, which is not the mark of British victory. On the other hand, Clinton aimed to get to New York and he did it.

Lee has been suspected of treason ever since. As a prisoner he had lived in New York and talked with the Howes. When exchanged, he probably had not sold out, but he may have thought he could be the peacemaker of the war. He had certainly become defeatist, and led men into battle in a war he thought could not be won. After the battle he forced the issue and was tried by a court martial which found him at fault, in a decision that was necessarily an expression of confidence in Washington. The Congress confirmed the court verdict by a large vote. Lee took it hard.

I understand that it is in Contemplation of Congress on the principle of Oeconomy to strike me out of their service—Congress must know very little of me, if they suppose that I would accept of their money since the confirmation of the wicked and infamous sentence which was pass'd upon me

I am Sir
Your most obd. Servant

There appears to be a deliberate stroke of the pen through the letters "obd."[29]

The evacuation of Philadelphia was a turning point. In North America the British concentrated on recovering the two southernmost colonies, and no northern battle of consequence followed Monmouth. The French alliance diverted attention to the West Indies. Gérard put it sourly, "The Americans often seem in effect to wish to be no more than spectators of the quarrel between France and England."[30]

Visiting Frenchmen, of course, knew little of the ferocious warfare of the frontier, where rebels were not spectators but survivors. The Indians were nearly all pro-British, because of the influence and protection of the Indian superintendents and of the licensed fur traders who were beneficiaries of the British western policy. At one time or other, war raged the full length of the frontier from the Great Lakes to the Gulf.

The northwestern Indians began to be troublesome in 1777, and in

July 1778 killed hundreds of settlers of the Wyoming Valley of Pennsylvania. In November they returned to Cherry Valley, New York, led by the white Walter Butler and the Mohawk Indian Joseph Brant, where they captured and killed about fifty. (Brant, measured by percentage of victories, may well have been the most successful leader on either side of this war.)

It was Washington's view that the Indians would be pacific only as long as they feared the United States. Hence the Congress should strike severely against those Iroquois nations that were "most formidable and mischievous," and, by sparing the less hostile, divide the Iroquois.[31] General John Sullivan led the Continental force charged with quieting the Iroquois, and defeated them near present Elmira, New York, in 1779. After the battle his army systematically ravaged the Iroquois food supply. His ultimate hope was to press on to Fort Niagara. It was the key to the war in those parts because the British commanded Lake Ontario and used Fort Niagara as their Indian allies' staging area, but Sullivan was unable to get farther than the Genesee Valley. Nevertheless, Sullivan's expedition permanently reduced the Iroquois threat.

In spite of the obvious hazards, there was a steady flow of migration to Kentucky during the war. Kentucky swelled and contracted alternately as Indian threats waned and waxed. Settlers lived in stations with palisaded forts in the centers of the farming regions. These were invulnerable to attack with weapons of less power than artillery. The British officer who served as director of Indian operations against western settlements was Lieutenant Governor Henry Hamilton, who made his headquarters at Detroit and was called "the hair buyer" because of a belief "That Gov. Hamilton gave standing rewards for scalps, but offered none for prisoners. . . ."[32]

Governor Patrick Henry of Virginia commissioned George Rogers Clark a colonel with the mission of preserving Kentucky, which was still part of Virginia, but gave him a microscopic force. Clark, with about a hundred men, moved west by water and took the French villages of Kaskaskia and Cahokia. He convened both Indians and French in August 1778 to get recruits, with some success, aided in part by an endorsement from the local ex-Jesuit parish priest who verified the news of the French alliance.

The somewhat strengthened force moved east against Vincennes, where they waded through waist-deep icy water on the flooded

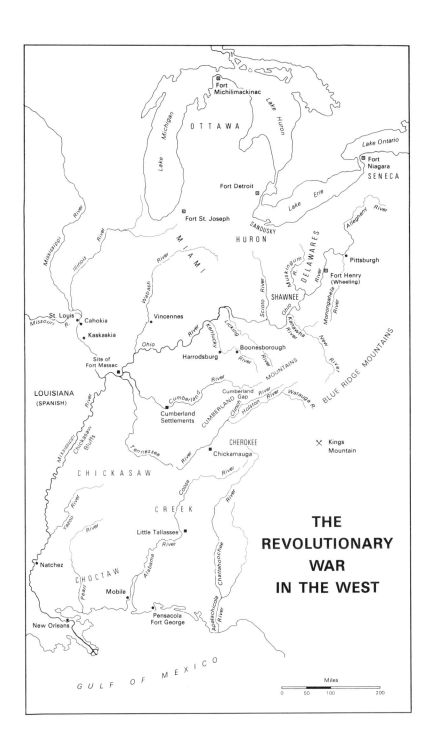

Fort Michilimackinac

OTTAWA

Lake Michigan

Lake Huron

Lake Ontario

Fort Niagara

SENECA

Fort Detroit

Lake Erie

Allegheny River

Fort St. Joseph

SANDUSKY

HURON

DELAWARES

Mississippi River

Illinois River

MIAMI

Wabash River

Muskingum R.

Scioto River

Pittsburgh

Fort Henry (Wheeling)

SHAWNEE

Ohio River

Monongahela River

Missouri R.

St. Louis

Cahokia

Kaskaskia

Vincennes

Ohio River

Kentucky River

Licking River

Boonesborough

Harrodsburg

Kanawha River

New River

BLUE RIDGE MOUNTAINS

Site of Fort Massac

LOUISIANA (SPANISH)

Mississippi River

Cumberland River

Cumberland Gap

Clinch River

Holston River

Watauga R.

MOUNTAINS

CUMBERLAND

Cumberland Settlements

Tennessee River

Chickasaw Bluffs

CHICKASAW

Chickamauga

CHEROKEE

River

Coosa River

Kings Mountain

CREEK

Yazoo River

Natchez

Little Tallassee

Alabama River

River

Chattahoochee River

CHOCTAW

Pearl River

Mobile

Pensacola Fort George

Apalachicola River

New Orleans

GULF OF MEXICO

THE REVOLUTIONARY WAR IN THE WEST

Miles

0   50   100   200

Wabash River bottoms to capture both the town and Hamilton, who turned out on closer acquaintance to be friendly and personable. Governor Henry had hoped Clark could take Detroit as well,[33] but neither supplies nor reinforcements could be had, and the Congress advised Virginia to use its little western force for Indian fighting only.[34] By 1780, Virginia was on the defensive on Kentucky soil again. The last western fighting beyond Kentucky was the successful defense of St. Louis against a badly organized British-led Indian attack in May 1780.

Thus no military decision was reached in the Old Northwest, but Clark's campaigns let Kentucky and Tennessee survive. The presence of British officers with Indian raiders left a legacy of hatred of Britain in those parts which lasted for generations. In the Old Southwest there were fierce Indian wars in 1777 and 1778. The Cherokee and Chickamauga, prodded to attack by the British, were crushed by frontier armies and ceded millions of acres as reparation for living where white men wished to live.

As for the British regulars, except for predatory raids on New England coastal towns they concentrated on the South. Georgia had been lax in recruiting. The militia seemed weak, and loyalist help seemed probable. A British amphibious operation took Savannah with little trouble at the end of 1778. As hoped, loyalists flocked to return to allegiance, and by accepting restoration of royal government Georgia became the only state of the union to relapse to colonial status. Georgia had been a dead weight on the rebellion because of poverty, and the Congress had put up nearly $2 million from its meager treasury to pay for running Georgia's war effort. But it had value to Britain as a source of food which otherwise would have been sent to the French allies in the West Indies, as a base for attacks against Charleston, and as a buffer to protect the Floridas. It seemed unlikely that American soldiers, without foreign naval help, could recover Georgia.[35] The British had opened a second front, and the war had taken a new turn.

The Continental Army with Washington had wintered at Morristown, New Jersey, under conditions as bad as those of Valley Forge, and in colder weather. Washington remained on the defensive in 1779, partly because Sullivan's operation against the Iroquois soaked up most of the country's military resources. The chief eastern operation was a counter-attack against a British seizure of Stony Point on the Hudson. General Anthony Wayne's men took it on the night of July 16–17, using bayonets only, but could not afford to hold it for long. Nevertheless, this spasm of American energy discouraged Clinton from going ahead with a plan to stamp out rebellion in New Jersey. And the Congress got a lift. Among the stimulating results of the storm of Stony Point was the capture of the colors of His Majesty's Seventeenth Regiment of Foot which were brought and displayed to the delegates ten days later. (The Congress refused to give the flag to the French officer who had gone along for the adventure and had lowered the colors himself.)[36]

In the north the elusive Continental Army not only proved hard to discourage but showed remarkable recuperative power at every season of the war.

C H A P T E R

14

Backward at Home,
Forward Abroad, 1779-1780

All British attempts to talk conciliation with the rebels had failed. The Howe mission of 1776 and the Carlisle mission of 1778 could not open official negotiations for the Ministry. Equally unsuccessful were unofficial feelers, such as John Burgoyne's early attempt to talk with Charles Lee at Boston Neck, and an invitation to the Congress from Richard and William Howe to visit Charles Lee in captivity in New York in the winter of 1776–1777. A Quaker merchant named John Brown went to York, Pennsylvania, in November 1777 to talk with Congressmen, but found himself in jail and then on the road home.[1] Every British mediator or sympathizer bogged down in the morass of Continental administration, which was almost government by buck-passing, and ended at "the usual blank obstruction."[2] All British attempts at pacification were futile and frustrating. Those Americans who were approached diverted applicants to the Congress, which said it would talk only when Britain recognized independence or withdrew its armed forces. But then came rumors of the Spanish intervention in the quarrel, and the advice of French Minister Conrad Alexandre Gérard, early in 1779, that the Congress draft its peace aims, just in case. We have looked at the outlines of the political fight that followed; let us now fill in the outline with the substance.

The drafting of possible peace terms began amiably enough with a cheerful dinner to celebrate the first anniversary of the French alliance, complete with the usual thirteen toasts (and a tab for $1,086).[3] Within three weeks the delegates had a committee report covering everything hoped for. It began with the requirements of independence and the withdrawal of British arms, then set minimum boundaries, insisted on fishing rights on the Grand Banks and the coasts of Newfoundland, required free navigation of the Mississippi River to the southern boundary and free commerce in some port below that point, and asked for the annexation of Nova Scotia if the allies agreed. (The Congress, in debate, struck out the reference to Nova Scotia and the insistence on the free use of a Spanish port on the Mississippi below the Florida boundary.) The first draft had some nonessentials which could be used for bargaining, including clauses on the East Indies, the slave trade, American colonizing outside the borders of the United States, the ultimate disposal of Florida if it fell to the United States, and details of cooperation with Spain if Spain entered the war. After the matter of independence, the boundaries were most important: the United States was to include all that lay between the Atlantic Ocean, the Mississippi River, Canada, and Florida.[4]

While there were things here that might not please France or Spain, one might expect reasonably swift adoption of the report by Americans. But no. The Congress had to spend more than six months on this document, not because of any ideological split but because of sectionalism and, equally important, because its appearance coincided with the Deane-Lee convulsion, which became a quarrel between what later observers call the Gallican and anti-Gallican factions.[5] It is also possible that well-informed delegates felt there was no urgency. John Adams had sent back word in late 1778 that British politicians could no longer safely oppose the war and that Britain would not leave America unless "driven or starved out. . . ."[6] James Lovell, six months later, wrote of "imagined Propositions of . . . a *doubtful* Event. . . ."[7]

The Sacred Cod of New England was a major character in this masque. The French were nervous about fishing because they too had Grand Banks interests, and every nation then thought its fishing fleet was the nursery of its naval manpower. New Englanders feared a French plot to do them out of their valued industry. If they had known of French promises to support *Spanish* claims, the fight would have been fiercer. The Yankees, mostly anti-Gallicans, wanted every fishing right and privilege that could be dreamed of, and argued about fish from February to mid-August in what may have been the roughest floor fight in the history of the Continental Congress. In July they managed to write in a clause that provided automatic war if the British bothered American fishermen in the future, ever. As early as March, men who wished an early end to this bickering asked Gérard to warn the Congress that France might have to make the best peace it could alone, if the Congress did not agree. But Gérard feared this threat would give the Americans an excuse for a separate peace of their own.[8] The fish faction became so heated in the matter that they even tried to write in clauses to guarantee fishing in all North American waters, including Hudson Bay. Finally, in August, they agreed not to make fishing an invincible necessity in the instructions,[9] but they receded only because they intended to put a reliable fish man in charge of negotiating any treaty.

The question of navigation on the Mississippi actually took more time than the fisheries, but never provoked so warm a quarrel. The question waited upon the end of the fishing disputes. It was a delicate matter in which the Americans might alienate the Spaniards, and at the end of September the Congress arrived at a problematic solution: if Spain conquered Florida, the United States would guarantee Florida if the Americans could have free navigation to the Gulf.

Minister Gérard was much troubled by the long battle over hypothetical peace terms, because it seemed to him that it was simply a toe-to-toe slugging match between Gallicans and anti-Gallicans. In reality it was partly the expression of an acrid antipathy between the believers in Silas Deane and the believers in Arthur Lee, and partly a sectional battle. The Southern states had some territorial concerns, but they seemed as well taken care of as possible while the Yankees felt no assurance whatsoever about the future of their fishing industry. Thus the Southern states were willing to see an earlier end to the war than was desired by the New England men, who wished to fight until they got what they thought they must have.

While keeping track of congressional maneuvering, and trying to influence its thinking without provoking offense, Minister Gérard had to take care of French commercial affairs, arrange supplies for the visiting French naval force, keep up with his Spanish opposite number in Philadelphia, propagandize for the glory of France, see to it that his kitchen did not disgrace Louis XVI, give military advice to the Congress when it was acceptable, and cheer on the Americans to fight their own war as much as possible. He may be excused for not being able to see clearly through the clouds of gassy rhetoric that enveloped the Congress, where every local material interest and advantage was wrapped in the new red, white, and blue starry banner, or deduced from some eternal, immutable, and divine principle.

Gérard found the American climate uncomfortable and his labors exhausting. He asked repeatedly to be relieved of his assignment in Philadelphia. The French Foreign Ministry granted his request, and sent a successor, the Chevalier Anne de la Luzerne, who arrived in September 1779. Le Sieur Conrad Alexandre Gérard seems to have been a weary success. He had friends in all parts of the United States, and the Congress ordered a full length oil portrait of him for hanging in its assembly hall (Lafayette was the only other foreigner so honored). There were many expressions of regret at his departure, and he could be satisfied with his work even if he left still somewhat puzzled by the place of the codfish in world affairs.

Before Gérard could leave, he and the Congress were caught up in the struggle to name a negotiator for this hypothetical peace. The anti-Gallicans or Deane-despisers, or codfish faction, wished Arthur Lee. To get him, they simply announced that the French Court and Gérard loved Lee dearly. Gérard, like a butterfly impaled on a pin, first tried to flutter loose by saying he had never expressed an opinion of Lee. Lee's friends threatened to call Gérard before the Congress to give him the opportunity to express an opinion, but Gérard warded this attack by showing to two members a statement from Vergennes that neither Vergennes nor the Spanish Court trusted Lee. A copy of this statement found its way to the table of the Congress. The anti-Lee delegates rid themselves of the Lee incubus by prompt insistence that the Congress now vote for envoys. After several ballots John Jay was chosen to go to Spain, John Adams (a safely fishy man) to go to France as negotiator of any peace, and Lee was left unemployed. This was the substance of Gérard's last report. It had not been easy. Both Adams and Jay were nominated to be negotiator of the peace, and neither had a majority after three ballots. The sending of Jay to Madrid was a compromise to break the deadlock.[10] Jay was the president of the Congress, and was now succeeded in that job by Samuel Huntington of Connecticut.

While getting ready to return to France, Adams received instructions to govern himself by the terms of the French alliance, by the advice of the French Court, by his knowledge of American interests, and by his own discretion. John Adams being the man he was, he would put a rather high value on his knowledge of American interests and on his discretion. He knew American interests, but he was *not* discreet. To anticipate a bit, there was really nothing for him to do about negotiating a peace when he arrived in Paris, so he poked into French affairs and offended Vergennes. In the long run this did not hurt the United States at all, but, as we shall see, it wrecked the friendship of John Adams and Benjamin Franklin.

II

Although the Continental cause seemed to prosper abroad, regress had set in at home. The French naval commander in American waters, Comte Jean d'Estaing, sailed in November 1778 for the West Indies, where the French and British had been swapping islands by force. After temporarily tipping the scale in France's favor, he steered for Georgia in September 1779 to help dislodge its conquerors.

After taking Savannah late in 1778, the British had things pretty much their own way in Georgia, and raided threateningly toward Charleston. Franklin hoped "General Fever" would help the rebel cause, but the occupation forces remained healthy. General Benjamin Lincoln was to cooperate with d'Estaing in 1779 in the hope of retaking Savannah, which would mean the recovery of all of Georgia. This operation was so thoroughly compromised by loose talk that Washington advised the Congress to clear the air by announcing it in a proclamation.[11]

The Franco-American force appeared at Savannah early in October, 1779, so confident that its leaders even argued whether the garrison should surrender to King Louis or to the Congress. D'Estaing summoned the British to surrender. They asked for a day to think it over, during which they energetically fortified their position and then said "no." The assault was a failure, and cost the life of Count Casimir Pulaski. The local guerrilla leader Francis Marion exclaimed, "My God! Who ever heard of anything like this before? First allow an enemy to entrench, and then fight him!"[12] The British had few casualties, but the attackers lost nearly eleven hundred dead.

Congressmen in Philadelphia showed no shock at the news—at least not in correspondence.[13] There was some military change, however, for the threat to Georgia had led the British to evacuate Newport so as not to be spread too thinly. On the loss side, as yet unknown, was the sending of Continental frigates which holed up in Charleston like mice in a humane trap, because they were too late to help at Savannah. Five days after the bad news from Savannah, the new French minister, the Chevalier Anne de la Luzerne, had his formal audience with the Congress. President Samuel Huntington mentioned the "prosperous course of the campaign," but he must have been speaking of diplomacy, not war.[14]

The situation in North America at the end of 1779 was much the same as at the beginning of the year. Now began the Southern inland rebel guerrilla warfare that made the fame of such leaders as Marion, Thomas Sumter, and Andrew Pickens. D'Estaing cleared for Europe, leaving Clinton free to use the coastal waters to ferry seven thousand men south for further operations. Washington saw the omens as unfavorable, and anticipated British conquest of all of Georgia and South Carolina, "both of which are so weak as to be in no small danger." Benjamin Lincoln had told him he expected little reinforcement.[15] Clinton arrived in South Carolina waters early in 1780 and did not repeat his mistake of the naval assault of 1776. This time he landed nearby and enveloped Charleston from the land side. Lincoln had time to escape from the trap but chose to submit to siege. He was the only northerner in the force; for a Yankee to abandon Charleston without a fight could have bad political effects. Beginning in March 1780 there were rumors that Britain would offer independence to the eleven other states in return for keeping Georgia and South Carolina.

The suspense began to mount, and reflected itself in the attitudes and fears of the members of the Congress.[16] Then, early in June, came the crashing bad news that Lincoln had surrendered Charleston, himself, his army, his naval force, everything, on May 12. The disaster quite obscured the Spanish triumph at Mobile at the same time. The

British had taken five thousand men (of whom two thousand were Continental regulars), three generals, three hundred pieces of artillery, two frigates with all their guns, and a great quantity of military stores. This was a greater loss than Burgoyne's and was to be matched in the history of United States arms only by Julius White's surrender at Harpers Ferry in 1862, the Bataan debacle of 1942, and the surrender of the 106th Division in 1944 in the Battle of the Bulge.

Charles Thomson, orphan boy, merchant, classical scholar, secretary of the Continental Congress, and the most rebellious of Philadelphia rebels, blamed the calamity on the poverty of the Congress, which had enough time but not enough money to help Lincoln. (The movement which led to the writing of the Constitution began within a year of the Charleston catastrophe.) Some American leaders thought they had lost the lower South forever, because they feared the rumored offer of independence, excluding Georgia and South Carolina, would be acceptable. To stop this kind of talk the Congress resolved (June 23) "That the said report is insidious and utterly void of foundation," and went on to promise perseverance. Perseverance had already started with the appointment of Horatio Gates, the victor of the north, to succeed the captured Lincoln.[17] As for Lincoln, he was released on parole and went to Philadelphia to ask for a court to sit in judgment of him. The Congress agreed to his request, but Washington said he could not arrange an inquiry with propriety until Lincoln was exchanged. The exchange did not occur until November, by which time the matter had been forgotten.[18]

The year 1780 was a gloomy year. The decline of public spirit showed itself in the vexations which buffeted Governor Thomas Jefferson of Virginia: militia mutinies, desertions, tax evasions, refusal to sell military supplies, and the unhappy condition of troops in Virginia, without arms, ammunition, tents, blankets, horses, or shoes. Inflation spiraled upward like smoke on a calm day; money appropriated by the legislature was practically worthless before it could be spent. Virginia regulars and Virginia militia found each other intolerable.[19] But no responsible leader in the United States showed any inclination to surrender, even though there was no light on the road ahead.

The war was going so badly in 1780 (after the most severe winter in the meteorological history of the United States) that the Charleston disaster may have been a disguised benefit. It sounded an alarm of crisis which revitalized those Americans who had fallen into apathy after six years of war. There were setbacks to come, but the Charleston surrender was the lowest ebb in the tide of the whole war. It certainly energized the Congress, which poured forth a stream of resolutions, all designed to concenter the country's strength on recovering the South.[20]

The only reason for cheerfulness was the news brought from France late in April by young Gilbert du Motier, Marquis de Lafayette, that France was sending an honest-to-goodness army to North America. The Congress became taut and nervous at the need to make a good showing in the presence of such an authentic regular force. Incidentally the British in America had the news before the Congress got it, and Minister Luzerne knew the British knew. He urged the Congress to send an executive committee to confer with Washington, something Washington himself had already invited.

Six thousand "French" soldiers came in mid-July, and with them ten ships of the line. (About a third of the "French" were German-speaking.) Jean Comte de Rochambeau commanded the force. Some of the delegates were embarrassed at the state of the American union at the moment. As one said, ". . . I fear it will serve only to reflect disgrace on us and render us unworthy of their notice in future. . . ."[21] The French expeditionary force rendezvoused in Narragansett Bay, where the Royal Navy promptly bottled it up for about a year. This has been regretted, but it may have been for the best since the Americans were certainly unready for any large-scale operations. The Congress had set money quotas on all the states except Virginia, South Carolina, and Georgia, which obviously had enough trouble already, and hoped to get up $10 million in thirty days. More realistically, the delegates also drew bills on Franklin and Jay in Europe for $25,000, to be hawked in six states. This was a reluctant step, but the crisis was great.

When the French arrived, the congressional committee to visit the Army could only report to the Congress that some states had not answered their mail. Unofficially some delegates had learned that a few states had decided not to fill up their Regular Army units to their paper strength, and there was even some desperate private correspondence urging that Washington be made politically omnipotent as the only solution. But most states gave assurances that they were at work on getting up their shares, and, in addition, the Army had enough to eat at present (though no assurances of future bread and meat). These slight promises as usual buoyed the Congress up to the unwarrantable optimism that had all along kept the war going, and which would win it in the end.

While the French lazed in Narragansett Bay and the Congress lived on hope, news came in September that a second French squadron had been blocked in Brest and would not come. Washington abandoned plans for any 1780 campaign and sent his militiamen home to save their pay. Their enlistments would expire, anyway, before he could use them in battle.

The new French commanding general was a good man for the job. Rochambeau had been on the verge of retiring in 1779 when he received his command. It was a good choice for this kind of war, which required his personal qualities of tranquility, honesty, and firmness. Furthermore, his men trusted his judgment, which is the first requirement for the maintenance of morale. Lafayette had wished the command for himself, often disagreed with Rochambeau's strategy, and did nothing to build up his superior in Washington's eyes, but Rochambeau's even temper kept Lafayette in his place without embarrassment and without unhinging the cooperation of the two armies once they were free to operate jointly.

III

For reasons only remotely connected with the American Revolution, the Russian government of Catherine the Great began to interest itself actively in the world war in the summer of 1780. The Russians hardly knew the United States existed, but they had plenty of knowledge of Great Britain, France, Spain, and all points between.

Vergennes worked hard after 1775 to persuade the monarchs of Europe not to tolerate British bullying on the high seas but to insist forcibly upon the rights of neutrals. Czarina Catherine founded a League of Armed Neutrality on March 9, 1780, and followed it in December with an offer to the French to mediate the war. She was not a whit concerned with the political aspirations of the Americans, but she was angry at the treatment of neutrals by both Spain and Britain. While blockading Gibraltar the Spaniards had taken all neutral ships in the vicinity, including some Russian merchant vessels which Vergennes got back for her, and the Czarina also resented the British unfriendliness toward the Dutch, whose neutral privileges had been profitable for Russian exporters. Thus her League was aimed at helping Russians and the customers of Russians. In politics the Russian interest lay in the ancient enmity with Turkey rather than in western Europe. The Armed Neutrality allowed Catherine to go it alone, free of the influence of foreign powers, their ministers, and their ambassadors. She had a grand contempt for her "Brother George" of Great Britain, but she carefully avoided recognizing his rebellious American subjects. The advantage of the Armed Neutrality was to guarantee that foreign ships could come to Russian ports to pick up cargos which bulked greater than the small Russian merchant marine could handle.

Three principles of the Armed Neutrality coincided with the Plan of 1776 of the Continental Congress: (1) neutrals could trade from port to port of belligerents; (2) enemy goods which were not contraband of war became free goods in neutral ships (contraband was defined only as arms and military supplies); and (3) to blockade a port a blockader must make it physically hazardous to enter, not merely issue a parchment declaration closing a port.

The Armed Neutrality of 1780 was an illuminating example of the interweaving of European interests which were the background of the War for Independence, but by 1780 the war was a world war and the United States was peripheral to the relations of Britain and Russia. Nevertheless, the United States immediately tried to join the League of Armed Neutrality, though hardly qualifying as neutral. News of the Armed Neutrality came as good news to America, and the Congress ordered its Board of Admiralty to draft instructions to the United States armed public ships to conform to the League's principles.[22] Then the delegates voted to send Francis Dana as minister to St. Petersburg to tell the Czarina that the Congress accepted the plan of the Armed Neutrality, and, if possible, to negotiate treaties of alliance and of amity and commerce, as much like the Franco-American treaties as possible.[23] Dana went, but the Russians ignored him.

The Congress was neither naive nor eccentric. *If* the United States could pull off this diplomatic *coup* it would amount to further legal recognition of the United States as a member of the family of nations. It was not an impossible gamble that Russia might recognize the United States as part of Russia's program of protecting Dutch carriers. And if that came to pass, the Netherlands might also recognize the United States. Russia had shown a determination to protect Dutch shipping against Britain. Dutch shipping helped the United States. Russian policy therefore might work out to the advantage of the United States. John Adams, the unemployed peacemaker, had left Paris for The Hague, where he was trying to borrow money for the Congress. Adams, no fool, thought Russian and Dutch recognition were worth trying for, and the Congress authorized him to agree to the terms of the League. But in the end the League ignored the United States in order to preserve its own pristine neutrality.

The Dutch had their troubles with Britain, what with carrying freight for Britain's enemies and appearing to help John Paul Jones. And then an Amsterdam banker and William Lee, both private citizens acting on their own, drafted a treaty of commerce which each hoped to have his country ratify. A British spy got a copy, his superiors thought it official, and the Royal Navy began being so beastly to the Dutch that the Netherlands found itself directly engaged in the spreading war by the end of 1780.[24] The Dutch had the only non-British surplus of saltpeter, and also sold steel and gunpowder to the Americans for tobacco or on credit. These supplies had gone via the Dutch West Indies. Thus a war with the Netherlands was useful to Britain in the short run. Sixteen months after the Anglo-Dutch war began, The Hague publicly accepted John Adams as the United States minister, though the United States had maintained a secret agent there, one Charles W. F. Dumas, at two hundred *louis* a year since 1778.[25]

At the end of 1780 Great Britain was formally at war with France, Spain, the Netherlands, and the United States. The Russians had organized a league of Russia, Denmark, Sweden, the Netherlands, and Portugal to protect neutral rights. (The Netherlands was no longer a neutral, and Portugal could not really be thought generally hostile to Britain.)

In the beginning the Dutch would not have been thought natural enemies of Britain, since about half of the British public debt was owned by Dutchmen as late as 1777, and Dutch bankers initially refused loans to the Americans. As late as 1780 commentators were sure the Dutch would do nothing to hurt Britain.[26] Actually, when once in the war, the Dutch hurt the British less than when they were neutral, because they were not strong enough to shoot their way to America through the Royal Navy. The entry of the Dutch gave a psychological lift to the Americans,[27] and they had been the first to salute the new United States flag, but that was the sum of the gain to America.

No other European nations openly joined the cause against Great Britain. Portugal, despite nominal membership in the Armed Neutrality, was so helpful to the British that the Congress spiritedly offered to help Spain conquer Portugal in return for a treaty of alliance. The Swedes helped the French and Americans by increasing their exports to the western hemisphere 2,400 per cent in the years 1777–1783, but, though Swedes served in the French, Dutch, and Spanish forces, about fifty officers also served in the Royal Navy until the Anglo-French war began. Then they resigned rather than fight the French, which shows their sympathies lay with France and no other foreign power.[28] King George was Elector of Hannover, but American ships twice managed to get cargos out of the Electorate because of the rundown condition of the local artillery. North German trade with America grew as did the Swedish; eighty ships from Hamburg and Altona in 1775, 190 in 1779.[29]

All in all, the British bore a heavy burden. For generations past (and to come) British policy had been to avoid maritime war unless a continental ally was available to restrain the French from putting all their resources into seafighting. Now the policy had been abandoned, and Britain had to spend much energy in defense of the West Indies. All the world seemed anti-British excepting Portugal. It was not quite all the world, but it was the world of nations that had three things in common: they were trading nations, they had imperial outlooks, and they were tired of Britannia's rule of the North Atlantic Ocean. (Portugal met these standards too, but Portugal feared Spain more than Britain.)

Great Britain also had some alarming domestic distractions. The years 1779–1780 were critical. Despite the foreign threats, the government could get cooperation on some important matters only from its sycophants. It dealt ineffectively both with America and with Ireland. Except for the accidental help of epidemic diseases among the enemy, the country might well have been invaded in 1779. Most of King George's limited imagination was applied to schemes to keep his reluctant, loyal, and incompetent Cabinet together. In eight days of June in 1780, the Gordon Riots against the toleration of Catholics caused eight hundred deaths by violence. This may have been temporary good luck for the Crown, for when the King dared an election the reaction in favor of law and order gave the government a six-vote majority, at a cost in election expenses of 103,000 pounds. This was called a mandate to carry on as before, and all idea of peace was cast aside.[30] The government's optimism was absurdly illustrated by the remark of a ranking Englishman to a French visitor that England would recognize American independence only when France captured the Tower of London, and England would only trade Gibraltar for Madrid.

But the British Empire was in deep trouble. When the French and the Americans threatened to command the waters off the east coast of North America and the West Indies, the British had to weaken the home fleet to defend the West Indies, and with this strategy they had to hazard Gibraltar, the American "colonies," and the rich, sweet trade of the West Indies. We must be humble and admit that in the late eighteenth century the West Indies were more important in European eyes than the continent of North America. It is a tenable hypothesis (remaining to be tested) that the United States won its independence because the French threat required a great diversion of energy and treasure to the West Indies.

By 1780, philosophy seems to have been playing a minor role in the War for Independence. Most minds had been made up by that time. Ideological propaganda filled provincial newspapers, but power politics, bayonet drill, and gunnery practice occupied more attention. At this stage of the war the only way the American rebels could have been kept in the British Empire was by skilled persuasion, friendly cajolery, magnificent concessions, and magnanimous gestures. Such methods required personality traits wholly lacking in King George and in Lord North's Ministry.

15

The Worst of Times, 1780-1781

The surrender of Charleston by General Benjamin Lincoln in May 1780 marked the lowest ebb of the American military tide. The tide did not turn until after another disaster at Camden, South Carolina, on August 16. Needing a new commander in the Southern Department, the Congress turned to Horatio Gates, then senior officer at Boston where he spent his time politicking with Samuel Adams against John Hancock while "that Medusa his wife"[1] prodded him up the social ladder. Even before the bad news from Charleston, the Congress and George Washington had started the pitifully small reserve of fourteen hundred New Jersey and Delaware Continentals southward under Johann De Kalb. Gates joined them on July 25 in North Carolina. Washington would not have chosen Gates, since he had arrived at a settled dislike of the man by 1779, when he wrote of his "malevolence and opposition . . . little underhand intrigues . . . equivocal and designing manner. . . ."[2] Under Gates, De Kalb was to command the regulars while Gates tried to extract militia and supplies from the governments of the Southern states. This was an unpromising assignment, as De Kalb was already short of rations and getting little cooperation from the civil authorities.[3] By the time Gates joined his command, it was in trouble. Roads were poor, farms were few, and the addition of militia worsened the supply problem.

The British had collected supplies and troops at Camden on the main road from Charleston to the interior. As Gates's force neared, Charles Lord Cornwallis moved his troops to surprise Gates, and Gates moved to surprise the British. When they met, Gates's militia made a poor showing, and the Continentals were practically wiped out. De Kalb died of several wounds (but of none in the back). Gates put all blame on the militia: "They ran like a torrent and bore all before them."[4] The "torrent" bore Gates himself 180 miles to Hillsborough, North Carolina, a mileage which destroyed his reputation for valor. One of his friends said Gates had to hasten because he was unguarded in loyalist country, and only the North Carolina Assembly at Hillsborough could get him more men.[5] Washington and the Congress accepted the explanation that the militia caused the failure, but Gates was neither cleared by a court nor employed again. Bitter Dr. Benjamin Rush, who resented the glorification of Washington, said Gates ruined his reputation by beating Burgoyne, because it excited the envious who enjoyed his defeat at Camden.[6] Nathanael Greene succeeded to the Southern command.

While still depressed by the news from the South, the rebels had more bad news from the north: the defection of General Benedict Arnold. It had occurred to the British that gold might work where lead had failed.[7] Sir Henry Clinton and his aide Major John André both left lists of prospects; they listed Washington as untouchable, but, except for Arnold, the others they named probably were equally incorruptible.

It would be more pleasant to say that Arnold did it in a fit of understandable anger, but he negotiated on his sale for nearly a year and a half, and we must put him down as a money-hungry sorehead. Five brigadiers had been promoted over his head in 1777, on geographical distribution, a fact which he took as a slight. His use of public vehicles for private baggage, and some other questions, provoked an inquiry early in 1779 which discovered nothing important but the baggage matter and drew a mild reprimand. Arnold thus had another grievance.[8] He was so unpopular in Philadelphia[9] that he asked the Congress, in the fall of 1779, for an armed guard to protect him from Philadelphians.[10] Fed up, Arnold asked Washington for command of West Point, got it, drew $25,000 in back pay,[11] and left to sell the fort.

The Congress recommended fortifying West Point in 1775, and by 1779 it became the strategic base of the northern Continentals. Washington thought of four ways the British might try to take it, but did not think of purchase.[12] During the long negotiations with Arnold, Clinton feared an attack on New York City, for which West Point would be necessary to the Continentals. His fears were not groundless,[13] but the Congress could not supply the fortress properly in 1780, so the threat to Clinton's base was not a present danger.[14]

Arnold offered West Point for ten thousand guineas and a general's commission. André acted for Clinton in the business, and Clinton sent him to visit Arnold for final planning. Protected by Arnold's pass, André cloaked himself and crossed the American lines, but the ship which brought him had to lie downriver to escape American artillery fire, and André had to try to return overland. He put on a long blue coat, tucked the plans of West Point in his stocking, and set out for New York on horseback. Two days later an irregular patrol picked him up between the lines. When Arnold received the routine report of the detention of a suspected spy, he fled to New York City by water. Upon Arnold's unexplained flight, Washington hurried to West Point, fearing the British might attack it while "the wind is fair."[15]

But that was the end. A court of fourteen general officers (two of whom were European and knew the international customs of war) condemned André to death. As Steuben put it, he "confessed everything, but a premeditated design to deceive," and, "It is not possible to save him."[16] He was hanged on October 2, 1780, and is memorialized in Westminster Abbey.

The Congress impounded all papers relating to Arnold and then let the news out.[17] It was claimed that "many of his scandalous Transactions are brought to Light that were before concealed,"[18] and eagle-eyed hindsighters recalled many suspicious past circumstances.[19] Philadelphia, where the citizenry loved him least, burned Arnold in effigy with elaborate ceremony.[20] Benjamin Rush had shared lodgings with him and later said his language was "indelicate" and he had a vulgar accent.[21] Washington now discovered Arnold had always been "hackneyed in villainy. . . ."[22] These judgments were after the fact, but there is plenty of pre-1780 evidence of

Arnold's truculence and avarice, from fellow townsmen. After 1780 he may have been unhappy in his scarlet coat, but he was a fierce and ruthless combat general.

Arnold's corruption is really not surprising. It is more surprising that few succumbed in the same way. As for the Continental cause, things were not as gloomy as they seemed. Five days after the hanging of poor André there was a victory at King's Mountain (October 7, 1780) which marked the turn of the tide, but no one knew that yet.

I I

The military weakness of the Continental forces in the worst year, 1780, was not the result of British triumphs. The British victories came because of Continental impotence, which in turn was not the effect of any natural cause—as famine or plague—but of ineffective management. The American leaders were not stupid, but they were groping for a system. Lacking any real authority except in the state governments, the American effort was really thirteen efforts of varying enthusiasm, intelligence, and resources.

From Burgoyne's defeat in 1777 to the end of 1780, efficiency declined. After the unearned failure at Monmouth Court House in 1778, and the transfer of British troops to the West Indies and Georgia, Washington asked for a conference with the Congress to plan for 1779. (Private letters show the Congress had a higher regard for Washington than he had for the Congress.) The decision was to hold the defensive on the seaboard, because any eastern offensive based on the assumption the British would voluntarily quit impregnable New York must end in disaster if the British stayed in New York.

This was not a defeatist decision. It was from hunger. Of all American failures, the failure of this rich little country to supply the Army was the greatest. The story of supply shortage is too dreary to relate in detail; a short sketch will illustrate. The Congress wrote letters of requisition to the states which were to gather supplies in magazines. If the states cooperated, the Army lacked the transport to collect the stuff. The supply records verge on the ridiculous. The Board of War once met on the problem of supplying horses for dragoons, which sounds grave enough, but a reading of the minutes shows that the board was hoping to replace twelve horses killed in battle, triumphantly located seven available public animals, and solemnly urged the Congress to buy five more.[23]

Washington's force had enough grain to make five days' bread on St. Patrick's Day, 1780, and, if he were very "economical and scanty," he could make the pickled meat last for forty days. At the moment the comfortable farming state of Connecticut was not feeding its own regular regiments; in fact it had no state supply officer.[24] The shortage of horses and wagons was so great that Washington could not have gone into the field against the enemy; if the redcoats wanted a fight they would have to come to him. Early in May the troops were four months behind in their pay, which worsened the supply situation, since, in a pinch, a hungry but fully paid soldier could usually find a sutler or a neighboring farmer to sell him something to eat.[25] By late summer of 1780, Washington could only feed the Army by marching it from temporary camp to temporary camp, exhausting the food supply of the neighborhood instead of more properly drawing on the country as a whole. If this kept up the Army would become a horde of plunderers. It was at this point that Washington sent the militia home; obviously he would not be fighting soon. Even the press knew he was "pretty much pinched for Provisions."[26]

The condition of the private soldier in 1780 was probably the worst of the whole war. He had endured much. In the winter of 1780–1781 he was to show there were limits to his patience and resignation. To look ahead a bit, in May 1781 the northern troops were entirely out of meat and had but thirty-one barrels of flour; they could not get the supplies which were known to be in remote magazines; and the state provision buyers were not bringing in the beeves that had been requisitioned and that, unlike barrels of flour, could walk to the Army.[27]

Anyone who has heard soldiers talk about food will know that the Continental Army must have had a personnel problem. And it was not only food, but clothes and pay and shelter. The whole military problem was made harder by provincialism. State officials dearly loved militia because they were usually at the disposal of state governments and were rarely called to serve at Continental command. Washington firmly believed, while at Valley Forge, that Continental use of militia slowed the state officials' recruiting of regulars.[28] The Congress proposed an Army, but the states disposed their men as they saw fit. For example, early in 1779 the Congress authorized bounties for men who re-enlisted for the duration, and for new recruits, but rejected a statement discouraging state bounties paid for Continental enlistments as a hopeless proposition. Washington said Continental recruiting could not be helped by bounties unless state bounties were abolished.[29] The point was that the Congress should pay bounties for *duration* enlistments and re-enlistments *after* the states had thrust the men into the Army for a year, bountyless. If both states and the Congress paid bounties, the one to get them into the Army, the other to keep them, the expense would be ruinous. What was wanted was temporary state recruiting without bounties, then congressional bounties for permanently signing on. After digesting Washington's views, the Congress fixed the Army at eighty regiments, apportioned among the states by population, ranging from fifteen from Massachusetts down to one each from Delaware and Georgia. How easy to raise an army on paper, but how hard in reality. As Washington told the Congress, men could be encouraged by bounties or they could be forcibly drafted. If he was to take the offensive, the Congress could use both methods. For defense the bounty would be enough, except that state bounties weakened Continental recruiting for permanency. He would still like to have a Continental bounty only, and have the state bounties abolished.

On reflection, the Congress tried to meet his wishes by providing a bounty of $200 for enlistment or re-enlistment (for the duration) after January 23, 1779, with the money to go to the state if the state had already paid such an amount. This might tranquilize state politicians, but it surely was no inducement to the enlisted man. Nevertheless, the new rule went out in the mail with an earnest exhortation to state officials to get their men up in time for use in 1779, for, if they did, the next successful campaign would end the war.

It did not work. The Army was supposed to get two thousand men from Massachusetts; it got 875 by the following August. From Connecticut came a mighty handful of twenty. Only one state, New York, had produced a substantial number, and they were out west with John Sullivan, engaging the Iroquois. Meanwhile, the Army was so short of food that if the militia flocked in to make up the manpower shortage there would not be enough to eat. If the militia did not come there would not be enough men for battle. If the British in New York City sallied forth, Washington implied, they could only be repulsed by hungry militia.[30]

Washington tried again. He suggested an annual draft which would place the men with the Army by January 1 each year. Then the officers would try to persuade them to re-enlist for the duration, for the previously authorized bounty. This would work only if the state bounties disappeared, but nothing came of the proposal.

By January 1780 the Congress was so broke it proposed to discharge the men whose enlistments were to expire in April and cut the table of organization back to sixty regiments. The French minister frowned at this and asked the Congress what its maximum strength might be figured at. The Congress thought it could keep 25,000 regulars in the field, plus all militia wanted, if the states would tax themselves and if Americans would buy United States treasury notes to pay the Army. (But taxes and domestic loans were not to be had.)

Four months later Washington said the Army would have dissolved long before except for patriotism, and the Congress could not rely on this cement forever.[31] And three months later he wrote that all combat responsibility must be the Continental Army's, and the Army was too small. This must be made clear to the state governments which had trusted too much in militia.[32] He had not received a single state draft by mid-1780, nor as many as two hundred recruits from all states north of the Mason-Dixon line.[33] He was supposed to have 16,540 men with him; he had 6,143, which was barely enough to defend his position without thinking of offense. Meanwhile, the Army lived from day to day by impressing food from the neighbors.[34] By September, Washington's letters to the Congress almost visibly show him shrugging his shoulders. Half his men would be leaving in a few months. "The honor of the Congress and the States as well as my own reputation, forbid me to enter into engagements, which I have no assurance of our being able to fulfil."[35] This somewhat delphic sentence meant he was making no military plans at all.

The officers also pressed some grievances, most of which seem legitimate. For example, in the beginning every major general was to have an aide with the rank of major. As time passed these aides discovered they were frozen in grade and pay. By late 1779 they petitioned the Congress to notice their immobility. The roster of signatures of these young men contains some names which later achieved distinction[36] (they were ultimately emancipated by the Congress and free to float upward as talent might deserve). On the other hand, some officers seem to have begun to abandon a republican simplicity of dress, since the Congress found it necessary to prohibit gold lace, silver lace, and embroidery as well as the wearing of parts of British officers' uniforms, though superiors might permit badges to distinguish officers from enlisted men.[37] Finally, the generals made a plea, pointing out that previous respectful petitions for redress of various grievances had been ignored. They reviewed their own complaints, of which the greatest was that inflation had made their salaries worthless. This petition bore the signatures of Greene, Lord Stirling, Alexander McDougall, Von Steuben, Henry Knox, Edward Hand, William Irving, Anthony Wayne, and Robert Howe, and the endorsement of Gilbert du Motier, Marquis de Lafayette.[38] A good deal more would be heard on this point, and not only from generals.

Given the best will and intelligence in the world, the Congress could not have done much better within the limits of the republic as then shaped. Committees studied and reported, other committees tried to implement, and state legislatures acted or slept, as they chose. The Congress was contentious and long-winded, puzzled by strange financial and diplomatic problems, and its membership rotated rapidly—for example, in 1779 alone there was a 50 per cent turnover. It moved with the speed of cooling lava. To illustrate, Washington's November proposals of 1779 for the campaign of 1780 became committee reports by mid-December, and led to resolutions that the states fill their quotas by February 1, 1780. Of course there was no sanction to support the resolution, and, as we have seen, the men did not appear.

The military problems of the war permanently affected Washington's political philosophy. When the Congress asked him, early in 1780, to tell the states how many regulars each had in the field, he replied that he had sent them the facts the previous November. If he repeated the process, the states which waited on the new figures before acting would not have men in the field in time to be of use. After all, some states were quite remote, and some legislatures might not be in session when his figures arrived.[39] The Congress, as if sensing explosive possibilities, sent a small committee to confer with its annoyed general. When the committee arrived, Washington was dissatisfied because it lacked executive authority. Not until the end of April 1780 did a new committee with power to act arrive at his headquarters. Its members were Philip Schuyler of New York, John Mathews of South Carolina, and Nathaniel Peabody of New Hampshire.

There was no quick improvement, and even the French minister began to fret. Anne de la Luzerne asked the Congress just how it was backing up its earlier resolutions. The Congress responded to his prodding by passing several more resolutions which called on the states to comply with earlier resolutions. If the states could be roused this would rouse them, but they remained dormant. About the only useful power the Congress had in mid-1780 was the power to borrow money abroad.

From March to August of 1780 the Congress constantly planned and replanned the Quartermaster Department in contradictory ways, none of which worked. Nathanael Greene resigned as quartermaster general in a waspish note which angered the Congress to the point where there were proposals to dismiss this first-rate combat commander from the Army. But passion cooled, and the authentically third-rate Colonel Timothy Pickering became quartermaster general in August. By this time, of the congressional committee at Army headquarters only one delegate remained, John Mathews, and he was reprimanded for too much zeal. His response was a hot letter telling the Congress to forget punctilio and get moving. The Congress, sensitive of its dignity, fired the committee by a vote of 10 to 2, and Mathews on resuming his seat found himself rather unpopular.

What saved the cause, despite the paralysis of the Continental Army, was that Clinton believed Washington could always oppose him with ten thousand men if the British moved out of New York. Therefore Clinton confined himself to raiding and tried no large offensive, while his naval counterparts kept the French blockaded in Newport.

Washington analyzed the American difficulties in a manner portentous for the future of the United States. He thought little of a nation with thirteen heads. Each state was careful not to outdo any other.[40] The weakness of the Army prolonged the war, because, if the Army were well organized, the enemy would become discouraged. But the Army's fluctuations of strength encouraged the other side. The solution was to put all military effort directly under the Congress. Every other policy had failed, and the Continental Army was becoming thirteen armies. Each state treated its regulars differently, and this alone was cause for concern.[41] It would really be better if the Continental Army were either thirteen armies or one army, but sometimes it was a mixture of both kinds. Washington had tried to make it a national army but found it politically very hard. "After the States have brought their Troops into the Field, the less they have to do with them or their supplies . . . the bettr. it will be for the commn. Interest. . . ."[42] That was a private comment to an ex-general in the Congress. For two years the Congress had been declining in Washington's esteem, though he still held to his republicanism. He had an abstract respect for the civil authority of the Congress, but his respect no longer extended to persons.[43] In the frustrating years 1778–1780 he learned a great deal about practical politics in a republic, and came to the conclusion that the republic of the United States of America was defectively organized. He had a belly-full of states' rights.

The year 1780 would have been a good year for an American Caesar or Bonaparte. If he had the force at Washington's disposal, and received the treatment Washington and his men received, he could easily have found means and reasons to set up a military dictatorship. Here was a constitutional crisis of the first order which passed off without detonation, simply because Washington was who he was. (In a similar crisis in 1861 the republican ideal again survived only because of the personality of the man who did not choose to subvert it.) It seems safe to say that the events of 1780 made George Washington a confirmed nationalist and led inexorably to his presidency of the Constitutional Convention and to his inauguration as President of the United States. His self-restraint was the only obstacle to earlier aggrandizement.

It was the structure of polity that was wrong, not the intent. The Congress—to avoid political euphemisms—was a beggar institution. With no certain source of revenue, it had devalued the dollar to two and a half cents in March 1780, wiping out much paper debt but, of course, bringing in no legal tender. That same month a motion to ask the states to allow their mendicant Congress to levy a duty of 1 per cent on imports and exports got two votes in the North Carolina delegation, and one delegate vote each from New Hampshire, New Jersey, and Maryland. In June the Congress did adopt a resolution hinting that the states might give the Congress larger powers, voting probably as a response to Washington's impatience. A reasonable man could believe the United States was becoming disunited.

The Congress could do little but plan, which may be the reason it was earlier than usual with the annual plan for the following year (1781, in this instance). On October 3, 1780, the Congress adopted its program for the next season of war. The states were to fill up their quotas with men for the duration, or at least for one year. Since the money economy had broken down entirely, the states received quotas of supplies in kind, and might choose to contribute money or supplies. For example, a quota of 299,999 gallons of rum was distributed among the states (it is hard to avoid speculating on the reason for omitting that last gallon). If the states taxed themselves the plan would work. If they printed more paper money it might be the end. Calculating the risk, the Congress sent out the proposal to the states, dated November 9, 1780, and written in milder language than usual.

By this time Jean Comte de Rochambeau had made his strategic estimate of the situation. "Send us ships, troops and money," he wrote to Charles Gravier, Comte de Vergennes, the Foreign Minister of Louis XVI, "but do not depend upon these people, nor upon their means."[44]

In a country like America it was impossible to hide the hardships and helplessness of the Continental Army. Common knowledge of American miseries encouraged British officers to report the failing of the American rebellion. By mid-1780 both Georgia and South Carolina seemed within the permanent grasp of the British. Ethan Allen of Vermont was becoming a separatist. Arnold had sold out. Silas Deane was now working for Britain. The Continental Army was restive and might become untrustworthy. Worse, the King of France was getting short of money, as the British learned when they captured Henry Laurens at sea late in 1780 and read his private papers. Even in 1779 it had seemed necessary for the provincial press to deny rumors of proposed reductions in the size of the Continental Army.[45] The final ignominy of the congressional supply system was the revelation in mid-1780 that the ladies of Philadelphia had been collecting food and clothes for the Army, and, for a brief period, outdid the Congress. The material help was slight in the long run, but an officer took the time to write his thanks for a mark of respect to the Army which felt neglected and forgotten.[46]

III

Armed men who feel neglected and forgotten have a ready means of calling attention to themselves. On the afternoon of January 3, 1781, when the Congress rested from its paper-shuffling, came alarming news that on New Year's Day the Pennsylvania Line, near Morristown, had replaced its officers with a board of sergeants and marched toward Princeton. The delegates immediately reconvened and appointed a committee to talk with the government of Pennsylvania.

The Pennsylvania regiments had a higher proportion of foreigners than most. Native-born Americans might endure neglect a little longer than foreigners, but, as Washington wrote, "it will be dangerous to put their patience further to the test." They might be waiting to see what profit mutiny brought to the Pennsylvanians.[47] Clinton sent two agents to visit the mutineers with a promise to pay them everything the Congress had promised them, but the severely self-disciplined Continentals handed the visitors over to General Wayne.[48] Clinton's agents were tried and hanged within a fortnight.[49]

The key to the mutiny was the meaning of the words of enlistment: for three years or the duration of the war. The soldiers thought it meant a maximum of three years, while the officers intended it to mean a minimum of the duration of the war. President Joseph Reed of the Pennsylvania Executive Council accepted the soldiers' understanding and promised discharges to all who wished. He added that those departing could keep their bounties and would also get certificates of back pay plus some clothes.[50] Half the Pennsylvania Line left the service. The British did not give up but sent another invitation to the neglected and forgotten by wrapping a letter in a sheet of lead and dropping it on the Princeton campus where the soldiers found it.[51] Clinton was wasting his time. The mutiny was not pro-British but against the officers.

The Congress sent a circular letter to the states on January 15, telling the state governments that state failures to honor requisitions had caused the mutiny, which was exactly the case, and individual delegates sent the word home privately. The episode should have been an argument sufficient to win congressional power to levy a customs tax, but it failed to effect fiscal reform.

New Jersey regulars at Pompton mutinied on January 20. This time Washington was ready. He sent General Robert Howe with six hundred men from West Point, who surprised the mutineers on January 27, disarmed them, and forced them to accept the command of their officers again. Two mutineers were hanged. A similar outbreak in May, again in the Pennsylvania troops, was suppressed in the same way.

A congressional investigating committee found nothing of British influence in the Pennsylvania mutiny of January (nor were the British involved in the later ones). The mutineers kept good order and said that if a British force moved against them they would fight under General Wayne. But if the militia attacked them "they would burn and waste the Country without mercy." The militia showed a notable tranquility.[52]

Washington suggested that one disciplinary weakness of the Army Regulations was the absence of any punishment between a hundred lashes and death, which brought many capital convictions but few executions. The narrow choice tempted the officers to arbitrary punishments.[53]

Congressional helplessness and state indifference really caused these mutinies, but the men were not political analysts and they resented their officers as the enemies at hand. They felt they had been tricked into re-enlistment by officers' misrepresentations. The British thought the mutineers were fed up with the Congress and tried to exploit that as the complaint. It is clear that the mutineers would not have behaved violently unless Washington or the Congress reacted with terrorism, which did not happen. The fact is, the men's grievances were greater than they understood.[54]

By late 1777 the Continental Congress had printed $38 million in paper currency. Inflation had become painful and was made worse by state currency based on hope and persuasion. Price regulation had failed, domestic loans brought little, and lotteries produced trivial sums. If the Congress could sell American produce in Europe, public finance could improve, but the Royal Navy had strong views against American exports. The financial deterioration was not owing to congressional languor, for this body worked at arguing and voting as hard as any legislature, and was a typical parliament in everything except power; ". . . there are here as in most other Assemblys some very Sensable Speakers, and some very loud Talkers."[55]

As we have seen, things went from worse to worst in the following years. Near the end of the gloomy year of 1780 a new Committee of Finance revived the notion of an import duty, and by February 1781 the Congress was able to adopt a resolution asking the states for power to levy a 5 per cent *ad valorem* import tax to meet congressional obligations. South Carolina and Georgia were back under the Union Jack, hence eleven votes would be enough to pass the proposal. It would bring in, the delegates thought, 600,000 or 700,000 hard dollars a year—hardly enough to meet the needs, but in any event it lost by the single vote of the Rhode Island Assembly. It was loosely estimated that there was about $7 million worth of silver spoons and such among the states which might have been confiscated,[56] but no rebel ever suggested taking that kind of wealth to support the war. Furthermore, if title to the public domain had been vested in the Congress before 1781, something in the way of a revenue might have been drawn from land sales. Localism blocked a tariff and a land policy. Respect for property made seizure of precious metal unthinkable. These negatives teach us much about the American Revolution.

Naturally the delegates looked abroad for help, as they had been doing since 1775. In September 1777 the Congress voted to pay interest on treasury certificates by means of drafts against the American commissioners in Paris; the vote by roll call was 19 to 6. The commissioners were to get the money where they could when the bills fell on their desks. The Congress was writing its own credit card for a charge account with the French royal treasury, not knowing that France was borrowing money to stay alive. In December the Congress asked its overseas representatives to try for two million pounds sterling for ten years from France and Spain combined. Then the Congress went ahead and used the potential money to pay interest on domestic debts, and to sink twenty millions of Continental dollars. Delegates also voted to borrow two million pounds sterling from Tuscany. This was to be kept secret. It was. It is not hard to keep zero secret. Ralph Izard, commissioner to Florence, spent his European tour of duty in Paris. He and the covey of commissioners there were expected to live in a fashion befitting representatives of a sovereign nation—at French expense. More dream money floated in imagination when John Jay went to suitor for funds at Madrid, and Henry Laurens went off to the Netherlands to borrow (he was captured by the British). The Congress fobbed off bills "worth" 200,000 pounds of this unborrowed money while Jay was still afloat and before Laurens embarked. European bill-of-exchange holders were waiting for Laurens with this paper when he got out of the Tower of London in 1782. These financial straits had a certain cultural benefit in that they gave many a backwoods Congressman a cosmopolitan viewpoint. For example, Laurens had a rather intricate assignment. He went as special envoy not only to try to touch Dutch bankers for a shaky loan but also to tell Jay not to yield anything of value to Spain *except* in return for a Spanish agreement not to make a separate peace and a Spanish grant of a handsome loan, or, better, subsidy. It all seems a long way from Concord Bridge.

Americans were not exactly desirable debtors. The Congress had devalued the dollar to two and a half cents on March 18, 1780. The action caused great pain not only to American speculators and war contractors but to foreign bankers and finance ministers. Vergennes took this up with John Adams instead of Benjamin Franklin, probably to pick a quarrel with Adams, since Franklin was the accredited minister. He got his quarrel. Luzerne, in Philadelphia, was unable to persuade the Congress to repudiate Adams's peppery defense of the action, which was that there was no reason to distinguish among creditors of the United States, as Vergennes said would be more proper. Those pre-borrowed and ante-spent bills on American commissioners in Europe were soon circulating in Europe at a little better than sixty-five cents on the dollar.[57]

After the devaluation of the dollar, the Congress asked the states to repeal all legal-tender laws, by a roll call of 26 to 1, in order to protect creditors from being forced to take worthless paper. In April 1781 there was even a recommendation to make wheat or flour or beef the standard of exchange instead of the cloudy abstraction called the dollar. The dollar was blowing away with the wind like sea smoke. The plunge was steep and quick. In May, 225 paper dollars equaled one gold dollar. A few weeks later it was 900 to 1. According to folklore, Philadelphians poked elaborate public fun at the paper currency. Young John Breckinridge wrote to his mother in June that no one would take it in Virginia or Pennsylvania. "If you can avoid taking the Continental money, it would be best, for in a little time it will not pass."[58]

Even before this the Congress had come to an important decision. It no longer trusted its Board of Treasury, the commissioners of a body called the Chamber of Accounts did not get along with the Treasury Board, and the Treasurer of Loans charged the board with incompetence and arrogance. These officers with resounding titles and no power had all failed. What was really needed was an executive to run the money side of the war.

In the Congress was such a man, Robert Morris, partner in Morris, Willing, and Company of Philadelphia, merchants. The word "merchant" then meant an importing-exporting wholesaler. Morris had decades of experience in business, importing and exporting whatever was profitable, including five parcels of black people in the years 1758–1765, starting with a few from the West Indies and then getting directly into the African trade which provided the firm with inventories totaling 240 blacks in the early 1760's. Entering the Congress in 1775, Morris became chairman of the Secret Committee of trade as soon as the ports were open. From 1775 through 1777 this committee spent more than $2 million, of which almost a fourth went to Morris' firm, according to contracts made with Morris for the government by Morris for his company. With this income Morris, Willing, and Company expanded by adding partners in New Orleans, Martinique (William Bingham), and Paris (Silas Deane). Their cargos traveled in United States warships, mixed in the holds with public property. Apparently Morris conducted his business more prudently than his committee conducted that of the Congress, for when the Congress was broke he was solvent. Most representatives of the United States abroad also represented Morris, Willing, and Company. In an age when commercial information was private information, Morris was well situated to profit from inside knowledge.[59]

Morris and his fellows of the mercantile line up and down the coast did a fairly good job for the cause of independence. As long as they could, they took the two-and-a-half-cent dollar for gold and silver, Boston businessmen searched out scarce supplies, and New England merchants loaned thirty thousand pounds in hard money for supplies in August 1780. Baltimore merchants raised the money to buy uniforms for Lafayette's troops early in 1781, and Virginia merchants at the same time offered money to buy arms.[60] The colossal inflation of 1780–1781 threatened merchants with extinction, because such a large part of their assets was debt which they had contracted earlier, much of it in those loan-office certificates issued in anticipation of European financing. And what could be more foolish than to lose independence by bad management? Being in politics, they worked at politics to survive. The obvious tactic was to put a skilled business-man in charge of public finance. The final approval of the Articles of Confederation offered a chance to choose a superintendent of fi-nance.*

Not one vote in the Congress was cast against the choice of Robert Morris for the post, though Samuel Adams and Artemas Ward of Massachusetts abstained from voting. Morris laid down two condi-tions: he would continue his private business, and he would have the last word in hiring and firing anyone who handled public money. Hearing objections, he suggested they choose another man. The ob-jections dissolved. By this choice of Morris and his circle to manage the finances, the Congress had taken another step in the American Revolution, as distinguished from the war. It was a step away from localism and toward nationalism.

Morris' formal acceptance came on May 14. Many delegates feared they had chosen a dictator. Others expected magic. Morris himself was optimistic, though he later admitted that appearances were more promising than the reality he discovered, which was that states' rights ideologues back home were less tractable than desperate Con-gressmen. Morris began to organize his department by substituting his personal credit in a form called "Morris Notes" for the vanished credit of the country. In denominations from $20 to $80 they circu-lated as currency. His employees attacked the huge paper pile of claims against the Congress. He abolished Army commissaries and began to contract with private suppliers; he recalled the treasury regulations making congressional paper legal tender; and he removed embargos on exports. His long-range program encompassed econ-omy, taxation, borrowing. He hoped the states would tax themselves to finance the Congress. Meanwhile, he would make do with domestic and foreign loans up to the limit of the need for revenue.

Within three days of his acceptance he came up with a plan for a bank which the Congress quickly approved but did not charter until the end of 1781. (There was honest doubt that the Congress could in-corporate anything.) The delegates asked the states to prevent other

---

* The ratification of the Articles is a subject of the next chapter.

banking competition, and voted that the bank's notes be receivable for taxes, duties, and the country's debt. The bank opened in Philadelphia in January 1782. Morris lived up to his station as the American equivalent of a prime minister, and a young French officer from the Rhineland praised his cellar, which is the highest praise possible.

Morris' influence was felt most concretely in Army supply. He found supplies lying around the country which cost more to move than they were worth. With the consent of the Congress[61] he sold them and applied the proceeds to buy from private sources near the Army. Washington came as close to exultation as his reserve permitted. ". . . The measures you are pursuing for subsisting the Army perfectly accord with my Ideas, and are, I am certain, the only ones which can secure us from distress or the constant apprehensions of it."[62] By the end of the year the soldier and the financier were close enough for the Washingtons to have Christmas dinner with the Morrises.

Less apparent, but quite real, was the influence of the new Bank of North America. As superintendent, Morris bought bank stock for the United States and deposited public funds in the bank. Then he borrowed the deposits back at 6 per cent. The bank shares yielded 9 per cent profit the first year. The United States owned five-eighths of the bank, and thus received 5.6 per cent of the gross profits, or, in the cycle of cash flow, showed a net loss of .4 per cent. In return for this service charge the United States received the use of a depository, gained a currency that people would accept, and stimulated business. This latter point was of vital interest to about five Americans in each eighty. The bank had nothing to do with victory, because the serious fighting was all over when the bank opened. Its capital was $10 million by its charter, but Morris could only scrape up seventy thousand hard dollars to start. Then he received, as Superintendent of Finance, $250,000 in gold as a loan from France, which Superintendent Morris deposited with banker Morris for safekeeping. Banker Morris then loaned some of the money to Superintendent Morris (an excellent credit rating *he* had) and kept the rest on deposit as a useful working balance on which the Congress could depend. While it lasted, the bank made about $6,000 gross profit from handling the Confederation account, which is not much.

Morris believed in debt as a stabilizing influence which gave creditors an interest in keeping the United States alive and solvent. He practiced his doctrine. Up through 1780 the country received nine million *livres* from France; in 1781 alone it got fourteen million more.

The Superintendent of Finance was the eldest of a trio of practical-minded financial thinkers who together shaped the mold of American public finance, the others being Morris' younger partner William Bingham (who died the richest of Americans) and Colonel Alexander Hamilton. Hamilton, in a long, long letter, suggested the formation of the bank at the very time it was being studied. Morris replied gratefully, on the day the Congress approved: "Communications from Men of Genius & abilities will always be acceptable and yours will ever Command . . . attention. . . ."[63] Morris' approval, and the quick success of the bank once it opened, were not lost on young Hamilton.

Robert Morris worked hard for the United States and did not expect to work for nothing. He emerged from the War for Independence as probably the richest man in the country (although bankrupted in the 1790's). Some of his practices would not be tolerated today because his interests conflicted. He was also rather secretive with the Congress, and usually had more cash on hand than he reported in order to be able to pay off war contractors instead of being sidetracked into arguments about soldiers' back pay. He has been installed in the pantheon of American heroes, but his devotion to the public welfare was not precisely disinterested. At the peak of his career he combined the powers and abilities of one of the fabled wolves of Wall Street, a modern secretary of the treasury, the chairman of the Federal Reserve Board, and an old-fashioned boss of a state political machine. With firepower he would have been above even George Washington.

While his accomplishments should not be underrated, it must be remembered that Morris did not have to finance any major military campaign in his last two years of office (1782–1783) and was able to run the country's business calmly with a real income of $6,700,000. Whether his system would have worked earlier is very doubtful. He saved the credit of the United States by the identical program later used by Hamilton in the 1790's, so far as it could be worked. Morris operated within stricter limits than Hamilton would, hence was not as successful. If he had succeeded completely—to speculate on the unknowable—the Constitution of 1787 might not have been drafted, for with the national debt systematically funded and a congressional revenue assured, a stronger central authority might not have seemed necessary. His public life came to an end in 1783 when he proposed to fund the debt of the Confederation as Hamilton later funded the debt of the United States. Congressional localists would not accept the plan, and Morris resigned. His achievement was to restore the credit of the United States in 1781 and 1782. Credit was the necessary means to the end of preserving the Continental Army until the British Army left the country.[64] To that extent his work was necessary to victory.

This is a convenient point at which to total the income of the Congress during the winning of independence, 1775–1783, expressed in specie value and not considering the several state treasuries.

Paper money	$37,800,000
Domestic loans	11,585,506
Foreign loans	7,830,517
Taxes	5,795,000
Miscellaneous	2,852,802
	$65,863,825

No wise man would stake his life on the accuracy of these figures. Most argument concerns the real value of the paper money, but this table is pretty close to reality.[65] It works out, roughly, to $33 a head for free whites.

16

Of Real Estate
and Nationalism, 1780-1781

The wild lands stretched west from the Appalachian front, and no one knew who owned them. By vesting them in the United States the Congress gave the United States its strongest impulse toward nationalism, made an empire, and created a common market which would enrich its people to undreamed levels. But it was not a sure thing in the late 1770's. Speaking as prophet, Thomas Paine had said the lands once were the property of the Crown, but, since all the former colonies were fighting, all should profit from the inexhaustible wealth which would pay for the war and make taxes unnecessary for generations to come. He overstated their value but not the logic of their ownership. Some men took shorter views. The unratified Articles of Confederation, which had been approved by the Congress in 1777, assumed that the states kept their land claims to the West, and provided only a court to settle boundary and title disputes.[1] Ten states had ratified the Articles by the end of the summer of 1778. New Jersey, Delaware, and Maryland balked. What they had in common was a lack of western land.

Virginia's seventeenth-century charter boundaries could be read as giving immense tracts to Virginia within the area claimed by every later northern colony except Maryland, New Jersey, Delaware, and Rhode Island. Neither the landless states nor those with plausible western claims liked Virginia's vast imagined boundaries. If Virginia's claims stood, Paine's prophecy would come true for Virginia only. As a matter of abstract political economy this would be unfair, because every state had promised land bounties for Continental soldiers.[2] Those states which had no western claims, and those which might lose out in controversy with Virginia later, would be hard put to make good their promises except by buying from Virginia. Maryland consistently favored giving the Congress authority to settle the western boundaries of the states. After decisive failure to gain that concession, Maryland sullenly fell back to the position that all states should yield their western lands to the Congress, though Maryland stood alone when New Jersey, Rhode Island, and Delaware ratified the Articles in 1778 and 1779.[3] New Jersey had not changed its attitude, and would have preferred to see the Congress holding title to the West—partly to help raise some Continental revenue independently of state taxation—but ratified the Articles on November 20, 1778, as a kind of self-denying act which postponed further consideration of the Western problem for sake of the common good.[4] New Jersey's ratification followed the failure of a move to set off twenty to forty million acres to be sold for benefit of the United States; the unsuccessful proposal was the shadow of a coming event, because it also would have provided for the erection of new states. Rhode Island and Delaware also ratified, which left Maryland in solitary stubbornness, blocking the Articles of Confederation by its single abstention.

Meanwhile, Virginia was distributing western land generously. As cash grew scarce, the Congress desperately appealed to Virginia (October 30, 1779) to reconsider the land warrants already issued, and not to issue any more, which at least shows that some members had not given up on the idea of cashing western acres to pay for the war. The Congress resolved that further appropriations of undeveloped land by states would be troublesome. North Carolina and Virginia voted "no," and Virginia returned a rather curt reminder that it reserved its own land for itself. Buried in the response was a hint that something less provincial and more continental might be arranged for the future. This was not so much altruism as a reaction to growing unpopularity, because Virginia's serene acceptance of

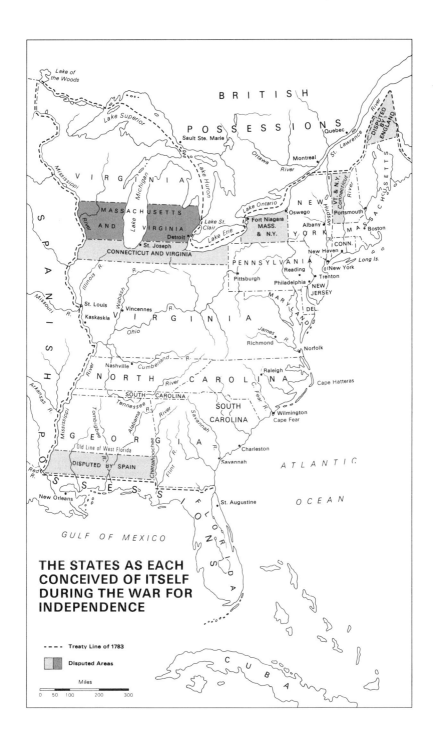

THE STATES AS EACH
CONCEIVED OF ITSELF
DURING THE WAR FOR
INDEPENDENCE

- - - Treaty Line of 1783

Disputed Areas

Miles
0   50 100   200   300

her own vast claims to an imperial wilderness had only emphasized her largeness and provoked jealousy.

So much for high policy. Private interest also needs scrutiny.[5]

Interstate rivalries in the Congress were not between large and small states but between landed and landless states. The landed states claimed land for themselves, and the landless—alas—claimed it on behalf of one or another land company. The middle states were pretty well controlled in this matter by investors in real estate speculations. One should not be surprised to find land speculators in the Congress. The land reforms of the Crown in 1774 opposed land speculation and promised protection to actual settlers (white, that is) by means of advertised auctions. In the absence of securities exchanges and organized investment banking, land was the only security which promised capital gains. Practically all rich colonials were in the real estate business, and the Crown's move against the engrossing of large tracts for unearned increment must certainly be included in the list of causes of the War for Independence.[6] Land speculation was a characteristic part of economic life in America, and the British were proposing to abolish a respected practice.[7]

But after independence the would-be speculators who lived outside of Virginia found themselves worse off, because Virginia had no interest in their enrichment. Which brings us to Maryland's intransigence. Maryland leaders, including a governor and at least two congressional delegates, were deep in land schemes. They associated themselves with Philadelphians, including James Wilson and Robert Morris, and organized into two companies, the Illinois Company and the Wabash Company. Each had privately "purchased" land from the Indians (which gives an unquiet title in land law) before the war. They merged as the Illinois and Wabash Company in 1779, and had an interest in the Indiana Company which had "bought" land from the Indians in present West Virginia. All of this acreage lay within the alleged boundaries of Virginia, and there was no hope of getting Virginia to validate the titles. Virginia did not believe in direct "purchase" from Indians; such a title passed from Indians to the Crown to Virginia to the individual landowner.

Among the share owners of the Illinois and Wabash Company were French Consul John Holker and Sieur Conrad Alexandre Gérard, the first French minister to the United States. They were quite clubby with Maryland Congressmen, though Gérard's successor was rather chilly toward Maryland. One of their Maryland friends was Daniel of St. Thomas Jenifer, a western investor who followed the French line in the Congress faithfully, even going so far as to support the right of the Spanish to conquer everything west, and to conquer Georgia if it remained British. It might, he thought, be easier to deal with a Spanish king than with those self-centered Virginians.

Virginia's case would be stronger in the eyes of posterity if Virginia had followed an orderly policy devised for the common good, but the Old Dominion had messy land practices which led to the issue of bales of land warrants to veterans and speculators who never saw their land. Instead they sold the warrants to other speculators and monopolists. Virginia land paper functioned something like modern stock warrants and convertible debentures in the dispersed money market of the day. The policy was wasteful and inefficient. Grants exceeded the area available, and entry procedures were lax. Surveying was so crude as to encourage fraud, duplication and overlapping, plural grants to single persons, concentrations of great holdings in few hands, and much absentee ownership.[8]

Less easily grasped than the abstract injustice of Virginia's overwhelming boundary claims, and the concrete pangs of non-Virginian land speculators, is the fact that the polity of Vermont was a principal obstacle to the ratification of the Articles of Confederation. The question was, who ruled Vermont? New York and New Hampshire both claimed it fell within their boundaries, and some Vermonters said they were their own masters. Some New Englanders sided with New Hampshire, some with Vermonters, but none helped the New Yorkers to make their claim good. Maryland and Pennsylvania delegates tended to be wary of Yankees, so the New England men delayed solution of the western lands problem in hope of settling the question of Vermont by trading for Pennsylvania and Maryland votes. If they settled the western land matter quickly, they could not count on help in the Vermont business from any delegates outside New England.

In passing it may be observed that the Vermont boundary problem dated from the wording of the Duke of York's grant of the 1660's, in which his eastern boundary was the Connecticut River. This was later adjusted to the present boundary between New York and Connecticut, but Vermont had not yet been born, and its boundary remained to be set.

If given their choice, some Vermonters would have preferred a war with New York rather than with Britain. New Yorkers asked the protection of the Continental Congress, or else their lives and property would be "at the Disposal of Ethan Allen which is more to be Dreaded than Death, with all its Terrors." Allen said that before he yielded he would "fight, nay even run on the mountains and live on mouse meat."[9] When New York put a price on Allen's head in 1772, he offered a reward for the capture of the men who did it, and invited them to Vermont. Was Allen moved by provincialist patriotism? Perhaps. But he and his followers claimed to own 300,000 acres of Vermont land not granted by New York. When war with Britain came, the Vermonters were torn between their political affinities and their economic interests. Claiming that the King had always intended Vermont to be a separate colony, they drafted a constitution and applied to the Congress for admission in 1777.[10]

New York delegates were indignant at Vermont's pretensions. They claimed admission of Vermont as a state would be congressional dismemberment of New York, a thing intolerable. The Congress backed away, but Connecticut delegate Roger Sherman became the champion of Vermonters.[11] Years passed with no success for Vermont. A man signing himself "Bev. Robinson, Col. Loyal Americans," wrote to Ethan Allen from New York City in 1780 and again in 1781 suggesting that Vermont return to allegiance as a separate colony; Allen would be a British brigadier with subordinate officers of his own choice.[12] Allen, in 1781, passed the letters on to the Congress, stoutly affirmed the independence of Vermont, and said he would persevere in that cause even if he had to "retire with hardy green Mountain Boys, into the desolate caverns of the Mountains and Wage War with Humane nature at large."[13] He and his had already threatened a separate peace in 1780, and were encroaching on lands which indisputably belonged to New York and New Hampshire. In the summer of 1781 the Congress learned of Anglo-Vermont armistice negotiations. A committee advised that both New York and New Hampshire surrender their claims to the region. The New Yorkers were adamant, and Governor George Clinton, serious for once, threatened to withdraw the New York delegation from the Congress.

Allen's problem was that he and his brothers claimed to own the northwest quarter of Vermont. The value of their holdings depended on ability to export via the St. Lawrence River. To get this he tried to conquer Canada, made an armistice some months before the end of the war, attempted a commercial treaty with Britain after 1783, proposed an American colonization scheme for the St. Lawrence valley, and, finally, in the 1790's, proposed the joint conquest of Canada by France and Vermont.[14]

Sherman's interest was aroused because some Vermonters were migrants upstream from the lower Connecticut River valley. Some of them despised the Allens, and in 1778 this element was pleased to have the Congress delay action on Vermont's application for statehood. Probably three-quarters of the people in the region were indifferent to Allen's hopes. When the Vermont constitution was written, Governor Clinton of New York had been briefly conciliatory, and offered in 1778 to confirm the Vermont land titles if the Vermonters would become part of New York. No Vermonter seems to have been agreeable to that proposition. If the Congress in 1779 or 1780 could have solved the Vermont question to New York's satisfaction, it would probably have provoked an explosion in Vermont. On the other hand, New York leaders were irascible, and John Jay hinted to the Congress that New York might not tax for the Congress if the assembly believed that the Congress dealt unfairly with New York in the Vermont affair.[15] Jay moved, and gained the unanimous passage of a resolution (September 24, 1779) that New York, New Hampshire, and Massachusetts should legislate to give the Congress authority to conduct hearings on the dispute, suspend the local use of force, suspend attempts by rival states to enforce law in Vermont, and stop patenting land grants in the region. Jay's private opinion was that the controversy was kept alive by influential leaders who held Vermont land claims and would like a fifth New England state in the Congress to strengthen New England influence. But Jay's resolution led to nothing because of the debility of the Congress at the time.

The merits of the case need not concern us. The Vermont question was not settled until the 1790's. During the War for Independence the quarrel was absorbed into congressional politics. There was to be no solution because Virginia thought the cooling of the heated controversy could only lead to the addition of yet another state to join those envious of states with western land claims. The national importance of the quarrel was that it delayed the Articles of Confederation by alarmingly suggesting the possibility of creating a new state in land claimed by other states, and thus was a working model of the whole western dilemma. Vermont, under its 1777 constitution, was a mirror of revolutionary radicalism, but lost all its friends by its truculence and by the Allens' flirtation with the British.

II

The Congress went right on working, in its spasmodic way, to get the Articles ratified. The problem had seemed immediate in June 1776, and nothing had happened since to lessen the urgency. There was energy and intelligence enough among the rebels, as shown by the drafting of state constitutions which worked, but the difficulty lay in the conflicting interests of energetic and intelligent men when they applied themselves to interstate problems. Virginia's land claim remained the great obstacle in the minds of men interested in creating a public domain, whether for nationhood or for profit.

While others lost patience with Virginia, Virginia lost patience with Maryland and proposed in May 1779 to go ahead and confederate without Maryland. The Connecticut delegation brought in a similar proposal, but with the added proviso that Maryland should not be disqualified permanently. The North Carolinians seemed to be in agreement until delegates generally became aware that a partial confederation would in fact be a disunion which would probably encourage the British. Henry Laurens of South Carolina proposed a national convention to review the entire organization of the war effort. Alexander Hamilton, in September 1780, argued for a convention to rewrite the still unratified Articles of Confederation, and General Nathanael Greene, commanding the shattered fragments of the armed forces in the Southern Department, asked for a convention.

Laurens, Hamilton, and Greene were asking the Congress to request power. If the Congress had simply assumed an implied power to do all things needful it might have pulled off the *coup*, but a resolution to beg the states for more power died on the table in October 1780.

There was even state pressure for action. A convention of state officials at Hartford in November 1780 received a resolution from the New York Assembly which urged the Congress to use the Army to enforce compliance with its requisitions. The men at Hartford agreed and passed the idea on to the Congress by way of the New York congressional delegation. Something in the atmosphere of the Congress throughout the whole war promoted that vice of timidity which we like to mislabel as the virtue of prudence, and the New York delegates shied away from the proposal. It died.

The paralysis of the Congress was partly due to the absence of energetic centralizers in the years 1779–1780. Silas Deane had returned to Europe, and Robert Morris was out of the Congress after October 1778. The desperate conditions of 1780 recalled national-minded men to a sense of duty and brought Morris and others back into public life. Without them, regardless of "liberal" or "conservative" labels, it seems unlikely that the United States could have survived. By the end of 1780 they were booted, spurred, and back in the saddle. Thus the ratification of the Articles, when it came, coincided with the lowest ebb of American fortunes. Only when the flame of revolutionary enthusiasm seemed but ashes did the rebels rouse themselves to reform their defective system.

New York broke the deadlock. As early as November 30, 1779, Robert R. Livingston wrote to Governor Clinton that there seemed an inclination among New Yorkers to sacrifice a part to save the whole, which seems a representative view. The New York Assembly, on February 19, 1780, took the important procedural step of waiving its claim to the West in favor of the United States. This was more procedural than substantial, since New York's gossamer claim rested only on grants from the Iroquois,[16] who seem to have liked to give away distant lands to elevate their own status as lords of the earth. The claim was contrived in order to give it up as a dramatic gesture. The New York technique was to let its Congressmen decide the western boundaries of the state, providing that anything New York lost would be for the benefit of the United States. The New York delegates announced this to the Congress with the pointed remark that it would be unfair to Yorkers if the New York delegation yielded something of value, unless the other states did as well.[17]

Connecticut moved next. The government of Connecticut had shuffled many crackly old parchments and pasted up a claim from the Atlantic to the Pacific (cut at the Mississippi River by the Treaty of 1763), which even included the old Plymouth patent and purchases made accordingly, as well as the sea-to-sea charter given by

Charles II in the 1660's. Part of the claim fell within the bounds of Pennsylvania (a dispute settled later), and that which ran west of Pennsylvania fell within Virginia's claim. In October 1780 Connecticut resolved to follow the example of New York by ceding its western claim to the United States, reserving a part of present Ohio as the "Western Reserve" to satisfy outstanding grants to individuals.

Virginians were thoughtful. Richard Henry Lee, who had first moved Confederation in 1776, was willing in 1778 to give up Virginia's claim to land north of the Ohio to benefit both Virginia and the union, on the ground that Virginia's boundaries might be too extended for effective state government in the future. Thomas Jefferson's imagination was stirred by prospects of a huge national domain of expanding republicanism. Joseph Jones and James Madison, delegates from Virginia to the Congress, agreed with Lee and Jefferson, and it was this cast of thought that led to a resolution by the Congress in 1780 which provided for the establishment of new states in the West when it became the territory of the United States. Considering the cessions of New York and Connecticut, Maryland's arguments, congressional discussions, and the prospect of congressional jurisdiction over land titles in the West, Virginia finally agreed to give a quit claim to everything north of the Ohio (with some acreage reserved for warrants already issued) on January 2, 1781. The Virginia decision provided that the Congress would not challenge Virginia's jurisdiction over present Kentucky, but the Congress rejected this condition and Virginia went along with it. The Virginians seemed more concerned with frustrating out-of-state land speculators than with governing Kentucky, since the Virginia legislature had explicitly canceled all "purchases" from the Indians by an act of 1776, and insisted in 1781 that the whole of the unsold western lands become the property of the United States.[18] Virginia never admitted that its claim had been illegal. As Madison put it, law was on Virginia's side, but equity favored the other side. Very likely the cession was encouraged by the painful and lonely experience of a British military invasion commanded by redcoated General Benedict Arnold.[19] Edmund Randolph wrote that he sensed "disgust and jealousy" of Virginia in other states, and believed it would be pleasant to have friends when it came to settling accounts of war expenditures.[20] An important part in the dramatic Virginia policy change was that of James

Madison, who had become a nationalist by this time. Elected to the Congress in 1780, he was present at nearly every meeting through December 1783, and despite his diminutive size was becoming an impressive American politician—quiet, logical, well informed, good humored, and aware of the behavior of mankind in the exercise of power. He even wished to have the Confederation title to western lands written into the peace treaty after the war, although he did not wish his views on this advertised in Virginia.[21]

The ferment was working in Maryland. Ex-Governor Thomas Johnson had come out of retirement in 1780. He could have entered either the Congress or the Maryland legislature; he chose the legislature. As soon as Virginia passed its resolution of cession, Johnson set to work to get Maryland to sign on the ship of state. It took him just four weeks to secure passage of a ratification resolution (January 30, 1781). Its passage may have been easier because the Chevalier Anne de la Luzerne, second minister of France to the United States, had told Maryland that France took a dim view of Maryland's reluctance to ratify. Inasmuch as Maryland wished French naval help in the Chesapeake, this must have been sobering. In the Congress the New York delegates now announced the new and final boundaries of New York, as they had authority from home to do. Maryland delegates John Hanson and Daniel Carroll signed the Articles of Confederation on March 1, 1781, and at long last the United States existed under a basic charter with specifically delegated powers.[22]

To look ahead, North Carolina yielded its jurisdiction, but no acres, because all of the public land running west to the Mississippi went to private owners. Georgia did not make a cession until 1788, and then in unacceptable form. Its cession of what Georgia still owned became complete and acceptable in 1802.

The seven states which ceded western lands or claims to lands gave the United States a total of 259,171,787 acres. South of the Ohio River all of the land went into private hands before the states gave up their powers, hence all they yielded was political authority. This was not a tinsel prize or theatrical flourish, since only in the unorganized West did the Congress have real authority. Hitherto it had none, except in Army camps and public ships.

The land was a common ownership gained, as Maryland phrased it in 1776, "by the blood and treasure of all."[23] The cry of looters of the public domain, that it should be "returned" to the states, is deliberate deception or ignorant nonsense. West of the Appalachians, excepting Texas and Hawaii, the states that were later formed were the creations of the United States, and the public domain was never theirs.

Even before ratification the Congress had begun to move toward something like executive operation. As in the Board of War, the attempt to use executive committees which mixed delegates and outsiders had not worked well. The Committee on Foreign Affairs had dwindled by mid-1780 to the overworked James Lovell alone. Lovell worked so many nights with quill and paper that he reserved alternate weekends for sleep. That year diplomatic business increased and the Congress had to try reform. The inevitable committee formed, met, and reported a recommendation (August 29) for *another* committee to plan a new arrangement of the civil executive. The first fruit was a resolution (January 10, 1781) to establish a single Secretary for Foreign Affairs. The King of France had the chief outside interest in congressional diplomacy, being the largest single investor in the American Revolution. His Minister Luzerne moved to defend the French interest which seemed threatened by the candidacy of Arthur Lee for the new post. Luzerne had to tell the president of the Congress that he did not trust Lee. This led to a long standoff, with Luzerne supporting Robert R. Livingston of New York for the job. Livingston got it on August 10, 1781. Those whose sentiments incline them to admire the Lee-Adams faction more than the element represented by Morris, Jay, Livingston, and such, have thought Luzerne's interference was unconscionable. It is hard to see how the war could have been won the way it was won, or how the bond of alliance could have been preserved, without the active participation of the French in American affairs. The United States was a beggar client of France by 1780, not out of necessity but because it chose to let the French carry the financial burden. With provincialism all-powerful, the Congress could do nothing else. And the thorough, imaginative, and systematic Livingston was very well qualified for the job of Secretary for Foreign Affairs.

Long before Livingston took his post, the other executive offices were created by the Congress.[24] The Congress established Departments of War, Marine, and the Treasury. Robert Morris, as we have seen, took over the Treasury on May 14. General Alexander McDougall of New York received the appointment of Secretary of

Marine, but when he insisted that he keep his Army rank—which was not acceptable—the Marine Office became a subdivision of the Treasury. General Benjamin Lincoln of Massachusetts became Secretary of War on October 1.

The Articles required a change in congressional voting procedures. No longer could a solitary delegate cast the vote of his state; it now took at least two. When, as happened, one or more states had only a single delegate present, the Congress resolved itself into the Committee of the Whole in which all could vote, though single delegates could not vote on the reports of the Committee of the Whole. A single delegate thus could speak, serve on committees, and have some influence until a tardy delegate or two reinforced him and restored the state's vote on final passage of resolutions. There was tacit acceptance of the principle that the three-year terms of delegates present began at the moment of ratification. The Congress also decided, after dull and tiring argument, that a quorum was nine states, and that the vote of seven states was needed for the adoption of a measure. Within months, absenteeism compelled reduction of the quorum to seven states.

The Congress formalized its name as "The United States in Congress Assembled," but it was only a change of words. The sitting members continued in office, and President Samuel Huntington went on presiding until he resigned on July 6, 1781, to be succeeded by Thomas McKean, a delegate representing Delaware.*

Thus in the last year of serious warfare the Continental Congress arrived at a workable organization. As so often in public affairs, a reform which took a long time was a reform which would have prevented the abuses of the past but was not very forward-looking. If change could have come in 1777 it would no doubt have helped the Congress to avoid blunders and to gain many advantages, particularly the ability to deliberate free of petty and vexatious administrative problems. But the machinery they set up to run the war did not operate fully until a few weeks before the end of important combat. The obvious reason for the years of delay was that the War for Independence was a war against centralized authority, and the state governments were reluctant to substitute yet another central authority.

* The Congress resolved to begin its "Federal Year" on each November 1. McKean was succeeded by John Hanson of Maryland on November 1. For this reason some have called Hanson the first President of the United States.

III

As soon as Maryland signed the Articles of Confederation, a battery at the State House fired a thirteen-gun salute. The guns of the United States Frigate *Ariel*, Captain John Paul Jones commanding, then lying in the Delaware River, responded with thirteen more explosions. The delegates called upon President Huntington in the afternoon to congratulate him, accompanied by the Pennsylvania Assembly and executive officers, and by some Army officers who happened to be in the city. Huntington fed them festively. That night fireworks at the State House and from *Ariel* flamed in the sky, and "great joy appeared in every Countenance but those of the Disaffected." Perhaps the celebration included more than lunch and fireworks, for Congressman Thomas Rodney sent the good news to his wife by a letter in which he saluted her as "Sir."[25]

If the Congress of the United States had lawful authority, it was derived from the right of revolution as expounded in the Declaration of Independence. The Articles of Confederation came late and only defined the authority explicitly. Consent to the resolves of the Congress was implicit, if vague, in its convening. The drafting of the Articles was part of the Revolution, and a part which well illustrated the internal political differences of the organization of rebels, both in the states separately and in the country as a whole. But the Continental Congress and the Articles of Confederation are not comprehensible if studied only for weaknesses or to prove that what came later was better. The Articles are, in a sense, a measurement of the degree of agreement the rebels could achieve.[26] It is not enough to dismiss the delegates with the remark that they agreed more than they differed, and then plunge into the movement which led to the Constitution of 1787.

The Articles also touch upon the question whether the Revolution was democratic. Merrill Jensen urges that it was. His case may be summed up fairly as follows. The fact of being supplanted proves neither the success nor the failure of the Articles of Confederation. The quarrels over the Articles were quarrels between conservatives and popular leaders. In the minds of popular leaders, local self-government meant agrarian democracy. The popular leaders were unwilling to erect another Parliament, and the Articles were their monument because they were the constitutional expression of the Declaration of Independence. The Congress they created was a conference of the agents of sovereign democracies. The changes in the United States which followed the ratification of the Articles did not happen because of a shift of opinion but because of a shift of power. The popular leaders had won their local self-government and then relaxed, whereupon the conservatives took charge and moved the country to accept the federal Constitution.[27] The thirteen sovereign democracies proved too inconstant to defend their victory in the years after 1781.

But the notion that the supremacy of state legislatures makes for liberty seems a dubious proposition. (Of course, "democracy" and "liberty" are not synonyms, but many people see democracy as a system of egalitarian values, not as a political structure.) Government can be too weak to protect the helpless. The Continental Congress received many pathetic petitions from people entitled to compensation for sacrifices and disabilities incurred in the common cause, for which no local government would assume responsibility.[28] There is such a thing as a democratic commitment based on the dignity of man, protected by assuring the immunities of citizens, by a free press, by the use of force to keep the peace in such a way as not to use more violence than necessary, and by respect for dissent. The wartime state governments did not show such commitment, despite the grandeur of the language of their several bills of rights. They smashed presses, tolerated mobbing, passed bills of attainder and outlawry. Their goal seemed home rule for the individual states, and nothing ethical about it. The tyranny of the majority was not effectively restrained.

In estimates of the work of the Congress, its failures have received much attention. Certainly it was weak in the year the Articles of Confederation went into effect. When Huntington resigned the presidency it took awhile to find a replacement, so little was its prestige. Men began to avoid election as delegates because the work was an unrewarding drudgery at a time when it was easier to gain reputation and fortune in the states. Early in 1781 there was another attempt to amend the Articles to give the Congress power to levy a 5 per cent customs tax. Income was essential to servicing the debt; without a taxing power there was no reason for creditors to trust the United States. Worse, from the viewpoint of reformers, the states might assume the debt, and when the fighting ceased there would be no reason at all to have a Congress.[29] There were also proposals in March 1781 for punitive action against financially delinquent states, going so far as to suggest the use of embargo and blockade. Nothing came of them, but they illustrate the feeling of frustration in the hearts of some delegates in 1781.

Although Superintendent of Finance Robert Morris fed the Army, he failed in his dream of strengthening the union. He was the conservative leader, he knew the ways of the Congress, he was respected (though unloved), and he became practically prime minister from 1781 to 1783. Above all, he feared the assumption of the Continental debt by the states. "There is in it a principle of disunion implied which must be ruinous," he said.[30] Morris advanced the notion that creditors would have to consent before the Congress could authorize the states to take over the debts, and in 1782 the delegates did refuse to allow the states to assume payment of money owed to the Continental Army. In short, at Morris' urging the delegates clung to the debt as to an asset. When the fighting ended the Continental loan office owed $11 million to its certificate holders. Debt was a stabilizing influence, for public creditors make unlikely political revolutionaries. Morris thought this stabilizing effect had not been enough emphasized.

The Articles of Confederation were not enforceable. A committee reported in August 1781 that twenty-one particular points of the Articles needed execution, and that the states should give seven additional powers to the Congress. This report was neither adopted nor debated. The delegates appear to have shown a rather indolent reaction to crisis, but the Congress had a customs-tax amendment pending which had still not yet been defeated. If they had known it would fail, the delegates might have acted more vigorously.

Morris proposed to fund the Continental debt. The loan-office certificates had depreciated, because the loan office could not meet the interest payments. Morris suggested accepting the old certificates at face value in exchange for new bonds, upon which he would begin to pay the interest. Domestic productivity and the country's foreign credit rating would both improve. The new bonds would provide capital for banking, which in turn would produce bank notes as an acceptable currency. The Bank of North America which Morris founded in 1782 had gone about as far as it could go, since it could not accept public securities which were untrustworthy. Using gold (from a French loan), he had issued about a million in bank notes which circulated freely. More could not be done unless United States certificates could be relied on as reserves for banking. He was proposing what Hamilton later succeeded in doing, and as early as 1783, was even willing to assume the state debts too. The delegates in the Congress knew what he intended; whether it was widely understood elsewhere is unknowable.

Morris' whole edifice would depend on getting a tax power, and by the time he was ready to work for that, the war was over. Thus his proposed tax would be for paying debts, not for winning battles. And, as any fund-raiser knows, raising money to pay off an old debt is as hard as raffling off a junk automobile.

Morris offered his resignation as a way of using leverage, secure in the belief his private credit was necessary to the Congress so that the delegates would reject his resignation and accept his funding plan. The funding plan failed, and, after scraping up the money to see the Army through to the end, Morris left public service. He broke off the connection between the Bank of North America and the Congress, and—after eight years of financial improvisation—the United States had a staggering debt and no other asset but undeveloped, unmeasured land. How that debt became something of value is the story of President Washington's first term.

As we have seen, the notion of reorganizing the central direction of the war gained support in the darkest year, 1780. It appealed to several elements. In the middle states there were people who intensely disliked their local popular governments and looked to a central authority for relief. Businessmen found the Continental economy chaotic. The public creditors had reason for dissatisfaction. The officer corps of the Continental Army was suffering acutely, both in body and spirit. These people were articulate and made their views known. Congressman James Madison supported Morris because he knew weak government did not promote liberty as he defined liberty. Alexander Hamilton was an intellectual disciple of Morris. George Washington was very, very tired of the localism that hindered the operations of the Army. Thus, with differing motives, there gradually accumulated a body of intelligent reformers who in time could merge political and economic objectives and make them inseparable. But their victory lay in the future. Meanwhile, the effect of their writing and talking was to disparage the Continental Congress.

The Congress was not all that bad. It was more than a council of ambassadors, and it made many decisions on its own which contributed to the winning of independence. Considering the requisition system in vogue, it did as well as it could, short of converting the country to a miniature Prussia through use of the Army. But its weaknesses received the most attention, and Alexander Hamilton, writing as propagandist in 1788, could see nothing but "the dark catalogue of our public misfortunes,"[31] all blamed on the system of the Congress under the Articles of Confederation. Until the second third of the twentieth century, Hamilton's view prevailed.

Before the ratification of the Articles, the Continental Congress was all the central authority there was, operating through committees and mixed executive bodies. It declared independence, commissioned generals, maintained a navy, set up a diplomatic service, negotiated treaties, directed the Post Office, issued currency, borrowed money, called on the states to write their constitutions, and drafted the Articles of Confederation. This is rather more than a gloomy list of public miseries. Many of these decisions and policies were entirely congressional, without any part played by the states individually. The weaknesses were so well advertised because the Congress, convened as an emergency body, spoke with an uncertain tone and suffered from a rapid turnover of membership. On balance it worked hard, compromised most differences, and tried to serve the common purpose. In this it was much distracted by its clumsy attempt to function as an executive through numerous committees, some of which were also quasi-judicial. If the executive departments had come earlier, the Congress could have made a more substantial record.

An example of what might have been was the settlement of the boundary controversy between Connecticut and Pennsylvania, which was decided strictly according to the provisions of the Articles of Confederation in a trial at Trenton in the winter of 1782–1783. Pennsylvania won, and there was no turbulence.[32] Another was the methodical establishment of a table of organization and state quotas of regular soldiers to garrison the posts in the western lands where the Congress had a true authority.[33] These sober acts were only possible because of the Articles of Confederation. With a few amendments the Articles could have served as a federal Constitution for the next several generations, *if* one of those amendments had provided a revenue.

It is even possible to acclaim the Congress for remarkable achievements which deserve stronger praise than the usual did-the-best-they-could. The delegates chose George Washington and stood by the appointment through some depressing periods, leaving him free to act. Their bucolic militia diplomacy won what may have been the principal diplomatic success in American history. And, after the ratification of the Articles, the Congress specifically and usefully listed the instances in which the Confederation failed to observe the law of nations.[34] The Continental Army blue and buff—more often seen in calendar and schoolbook art than in the field—has pushed the more drably dressed civilians into the background. There has been a tendency to overrate the soldiers and to underrate the civilians.

In practice the Congress had stayed within the principles of the Articles of Confederation from writing to ratification, so the ratification required no important changes. The operation of the Articles, however, had a psychological effect, convincing the public there was a definite structure named the United States. This was the seed from which grew the first of the modern nation-states, anticipating the French by a few years. Even before ratification, a letter in the press had made a brave effort to incarnate a sovereign in the Congress, calling it "that great council of our empire,"[35] but after ratification it was easier. The New York Assembly asked its constituents to show by deeds rather than words "their inflexible determination to support with their lives and fortune [*sic*] the constitutional authority of the United States in congress assembled."[36] If nationalism is a good thing, the Congress and the Articles were steps in the right direction.

Some have argued that the Congress was merely a council of state ambassadors. It is true that several states declared independence in their own names, some sent diplomatic agents abroad, some tried to borrow money from foreign bankers, most instructed their delegates in the Continental Congress on how to vote on specific questions. Looked at this way, the War for Independence was a congruence of state revolts loosely directed and guided by the Continental Congress. In the minds of the more provincialist leaders of the time, it never went much beyond that, even when British and German armies were marching about the land.

Nevertheless, the War for Independence left a lasting impression on many of those who were caught up in it, because at center it was a continental war. A large number of later Federalists were wholly engaged in the war, whether under arms, in finance, or in diplomacy. Warfare, the revenue question, and foreign relations all demanded a continental viewpoint. Men with such a viewpoint tended to be younger than their political opponents. For many, the Revolution was the beginning of their political careers. Being younger, they survived to complete the political revolution.[37]

By and large the delegates to the Continental Congress were probably more able than the members of Lord North's Ministry, many of whom seem to have been the proxies of more powerful and competent personages, or else political hobbyists. If the Continental Congress had had as efficient a taxing machinery as North's front benchers, the contrast would be sharper.[38]

The Continental Congress and the soldiery it mustered won the independence of the United States. Revolutions occur when a monopoly of power is destroyed and a habit of obedience is broken. The worst that can be said of the Congress is that it was able to break the habit of obedience to the King, but lacked the power to compel obedience to itself. Its successor, which could not have existed except for the work of the Continental Congress, was to get that power.

17

The Long Lane
to Yorktown, 1780-1781

Because of stubbornness, resilience, and recuperative power, the United States survived the gloomiest year of the war, 1780, and in fact managed to end the year on a rising flood of success which began at King's Mountain, out west on the Carolinas' boundary, October 7, 1780. The loyalist leader Major Patrick Ferguson, recruiting loyalists, got into a fight with back-country rebels and lost the bloodiest battle since Bunker Hill. Ferguson was killed, and his whole force of eleven hundred killed, wounded, or captured, at an American cost of but eighty-eight casualties. It was a grudge fight between American rebels and loyalists. The victors shot scores of prisoners and hanged a dozen in reprisal for British executions of deserters taken in arms against them.

Charles Lord Cornwallis was blamed for leaving the force unsupported so far inland, and the British cause suffered since Carolina loyalists lost faith in British protection. On the American side the meaning of the battle was missed by most, except that one observer thought "that Ferguson's defeat will prove the Prelude to a second Burgonade."[1] Nevertheless, Lord George Germain made Cornwallis practically independent in his theater, and the British optimistically took up the project of reasserting control over North Carolina.

The easy victory at Camden over Horatio Gates had made Cornwallis overconfident. He was continually harassed by guerrilla bands under Francis Marion, Thomas Sumter, and Andrew Pickens, who were incapable of pitched battles but could make all roads dangerous, put messengers in peril, and terrorize loyalists. Each was half brigand and half soldier, hard to repress, impossible to catch. For such men British regulars had misplaced contempt. Pacification and conciliation was the British task. The rebel job was to inflame the people.

Inflammation was far more successful than pacification. An unknown officer at the Southern headquarters of the American forces wrote of the local combatants who warred so ferociously that "blood and slaughter" would depopulate the country.[2] The whole area saw a nastier kind of warfare than usual. Those Americans willing to fight for one or the other side seemed about equal in number, and treated each other atrociously. Lawlessness became a principle of conduct, force was a supplement to politics, and both sides were inhumane, as usually happens in wars fought for local political goals. Most Southerners were in the fight for political reasons (and a few for loot). Those in red coats behaved the worse. The only northern units of the Continental Army that served in this theater were the Pennsylvanians, who fought in no major battle, but once tried to mutiny and deliver their commander to the British.[3]

Nathanael Greene came south to assume command in place of Horatio Gates after the crushing defeat at Camden, arriving in Charlotte, North Carolina, early in December 1780 with what he could collect in men and supplies. He was Washington's choice. As a Rhode Island militia officer he learned war from books and from a hired British deserter who served as his drillmaster. Rhode Island made him a brigadier in 1775, and after the fall of New York in 1776 he helped Washington to think his way through to the adoption of Fabian strategy. Greene was a true Fabius in the South after 1780—informed, imaginative, and leader of a slippery force.[4]

He had only a few hundred regulars and had to rely on a variable militia force whom he reflectively equated with the locusts of Egypt. In his professional judgment the militia of North Carolina alone could soak up all the revenues of the United States because of their skill at wasting supplies. But his officer corps was peerless, and the

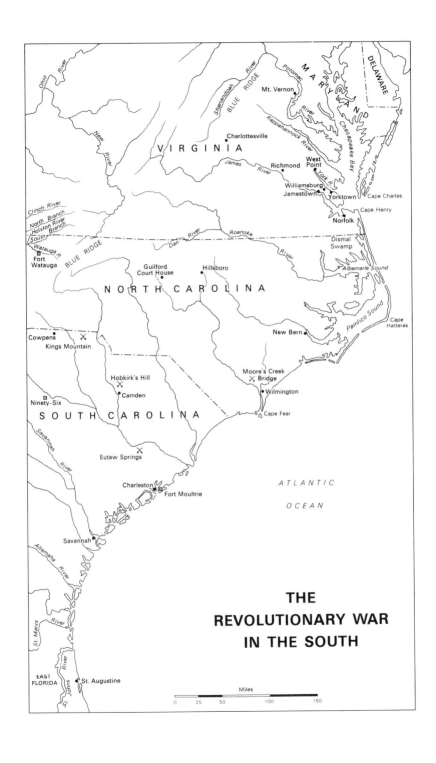

THE
REVOLUTIONARY WAR
IN THE SOUTH

Miles

0   25   50   100   150

best officer was Brigadier Daniel Morgan. Greene divided his force, putting half on either side of the route Cornwallis must take to invade North Carolina, with the western wing under Morgan's command. Cornwallis sent Colonel Banastre Tarleton with a loyalist legion to bag Morgan or chase him away. Morgan bagged Tarleton in the battle of Cowpens, January 17, 1781.

Tactically considered, Cowpens was the battle best fought by the Americans in the whole war. Morgan was not a master of the European volley-and-charge tactics, nor were his men fitted for such fighting. He put his militia in the front and had them fire a few rounds and fall back through his formed regulars. Their dropping back lured the British within range of the massed Continental infantry, who took the loyalist troops in front and on both flanks simultaneously, enveloping them on three sides, while Colonel William Washington's cavalry and the realigned militia cleaned out the rear of the British. It was a classic triumph, as the figures show: Tarleton, a hundred killed, 229 wounded, six hundred captured; Morgan, twelve killed and sixty-one wounded. The shooting lasted less than an hour. This was the only field on which Morgan was completely in command; in all other battles he was subordinate, so we know nothing of his strategic abilities, but tactically he was without superior.

Morgan and Greene immediately danced away from their lumbering opponents. Cornwallis, with grim determination, burned his heavy baggage and set his redcoats at forced marches, but he could not catch Greene and Morgan before they reunited and crossed into Virginia. Cornwallis summoned loyal subjects of the King, but they were timid about enlisting under him. Meanwhile, Greene added to his strength and surprised Cornwallis by coming back into North Carolina, bringing his whole force to Guilford Court House. Morgan was ill and off duty, but Greene adopted the Cowpens technique of a temporary screen of militia across a front of Continental regulars, and it worked well. The battle of Guilford Court House, March 15, 1781, was a pyrrhic victory for Cornwallis, costing him from a quarter to a third of his force, and gaining him nothing, as Greene saved his army by pulling away again. Cornwallis' distress is shown in the fact that he abandoned some of his wounded and left in a hurry for Wilmington, where he could get supplies.

Greene was too weak to pursue Cornwallis, but from March to

September he cleaned out the back country. He fought three battles, retreated from each field, and made the interior too uncomfortable for the British, who, continually harassed by the partisan bands, abandoned all interior posts. Greene had recovered everything but the shoreline without himself winning a battle. His formula was to preserve a fast-moving force while making life miserable for the British forces. He erred tactically in every battle but never made a strategic mistake. With a small, badly fed, underequipped force he reversed the Southern balance in the year after Camden. His was a peculiar but brilliant record: he never won a major battle, and he never lost a major campaign. His reputation is secure. Guilford Court House evoked again the popular new verb: "If Greene is so strong as to attack the enemy, he has only to keep up the ball awhile, and he must effectually ruin his Lordship. Two more such victories would probably Burgoyne him and his veterans."[5] Cornwallis was about to be Burgoyned, all right, but not by Greene.

When the British force limped back to Wilmington after Guilford Court House, ragged, and wearing brown-stained bandages, it looked more like a defeated than a victorious army. His Lordship had started with three thousand men. He had but seventeen hundred left, and they were in poor physical condition. Up in Virginia there were five thousand British troops, commanded by a general whom Cornwallis outranked. Perhaps the earl let himself be tempted by the thought that the Virginia theater had an army better suited to his station in life.

II

While Cornwallis was doing pretty much as he pleased, his nominal superior, Sir Henry Clinton, had other ideas on winning the war. He preferred to destroy American commercial and economic life. In December 1780, Clinton sent General Benedict Arnold with fourteen hundred mostly loyalist regulars to Virginia, where Arnold acted energetically and damagingly. George Washington and Jean Comte de Rochambeau sent Gilbert du Motier, Marquis de Lafayette, with reinforcements to try to trap Arnold for hanging. Clinton countered with another three thousand men. Virginia's green woods and fields, presided over by Governor Thomas Jefferson, were becoming ever more important scenes of war. Cornwallis, locked in Wilmington by his own military weakness, could not resist the attraction of a more active theater. His men and those in Virginia were the only mobile British troops, since all others were in fixed garrisons, but those six thousand could go anywhere safely as long as Britannia ruled the waves. Cornwallis and his men marched northward on April 25, 1781. Once in Virginia Cornwallis assumed command of the hunt of young Lafayette until Clinton revived a frayed old order to build a naval base on Chesapeake waters. Cornwallis issued picks and shovels, and started work at a place named Yorktown.

Meanwhile, a French squadron from Brest, under François de Grasse, Marquis de Grasse-Tilly, had slipped safely into Martinique, taking advantage of Admiral George Lord Rodney's temporarily distracting obsession with looting the Dutch island of St. Eustatia and its millions in prize money. While Cornwallis was yet stalking Lafayette in Virginia, de Grasse wrote to North America offering some naval help. Here was a tide in the affairs of men which the generals gladly took at the flood. French soldiers and sailors had been idling at Newport since July 1780, having plenty of fun but serving only to keep Clinton nervous about the safety of New York City. Upon receipt of de Grasse's offer, Washington longed to attack New York but agreed to meet the French guests in the Chesapeake. Rodney, dreading a New York winter, fearless of the French, and anxious about his Dutch prize money (then being litigated in English courts), went home while Cornwallis' men went on sweating over the new redoubts of Yorktown.

It was de Grasse's own decision to come north to help, but he made the decision with the help of a memorandum from the French minister to the United States, the Chevalier Anne de la Luzerne, who knew the American military situation and was a veteran soldier himself. Security was pretty loose, and the British naval commander at New York, Admiral Thomas Graves, dismissed an accurate report of French intentions as an idle boast. Washington was certainly weak in manpower; in the first five months of 1781 the Continental Army received only 2,574 recruits.[6] Recruiting was improving, however, and Pennsylvania, for one, had gone to a straightforward conscription of men for the regular Army.[7] The Continentals would not be as weak as they had been in Graves's former experience, though as late as August Washington was still fretting about his shortage of men.[8]

Washington now had new resources, for Robert Morris had become superintendent of finance. When Washington suggested that the men should have some cash before setting out for the South, Morris raised thirty thousand hard dollars for a payday (twenty thousand of which he borrowed from Rochambeau).

Except for the accumulation of military strength in Virginia, there was no visible sign of a dramatic break in the long drudging war. Even so well informed a man as young Congressman James Madison, only ninety days before the siege of Yorktown, confidently predicted more important operations in the neighborhood of New York City. That was also the view of the British high command.

In the West Indies de Grasse drew off the garrison of Saint Domingue after arranging for Spanish soldiery to guard the island, and borrowed the equivalent of his payroll from Spanish officials. He sent word to Washington and Rochambeau that he would arrive in the Chesapeake about September 1. He was at Elkton, Maryland, on September 3. Washington organized a defense of the Hudson, then started off through New Jersey with two thousand Continentals and five thousand French before Clinton realized that New York was not to be attacked. The New York press claimed that New Jersey felt abandoned "to the mercy of our enemies," and accurately reported the rebels' progress southward through New Jersey.[9] (Clinton's constant pressure on the Hudson defense force left behind by Washington led to the death of the only Congressman killed in combat during the war, Dr. Nathaniel Scudder, colonel of New Jersey militia, who lost his life in a skirmish at Shrewsbury in October.)

With two engineers out ahead of the force to find the best marching route, Washington pressed south with assurance. He confidently asked Morris for flour, salt meat, rum, and five hundred guineas in gold for espionage.[10] Although he grumbled about the depreciation of money, Morris met the needs almost as a matter of course; things had changed much in a year.[11] The Franco-American force marched through Philadelphia, reviewed by the members of the Congress at the State House door, to whom the French troops gave the salute reserved to kings. The watchers could only guess at the objective, but they realized something big loomed ahead. The young French officers were pleased with themselves. "All the ladies were assembled at M. de la Luzerne's residence, where they watched the army pass and were enchanted to see such handsome men and to hear such good music."[12] From the head of the Chesapeake, de Grasse ferried many of the troops to the James-York peninsula, and others marched along the western shore, some camping for a night in the present yard of the United States Naval Academy. On dry land, from Newport to the Chesapeake, the French troops averaged 14.8 miles a day, about three-quarters of the daily stint of Caesar's legions on campaign. A Continental soldier described them: "They stepped as though on edge. They were a dreadful proud nation."[13]

When all of the troops under Washington and Rochambeau gathered near Yorktown they numbered about sixteen thousand, of whom slightly less than half were French. Militia patrolled the roads and garrisoned important points for miles around. Yorktown, on the York River, an arm of the Chesapeake, was a strong position for small-scale operations. Cornwallis had an outer line but withdrew to his inner defenses except for two advanced redoubts to the east where high ground made the town easily accessible. The French engineers, with naval guns for besieging, knew their business, and went to work to pry Cornwallis loose with professional finesse.

Cornwallis had army rations for men but was short of forage for his draft animals. The besiegers settled in position on September 27, and within five days spied dead horses within the British lines. The French engineers began their attack-trenches on October 5 and moved ahead methodically. British gunners, beginning on October 6, made the diggers duck by flashing powder near the vents of their guns, as though to fire. But they fired little, perhaps because short of ammunition. On October 11 a young Virginia officer noted in his diary that many blacks "have died, in the most miserable Manner in York."[14] The British may have regarded them as expendable draft animals, since the death rate among whites was not notably high.

The French and Americans (under Colonel Alexander Hamilton) each seized one of the two external redoubts, included them in the siege works, lost them to storming parties, and recovered them without serious loss. On October 19 a patrol found a grounded boat containing a British officer's baggage, in which were letters saying rations were short and ammunition exhausted.

Cornwallis' force had not left by water under the comforting escort of the Royal Navy, because the Royal Navy had been blocked

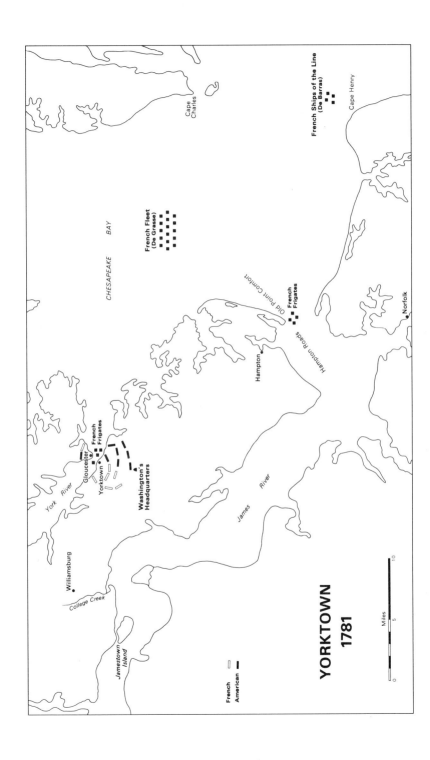

YORKTOWN
1781

French ▫
American ▬

French Ships of the Line
(De Barras)

Cape Henry

Cape Charles

French Fleet
(De Grasse)

CHESAPEAKE   BAY

French Frigates

Old Point Comfort

Hampton Roads

• Norfolk

• Hampton

French Frigates

Gloucester
Yorktown
Washington's Headquarters

York River

James River

• Williamsburg

College Creek

Jamestown Island

Miles
0   5   10

out of the battle by de Grasse. That is the decisive fact of the York-town campaign. The outcome of the siege had been settled three weeks before it began, in the battle off the Chesapeake, September 5, 1781. A British squadron shadowing de Grasse from the West Indies brought news of his arrival only after he was visible from American shores. It was not until September 5 that the British could get down from New York to the Chesapeake, where they found the French anchored. The French stood out in light airs to fight, and the British captains botched Admiral Graves's tactical plan. Only the leading British ships got into the fight, and those few suffered severely. The fleets drifted apart after a few hours of hammering. There was no more fighting, though they lay becalmed within sight of each other for several days. Cornwallis was stranded; naval help could not reach him.

The loss in sea casualties was about equal at six hundred each. HMS *Terrible* foundered a few days later, and the masts of the ship *Intrepid* were crippled. Graves had to go back to New York to refit, while de Grasse resumed his position at the entrance to Chesapeake Bay. The necessary siege guns and some welcome French naval support came down from Newport, which had been left unlocked by Graves. The British squadron, partly because distracted by a visit from royal Prince William, could not refit and return until October 21, which was too late.

There was but one possibility of escape for the landlocked army of Cornwallis—to cross the York and march swiftly northward to New Jersey where Clinton might be able to help. But foul weather prevented the river crossing, and Cornwallis ordered his drummers to beat "Parley." He surrendered on October 19, 1781. His situation was not wholly desperate. He still had a week's rations and his fortifications were still inviolate, but he was short of ammunition. We will, of course, never know whether he could have held out until the Royal Navy had a second try at extricating the force.

The terms of surrender were identical with those extracted from General Benjamin Lincoln by the British victors at Charleston, and at Washington's direction Lincoln received the surrender. Washington's rank and title were certainly established by this time, for Cornwallis' opening message bore the superscription: "To His Excellency Gen. Washington, Commanding. . . ."[15]

News of the surrender arrived at Philadelphia on October 22, and a rider brought Washington's official despatch on October 24. Washington's report was almost excessively restrained. It was enormous good news, but he held himself in, and very little cheerfulness broke through.[16] Perhaps he was moved by what a witness called the "present miserable melancholy plight" of his captives.[17] The members of the Congress were happy enough to chip in a dollar each (in hard money) to pay the expenses of Lieutenant Colonel Tench Tilghman who brought the news, and to vote him a horse "properly caparisoned, and an elegant sword,"[18] after he explained each article of the surrender to their satisfaction.

The Americans and French were good winners. They let Cornwallis keep a ship for despatches, and sent him on parole to New York (he took with him a load of objectionable loyalists). The ship, under flag of truce, brought back letters of thanks for the kindnesses of American and French officers, and a quantity of cheese and porter as tokens "in appreciation of . . . handsome treatment." Rochambeau had loaned Cornwallis 150,000 pounds, which was promptly repaid.[19]

The bagging of five or six thousand redcoats required that there be a good deal of correspondence in 1782 between the captors and the British headquarters at New York, carried on by flag-of-truce ships. These served to cover smuggling, escape of loyalists, slave trading, refit of ships, and the sale of tobacco to the British, all very vexing to the government of Virginia.

Washington wished to extend his victory march by quickly attacking New York or Charleston, but de Grasse thought he should restore the borrowed garrison of Saint Domingue and sailed south. Rochambeau's men wintered in Virginia, while Washington took up his post on the Hudson where, we may suppose, he still yearned for a triumphal re-entry into New York.

Those Americans who believed in the cause of independence seem to have recognized the meaning of Yorktown instinctively. The surviving records of the reception of the news reflect much greater joy than the people showed on getting the news of the treaty which confirmed the victory. The delegates

Resolved, That Congress will, at two o'clock this day, go in procession to the Dutch Lutheran church, and return thanks to Almighty God, for crowning the allied arms of the United States and France, with success, by the surrender of the whole British army under the command of the Earl of Cornwallis.[20]

President Thomas McKean wrote a florid and fulsome letter of praise to Washington, worthy of an Elizabethan courtier.[21] Madison saw the significance of the victory, calling it a "glorious success,"[22] and saying, "If these severe doses of ill fortune do not cool the phrenzy and relax the pride of Britain, it would seem Heaven had in reality abandoned her to her folly & her fate."[23] The Connecticut delegates told their governor it was a "great event,"[24] but Congressman Samuel Livermore of New Hampshire complained to the president of New Hampshire about his gout, sent only a newspaper account of the Yorktown triumph, and closed by saying, "My wish is to get home, from this intolerable expensive place, if once Vermont business was done."[25] First things first with Livermore.

There was also a faction in the Congress which actively promoted the hanging of Cornwallis for alleged atrocities in South Carolina. Its opponents claimed they had great difficulty in blocking the movement which would have required of Washington the "resigning his Command or forfeiting his Honor and Reputation. . . ."[26]

The city of Philadelphia celebrated with all its might. Flags flew, guns boomed, delegates and diplomatists went to church, the city glowed with lights, and "people of all ranks seemed to contend who should distinguish themselves most, in demonstrating their joy on this important event." Unluckily, rain set in, and fireworks had to be postponed until October 25. The talented and popular artist Charles Willson Peale ornamented the front of his house with a painted transparency full of patriotic symbolism, covering the whole of three storeys, and reading at the top "For Our Allies, Huzza! Huzza! Huzza!"[27]

The news spread outward. Boston had it by October 27, and church bells rang all day "with as merry a peal as we have heard since they rang the departure of Francis Bernard." In the harbor, ships flew the flags of most nations, and both artillery and ships' guns fired salutes. Public houses displayed the flags of the United States, France, and Spain. Everybody—"a wretched few excepted"—obviously felt triumphant.[28] In Fishkill, New York, the citizens consumed a roast ox and "plenty of liquor," drinking many toasts, displaying the allied flags, shooting their heavy guns, and lighting the sky at night with illuminations, rockets, firecrackers, and bonfires "which gave agreeable amusement to the numerous spectators."[29]

The loyalist press meditated for a week before commenting that the Continental Army was in the French service, paid with French gold, and entirely out of the control of the Congress. The French mistrusted the Congress and would allow only Washington to handle the cash. Thus the only ruler in America was "the *Frenchified* Washington."[30]

The surrender of Cornwallis may have come at the eleventh hour of the War for Independence. The French deserve much, but not all, credit for the victory, and the French Foreign Minister had said he would send no money, men, or ships after 1781. Whether he meant it we cannot know; it may have been a form of pressure to get the Americans to tax themselves. Altogether the French sent 63 ships mounting 3,668 guns and manned by 33,000 sea officers and men; the land forces numbered about 12,500, but they never had more than 8,400 soldiers in America at any one time. Looked at narrowly, one could say they merely equalized the original advantage the British received from renting German troops; but the Americans could not have won the war in the way they did without French financing and without French seapower. After the French came into the war, the Royal Navy lost control of the North Atlantic briefly in each year. One of those brief spans was the crucial period from September through October of 1781. This seems to have been the key point. The *de facto* division of the British Army into two North American commands compounded the weaknesses and made everything easier for the French and the Americans.[31]

Cornwallis' disaster was decisive in Britain. Before Yorktown the British were generally satisfied with their military leadership in America, though Cornwallis was rated higher than his superior, Clinton. Informed people could see hazards in the Cornwallis campaign. His defeat provoked several explanations. Clinton received blame for letting Washington and Rochambeau pass New York, and then not sending help to Cornwallis. The Navy had not properly commanded the Chesapeake. The Ministry had bungled. Washington had outgeneraled his opponents. The loyalists had let their British helpers down. None of this reflected on Cornwallis, who was cleared of guilt and became a popular hero. But the British ruling public was war-weary and began to see the conquest of the United States as impossible.[32] This loss of confidence was greater than the purely military situation in America justified, though the difficulties of the Treasury (not widely publicized) show that the British war effort was faltering. At any rate, the surrender of Cornwallis did what no other defeat since 1781 has accomplished: it convinced the British people they had lost a war at Yorktown, a few miles from Jamestown where the Anglo-American story began.

The war, to be sure, was not over. The British held a base in Maine, made their headquarters in New York City, controlled Westchester County and Long Island of New York, held Charleston, Savannah, and part of east Florida, and had small garrisons at Lake Champlain's northern end, Oswego, Detroit, and Mackinac. Washington wished to go on fighting because a large effort to expel the enemy would be no more costly than a "lingering War."[33] He and the Congress went ahead and planned on warfare through 1782, though Washington's operational plans were clouded by doubt of support from France. Counting 9,000 British troops in Canada, the enemy had a total of 26,000 men in America. Washington reflected on the advantages of carrying the war to South Carolina and Georgia, invading Canada, trying to reduce Halifax, surprising Bermuda, or investing New York, Charleston, or Savannah. But it was plain that his heart yearned for New York.[34] Relying on Lafayette's advice, he suggested that nothing would so encourage the French to help as congressional "pointed assurances" of a good Continental Army for the duration.[35] And while awaiting the next turn of events he improved the occasion by reshaping the high command of the Army, there being a shortage of brigadiers at the moment.[36] Through Lafayette he conveyed to the French government the no doubt pleasing thought that if all went well in America in 1782, Great Britain would be ruined.[37] Plainly, the commanding general of the Continental Army, no terrier, was all bulldog. Not that he enjoyed war. Lacking recent information on the state of European politics, he wished the United States to be in as strong a position as possible for negotiating peace if and when the opportunity came.[38] Washington could not know, but opportunity was raising its knuckles to knock.

18

Free, Sovereign, and Independent States

To suppress a rebellion requires good judgment, sufficient power, and a firm will. The British Ministry never had the judgment, and lost the power after 1777. But its will remained firm until the latter half of 1781, mostly because of optimistic misinformation from British officers and American loyalists. By 1781 there were doubts that the perennial optimism of the loyalist New York City press, for example, was founded on reality.[1] After news of Yorktown reached Parliament on November 25, the Lords still were firm for war, but Frederick Lord North's majorities in the Commons withered steadily. The election of 1780 had been crucial for the government but merely kept it alive, not stronger. The Yorktown despatches quickly reduced North's majority to forty-one as the independent squires gave up on the war. In January 1782 the majority waned to nineteen. Colonial Secretary Lord George Germain accepted the title of Viscount Sackville and resigned on February 11. Eleven days later a motion to stop the fighting failed by a single vote, and on March 4 a similar motion carried without a division. North and his ministers quit on March 20. New York's loyalist colony read the dismaying news of the 193 to 194 vote of February 22, on May 1.[2]

Early in 1782 the military situation was this: Washington brooded outside of New York City, Rochambeau and Lafayette were back in France, and de Grasse was in the West Indies concerting an attack on Jamaica with the Spanish (it never came off). The British could not be levered out of America, but British taxpayers were tired of the war. They were even getting bad news from the Indian and Pacific Oceans. Britain still held Gibraltar, but it was not as valuable as it became later, and the British might have traded it for something of value except that they never had a good enough offer. Every power except the Dutch had conquered islands, posts, ports, and coasts from each of its enemies, but only the United States had come close to its goal; the anti-British world was ahead in pawns, pieces, and *de facto* American independence.

The resignation of North came four long months after news of Yorktown, not because North was stubborn but because the King wished him to stay. George III hated to admit defeat, composed an abdication message, is thought to have alerted his yacht skipper for a passage to his Electorate of Hannover, but then, as has been said, took another look at the Prince of Wales and decided to do his duty. Peace offers were tendered throughout the war, and after 1777 North was willing to deal, but not King George. Thus the King prolonged the war. North finally had an excuse to go when he had to pay 20 per cent interest on his 1782 public loan.

Charles Watson-Wentworth, Marquis of Rockingham, became First Lord of the Treasury, but in the King's mind shared power with William Petty, Earl of Shelburne, Secretary at State for Home, Colonial, and Irish Affairs. Shelburne was a loner without much personal following, and seemed to lack both skill and desire to build a faction. Charles James Fox was Secretary at State for Foreign Affairs (the old "Northern Department," i.e., everything dealing with sovereigns).[3] These men were not precisely enemies of the United States, but Shelburne did not favor independence. He was a natural-born plotter but seems sincere in trying to arrange a comfortable relation with America inside the Empire. Fox favored independence, and quickly, to force the French to terms. The French had some ideas of their own. They thought changed circumstances in India, for example, required some revisions of the 1763 treaty. The Americans believed independence the absolute necessity of their cause. Britain preferred to divide the French and the Americans above all else. Until Rockingham died after ninety days in office, there was only talk, talk, talk.

Shelburne succeeded Rockingham, and the British interest now had a single head. That prime interest was to isolate France in the diplomatic world, which boded much good for the United States.

The Americans learned of the fall of the North Ministry by news coming in a ship which arrived in New York on May 5, bringing also Sir Guy Carleton to command in place of Sir Henry Clinton, and to act as "*commissioner for making peace or war* in North America. . . ."[4] This was really a military ruse to get the troops out of North America in the double hope of separating America from France, and using the troops against France and Spain elsewhere. Carleton asked George Washington for a safe conduct for an agent to visit Washington's headquarters; Washington cautiously referred Carleton to the Congress.[5] James Madison noticed the exchange with the wise comment that any request from Carleton would be rejected. Washington was merely to forward future correspondence to the Congress.[6] There was to be no negotiation in America. The diplomatic action was in Europe.

II

The War for Independence had become but one theater of a world war, and, except to Americans, not necessarily the most important. With better military fortune in other theaters, the French and Spanish might have been willing to continue the war for a long time with or without America. To get Spain into the war the French had talked of various rewards—Gibraltar, the Floridas, Jamaica, a share of Newfoundland fisheries, the land between the Appalachian crest and the Mississippi. The trans-Allegheny West was a prize to which only the French were indifferent. Since Spain had not been able to take Gibraltar, the American West would be a pleasing compensation for its efforts. The French really did not mind leaving Gibraltar British; it kept Spain usefully nervous and jumpy. The Americans said the West was part of the United States. The French hinted that the western boundary of the United States was set at the Appalachian divide by the Royal Proclamation of 1763. Perhaps the Americans could satisfy themselves with the land between the Cumberland and Ohio Rivers, which did not quite reach to the Mississippi? All these things were seen as in diplomatic dreams, but they show that the American Revolution was but a detail in a vast landscape.

In 1780, unknown to the Foreign Ministry, Jacques Necker, the finance minister, had waged a private peace offensive, probably as an economy drive to balance the books and thus earn the smile of King Louis XVI. His undercover peace feelers blunted themselves on the stone wall of American insistence on independence, and only encouraged the British to think France was in bad money trouble. He was fired for his official stinginess, not for diplomatic meddling.

In that same year the Spanish and British had some talks. Vergennes could not learn the substance of their conversations, and from 1780 to 1783 he tried many schemes to get the possibly incriminating documents. The only result was the capture and bloody execution of his best spy in England, and the wrecking of his intelligence network there. Vergennes even fell into the trap of accepting a double agent planted on his embassy in the Netherlands, whose mission was probably to inflame French suspicions of Spain. This stealthy disorder in Europe serves the story of American history only to establish that every political leader in Europe distrusted all foreigners (including allies), and some of his fellow countrymen.

Into this hugger-mugger came John Jay in 1780 as United States minister to Spain. Spain was dealing with Britain through a double agent, in the hope of getting Gibraltar. Jay was treated with a frigidity that cost Spain much in the long run, for Jay learned both power politics and skepticism. Skepticism was the healthiest attitude he could have. For example, when he later met Vergennes he met a man who believed Silas Deane's observations that the Congress lacked respect and the American rebels lacked perseverance. The French world view was compounded of too little fact and too much suspicion, which is not a bad description of paranoia.

Another important American with no illusions about European altruism was oaken John Adams, whose only concession to continental ways was to give up chewing tobacco in royal palaces. After a quarrel with Vergennes he went to the Netherlands to borrow money, not only for sake of the money itself but also to lessen American dependence on the French. His suspicions of America's best friend were sharpened when he heard about a proposal for a peace congress at Vienna, which then flickered in dimly lit baronial brains. He said American independence or British evacuation of North America, one or the other, must be accepted first, and the French alliance was to bind as long as any truce lasted. That killed the Vienna meeting in advance.

Early in 1781 there were rumors that Britain would stop the war but keep Georgia and South Carolina. If the price were right, the French foreign minister would have been willing to partition America. To other Frenchmen too, this was a very attractive idea, but the Chevalier Anne de la Luzerne, minister to the United States, cooled French interest by pointing out that to divide America would strengthen Britain, while a whole America would be an advantage to France. Nevertheless, the French would have been willing to deal directly with state governments instead of the Congress. It was the complete secession from the British Empire that appealed to the French, not the prospect of a strong union.

In Philadelphia the French were served about as well as possible by their Minister Luzerne, a capable, careful, and intelligent man, whose influence in the Congress was pervasive, and, naturally, was exercised in the interest of King Louis XVI. Apparently life in Philadelphia made the members of the Congress more susceptible to his cuisine, music, and general hospitality. "A rich commercial city," he wrote, "offering the most frequent opportunities for pleasure and dissipation is not suitable to the representatives of an infant republic which can sustain itself only by economy, activity, and application to work."[7] While his advice was often wise, he did nothing to toughen the moral fiber of the infant republic.

What Luzerne did was to insinuate himself into the congressional contention between the followers of Silas Deane and the supporters of Arthur Lee. French influence eliminated Lee, and Deane's indiscretions finished him, so superficial peace reigned by 1780. By that time Franklin was minister to France, Jay was minister to Spain, and John Adams minister to negotiate peace with Britain, if and when. The French decided to assure the appointment of a peace delegation which included more than John Adams. This project developed into an exercise in parliamentary choreography in June 1781. First the

Congress elected John Adams again. Then the delegates decided to add two more commissioners and agreed that Jay should be one of them. For the third member the vote was Jefferson five, Franklin four, and Henry Laurens one, and the totals held that way for three ballots. A motion to put both Jefferson and Franklin on the delegation passed, making a four-man mission. Next they added Laurens to make five.[8]

At the moment the only member known to the French to be cynical about French benevolence was John Adams, who knew that neither France nor Spain wished the United States to amount to very much. (The Spaniards, at the moment, were teaching Jay the same lesson.)

No foreign diplomat since Luzerne has had as much positive influence on the decisions of the United States as he had. The Articles of Confederation expressly gave foreign policy into the hands of the Congress, but Luzerne had no scruples about dealing directly with state governments. Much of the American diplomatic correspondence was open to the French, because Vergennes had the cypher used by John Adams for out-mail, and the cyphers used by Jay and the Congress in correspondence. Luzerne also had the cypher used by Laurens. Such meticulous espionage was not really necessary, because the Congress was a leaky vessel so far as security was concerned, and believed rather credulously in the benevolence of the French government. Both Luzerne and his predecessor could usually learn what they wished to know about congressional motivation and goals merely by asking.

In the end, Jefferson did not choose to go to Paris.

Laurens departed but fell into British hands. He was a rich merchant of Charleston who had formerly been a slave trader. In this respect it can only be remarked that he was probably the first prominent man in the lower South to say he did not approve of slavery. Because he had been president of the Congress, the British thought they had caught a very important prisoner, and they lodged him in the Tower of London on suspicion of treason from October 1781 until the end of the year. According to his son and Edmund Burke, Laurens' health suffered from confinement, and after a rumpus in the Commons Burke secured his release on parole from the Court of King's Bench,[9] under terms which convinced the senior Laurens he was prohibited from talking with close relatives.[10] In November 1782 the two governments exchanged Cornwallis and Laurens, and Laurens went to Paris in time for the final drafting of the terms of peace.

III

A friend of John Adams once said he was unfit for diplomacy, since he could not dance, drink heavily, gamble, flatter, promise, dress like a courtier, swear, and flirt with ladies. He lacked all the essentials for the role. There were thousands of men in Europe better fitted than he, though only a tenth as intelligent. From the earliest of his writings until his death, Adams, while sometimes deflected from logic by his passions, recorded a respect for reason and a hunger for fame. It has been observed that he never wrote a dull letter. Although usually considered one of the radical rebels, he was no democrat, nor was he an original political philosopher. Like the lawyer he was, he piled up precedents from ancient practices and thinkers to show how the United States could achieve what it ought to achieve. This made him at once a conservative and a revolutionary.[11] In religion he bumped against mysteries and dismissed them with the remark that it would be presumptuous to dogmatize about such things which only God can understand. In theology he had one attitude that would make him even more suspicious of the French: "A free government and the Roman Catholick religion can never exist together in any nation or Country. . . ."[12] He had a low opinion of the French, and not much higher regard for his colleague Franklin. As for Europe in general, he said Benedict Arnold would have been true to the cause if he had had the benefit of a tour of that continent. Through the Revolution he believed the American people were generally a virtuous lot, and he identified the antagonism toward Britain with a love of liberty and a wish to promote the common good. Later he came to believe his fellow countrymen had changed for the worse, which explains why his political thought after 1790 seems unrelated to the aspirations of 1775 and 1776.

After returning to Paris from the Netherlands in October 1782, John Adams persuaded Franklin that American thoughts, words, and deeds should be kept from the French. Franklin accepted the policy, because the French were pretty secretive themselves. This was a fruit of the quarrel between Vergennes and Adams, which was surely picked by Vergennes in order to get rid of Adams. Adams had no official status at the French Court when Vergennes chose to chide him about American fiscal policy and got such a hot response. Despite Franklin's rather weak support of Vergennes, the Congress had gone no further than to surround Adams with other negotiators, who, because Jefferson did not go and Laurens was captured, were only two, Jay and Franklin. Jay became as suspicious as Adams, and together they kept Franklin from falling into the arms of the French Foreign Ministry.

The browbeating of Adams by Vergennes, and Luzerne's attempt to neutralize Adams's influence by packing the delegation, was a French strategic error. Adams was a greater man than any Frenchman who held political power then, and their behavior put him on his guard against any sentence uttered by a French official.

Franklin, of course, was no weakling. He was not always morally consistent, but he was shrewd, and he had a tough common sense in politics and social matters. Outside of science, in which he stood in that century's front rank, his suppleness of principle suggests that conventional European diplomacy was his strength. Franklin showed an understanding of the correct American tactics in July 1782, after talking with Jay but before Adams came to Paris, when he dug in his heels and said that independence was America's absolutely indispensable diplomatic principle and goal.

Jay had been in Spain from 1780 until 1782, holding out in favor of alliance with Spain before any deal be made with Spain. The Congress was willing to yield its claim to the Mississippi River in exchange for substantial Spanish help in 1781, but Jay said he would have to see a treaty of alliance first. In this way he postponed the issue until he joined the peace delegation in Paris. He firmly opposed letting the United States carry any of France's diplomatic burdens. If the French committed themselves to third parties in any way, the American mission would not accept those commitments as binding on their own negotiations. Once the American war had become merely a strand in the European political tapestry the French alliance could be a liability. Jay was wise to be suspicious. His observation of European monarchies in action certainly forestalled any temptation to be anything but republican and nationalist. He had learned that every time he yielded to Spanish arguments the Spaniards took it as a sign of weakness and raised new requirements. His diplomatic education was a series of exasperations. It is now plain that Spain would have sold out anybody, would even have delivered Louis XVI to the Tower of London in handcuffs, would have done all harm short of war to prevent American independence—if Gibraltar could be had in return. Jay was not edified. He decided to believe in peace when he saw it, and as late as the end of August 1782 he advised Maryland's purchasing agent to keep on stockpiling military supplies in America.[13] The leading authority on the peacemaking thinks Jay's skepticism made him the key man in the negotiations. It is commonly believed that his French Protestant upbringing made him suspicious of France, but he was equally cynical about Britain because of its double-dealing in the years 1780–1782.

It is axiomatic in the politics of a republic that one does not make an enemy unnecessarily, but no such principle governed the Spanish monarchy. It seems to have gone out of its way to make Jay feel uncomfortable. Jay thought he should not have to haggle with a nation that was also at war with Britain. True, Spain was secretly dickering with Britain for its own profit, but Jay should have received silkier treatment, if only because a reconciled British Empire could destroy the Spanish Empire at will. Instead of keeping his friendship, the Spanish tampered with Jay's mail and compelled him to draw on Franklin in Paris for his bread and rent. The myopic Spanish did not even see the significance of Yorktown. For Jay it was a relief to depart for Paris in May 1782.

In reshaping its delegation the Congress had drafted new instructions. The need for them arose because European powers were proposing a mediation of the quarrel. If they could get away with it, the neutral arbiters would proceed to vest the belligerents with the territory under their actual control at the moment, on the principle which international lawyers call *uti possidetis*. Luzerne posed a delicate question: would the American ministers receive instructions to consult with France at every turn and twist of the process, and to follow French advice?

The Congress had to answer cautiously. Two requirements seemed necessary: the recognition of the independence of the United States, and the continuance of the French alliance. It did not seem prudent to shackle the negotiators with fixed requirements on boundaries and other questions. Luzerne assured the Congress that the French Court would defend American interests as zealously as French interests; could the Congress promise him it would do the same for France? The Congress decided to instruct its envoys to be completely candid with the French, to do nothing about a peace without French knowledge. Luzerne managed to persuade them to insert a final clause which no proud country would accept today.

The episode boils down to the fact that the French wrote the American instructions. About a third of the delegates opposed the act. John Adams resented the French influence and thought America should blush. Jay thought the instructions were beneath the dignity of the United States and tried to resign his commission, but the Congress refused his resignation. In the end the proposed great-powers mediation faded from serious discussion. The enlargement of the American mission and the French drafting of its instructions were the only fruits of the projected interference of other continental powers.

Before being tailored by Luzerne, the congressional instructions told the American envoys to act in "concurrence" with the French. After Luzerne's persuasion, this was changed to read "ultimately to govern yourself by their advice and opinion . . . in your whole conduct." A roll call being requested, this amendment carried 7 to 2, with Pennsylvania split and Rhode Island lacking a second delegate to vote. By individuals the vote was 20 to 9. Of the nine nays, six were from New England, two from Pennsylvania, and one from Virginia (James Madison voted "aye").[14]

The French interest was not wholly confined to continental power politics. The Treaty of 1763 had practically barred the French from the Newfoundland fisheries, a fact remembered with pain in France. Certainly there was an interest in recovering access to a trade that all nations called a nursery of seamen. It might yet happen that the United States would conquer Canada, in which case the settlement of the fisheries question would be easier for France if it could be separated from the question of Canada.[15] The French had long wished to oppose New England pretensions to special rights in the use of Newfoundland waters and shores for the fishing industry. How little the Congress understood French desires is shown by a belated revision of the instructions in January 1782, seven months after it had accepted Luzerne's proposed instructions, in which it reminded the mission in Paris of the importance of both boundaries and fisheries. The Congress innocently counted on French support for American claims to a vested right to catch and dry cod near and on Newfoundland. The delegates were invincibly ignorant of the French disposition and still clung to the belief in French benevolence. If the peace mission in Paris had obeyed instructions to the letter, the United States would have remained a French satellite.

Vergennes had tried to get the Congress to dismiss Adams. Failing that, Luzerne manipulated the Congress to saddle Adams with four other peace negotiators and a set of instructions which should have been stamped "Made in France." After all this was arranged, and only then, the French Foreign Ministry, with a feigned air of reluctance, said France might have to settle *its* war by agreeing that each warring country should keep what it had conquered, which would leave redcoats in many posts in America, including New York City and Charleston. John Adams became almost as anti-French as George III. While the French were reorganizing the American peace mission, they also managed to get the election of Robert R. Livingston as secretary for foreign affairs, but he turned out to be no French pawn, being a strong-willed Hudson Valley baron with a mind of his own. With Jay and Adams as members of the American negotiating delegation, Vergennes had lost two votes already. But he had driven an icicle into the personal relations of Adams and Benjamin Franklin, United States minister to France, when he had persuaded Franklin to write to the Congress that Adams had offended the French and that more tact was needed. Adams added Franklin to his private lifetime blacklist, but did not let his anger affect the performance of his official duties.

In the winter of 1781 Vergennes had considered the partition of America. By the following spring he was thinking of arranging a peace settlement for each state separately. Letting this be known, he had to listen to a lecture by John Adams on the nature of the Confederation. Perhaps shaken by this experience, Vergennes began to think he did not care to speak for America at all, because the United States might disavow France. This fear of American repudiation—which could only strengthen Britain—had nothing to do with love of America, but it left the American envoys free to go ahead on their own. When Shelburne came into the headship of the British Ministry in July 1782, the Americans, as Madison intelligently noted, were in a position to deal with a man whose policy was so flexible that it could be adjusted to any event.[16]

IV

In the last days of the victory winter of 1781–1782, an Englishman in Paris approached Benjamin Franklin with an offer to carry a message to Shelburne. Franklin wrote a letter, dated March 22, and received by Shelburne as Rockingham was forming a new Ministry. The Ministry read Franklin's note and decided that Shelburne should reply by sending a personal representative to Paris. The man sent was Richard Oswald. Oswald was an octogenarian. He had been a merchant and remembered the friendly profitable days before the 1760's. He also foresaw the growth of the United States, which he somewhat overestimated as sure to reach eighty million people by 1860. Such a nation could be a useful friend. While he was inclined to be generous toward America, the Ministry's trust in him was not misplaced. Except for an earlier erroneous undercalculation of American willingness to fight for long, his judgment had been excellent.

Oswald's original commission authorized him to treat with representatives of the "Colonies or Plantations." When Jay arrived at Paris he was sensitive to this language and refused to talk as a colonial. Both Franklin and Vergennes thought the wording harmless, but that simply made Jay doubt Vergennes. It was Jay's firm conviction that independence was the starting point, not a matter to be negotiated. He brought Franklin around to his view. The Ministry decided to admit the independence of the United States as a prior condition, and to try to restore the status of 1763 everywhere else. Oswald returned to Paris to arrange for a general peace conference.

There was a minor difficulty inside the Ministry, since Shelburne's jurisdiction extended only to colonies, while the fat, sloppily dressed, jovial Charles James Fox had charge of relations with independent nations. Fox was almost offensively pro-American, wearing blue and buff as his political colors. He sent Thomas Grenville to Paris to talk with Franklin and Vergennes, and to admit American independence as a starting point. Although the difference between Shelburne and Fox has received the most attention, the salient fact of this meeting was that Vergennes told Franklin and Grenville to go ahead by themselves on American independence, that their conversations were not the business of the French. Grenville had no authorized powers to make commitments, so this preliminary conference was indecisive. Meanwhile, Oswald was shuttling back and forth between London and Paris, representing Shelburne's views, and nothing of consequence could be settled through May and June. Jay and Franklin had established that independence was a precondition, and the British had the cheering news that Rodney had smashed de Grasse in the battle of the Saintes (April 12), hence there would be no Franco-Spanish assault on Jamaica and no French hope of dictating peace to Britain.

Then on July 1 Rockingham died, to be succeeded on July 11 by Shelburne, which ended the rivalry between the Colonial and Foreign Offices.

Jay asked Benjamin Vaughan, an English friend of Shelburne then in Paris, to tell Shelburne it would be wise to deal separately with the Americans. He was not proposing a separate peace, but it came to that in the end. And Jay sent along a freezingly anti-Spanish suggestion. Florida was British in title but Spanish by possession. Jay would recommend that Carleton be allowed to attack it, and if Carleton conquered Florida, its northern boundary would be moved to 32 degrees, 28 minutes north latitude (which would add the southern third of present Mississippi and Alabama). Jay showed a vindictive feeling toward Spain in this matter; it was not really to American interest to have Britain as neighbor at each end of the country. But Shelburne wanted war no more; however, he did keep the American question separate, and in his own hands.

Shelburne did not favor American independence. His ideal price for recognizing it was a complete break between France and the United States, and he preferred to deal with the states separately. He would have liked to impose a tough treaty, and *then* admit independence. Jay said independence must come first, in order to get the British Army out of North America. Simultaneously, the French and Spanish were stalling for time to finesse the trans-Allegheny for Spain. Jay, impatient, wished to go it alone, and in August he managed to implant the notion that Britain could get better terms from France if peace with America were an accomplished fact.

Vergennes had now concluded that an early peace would be best, and he and the Spanish amused themselves by drawing lines on the map of the United States, which Jay ignored. The British captured a

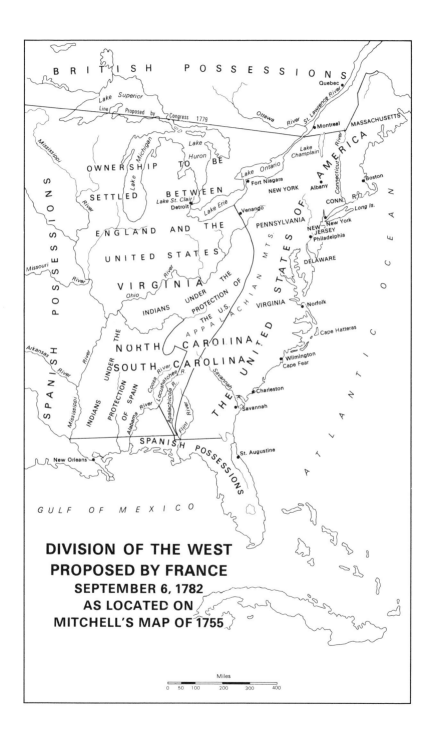

DIVISION OF THE WEST
PROPOSED BY FRANCE
SEPTEMBER 6, 1782
AS LOCATED ON
MITCHELL'S MAP OF 1755

letter from François Barbé-Marbois, of Luzerne's staff in Philadelphia, most uncomplimentary to the Americans, which they gave to Jay. Gérard de Rayneval went to London for Vergennes on what has been called "the double-cross mission," September 1. He proposed a new set of boundaries in the West which would give the United States the land between the Cumberland and Ohio Rivers, with a corridor running south to Florida back of the Appalachian Front. The Old Southwest would be a Spanish Indian protectorate; the Old Northwest would be a British Indian protectorate. This would compensate Spain for not getting Gibraltar, which still held out stoutly. Rayneval had explained the idea to Jay but kept his trip to London secret. Jay learned of it, and, we may suppose, it did not surprise him. Rayneval's overriding purpose was to see whether Britain would make a peace to restore France to its former dignity in the world, but the Franco-Spanish opposition to American claims was genuine.

Shelburne now decided to gamble on separate negotiations with the Americans. His men in Paris assured him there could be no peace unless independence were acknowledged. The private negotiations began on September 23.

Shelburne had tried to postpone independence by suggestions of a close alliance, or common citizenship, or a "federal union." Federal union was a popular idea among opposition politicians. Shelburne had written to Oswald, "My private opinion would lead me to go a great way for Federal Union; but is either country ripe for it? If not means must be left to advance it."[17] He left means to advance it by writing a conciliatory treaty. Oswald told him the American mission in Paris was getting irritable, and if he hoped for a conciliatory peace he had better get on with it before American necks were stiffer.

By the end of November the provisional draft was finished, and Jay managed to persuade Franklin to keep his mouth shut while the work was done. The preliminary concession of independence was a great diplomatic victory, for, after all, that was what the war was about. American independence was a large item in everybody's agenda. France wished its concession as late as possible so America would not quit the war. Spain wished to put it off until the Gibraltar matter was properly settled. Britain's ideal solution would be first a truce, second a treaty which included independence, and third an armistice until things were tidied up. The delegates of the United States stood firm for independence at the outset, in order to get the

British forces out of the United States before the Continental Army fell apart—as it probably would during a long truce.

After independence and the boundaries, the Americans had some interest in Canada and much interest in loyalist claims. Franklin worked out a systematic argument that Britain should yield Canada, but the improvement of the British military situation made his logic unconvincing. Franklin had bungled, earlier, in offering to assume claims of the loyalists in return for Canada. It would have been better not to have mentioned the loyalist claims in advance because that might seem to legitimize them, but Oswald and Shelburne kept it quiet and did not embarrass him.

No peace which bound the states to satisfy loyalist claims for property losses would have been "conciliatory." The matter came up later in Paris, but Franklin killed it by suggesting a balancing of rebel claims against loyalist claims. This was a most unattractive proposition to the British, who satisfied themselves with a token clause in favor of loyalists.

When the draft was finished it still had to satisfy the French, who, in turn, had to keep their Spanish allies happy. Very surprisingly, the Spanish minister in Paris, Pedro de Bolea, Conde de Aranda, made peace possible by defying his instructions, forgetting Gibraltar and taking Florida instead. The award of the trans-Allegheny to the United States by Britain had put Spain in a weak position, and the minister felt he must at least get Florida. This was taking a personal risk, but his hazard made peace possible.

Back in Philadelphia, the Congress was unaware negotiations had started until after they ended.[18] The delegates were considering a change in the membership of the Paris mission and its instructions, to remove the stain of Francophilia. Franklin would have to go because he was a western land speculator, and Jay too because he was pro-French. This could have been very embarrassing all around, but James Madison persuaded the Congress to stand pat. Gradually, private letters, British documents, and West Indian newspapers arrived with rumors and statements of negotiations. A public letter to the Lord Mayor of London, dated December 3, spoke of a preliminary draft completed on November 30. This was contradicted by a French report that the negotiations might not lead to peace. Finally, after five months of official silence, Captain Joshua Barney arrived on

March 12, 1783, with despatches from the mission and a copy of the provisional treaty of November 30.

Because it was an excellent treaty and because it was made by Americans, it has been assumed to have been the product of moral superiority. The fact is that Franklin, Adams, and Jay had won a great victory, and they won it by learning the rules of the European diplomatic game and playing the game to win. It was a team effort, and they were the best team in the world at the moment. What was superior was not American morality but American republicanism, which allowed the choice of the most competent negotiators without regard for their pedigrees. Hereditary aristocracy did not have a chance against the talent available to the Congress.

The provisional treaty declared the United States free and independent. It established the national boundaries and confirmed American fishing "rights" in Newfoundland waters. Concerning the loyalists, it promised there would be no impediment to the collection of debts, the Congress would recommend the restoration of confiscated property, and the states would cease confiscations and further prosecutions. The British Army would withdraw. The navigation of the Mississippi River would be free to both parties. Finally, any conquests after November 30, 1782, would be restored. The conferees in Paris signed an armistice on January 20, 1783, which was known in America late in March. The Congress approved the armistice 10 to 0; by individuals the vote was 26 to 1.[19] The definitive treaty, dated September 3, 1783, began, "In the name of the Most Holy and Undivided Trinity," and added a clause requiring ratification in six months; otherwise it was identical.

The boundaries were approximately those of the present United States east of the Mississippi, less Florida and the southern parts of Louisiana, Mississippi, and Alabama. The northern boundary at its northeast and northwest corners provoked later controversy, but it was obscurely drawn only because of ignorance of geography. More important than potential controversies in the north was a secret clause on the boundary of Florida, which the Congress accepted without roll call.[20]

It is hereby understood and agreed, that in case Great Britain, at the conclusion of the present war, shall recover, or be put in possession of West Florida, the line of northern boundary between the said province and the United States shall be a line drawn from the mouth of the river Yassous, where it unites with the Mississippi, due east to the river Apalachicola.

In sum, if Florida were British it was to be bigger than if it were Spanish. The difference between the two lines was roughly ninety miles. Jay got even with the Spaniards.

The fishing settlement permitted Americans to fish in Newfoundland waters and to dry or cure their catches on the unsettled coasts of Labrador or Nova Scotia, but not Newfoundland. It was the work of John Adams, but it was not immediately satisfactory and provoked disputes lasting until 1911.

The clauses which seemed to benefit the loyalists were eyewash, inserted to save King George's face. He could now say he had done everything possible for them.

On the American side the document was the product—in order of influence—of Jay, Franklin, Adams, and Laurens. Shelburne, through Oswald, did the thinking for Britain. Considering that the United States was still an occupied country, and that Great Britain was in no immediate danger of military destruction, it was a generous settlement.

19

Independence Won

The French Court did not applaud the Anglo-American Treaty of 1783 which acknowledged American independence and ended the war. Although the French Foreign Minister, Charles Gravier, Comte de Vergennes, had approved separate negotiations, talking was not the same as signing. The Franco-American Treaty of Alliance explicitly forbade separate peace. Vergennes mildly rebuked the United States minister, Benjamin Franklin, for coming to a final agreement with Britain. Franklin answered that nothing had been agreed upon which hurt the interests of France, and if the American mission had been guilty of anything, it was guilty only of a violation of etiquette. He added an oblique reminder that things could be worse: "*The English . . . flatter themselves they have already divided us*."[1] It would be best not to quarrel publicly. Vergennes, to another Frenchman, wrote, "We have never based our policy towards the United States on their gratitude. This sentiment is infinitely rare among sovereigns and unknown to republics."[2]

Actually, while John Jay, Franklin, John Adams, and Henry Laurens were writing the provisional draft with Richard Oswald, the British representative, Vergennes had been talking privately with other British agents in hope of frustrating some American hopes. But his position was awkward. If the French delayed a settlement, the issue of independence could raise a row in Parliament and the pacific

Ministry of William Petty, Earl of Shelburne, might fall. So the Anglo-American negotiators finished their work, and the French had to continue to lend money to preserve the alliance until they had a peace of their own. Otherwise the Americans and the British might be jointly unpleasant to the French. This was a triumph for a scorned provincial country. The United States made its separate peace and kept the French alliance.

For Shelburne himself it was not simply a matter of announcing peace and printing a treaty. The treaty, but not its terms, was made known to Parliament on December 5, 1782, and went off to America under a British passport which matter-of-factly referred to the "United States." As an American wrote, "Tis signed by the King of the British Penitents."[3] In Parliament, to make acceptance easier, Shelburne allowed some confusion on the question of whether the acknowledgment of independence was unconditional or contingent upon a satisfactory British peace with France. Naturally suspicious, the Americans became quite uneasy at this apparent deviousness. In the end all was well for the American interest.

Official news of the treaty arrived in Philadelphia in a packet on March 11, 1783. News of the peace was available generally in the American press in the early days of April, complete with the text of the provisional treaty.

Nobody could seriously quarrel with the terms. At first it was even suspected that Britain was overly generous in order to buy the United States out of the war so that full British attention could be concentrated on fighting the French.[4] There was a feeling that the United States was showing ingratitude, and this notion that the treaty was somehow anti-French received encouragement when the Chevalier Anne de la Luzerne, French minister to the United States, transmitted a disappointed note from Vergennes. The Congress debated the propriety of the separate settlement for nine days. Robert R. Livingston, Secretary for Foreign Affairs, let the negotiators in Paris know he disapproved of the separate negotiations (but he liked the terms), and feared the treaty might provoke the enmity of Spain. While the Congress was debating the correctness of American behavior, Luzerne received another note from Vergennes to the effect that Franklin's explanations were satisfactory.

That left but one other cause for dissatisfaction—the secret clause by which Florida's northern boundary would be farther north if it became British than if it remained Spanish. This seemed somehow dishonorable. The Congress would either have to keep the secret or destroy its own envoys. Delegates suspected it had been extorted from the envoys by the British in order to split the United States and France. Actually, it was Jay's revenge for innumerable Spanish snubs.

What does a Congress do if it gets a treaty intrinsically satisfactory but negotiated by suspect means? It refers the matter to a committee, which reports out a mild reproof, on which no action is taken. That was the therapy which the Congress applied to heal its own conscience.

The final ratification of the definitive treaty by the United States was technically though not wilfully illegal. After a long wait the Congress got nine states together and said they ratified the treaty by unanimous vote of the members present. But there was only one delegate each from New Hampshire and New Jersey. Because of the long delay, the Congress disregarded the clause in the Articles of Confederation that required two delegates present to cast a state's vote.[5] The date was January 14, 1784; the vote was 23 to 0. Next they had to deliver the signed paper by March 3, according to the six-months-ratification clause. It arrived at Paris on May 12, but no one made any difficulty.

Should the United States have been guided in every respect by the French? For once we have a laboratory control. The Dutch leaned heavily on the French, tried to get all losses returned, all damages made good, and to write the principles of the League of Armed Neutrality into their treaty. These goals were impossible; after all, partnership with France was no merit in British eyes. The Dutch felt betrayed. By contrast the American terms were a triumph. Ironically, they resulted from a reaction against French influence. Luzerne had pushed the Americans too far in the instructions he had dictated and had driven them, stiff-necked, into a separate peace.

II

The French Foreign Ministry, on reading the Anglo-American terms, was surprised at Britain's generosity. Vergennes wrote to one of his subordinates, "You will notice that the English buy peace rather than make it. Their concessions, in fact, as well in the matter of the boundaries as in that of the fisheries and the loyalists, exceed all that I could have thought possible."[6]

Approval was far from unanimous in Britain among those whose opinions counted—what might be called the ruling public. Merchants, loyalists, the Penn family, the naval stores industry, persons concerned with the future cooperation of the northwest Indians, and political opportunists murmured against the settlement. To get acceptance Shelburne played on war weariness, which was his strongest point. He talked of the great costs of continuing war, of danger to the public credit, and of the weakness of the Royal Navy. The problem of the opposition was to accept peace while disapproving it, which they did by voting approval of the treaty and a censure on the Ministry that made it. Shelburne resigned, and in the Ministry which succeeded his, Charles James Fox had responsibility for the last details. Without changing the essence of things, he managed to set awry the benevolent tableau so carefully staged by Shelburne. He completed the peace but flatly declined to make a commercial treaty with the fledgling United States. Thus Fox, who publicly took the American side when Frederick Lord North fought the rebellion, planted the seed of the War of 1812.

As well as can be learned from studying the British press, public officials differed from their social equals in private life. The ministers were more legalistic and conservative, more concerned to put France down, more anxious to preserve the British trade domination of the Western world. Men out of office wished to see a true conciliation which would separate France and America. They would have been willing to admit American independence as early as 1778, and then to make a generous trade treaty with the new nation.[7] It was this element which Shelburne, and almost no other public official, reflected. His position was politically weak. American operations were deadlocked, the French Navy had suffered a resounding defeat since Yorktown, Gibraltar was relieved, the French were obviously anxious for peace, and half of Shelburne's Ministry wished to continue the war. Looked at from their point of view, victory in a year or two was not impossible.[8]

King George III took the end very hard. As he wrote,

I cannot conclude without mentioning how sensibly I feel the dismemberment of America from the Empire, and that I should be miserable indeed if I did not feel that no blame on that account can be laid to my door, and did not also know that knavery seems to be so much the striking feature of the inhabitants, that it may not in the end be an evil that they will become aliens to this Kingdom.[9]

The Empire, of course, had suffered a wound, but it was certainly not mortal.

All of the combatants made treaties with each other in 1783, which made the American provisional settlement final. Spain failed to get Gibraltar after all, and has never forgotten the humiliation. The monarchies of Europe carried on as if they were a party of revelers on an excursion boat, drifting down a foggy river a short distance above a waterfall unknown, and thinking they could drift in luxury forever. They were, so to speak, but a few yards above the falls in 1783. For example, the remains of Luzerne were exhumed and thrown into his neighborhood river by French revolutionaries before ten years had passed. No European leader seems to have learned a thing from the American Revolution.

When news of the definitive peace reached Washington's troops, the men burned thirteen candles in each hutment, one for each state. The Philadelphians had more resources and staged an elaborate show. At the expense of the state, Charles Willson Peale built a triumphal arch covered with transparent paintings illuminated by eleven hundred lamps. At the first attempt to light it, on January 22, 1784, a premature ignition of fireworks set the arch afire, burning some of the spectators and killing an artillery sergeant. Peale fell off, breaking two ribs. They tried it again on May 10, without fireworks. The arch was replete with every possible piece of republican and royal symbolism to gratify both Americans and French. The design celebrated everybody—except the men who wrote the peace treaty.

Upon close reading of the terms of peace, Americans could not help being surprised at their liberality. Well-served and generally satisfied, they looked forward to greater things. The peace would be just a beginning. Now some way must be found to press forward. There was a prophetic note in Alexander Hamilton's remark, "The centrifugal is much stronger than the centripetal force in these states. . . ."[10] He and like-minded men were to change that.

III

While war was wholly wasteful, peace brought no profit to the treasury or order to the finances of the United States. Just before

Yorktown, supplies and money came from France with promise of more to come. The promise allowed Robert Morris to borrow from Rochambeau's chest of hard money. Thus the Superintendent of Finance managed to improvise survival until February 1782. That month he told the Congress some hard truths. The states had given no help with the interest on the public debt, hence there was no reason for any lender to trust the United States. The Congress had the privilege of asking for everything; the states had the privilege of giving nothing. No more money could be expected from France. The financial situation early in 1782 was so desperate that Morris did not wish to state it in writing, so he asked Congressmen to visit their state legislatures and tell the story. By April not a single cent of the previous autumn's requisitions had arrived at his office. By September Morris had received $125,000 of $6 million due.

The Congress appointed a grand committee (one delegate from each state) in July to report on the best way to support the credit of the United States. There was still hope of getting permission to collect a customs tax, but Rhode Island seemed to block the way. Congressman David Howell of Rhode Island was the most extreme supporter of states' rights in the whole Congress. It was probably more than coincidental that three months after Howell took his seat in the Congress, June 7, 1782, the Rhode Island legislature adjourned without acting on the customs levy. The situation of the Congress was shown by a letter from the Rhode Island delegates to their governor in September, telling him that not a cent had been paid into the treasury for more than a year by any state except Pennsylvania.

Lacking permission to levy an impost, the Congress, almost irrationally, called on the states for $1.2 million to pay interest on the debt. It was not possible any longer to draw bills of exchange on Europe, since there was no reason to hope for new European credits. Then in this dark hour word came from John Adams in the Netherlands that he was negotiating a loan from Dutch bankers. The Congress happily spent it before he closed the deal. What else? The Army was further behind in its pay than it ever had been before.

The Congress tried to press Rhode Island to yield to the request for a customs duty, and had to endure a torrent of Rhode Island congressional oratory to the effect that the war had been fought to preserve liberty, not to change one yoke of tyranny for another. In November the Rhode Island legislature flatly voted "no." A congressional committee set out for Rhode Island to try personal lobbying; while on the road it learned that both Virginia and Maryland had repealed their resolutions favoring the customs duty, hence the whole project was dead. The Virginia and Maryland repealers remain inscrutable.

Through the summer of 1782 there had been some faltering attempts to arrange a system of selling western land to remedy the fiscal starvation, but the process of settling boundaries would have been too slow in this emergency even if a program had been adopted. Furthermore, it would have been a kind of distress sale, of the sort that usually produces the least profit.

What aggravated the fiscal crisis was not so much the direct pressure of civilian creditors but the ugly thought of a hungry, angry, and mutinous Continental Army. The Army's money troubles were a permanent feature of the War for Independence.

In the hard Valley Forge winter of 1777–1778 the officers had begun to think seriously of their future. No doubt the failure of conciliation in 1778 intensified the speculation. The Congress voted half-pay for seven years after military service, but Washington recommended a promise of half-pay for life and renewed the recommendation early in 1779. Very likely only the optimism induced by knowledge of the French alliance quieted the officers by encouraging them to hope for early victory, for in May 1779 the Congress gave only two "aye" votes for a resolution assuring half-pay for life. In June the officers themselves petitioned for half-pay for life, which startled the Congress. The Pennsylvania and Maryland legislatures had already given such assurances to their line officers, so, against much opposition, the Congress voted to recommend that all states do the same, and also make some provision for widows. Some states went along, but state action could not help men holding commissions directly from the Congress. New petitions came before the delegates in the late summer and fall of 1779, but again in October the opposition beat a motion for half-pay for life. Half-pay for seven years after the war was the best the officers could get. And so the question stood until 1782.

Although the fighting was practically over in 1781, the Army strength stood steady through 1782 at from sixteen to eighteen thousand men.[11] Washington warned Robert Morris of the impatience of the officers, and he told the officers to tell their friends at home that taxation was the only sure remedy.[12] With peace negotiations under way, the Congress in August worked out a plan for the voluntary retirement of officers. Washington approved in substance, but pointed out that the officers were broke, in debt, and worried about the prospect of returning to their families in poverty. They knew that there would be no more promotions, that pay was far in arrears, and that the Congress had made no formal arrangement for seven years' half-pay.[13] By December the whole Army was in a sour mood. Although officers had so far kept the enlisted men in line,[14] nothing at all had been done for the rank and file.

At the end of 1782 there were delegates who would have agreed to turn the problems of the Army back to the states. This would have been the least intelligent solution, because it would have created thirteen armies and, very likely, destroyed the union. But what to do? It was believed that many officers were resigning,[15] and Rhode Island, it seemed, would forever block the enactment of a national customs levy.

At the end of December a deputation from the Army arrived with a petition to the Congress. General Alexander McDougall and Colonels Matthias Ogden and John Brooks were the deputies. Their memorial very bluntly asked for money, cited the discontent of the enlisted men, and advised against testing the patience of the soldiery. Among specific requests they included commutation of their pensions to six years' full pay. The Congress read it in January and argued it inconclusively late in February 1783.[16] Robert Morris, who would have to get up the cash, confidentially admitted that he was overdrawn in Europe by about $3.5 million.[17] The Congress faced a grave situation. At the moment it seemed that the Army's ugly mood could be deflected only with more French gold. Just when political independence seemed to be within reach, the country's economic dependence was plain.

The discussion of the Army memorial provoked much gaseous argument and a discussion which ranged over the whole tangled net of public finance. This talk may have been informative to the delegates, but it was no way to make aggrieved soldiers happy. Some of the proposals could not have matured until 1784, if ever. Meanwhile, a cloud hovered over the North River—the sulky Army in its quarters at Newburgh, New York. McDougall's deputation waited around until well into March. The colonels left, and McDougall said he would leave unless he had some good news soon.

Independence Won

What could the Army expect at demobilization? The officers' pay had never been satisfactory, being too low at first and then, after raises, being rendered worthless by inflation. Illustrations are available. After selling all of his property in 1782, General Arthur St. Clair was flat broke. While handing Martha Washington into her carriage, Quartermaster General Timothy Pickering was served a writ in litigation holding him responsible for all the debts of his department. He hid out while the New York legislature passed an act immunizing him from such a suit. Nathanael Greene had pledged his credit for Army rations in South Carolina. When the contractor went bankrupt his creditors came down on Greene and took the South Carolina real estate he had received as the gift of the state for his military services.

Through all of history sullen armies have, from time to time, remodeled the governments which they thought were abusing them. After Yorktown the Continental Army was well fed, well clad, and well housed. The officers and men had time to think dark thoughts about their troubles, their back pay, their clouded futures. Some men thought a change in the system, as we would now call it, might brighten their circumstances. Republics were an innovation, and it was natural that men thought in monarchical ways. Washington was the man most eligible for King of the United States, a thought which inevitably crossed other men's minds. In the spring of 1782 Colonel Lewis Nicola lauded monarchy to Washington and hinted that Washington would be acceptable to the Army. Washington would not hear it, and, of course, no other man could have a crown if Washington opposed the idea. Although monarchy was out of the question, anarchy was not. In 1775 the Army was loose and amateurish; in 1783 it was close-knit and professional. Few of its leaders wished to be civilians on any terms thus far made available to them. Some began to think of congressional slowness and unwieldiness as expressions of hostility and malevolence.

The cloud over the North River turned blacker, and on March 10 flickered with lightning. An anonymous paper appeared in the camp, calling on the officers to consult. There was threat in this Newburgh Address. It asked whether the men had brought freedom to a grateful country, "or is it rather a country that tramples upon your rights, disdains your cries and insults your distresses?" And the sound of a knife being sharpened: ". . . In any political event, the Army has its alternative."[18]

Here was immediate work for a law-abiding commanding general. Washington condemned the anonymous paper and called the officers together himself. Putting on spectacles to read a statement, he remarked that he had not only grown old in their service but blind. His short statement said such an approach would not do. He then read a letter from a delegate on the problems facing the Congress, and retired. In his absence the officers passed resolutions affirming their faith in the good intentions of the Congress and asking Washington to plead their case. Washington wrote a formal letter to the delegates in which he said his life would be permanently embittered if the Congress played the Army false. He also sent private advice to do something in a hurry, or else.[19]

There seem to have been three thrusts in the Newburgh episode: a plain soldierly dissatisfaction with the treatment of the Army, some hope in the Congress of getting rid of Washington, and, most easily documented, a public-creditor interest in shocking the Congress and the country into taking a firm position on the national debt. Ex-Colonel and now Congressman Alexander Hamilton was pleased to see General McDougall's deputation arrive in December 1782, complaints in hand, because it might lead to an overhauling of the Continental system. Hamilton had come to the Congress from New York in November, moving about the floor with catlike grace, speaking well and logically, though giving a certain impression that behind his blue eyes there was vanity and intrigue. He thought the Newburgh incitement could be healthy: ". . . I shall not be sorry that ill-humours have appeared. I shall not regret importunity, if temperate, from the Army." He candidly admitted that public creditors were stirring up the Army with the hope of lumping all the public debts and thereby influencing the states to accept a congressional decision on paying off the debt. But, Hamilton added, he certainly did not wish a civil war.[20] If the Army's debt was lumped with the civilians' debt, the Congress might be able to lead in erecting a stronger government.

Washington did not like it. He said the Army should not be put in danger of being sacrificed to the ambition of establishing a national debt. The officers suspected this would happen. The rumors should be stopped by treating the Army justly.[21] Even before things came out in the open at Newburgh, Washington had warned Hamilton that a collapse of the Army for lack of support would be followed by a flow of blood. The Congress must state the justice of the Army's claims and tell the states to make them good because the Congress could not, and the delegates should say nothing more. Unless the Congress received all necessary power, the blood spent in eight years of war would profit nothing.[22] When the Newburgh statements appeared, Washington sent them to the Congress, covered by a letter dated March 12, which, luckily for public morale, was the date on which the provisional peace treaty arrived. The delegates showed an acid sense of humor by referring the Newburgh papers to a committee of the five members who most strongly opposed the requests of McDougall's deputation.

The upshot was that the Congress voted the officers half-pay for life and the enlisted men full pay for five years. This would have to be mostly in interest-bearing promises, which at least had some discounted resale value to speculators. On motion of Hamilton, the Congress allowed the men to take their weapons with them when discharged. The delegates symbolically selected April 19 for proclaiming the official end of the war, and Robert Morris scraped up three month's pay for the men, nearly all of whom took immediate furloughs and scattered. Most had been gone from camp for six days when their promissory notes arrived. When pensions were later added, the total cost of the Continental Army manpower (finally ceasing in 1908!) was $70 million. The Congress proclaimed the discharge of all officers and men who had joined for the duration as of November 3, 1783.[23] Next it tried to resolve that a force of about five hundred be kept as skeleton garrisons of posts, and to guard stores, but failed of a quorum. Eventually the Army dwindled to a handful at West Point, where most of the stores and munitions were.

The quieting of the Newburgh ferment did not please everybody. Major John Armstrong, the assumed scribe of the discontented, feared the soldiery would disperse, the nation dissolve, the debts go unpaid, and a civil war follow, because the veterans and creditors would not accept repudiation.[24] He found Washington's intervention very annoying: "Of all his illustrious foibles, I think the affectation of Zeal in a cause he strove so anxiously to damn, is the most ridiculous; and like the lies of Falstaff, or Falstaff himself, it is gross and palpable."[25]

Before it managed to get rid of the Army, the Congress suffered its most debasing humiliation in being frightened out of Philadelphia by a body of troops. After due notice demanding satisfaction of their accounts, enlisted men who had refused the dispersive furloughs descended on Philadelphia and moved into the Continental barracks on June 21. The Congress convened, surrounded by four or five hundred men, and received an ultimatum which had been handed to the Pennsylvania State Council, then in session next door. The Congress adjourned and left its chamber, meeting no resistance from the troops, who seem to have been more intent on getting what was coming to them from Pennsylvania. Knowing that Pennsylvania could not protect the Congress if the troops grew ugly, the delegates angrily resolved to convene at Princeton on June 26 (no quorum appeared in Princeton until July 29). The tone of the Congress was its strongest quality: "Having been this day grossly insulted by the disorderly and menacing approach of a body of armed soldiers about the place within which Congress were assembled," the delegates went on to hint they could not expect the protection of the government of Pennsylvania,[26] a rather sorry admission of congressional impotence.[27] John Armstrong was rather pleased with it all: "The grand Sanhedrim of the Nation with all their solemnity and emptiness, have removed to Princeton, and left a state, where their wisdom has long been question'd, their virtues suspected, and their dignity a jest."[28] Benjamin Rush thought the soldiers showed restraint, because there was so much sympathy for them that people wondered that the whole Army did not join in. He thought they showed no anger against the Congress but were wroth with Pennsylvania. The net effect was that the Congress appeared to have panicked.[29]

The delegates did not intend to stay at Princeton, and finally decided to winter in more comfortable Annapolis. The situation caused some embarrassment, because while they were poised for decision the new minister from Sweden arrived to pay his respects. They managed to get through a formal reception in crowded Princeton, and then, on November 3, voted to move to the urbane little capital of Maryland on November 26.[30]

Washington issued a farewell order to the Continental Army, reviewing the course of the war and its remarkable result, and ending with thanks to the several categories of officers and enlisted men for specifically described services. To the noncommissioned officers and the privates he was grateful "for their extraordinary patience in suffering, as well as their invincible fortitude in Action."[31] Then (having seen the British safely off at New York) he set out to say goodbye to the Congress, with which he had worked so well in harness. The Congress had known it needed Washington, and Washington knew the country would fly apart without the Congress. Here was no Caesar poised at the bank of a Rubicon, but a Cincinnatus anxious to see a plow again—though, unlike Cincinnatus, he never did his own plowing.

The Congress gave a public dinner for Washington on the night of December 22, attended by about two hundred. There were the usual thirteen toasts and the firing of thirteen field pieces, followed by a ball in the graceful State House. On the next day, according to a stiff, pre-written protocol, the retiring general appeared before the Congress (which had nervously debated whether it was numerous enough to be properly representative—answer, yes). The script provided that "When the General rises to make his address, and also when he retires, he is to bow to Congress, which they are to return by uncovering without bowing." It went off exactly as prescribed on December 23.[32] (Much has been made, and rightly, of the general's bows to the civil authority.) The resignation and the surrender of his commission provoked "a most copious shedding of tears."[33] In fact, one witness testified, "The spectators all wept, and there was hardly a member of Congress who did not drop tears."[34]

IV

A group equally sad at the time, but for quite different reasons, was the body of loyalists. They had received rather rough treatment if they actively supported their King, and had responded in kind where they were able. Most of those who were "notorious" for royalism suffered loss of property, but few suffered death unless they actively took arms and died in combat. Rebels with a taste for brutality tried to coerce outspoken loyalists to conformity or flight by stoning, ducking, tarring and feathering, and other public humiliation. Thomas Paine thought the terrorists went too far. Their victims, he wrote, were but the dupes of greater villains, and true patriots should go for larger game—which he did, with his pen.[35]

In addition to sporadic terrorism, there were hundreds of state statutes penalizing loyalism: test oaths, denial of free speech, barring of loyal publication, denial of access to courts or the practice of law or teaching, levies of special taxes, restrictions of place of residence, exile, and, most interesting to rebels on the economic ladder, confiscation of property. In some states it was treasonable to accept a royal military commission, to enlist in a regular military element of the King, or to recruit for the British forces. These laws were not uniform, and penalties and enforcement varied from place to place and time to time.

The Congress gave the original impetus to legislation punishing loyalists, as a way of reply to the Royal Proclamation of August 1775 which announced that the colonies were in rebellion. The delegates advised the arrest and detention of any persons whose freedom could endanger the safety of a colony or "the liberties of America." This gave a quasi-legal sanction to the suppression of loyalism by the provincial congresses and committees of safety. Several of these local bodies passed acts of treason, piracy, and attainder, while overlooking a good deal of vigilante violence. Pennsylvania, that most American of colonies, hanged the most for treason—four.[36] The local leaders of the movement for independence found the grand jury an ideal instrument for pressing hard on loyalists.[37] The Congress followed with recommendations to the colonies to prohibit Tories from speaking and writing against rebellion.

In the prosecutions for treason throughout the war, the state courts usually followed the legal forms, the writ of habeas corpus was available, and the anti-loyalist actions were not outwardly a reign of terror or a witch hunt. Legal executions were less barbarous than British law allowed, and nearly all who were convicted were pardoned.[38] The only persistent ugliness was the tendency of the rebels to regard captured loyalist soldiers as political prisoners rather than prisoners of war.[39]

The royal governors got off rather more easily than might be expected, though they were certainly uncomfortable. Most lost their property; not one lost his life. They had been well selected, each because he was in some way thought to be acceptable to Americans. They were generally popular with American social climbers. If properly supervised by Lord North's Ministry, they might have been useful in arriving at a conciliatory settlement, but on their own they had no sedative effect on American excitement because not one was inclined to political theorizing or social reform. To the colonials it was plain they were agents, not principals, and for a revolution they received relatively mild treatment. The worst that happened to them was humiliation, temporary imprisonment, and loss of property.[40]

The rebels were much more interested in the property of the loyalists than in severity toward their persons. The process of confiscation in Suffolk County, Massachusetts, offers a useful case history. Once the sale of confiscated land began, it moved along rapidly. The chief beneficiaries were the creditors of the loyalists. The land went at bargain prices, and only about 40 per cent of the proceeds went into the state treasury. This redistribution of land titles was in no sense democratic; there were no more owners after the process than before, nor did the new owners subdivide their holdings for sale. Confiscation was not a scheme to benefit insiders. The land was sold only for hard cash, hence those who happened to have the cash at the moment benefited most. It was not a process of corruption, of getting a state revenue, nor of bringing about a social revolution. It was to satisfy creditors and to punish the loyalists.[41] It did not destroy the sanctity of property, since the debts of the creditors were property which was thus protected by the intervention of the revolutionary state government. And the whole business satisfied a longing for revenge, which is not necessarily confined to political affairs.

New Jersey, which saw far more war than Massachusetts did, followed a similar procedure, though insiders profited there by controlling the legal process of confiscation. The procedure was usually this: a defendant had gone to the British or had refused to take a loyalty oath, commissioners seized his land, a court decided whether it should be sold, and, if so, offered it for sale. Some of the commissioners, and especially Attorney General William Paterson, profited from their timing and foreknowledge of the sales.[42]

In Georgia, which had slight resources, the state government intended that loyalist confiscations, including the confiscation of slaves, should help to finance the war effort. Until 1778 the state government confiscated only the property of persons convicted of treason. In 1778 the British reconquered Georgia and re-established a royal government which seized the property of rebels. When the British lost their grip on parts of the province in 1781, the rebels reversed the process and started over, using such loyalist property as they could seize in order to support the state's paper money. Buyers bought on credit, and their notes were the backing of the paper currency, though it often turned out that the notes were not collectible. Georgia sales of loyalist property occurred as late as 1785. The proceeds ultimately went to every conceivable public purpose and to satisfy private creditors' claims. The accountancy of the matter is difficult, but it may have been more expensive than the benefits derived would justify. It was definitely not a democratizing process. Eleven loyalists lost a third of the total property taken, and twelve rebel buyers acquired about the same amount.[43]

All of these confiscations (excepting those after the treaty of peace) had the sanction of a resolution of the Congress, November 27, 1777, which recommended taking loyalist property to finance the war.[44] The general effect, however, was not to finance the war but to punish loyalism.

Except for propaganda and polemics, there seems to have been little official effort to conciliate loyalists and bring them around to rebel views. In 1777, Washington advised the Congress that it might be possible to weaken the British by seducing redcoated loyalists to desert the British Army. Accordingly, the delegates resolved that he could offer rewards to encourage deserters to come over with their arms and their horses.[45]

Loyalist counter-revolutionary action was rare. In Massachusetts a veteran of the Great War for Empire, Brigadier Timothy Ruggles, formed an association to oppose the acts of rebel committees, and once received help from the British Army when attacked by Plymouth Minute Men; but his group failed in the end. In Connecticut a meeting resolved that the Continental Congress measures were unconstitutional. The rebels ostracized the participants and stilled the resistance. There were loyalist associations in New York, which, as a British garrison town, was a safer base. The Associated Loyalists of New York organized themselves in companies and battalions, which were actually armed bands engaged in a rather ferocious guerrilla war. They once hanged an American prisoner of war in reprisal for the hanging of a loyalist. With permission of the Congress, Washington selected a British captain to hang in his turn, but he had been captured by the French which gave a loophole for his release. At this point the British dissolved the Associated Loyalists.[46] They were reducing war to its logical brutality.

Before anyone knew of the Anglo-American negotiations in Paris, the "Loyalists" (their own word) appealed to the King not to abandon the Americans to "the usurpation of Congress" which could never make them as happy as would a connection with and dependence on Britain. They spoke of cruelty and outrages as the characteristic traits and principles of "the present system of Congressional Republicanism" to which they had "an aversion . . . unconquerable, irreconcilable."[47] When word of the provisional treaty reached America, loyalists took it very hard, as shown in letters home which were printed in Britain and thus found their way back to the American press. One put it very well: "You have seen eclipses of the sun frequently, but never did you see such a darkness as hung over this place for two days, after the letter was published—horror and dismay painted in every face. . . ."[48] Within weeks, loyalists were flocking to New York, the headquarters of the British Army in North America.

The purpose of the movement was emigration. Loyalists had been leaving the country since the first shots of war. Virginia, for example, had enough emigration in 1775 to feel justified in making regulations. Emigrants could go to Britain if born there, but could not take any papers or account books. We may suppose they were mostly branch managers of British businesses who were thus prohibited from removing evidence of debts. In Massachusetts, emigration began with the evacuation of Boston on March 17, 1776, at which moment royal officials began to receive pensions. Those from Massachusetts who went to Britain were not happy with their treatment, as shown by their private diaries, but they concealed their disappointment in spirited letters to New England in which they proudly described the power of the kingdom. As British chances of victory lessened, the letters and diaries became pathetic with homesickness. Few, however, went directly to Britain. The largest fraction went to Canada.

At the close of the war loyalists converged on New York, asking the new commander, Sir Guy Carleton, for outbound transportation. The war was over for practical purposes, and civilians could move freely within the United States. The British commander naturally wished to do the right thing by those who had stood by King George III. Meanwhile the Congress was eager to get control of New York port, which had been British since August 1776. They had a motive to speed the British departure. Carleton asked the Congress to appoint somebody to help with the embarkations.[49] He thought it proper to provide transport for all who asked, to protect them from the violence they feared.[50] British shipping was needed for about 22,000 persons.

Washington cautioned his own side against rough treatment of the loyalists, because it would promote emigration to Nova Scotia, strengthening that province at the expense of the United States. And persecution would make the United States seem vindictive in victory while encouraging Britain to do more for the loyalists than otherwise.[51]

From beginning to end, perhaps forty thousand loyalists left the United States (though other estimates range up to a hundred thousand). About fifteen thousand settled in New Brunswick, and, despite severe hardships, probably not more than a thousand returned from New Brunswick to the United States. Few achieved genuine distinction after this second start in life. The luminary of the emigrants was Benjamin Thompson of New Hampshire, who became a scientist of repute on the continent and received the title Count Rumford of the Holy Roman Empire, after having served earlier in the British Army and military intelligence. He bore no grudge, as shown by his founding of the Rumford Professorship at Harvard.

The departure of the loyalists undoubtedly cost the country a handful of rich patrons of learning and the arts, but socially and politically their exodus made little difference. The vacuum they left attracted a rush of successors, as class-conscious and politically conservative (in all but royalism) as those they replaced. In every revolution the losing party suffers. The winners treated the losers in America better than the losers were treated in any modern overturn except in England's Great Rebellion of the seventeenth century. The treatment of the loyalists compares favorably with the treatment accorded the defeated anti-Nazis, Italian liberals, and Russian kulaks. Probably four out of five loyalists stayed put, held their tongues, and survived with only the eight-year penalty of loss of freedom of speech. There were more emigrants from the American Revolution than *émigrés* from the French Revolution in proportion to population—about five times as many. And the French revolutionaries confiscated, in proportion, only slightly more real estate. On the other hand, America had no guillotine, no reign of terror.

The peace treaty clause that promised to recommend to the states that they restore confiscated estates accomplished little. Some argued that the dissolution of royal government canceled land titles, and only adherence to the new order restored land titles—thus loyalists owned nothing.[52] Only Pennsylvania indemnified its loyalists, and other states prosecuted and confiscated even after the war. The debts to creditors were not settled until the first years of the next century, and then they were paid out of public funds, not by the private debtors in the United States. The British Crown treated the loyalists better. The cost to Britain of relocating refugees in Canada, added to cash paid out for them or to them directly, amounted to about $30 million by the end of the eighteenth century. Although most states did not return what they confiscated, by 1789 most had repealed anti-loyalist laws which conflicted with the peace treaty, and those loyalists who remained in the United States were often in positions of political leadership on the conservative side of American politics.

V

The next thing was to see the British safely away, which took an interminably long time. After Yorktown there were still 34,000 soldiers of the King in America, mostly in Savannah, Charleston, and New York. With the appointment of Sir Guy Carleton as the new commanding general in the spring of 1782, the order to these troops was to leave, even if it meant a premature surrender of their posts. But they were not all gone for another year and a half, partly because of a shortage of transports, and partly because of Carleton's conscientious protection of loyalists and freed blacks. (During this period a French naval force audaciously raided into Hudson Bay, capturing the Hudson Bay Company's Fort Churchill and burning its warehouse at York.)

There had been British garrisons in New York since 1776, in Savannah since 1778, and in Charleston since 1780. Theirs was not necessarily a hard life. For example, a New York newspaper in 1779 printed the following:

> To the GOLF PLAYERS
> The Season for this pleasant and healthy
> Exercise now advancing, Gentlemen may
> be furnished with excellent CLUBS and the
> veritable Caledonian BALLS, by enquiring
> at the printer's.[53]

The rebels wished every person in these garrison towns to be a burden on the British oceanic supply service for all necessities, but it was militarily impossible to stop provisions from moving into the towns.[54]

As the year 1782 dragged on quietly, the Congress feared a slackening of effort everywhere and adopted resolutions that the states should not "remit of their exertions." Washington published them in his orders to the Army.[55] Although free from the dangers of combat, the Army was still hungry, and, worse, the troops with Washington had to cut six thousand cords of wood for the coming winter, without a drop of rum to cheer and sustain them.[56]

All of the fight had gone out of the loyalists who were concentrated in New York in 1782. A privateer captured the outgoing mail late in 1782, and it is a pathetic collection, revealing the homesickness of divided families, sad uncertainties about long missing relatives, health reports relayed to worried kin, apprehensive inquiries about life in Canada, and records of the discomfort of cramped New York: "Firewood is not to be got here at any rate, Scharsly."[57] New York and Savannah were probably impregnable, but Nathanael Greene was prepared to retake Charleston in the same manner as Washington and Rochambeau had taken Yorktown, if he could get French naval help. But the French fleet had sailed off to its doom in the West Indies.

The only active theater of operations after Yorktown was south of Virginia, where hungry and ragged rebels fought a guerrilla war known as "The Tory War," which deteriorated into bloody marauding. The evacuation of Savannah, July 11, and of Charleston, December 14, 1782, stilled this conflict by killing the last hopes of the loyalists. But as late as March 1, 1783, the people of New York were still uncertain of their future and were studying the arts of getting royal compensation for losses suffered for loyalty, and getting royal help in the settlement of accounts between debtors and creditors.[58] By the end of the year the change in the political climate was made obvious by the joint proclamation of Carleton and Rear Admiral Robert Digby, which warned everybody to avoid insulting the flag of any "foreign nation" in the harbor. The occasion of the warning was the destruction of a flag of the United States.[59]

The British cleared out of Manhattan on November 25, and Washington and Governor George Clinton came to town. On December 4 the royal transports and warships were taking the last troops and loyalists from Staten and Long Islands. That same day Washington said goodbye to his officers in Fraunces' Tavern before leaving for Annapolis to resign his commission. The British ended their Manhattan residence with a practical joke. Some redcoat cut the flag halliard and greased the pole at Fort George to make it difficult to haul up the stars and stripes.

To the credit of Carleton and Digby, they took with them not fewer than 2,272 blacks who had been promised their freedom for coming over to the King. Carleton was quite firm on the need to keep this promise. Their listing and clearance took from April to November 1783, and was done by a joint commission of American and British officers.[60] The figure 2,272 is the minimum; perhaps as many as seven or eight hundred more got away without waiting around to be listed.

The departure of the British forces and loyalists from New York was the last military operation of the War for Independence on the Atlantic seaboard. The winning of independence was complete.

20

Why It Came Out as It Did

The War for American Independence was a long and drag-ging war, which might be called a war of psychological attri-tion. From it came no revolutionary change in methods of warfare. No soldier of the war is in the pantheon of those who venerate military geniuses. Some of the rebel captains showed remark-able perseverance, but not one could be called brilliant. On the British side a series of mediocre generals upheld King George's cause. No grinding dramatic siege (like Gibraltar's) occurred in the western hemisphere, and, indeed, there was very little to excite the imagina-tion. Old-fashioned conquest was not the true goal of either side. It was the task of the British to restore the habit of obedience, with sufficient police power over territory to make it stick. Conversely, it was the work of the rebels to prevent a restoration of the King's authority. The war did not mount to a dramatic climax from one suspenseful step to the next. Rather, it proceeded like sporadic fire-works in a blackened sky.

At most times the British could take and hold any seaport if they did not underestimate the foe, and they could move well inland in the South for short intervals; but they could never occupy any large and thickly populated area permanently. By hindsight, the patch-work strategy of marching armies hither and thither seems the worst choice. A tight blockade, relatively inexpensive and painless to

Why It Came Out as It Did

Britain, might have tired and frustrated the Americans into accepting a British-designed conciliation, but it was not tried and we cannot know. We do know that land operations by a heavily equipped European-style army required slow movement against a more lightly burdened and faster-moving enemy. The American action was almost always successfully evasive; only one large American force was ever trapped (Charleston, 1780), though two large and fully equipped British armies had to surrender—Burgoyne's (1777) and Cornwallis' (1781).

The conduct of the opening campaigns seems to have led straight to British defeat years later. The failure to pinch off the sprout of rebellion in the beginning was the result of the British vision of the American rebellion as primarily political rather than military. The political problem was the future reconciliation of the colonies. A crushing military attack might have made conciliation impossible. But the British Ministry botched its conciliatory gestures, and its abortive political solutions only made the ultimate military solution impossible.

When they did get to waging serious warfare, the British were rather milder than victory demanded, probably because they were fighting fellow subjects rather than foreigners. The British needed a quick victory before the Continental Army could be perfected and before foreign intervention could lengthen the odds. Within the rules of international law they could, for example, have exterminated the garrison of Fort Washington in 1776, with chilling effects on the recruitment of Continental regulars. They could have sacked all seaports, thus cutting off privateering and merchant shipping. They did not really have the time nor the numbers needed for the strategic chess play of the Howes and of Burgoyne. An example of wasted manpower and time was the diversion of ten thousand men to Quebec in 1776, far off on the edge of the battle scene.

With the limited brainpower at the King's disposal, the government leaned on improvisation and luck. As always, whether in war or poker, luck ran out. If the British had thought about gambling in the way that later mathematicians have, they would have altered their gamesmanship when the French came in, at the latest. But they played on in the same way until the disaster at Yorktown.

British leadership, from beginning to end, takes so much explaining that a republican may be excused for thinking that hereditary aristocracy provided too small a pool of talent for running a large empire. To start at the top, George III, the man ultimately responsible, showed smallness and nothing else; in the end he blamed the decadence of Englishmen for the defeat. One could wish it were that simple. His principal aide, Frederick Lord North, was a man of good humor, good intentions, a sincere wish to please his master, and more devotion to duty than some of his colleagues; he had all the qualities of an efficient postmaster general. The Colonial Secretary, Lord George Germain, earlier called Lord George Sackville, expanded his jurisdiction until he became more important in this war than the Secretary at War. Since his side lost, he has traditionally received the direct blame. In late years there has been an attempt to rehabilitate him by saying that his original military disgrace in the Great War for Empire (1759) was politically motivated, that he could not be expected to understand the force of the idea of revolutionary republicanism, that he could organize an overseas shipment of troops as well as anybody, and that he shared responsibility with the King, North, and the generals. But Germain was responsible for coordinating military operations in America. They were not coordinated. No argument yet brought forward seems to weigh as much as the judgment of the court of twelve lieutenant generals and four major generals which in 1759 agreed on the following statement:

The court, upon due consideration of the whole matter before them, is of opinion that Lord George Sackville is guilty of having disobeyed the orders of Prince Ferdinand of Brunswick, whom he was by his commission and instructions directed to obey, as commander in chief, according to the rules of war; and it is the farther opinion of the court, that the said Lord George Sackville is and he is hereby judged unfit to serve his majesty in any military capacity whatsoever.[1]

The accompanying case record makes Germain seem an incarnation of the moronic stage Englishman who infested the American comic theater a century ago. His record boils down to this: He was evicted from George II's army for cause. Twenty-odd years later he received a consolatory title and was kicked upstairs out of the office in which he had directed a war which failed. He had two losses and no wins. If he had ever won anything important it might be worth the effort to go behind the unbroken record of his flat failures to seek out hidden merits.

There were some good civilians in the British government—the subministers who served the Ministry, the admirals, and the generals, who were on balance rather more capable than their baronial chiefs. They were no band of geniuses, but they showed more initiative, competence, and efficiency than one might expect. They could not do their best in the jerry-built machine of government they served.

Now to the military. There were three successive commanding generals in North America during the whole of the period of combat, Thomas Gage, William Howe, and Henry Clinton. Gage's reputation for good judgment perished when he failed to prevent war (with insufficient force), and he departed early. Howe commanded from 1776 to 1778, won slam-bang battles, took New York and Philadelphia, and had little effect on the outcome. After taking Bunker Hill (when Gage was still in charge), his energies seemed to have exhausted themselves at a steady rate, like water leaking from a tank. The dreadful spill of blood on the slopes leading to Breed's and Bunker Hills may have made him a psychological casualty. On no occasion was he able to capture even a badly crippled enemy force of any size. Howe's successor, Clinton, commanded from 1778 through the remainder of the combat period. He was peevish and neurotic, disliking both untrammeled responsibility *and* a subordinate role. He might have been a good military governor of a small tranquil island. His nerves were shaken by the independent behavior of his second, Charles Earl Cornwallis, who showed more appetite for battle than any other British general officer in North America, but who was not very good at long-range planning. Clinton won a major victory at Charleston in 1780, and was senior to Cornwallis at the time of the Yorktown collapse, for which he was partly responsible. He showed a kind of negative wisdom not shown by Cornwallis when he concluded that loyalists could not be used as occupation troops.

One school of thought holds that the war was lost by poor diplomacy rather than by military errors. Britain fought this war in inglorious isolation. It was the only phase of the "Second Hundred Years' War," from 1689 to 1815, in which the British tried to defeat the French without the help of continental allies. France, Spain, and the Netherlands were openly at war with Britain, and no other power except Portugal was on good speaking terms. All other nations with merchant fleets, or dependent on merchant shipping, resented Britannia's rule of the waves. The upshot was that the French *marine militaire* made it impossible for the Royal Navy to rescue Cornwallis at the critical moment. This suggests several British failures: to patch up the quarrel with the Americans in time to deal separately with European enemies, to bring the Royal Navy to a high level of efficiency, to make British glory profitable to *some* continental power with a good army. As it was, from 1778 to the end, Great Britain had no friends abroad; hence French intervention could be decisive.

But there is a great deal more to explaining the outcome of this war than merely to catalog British incompetents and their blunders. Such critiques, which are numerous, ignore the fact that *somebody* frustrated the British hope of reasserting royal rule in America. In short, the British were beaten by somebody. To condemn American warfare, to credit French intervention, to discredit British strategy and leadership, is too strong a reaction against early hero-worshiping and flag-waving explanations of the winning of independence. The idea that the Americans may have won the war *does* seem to have the marks of historical fiction. Earlier writers who saw in it the finger of God or the working out of some mechanical law of history did little to help understanding.

In the War for Independence there were a good many determined and convinced men in every level of rebellion who kept their comrades at the job. The hard core of the Army never melted away. Tactics were often original. The commanding general was one of the most stubborn men in all history. The Continental Congress was often near despair but never allowed its despondency to be known to the public. The Congress was a convention of the best propagandists in the country, which used every known technique of press and pen to keep the spirit of rebellion alive. The only abject failure was in finance; there the foreign intervention was a necessary ingredient of the kind of success they won, though they might have won in some other untried way.

With no other foreign help than covert shipments of weapons and powder the Americans still could have interdicted communications, made transport by land next to impossible, used their familiarity with the terrain and climate to make life very miserable for occupying troops, and, in short, won by surviving—as brigands, banditti, and guerrillas have done so often. Without foreign intervention it would have been a different war, but not necessarily a losing war. The lesson of guerrilla warfare through the ages is that popularly supported forces do not have to destroy the enemy. They have merely to harass him without let-up. On the other hand, the British had to disperse the rebels to win. By rule of thumb one may suppose that 150,000 redcoats, supported by a Navy which continuously commanded the sea, could have harried the rebels to despair and dispersal; but the figure is absurd, since the British were hard pressed to put more than sixty thousand under arms in the western hemisphere. And at no time did the leading rebels relax their stubborn perseverance.

The civilians of the Congress and the military as personified by Washington worked as one. Each knew the other, each knew that close cooperation was necessary, each made the most of the other's abilities. To say that Washington won the war is to disregard other absolutely essential actors. It is good metaphysics to say that when parts are brought to a unity, one will dominate the others. Dante applied this philosophical truth to political theory. It properly applies to the American war effort. As the dominant figure on the American scene, Washington led the effort that won the war. But he did it less as a warrior than by his concerned improvisation, his steadying influence, his constant collaboration with civil authority, his close attention to every detail within his power to manage. Both the Continental Congress and George Washington were necessary. Washington's steady stream of official letters to the president of the Congress and his large flow of private explanations to friendly and influential delegates made him an active participant in the congressional debates on domestic affairs, and probably the most respected.

Usually an administrator who works under the supervision of cooperating but independent political bodies does not control the situation, regardless of how outstanding, forcible, and dedicated he may be. The career of such a man is most often shaped by forces beyond his control. If the independence of the United States was a worthwhile achievement, it was fortunate that Washington was not crippled by the dispersal of authority among independent states which he could not control. They certainly checked his power, in the sense that he could never suggest policy without preparing the ground by a good deal of political cultivation; but only an idolater of Washington could insist that things would have been uniformly better without the need for him to make careful political calculations of what would be acceptable to the ruling public of the new nation. It was also lucky that the circumstances did not require a lovable leader, for despite all attempts to humanize the man, Washington's private feelings are still buried in the deified romanesque marble which remains his public image—strong, weatherproof, but chilly.

For the American success, first credit goes to Washington, but he could not have done it alone. The skills of the rebels in operating the machinery of government in all the new states, and in keeping the Continental Congress together, were necessary. The impolicy of the British King and civilians, and the obsolescent strategy of the British generals and admirals, permitted the Americans to reach their goal. The distraction of European warfare would have prevented the reform of British military methods, even if Britain had been so inclined. The military, naval, and financial support of Britain's economic enemies were necessary if the Americans were to win the war by conventional strategy and tactics, though such strategy and tactics were not the only means which could have been chosen. A well-run guerrilla war might have achieved the same results, though it probably would have taken longer. The leadership of the American cause showed remarkable courage in never admitting the possibility of defeat, which meant that temporary collapses of morale were not losses of faith in the cause but were the result of unnecessary hardships inflicted on the troops. The several important mutinies (none of them pro-British) resulted from inexperience in administering a collective interstate operation.

It is only human to assume that important effects have very complicated causes. Explanations of the military result of the War for Independence have often been oversophisticated. The Continental Army did not have to destroy the British Army. It had but to survive. As long as it existed, the British had not won. The British had to destroy the Continental Army and control the sea continuously. They could meet neither requirement. As long as the United States kept its fighting spirit, it could not lose.

The Americans kept their spirit. The free white Americans seemed to have had an irresistible compulsion toward their object, which has been most often described as liberty. Liberty then meant freedom from dependence. That was the liberty they fought for and won: independence.

N O T E S

PROLOGUE

1. Worthington Chauncey Ford and Gaillard Hunt, eds, *Journals of the Continental Congress, 1774-1789*, 34 vols. (Washington, D.C., 1904-1937), V, 506-518, covers most matter-of-factly the events immediately preceding the publication of the Declaration.

2. Philip Davidson, *Propaganda and the American Revolution, 1763-1783* (Chapel Hill, 1941), is the best account of attempts to influence public opinion.

3. Washington to President of the Congress, July 10, 1776, in John C. Fitzpatrick, ed., *The Writings of George Washington from the Original Manuscript Sources*, 39 vols. (Washington, D.C., 1931-1944), V, 247.

4. *Providence Gazette*, November 2, 1776.

5. Letter signed "A.," 1776(?), *Rivington's Royal Gazette* (New York), October 11, 1777, the second issue of this New York newspaper, which had been suppressed in 1775 and resumed publication two years later under a different name.

CHAPTER I: AN ASSEMBLY OF THE ANGRY

1. Edmund Cody Burnett, *The Continental Congress* (New York, 1941; reprint ed., 1964), pp. 3-22, narrates the public acts which initiated the First Continental Congress. Benjamin Woods Labaree, *The Boston Tea Party* (New York, 1964), Chapters 10-13, covers the politics, from the Port Act through the First Congress.

2. H. M. Morais, "The Sons of Liberty in New York," in Richard B. Morris, ed., *The Era of the American Revolution* (New York, 1939; reprint ed., 1965), pp. 269-289.

3. John M. Murrin, "The Myths of Colonial Democracy and Royal Decline in Eighteenth-Century America: A Review Essay," *Cithara*, v (1965), 53-66.

4. Michael G. Kammen, "The Colonial Agents, English Politics, and the American Revolution," *William and Mary Quarterly*, 3d ser., XXII (1965), 244-263.

5. The history of Georgia politics on the eve of the War for Independence is admirably presented in W. W. Abbot, *The Royal Governors of Georgia, 1754-1775* (Chapel Hill, 1959).

6. John Richard Alden, *General Gage in America* (Baton Rouge, 1948), p. 212.

7. John J. Zimmerman, "Charles Thomson, 'The Sam Adams of Philadelphia,'" *Mississippi Valley Historical Review*, XLV (1958-59), 464-480, meets the need in part, but a longer biography would be useful.

8. Bernard Bailyn, "Butterfield's Adams: Notes for a Sketch," *William and Mary Quarterly*, 3d ser., XIX (1962), 238–256.

9. John R. Howe, Jr., *The Changing Political Thought of John Adams* (Princeton, 1966), sketches the political broadening of Adams's mind.

10. Thomson, the Adamses, Sherman, Dyer, McKean, Mifflin, Chase, and the Rutledges are all adequately sketched in *Dictionary of American Biography* (hereafter cited as *DAB*), as are most other leading American revolutionaries.

11. John Adams to Abigail Adams, September 29, 1774, in Edmund Cody Burnett, ed., *Letters of Members of the Continental Congress, 1774–1789*, 8 vols. (Washington, D.C., 1921–1936), I, 60–61 (hereafter cited as *LCC*).

12. John C. Fitzpatrick, ed., *The Diaries of George Washington*, 4 vols. (Boston, 1925), II, 164 n.

13. John Adams, Diary, September 3, 1774, in *LCC*, I, 3.

14. L. H. Butterfield, ed., *Diary and Autobiography of John Adams*, 4 vols. (Cambridge, Mass., 1961), II, 122–157, covers the proceedings, less completely than the *Journals*, of course, but with more humanity.

15. Worthington Chauncey Ford and Gaillard Hunt, eds., *Journals of the Continental Congress, 1774–1789*, 34 vols. (Washington, D.C., 1904–37), I, September 6, 1774 (hereafter cited as *JCC*). The yeas and nays were not listed individually until a roll call of September 9, 1777, *ibid.*, VIII, 725, and generally thereafter. Even then, of course, the roll was called only to determine how each state's solitary vote was to be recorded.

16. Galloway's proposal is most widely available in Samuel Eliot Morison, ed., *Sources and Documents Illustrating the American Revolution*, 2d ed. (Oxford, 1929), pp. 116–118. The standard work is Julian P. Boyd, *Anglo-American Union: Joseph Galloway's Plans to Preserve the British Empire, 1774–1788* (Philadelphia, 1941).

17. Quoted in Carl Bridenbaugh, *Cities in Revolt: Urban Life in America, 1743–1776* (New York, 1955), p. 351. Raymond C. Werner wrote the sketch of Galloway in *DAB*.

18. *LCC*, I, 6.

19. Although Galloway explained himself in 1780, the editors of *JCC* bound his text as of September 28, 1774, I, 43–51.

20. John Adams, Notes of Debates, September 28(?), 1774, *LCC*, I, 51–54; for Duane, see Sarah Simpson's sketch in *DAB*.

21. John Bigelow, ed., *The Works of Benjamin Franklin*, 12 vols. (New York, 1904), VI, 430–433.

22. The document is most easily available in Morison, *Sources and Documents*, pp. 118–122.

23. Duane, Notes of Debates, October 17(?), 1774, *LCC*, I, 77.

24. The Association is reprinted in Morison, *Sources and Documents*, pp. 122–125.

25. Edmund S. Morgan, "The Puritan Ethic and the American Revolution," *William and Mary Quarterly*, 3d ser., XXIV (1967), 3–43, opens a new line of interpretation to explain the often puzzling division of men into rebels and loyalists.

26. Burke to O'Hara, August 17, 1775, and January 7, 1776, in Ross J. S. Hoffman, *Edmund Burke, New York Agent* (Philadelphia, 1956), pp. 595, 615.

27. M. L. Robertson, "Scottish Commerce and the American War of Independence," *Economic History Review*, IX (1956–1957), 124. This study centers on the Glasgow merchants, but my extrapolation seems reasonable.

28. For example, *Massachusetts Spy* (Worcester), April 23, 1778.

29. *JCC*, October 21, 1774, I, 102.

Notes

30. Galloway to William Franklin, February 28, 1775, quoted in Boyd, *Anglo-American Union*, pp. 49–50.

CHAPTER 2: FROM INK TO BLOOD

1. An abridged version of Wilson's pamphlet, which has not suffered in the editing, will be widely found in Samuel Eliot Morison, ed., *Sources and Documents Illustrating the American Revolution*, 2d ed. (Oxford, 1929), pp. 104–115.

2. Harvey Wheeler, "Calvin's Case (1608) and the McIlwain-Schuyler Debate," *American Historical Review*, LXI (1955–56), 597 n.

3. Jefferson's essay is reprinted, among other places, in Paul Leicester Ford, ed., *The Writings of Thomas Jefferson*, 10 vols. (New York, 1892–99), I, 421–447.

4. Anthony M. Lewis, "Jefferson's *Summary View* as a Chart of Political Union," *William and Mary Quarterly*, 3d ser., V (1948), 34–51.

5. Charles Francis Adams, ed., *The Works of John Adams*, 10 vols., (Boston, 1856), IV, 46, "Novanglus."

6. "Novanglus" is also available in Morison, *Sources and Documents*, pp. 125–136.

7. Gage's tribulations are analyzed well in John R. Alden, *General Gage in America* (Baton Rouge, 1948); and see note 18, below.

8. These tense days are vividly described in Christopher Ward, *The War of the Revolution*, ed. John R. Alden, 2 vols., sometimes bound in one vol. (New York, 1952), I, 17–31.

9. Quoted from Richard B. Morris, *Government and Labor in Early America* (New York, 1946), p. 192, and see also "American Revolution" in index.

10. Willard M. Wallace, *Appeal to Arms* (New York, 1951), pp. 1–26. Wallace is much briefer than Ward, and perhaps better written.

11. Warren to Arthur Lee, February 20, 1775, Morison, *Sources and Documents*, pp. 139–140.

12. Hezekiah Niles, *Principles and Acts of the Revolution in America* (Baltimore, 1822; facsimile reprint, Maywood, Calif., 1961), pp. 25–30; quotation on p. 29, col. 2.

13. Benjamin Franklin, reprinted from Franklin Papers, Library of Congress, in Worthington Chauncey Ford and Gaillard Hunt, eds., *Journals of the Constitutional Congress*, 34 vols. (Washington, D.C., 1904–37), I, 123–124.

14. Edwin Wolf, 2d, "The Authorship of the 1774 Address to the King Restudied," *William and Mary Quarterly*, 3d ser., XXII (1965), 189–224.

15. Ross J. S. Hoffman, *Edmund Burke, New York Agent* (Philadelphia, 1956), pp. 169–172, 264. The text of the "Conciliation" is most easily available in Morison, *Sources and Documents*, p. 138 n.

16. Franklin to Galloway, February 25, 1775, *ibid.*, p. 139.

17. Hoffman, *Burke*, p. 174.

18. John J. Waters, Jr., "General Gage and the Opposition in Boston, 1765–1775," master's thesis, University of Notre Dame, 1959, pp. 87–110, is an excellent narrative of events during Gage's governorship.

19. Alden, *Gage in America*, pp. 226–250; quotation from p. 241.

20. John R. Alden in *American Historical Review*, LX (1954–55), 684–685.

21. David M. Ludlum, *Early American Winters*, 1604–1820 (Boston, 1966), pp. 89–90.

22. The documents of the Lexington episode began to appear even before the British reached Concord. Andrew C. McLaughlin *et al.*, *Source Problems in United States History* (New York, 1918), pp. 13–54, collected them to provide intellectual exercise for graduate students in history; the volume is widely available.

23. Revere to Corresponding Secretary, January 1, 1798 (including narrative of events of April 18–19, 1775), in *Massachusetts Historical Society Collections*, v (1798), 106–110; quotation from p. 110.

24. Edmund Burke received an eyewitness account; Hoffman, *Burke*, p. 584.

25. Quoted in Wallace, *Appeal to Arms*, p. 20.

26. Ward, *War of the Revolution*, I, 50.

27. John R. Alden, *The American Revolution, 1775–1783* (New York, 1954), pp. 46–47. This is the best one-volume work on the subject.

28. *Ibid.*, 48 n.

29. Read to Mrs. Read, May 18, 1775, in Edmund Cody Burnett, ed., *Letters of Members of the Continental Congress, 1774–1789*, 8 vols. (Washington, D.C., 1921–36), I, 93.

CHAPTER 3: UNDECLARED INDEPENDENCE

1. Quoted in Christopher Ward, *The War of the Revolution*, ed. John R. Alden, 2 vols. (New York, 1952), I, 52.

2. Jane Mecom to Benjamin Franklin, April 20(?), 1775, in Carl Van Doren, *Jane Mecom* (New York, 1950), p. 117.

3. Roger J. Champagne, "New York's Radicals and the Coming of Independence," *Journal of American History*, LI (1964–65), 21–40, describes this political problem as faced by leaders in one colony; many more such studies are needed.

4. Bernard Bailyn, "Butterfield's Adams: Notes for a Sketch," *William and Mary Quarterly*, 3d ser., XIX (1962), 253–254.

5. Franklin to Priestley, May 16, 1775, in Albert Henry Smyth, ed., *The Writings of Benjamin Franklin*, 10 vols. (New York, 1905–7), VI, 400.

6. Useful sketches of Hancock, Whipple, Langdon, Gerry, Huntington, Wilson, Dickinson, and Franklin are in *Dictionary of American Biography*.

7. The letters for these days are collected in Edmund Cody Burnett, ed., *Letters of Members of the Continental Congress, 1774–1789*, 8 vols. (Washington, D.C., 1921–36), I, 93–97 (hereafter cited as *LCC*); see especially Hewes to Johnston, May 23, 1775, *ibid.*, I, 97.

8. *Pennsylvania Evening Post*, July 19, 1775.

9. Philip Davidson, *Propaganda and the American Revolution, 1763–1783* (Chapel Hill, 1941), p. 96.

10. Worthington Chauncey Ford and Gaillard Hunt, eds., *Journals of the Continental Congress, 1774–1789*, 34 vols. (Washington, D.C., 1904–1937), May 15, 1775, II, 52 (hereafter cited as *JCC*).

11. *JCC*, June 10, 1775, II, 84–86.

12. *JCC*, June 14, 1775, II, 89–90.

13. Adams to Warren, July 6, 1775, *LCC*, I, 153.

14. Bernard Mason, "Robert R. Livingston and the Non-Exportation Policy: Notes for a speech in the Continental Congress, 1775," *New-York Historical*

Notes

Society Quarterly, XLIV (1960), 296–307, helps us to understand the discussion by presenting the outline of a lost speech.

15. Dickinson to Arthur Lee, July 7, 1775; autobiography of Jefferson; Jefferson to Wirt, August 4, 1805; memorandum of Charles Thomson, 1779—all in *LCC,* I, 157, 157 n.–158 n., 159 n.

16. The Declaration is readily available in Samuel Eliot Morison, ed., *Sources and Documents Illustrating the American Revolution,* 2d ed. (Oxford, 1929), pp. 141–145.

17. *JCC,* July 6, 1775, II, 128.

18. *JCC,* II, 128 n.

19. *JCC,* II, 154, 156.

20. *JCC,* July 26, 1775, II, 208–209.

21. *JCC,* May 29, 1775, II, 68. The text is included in Henry Steele Commager, ed., *Documents of American History,* 7th ed., 2 vols. (New York, 1963), I, 91–92.

22. Benjamin Thompson, in H. S. Commager and Richard B. Morris, eds., *The Spirit of 'Seventy-Six,* 2 vols. (Indianapolis, 1958), I, 153–156. It seems to have reached Germain, because it is now in the papers of the Sackville family, of which Germain was a member.

23. John R. Alden, in his *The American Revolution, 1775–1783* (New York, 1954), pp. 17–18, 18 n., collected these evaluations.

24. Quoted in Ward, *War of the Revolution,* I, 50–51.

25. B. D. Bargar, "Matthew Boulton and the Birmingham Petition of 1775," *William and Mary Quarterly,* 3d ser., XIII (1956), 26–39.

26. The pamphlet is analyzed in Lawrence Henry Gipson, *The British Empire Before the American Revolution,* 14 vols. (New York, 1936–68), XII, 335–336.

27. Dalphy I. Fagerstrom, "Scottish Opinion and the American Revolution," *William and Mary Quarterly,* 3d ser., XI (1954), 252, 254, 254 n.

28. O'Hara to Burke, June 5, 1775, in Ross J. S. Hoffman, *Edmund Burke, New York Agent* (Philadelphia, 1956), p. 585.

29. Ridge to Burke, September 25, 1775, *ibid.,* pp. 600–601.

30. J. E. Tyler, ed., "An Account of Lexington in the Rockingham MSS. at Sheffield," *William and Mary Quarterly,* 3d ser., X (1953), 106.

31. The opposition forensics are well sampled in Alden, *American Revolution,* p. 63.

32. For example, a letter from London, July 22, 1775, *New-York Gazette and Weekly Mercury,* September 22, 1775.

33. Burke to O'Hara, n.d., and July 26, 1775, Hoffman, *Burke,* pp. 182, 589.

34. *JCC,* November 9, 1775, III, 343 n.

35. The Royal Proclamation of Rebellion is available in Commager, *Documents,* I, 95–96.

36. Ira D. Gruber, "Lord Howe and Lord George Germain, British Politics and the Winning of American Independence," *William and Mary Quarterly,* 3d ser., XXII, (1965), 225–243, has the best sketch of Germain's initial intentions.

37. The vote was taken on November 16, 1775. George H. Gutteridge, ed., *The Correspondence of Edmund Burke,* 8 vols. (Cambridge, Mass., and Chicago, 1958–69), III, 237; the letters immediately preceding p. 237 are also relevant.

38. Frederick Bernays Wiener, *Civilians Under Military Justice: The British Practice Since 1689, Especially in North America* (Chicago, 1967), pp. 86, 86 n.

Wiener gives half his space to the courts martial of the British Army in North America from 1765 to 1783.

CHAPTER 4: MEN AT ARMS, 1775–1776

1. John C. Fitzpatrick, ed., *The Diaries of George Washington*, 4 vols. (Boston, 1925), II, 167 n.
2. John Adams to Abigail Adams, May 29, 1775, in Edmund C. Burnett, ed., *Letters of Members of the Continental Congress, 1774–1789*, 8 vols. (Washington, D.C., 1921–36), I, 102 (hereafter cited as *LCC*).
3. Worthington Chauncey Ford and Gaillard Hunt, eds., *Journals of the Continental Congress, 1774–1789*, 34 vols. (Washington, D.C., 1904–1937), II, 91 (hereafter cited as *JCC*).
4. John Adams to Abigail Adams, June 17, 1775, in Lyman H. Butterfield *et al.*, eds., *Adams Family Correspondence* (Cambridge, Mass., 1963–), I, 215; Charles Francis Adams, ed., *The Works of John Adams*, 10 vols. (Boston, 1856), II, 415–418; quotation on p. 417.
5. Bernhard Knollenberg, in *George Washington: The Virginia Period* (Durham, N.C., 1964), pp. 114–116, believes that Adams may have exaggerated his part in choosing Washington to command and that Washington was the obvious choice from the beginning. Adams's letter of June 17 (see note 4, above) makes no claims, and he was a far from discreet letter writer.
6. For the record, the general officers chosen to command troops were, as of June 1775, Major Generals George Washington, Artemas Ward, Charles Lee, Philip Schuyler, and Israel Putnam; Brigadier Generals Seth Pomeroy, William Heath, John Thomas, Richard Montgomery, John Sullivan, David Wooster, Joseph Spencer, and Nathanael Greene; Adjutant General, Horatio Gates; and Quartermaster General, Thomas Mifflin. These men were residents of seven states. F. V. Greene, *The Revolutionary War* (New York, 1911), pp. 14–16.
7. Marcus W. Cunliffe, ed., *The Life of George Washington by Mason L. Weems* (Cambridge, Mass., 1962); Gilbert Chinard, ed., *George Washington As the French Knew Him: A Collection of Texts* (Princeton, 1940).
8. John J. Meng, ed., . . . *The Despatches and Instructions of Conrad Alexandre Gérard, 1778–1780* (Baltimore, 1939), p. 458: "il me paroit mériter comme homme et comme Citoyen"; p. 582: "il sera plus circonspect. . . ."
9. Bernhard Knollenberg, *Washington and the Revolution: A Reappraisal* (New York, 1940), pp. 151–167.
10. Douglas Southall Freeman *et al.*, *George Washington: A Biography*, 7 vols. (New York, 1948–1957), is the multi-volume monument.
11. *Ibid.*, II, 379–398, has a good description of Washington's temperament at age twenty-seven.
12. Samuel Eliot Morison, "The Young Man Washington," in *By Land and By Sea: Essays and Addresses* (New York, 1954), Chapter VI, is by far the most useful characterization of Washington as a human being.
13. George Adams Boyd, *Elias Boudinot, Patriot and Statesman, 1740–1821* (Princeton, 1952), pp. 38–39, quotes Boudinot as recollecting that he was the one who urged the prosecution and admitting that Washington convinced him.
14. Diary of John Adams, August 31, 1774, *LCC*, I, 1–2.
15. Washington to President of the Congress, April 4, 1781, in John C. Fitz-

Notes

patrick, ed., *The Writings of George Washington from the Original Manuscript Sources*, 39 vols. (Washington, D.C., 1931–1944), XXI, 411–412, 412 n.

16. Hamilton to Schuyler, in Broadus Mitchell, "Hamilton's Quarrel with Washington, 1781," *William and Mary Quarterly*, 3d ser., XII (1955), 200.

17. Freeman, *Washington*, I, xv; II, 369–379; III, 444.

18. Letters to various correspondents, June 19 and 20, 1775, Fitzpatrick, *Writings of Washington*, III, 297–299.

19. *Ibid.*, III, opposite 292 (facsimile).

20. Washington to Trumbull, July 18, and to Massachusetts legislature, July 31, 1775, *ibid.*, III, 343–344, 379–381.

21. Washington to Reed, January 14, 1776, *ibid.*, IV, 280.

22. Freeman, *Washington*, V, 487–488.

23. Washington to President of the Congress, July 10, 1775, Fitzpatrick, *Writings of Washington*, III, 328.

24. The thinking of the British command is told in John R. Alden, *General Gage in America* (Baton Rouge, 1948), pp. 253–270.

25. Quoted in Christopher Ward, *The War of the Revolution*, ed. John R. Alden, 2 vols. (New York, 1952), I, 96.

26. Quoted in Edward Channing, *A History of the United States*, 6 vols. (New York, 1905–1925), III, 170.

27. Adams to Warren, June 27, 1775, *LCC*, I, 145.

28. Adams to Warren, July 24, 1775, quoted in Edmund Cody Burnett, *The Continental Congress* (New York, 1941; reprint ed., 1964), pp. 87–88.

29. Quoted in Channing, *History of U.S.*, III, 170.

30. Burke to O'Hara, July 26, 1775, in Ross J. S. Hoffman, *Edmund Burke, New York Agent* (Philadelphia, 1956), p. 589.

31. *JCC*, June 27, 1775, II, 109–110.

32. Washington to President of the Congress, October 5, 1775, Fitzpatrick, *Writings of Washington*, IV, 12–13.

33. Smith, Diary, January 18, 1776, *LCC*, I, 318.

34. Freeman, *Washington*, IV, 11–12.

35. David M. Ludlum, *Early American Winters, 1604–1820* (Boston, 1966), pp. 90–95, describes the weather from the beginning of Arnold's march. Kenneth Roberts, ed., *March to Quebec: Journals of the Members of Arnold's Expedition* (New York, 1940), is an excellent collection; we need more books like it covering other episodes.

36. Chase to R. H. Lee, May 17, 1776, quoted in Francis F. Beirne, "Mission to Canada, 1776," *Maryland History Magazine*, LX (1965), 404–420.

37. Freeman, *Washington*, IV, 95.

CHAPTER 5: The Balance of Obstinacy, 1775–1776

1. L. H. Butterfield, "The Milliner's Mission in 1775; Or, the British Seize a Treasonable Letter from Dr. Benjamin Rush," *William and Mary Quarterly*, 3d ser., VIII (1951), 197–198.

2. The British decisions are contained in John R. Alden, *The American Revolution, 1775–1783* (New York, 1954), pp. 62–66, 75, 75 n.

3. Richard J. Hooker, "The American Revolution Seen Through a Wine Glass," *William and Mary Quarterly*, 3d ser., XI (1954), 52–77.

4. Clinton Rossiter, "Richard Bland: The Whig in America," *ibid.*, X (1953),

33–79, is a fine analysis of the thought of a typical American Whig, active in all political conflicts until his death late in 1776.

5. Quoted in Julian P. Boyd, ed., "The Murder of George Wythe," *ibid.*, XII (1955), 514.

6. John Adams, Diary, September 15, 1775, in Edmund Cody Burnett, ed., *Letters of Members of the Continental Congress, 1774–1789*, 8 vols. (Washington, D.C., 1921–1936), I, 194–195 (hereafter cited as *LCC*).

7. Dyer to Trumbull, September 25, 1775, *ibid.*, I, 206.

8. Washington to President of the Congress, December 31, 1775, in John C. Fitzpatrick, ed., *The Writings of George Washington from the Original Manuscript Sources*, 39 vols. (Washington, D.C., 1931–1944), IV, 194–199, 197 n.

9. Worthington Chauncey Ford and Gaillard Hunt, eds., *Journals of the Continental Congress, 1774–1789*, 34 vols. (Washington, D.C., 1904–1937), December 6, 1775, III, 410–411 (hereafter cited as *JCC*).

10. J. Adams to James Warren, October 19, 1775, *LCC*, I, 236. Practically identical arguments against having a navy appeared in the 1790's. Marshall Smelser, *The Congress Founds the Navy* (Notre Dame, Ind., 1959).

11. Howard I. Chapelle, *The History of the American Sailing Navy: The Ships and Their Development* (New York, 1949), covers the subject about as well as possible.

12. *JCC*, October 5, 13, and 30, 1775, III, 277, 277 n., 293, 311.

13. *Ibid.*, November 10, 1775, 348.

14. *Ibid.*, December 13 and 14, 1775, 425–428.

15. *Ibid.*, December 22, 1775, 443–444. Hopkins' given name is usually spelled Esek, but the printed *Journals* have it "Ezek."

16. Smelser, *The Congress Founds the Navy.*

17. Washington to President of the Congress, November 11, 1775, Fitzpatrick, *Writings of Washington*, IV, 81–82, 83 n.

18. Carleton Savage, ed., *Policy of the United States Toward Maritime Commerce in War*, 2 vols. (Washington, D.C., 1934–1936), is the foremost work, but it discusses the Continental Congress only briefly.

19. The Regulations are in *JCC*, November 28, 1775, III, 378–387.

20. Samuel Flagg Bemis, *The Diplomacy of the American Revolution* (New York, 1935; reprint ed., 1957), pp. 3–15, still seems the best introduction to the subject.

21. Robert A. East, *Business Enterprise in the American Revolutionary Era* (New York, 1938), gives the best account of the counterpoint of war and trade (among other things); see pp. 127–130.

22. Benjamin Quarles, "Lord Dunmore as Liberator," *William and Mary Quarterly*, 3d ser., XV (1958), 494–507.

23. Bernard Bailyn, *The Ideological Origins of the American Revolution* (Cambridge, Mass., 1967), best traces the intellectual conversion. This work is an enlarged separate printing of the general introduction to Bailyn's *Pamphlets of the American Revolution, 1750–1776*, 4 vols. (Cambridge, Mass., 1965).

24. Lawrence Henry Gipson, *The British Empire Before the American Revolution*, 14 vols. (Caldwell, Idaho, and New York, 1936–1968), XII, 323–325, touches specifically on the mental block which prevented a British accommodation—which is, of course, one of his generalized themes (see *passim*).

25. Curtis P. Nettels, "The Origins of the Union and of the States," *Proceedings of the Massachusetts Historical Society*, LXXII (1957–1960), 68–83.

26. William H. Nelson, *The American Tory* (New York, 1961), pp. 116–120.

Notes

CHAPTER 6: Means and Ends

1. The composition of the white American population has been carefully estimated by several scholars and committees. See Louis B. Wright, *The Cultural Life of the American Colonies, 1607–1763* (New York, 1957), p. 46, for figures which rank the English first, with 60.9 per cent of the total. The blacks, at about 20 per cent, would be the second largest group, although this fact is rarely noted.

2. Jackson Turner Main, *The Social Structure of Revolutionary America* (Princeton, 1965).

3. Roger J. Champagne, "New York's Radicals and the Coming of Independence," *Journal of American History*, LI (1964–1965), 21–40.

4. Mack E. Thompson, "The Ward-Hopkins Controversy and the American Revolution in Rhode Island. An Interpretation," *William and Mary Quarterly*, 3d ser., XVI (1959), 363–375 (hereafter *WMQ* 3s).

5. Jesse Lemisch, "Jack Tar in the Streets: Merchant Seamen in the Politics of Revolutionary America," *WMQ* 3s, XXV (1968), 381–400.

6. Lawrence H. Gipson, "Virginia Planter Debts Before the American Revolution," *Virginia Magazine of History and Biography*, LXIX (1961), 259–277.

7. Jacob M. Price, "The Rise of Glasgow in the Chesapeake Tobacco Trade, 1707–1775," *WMQ* 3s, XI (1954), 179–199.

8. See Thad W. Tate, "The Coming of the Revolution in Virginia: Britain's Challenge to Virginia's Ruling Class, 1763–1776," *ibid.*, XIX (1962), 323–343.

9. Robert L. Ganyard, "Radicals and Conservatives in Revolutionary North Carolina: A Point at Issue, the October Election, 1776," *ibid.*, XXIV (1967), 568–587.

10. W. W. Abbot, *The Royal Governors of Georgia, 1754–1775* (Chapel Hill, 1959), is an excellent survey of a revolutionary generation in one colony.

11. For a partial collection of propaganda broadsides through the course of the war, see Miscellaneous Papers, Continental Congress Papers, Microcopy 332, Roll 9, Microfilm Publication of the Papers of the Continental Congress, Record Group 11, National Archives, Washington, D.C. (hereafter cited as Papers CC, Roll . . .). The best secondary work is Philip Davidson, *Propaganda and the American Revolution* (Chapel Hill, 1941).

12. Glenn Weaver, "Benjamin Franklin and the Pennsylvania Germans," *WMQ* 3s, XIV (1957), 536–559.

13. Alice M. Baldwin, *The New England Clergy and the American Revolution* (Durham, N.C., 1928), pp. 183–189.

14. Clinton Rossiter, "The Life and Mind of Jonathan Mayhew," *WMQ* 3s, VII (1950), 538.

15. Paul H. Smith, "The American Loyalists: Notes on Their Organization and Numerical Strength," *ibid.*, XXV (1968), 259–277.

16. Catherine Snell Crary, "The American Dream: John Tabor Kempe's Rise from Poverty to Riches," *ibid.*, XIV (1957), 176–195.

17. Courtlandt Canby, ed., Robert Munford's "The Patriots," *ibid.*, VI (1949), 438 n.–439 n.; *Pennsylvania Packet*, June 15, 1779.

18. Catherine Snell Crary, "The Humble Immigrant and the American Dream: Some Case Histories, 1746–1776," *Mississippi Valley Historical Review*, XLVI (1959–1960), 46–66.

19. The best available treatment, although rather brief, is William H. Nelson, *The American Tory* (Oxford, 1961).

20. See captured Quakers' papers, Papers CC, Roll 66.

21. Patterson to Smallwood, April 15, 1778, *ibid.*, Roll 180.

22. Smith, "The American Loyalists."

23. Clement Eaton, "A Mirror of the Southern Colonial Lawyer," *WMQ* 3s, VIII (1951), 528.

24. The Regulator complaints are documented in Samuel Eliot Morison, *Sources and Documents Illustrating the American Revolution*, 2d ed. (Oxford, 1929), pp. 83–87.

25. R. O. DeMond, *Loyalists in North Carolina During the Revolution* (Durham, N. C., 1940), is the standard account.

26. Champagne, "New York's Radicals," p. 27.

27. Bernard Mason, *The Road to Independence: The Revolutionary Movement in New York, 1773–1777* (Lexington, Ky., 1966), pp. 254–257.

28. Thomas P. Robinson and Lawrence H. Leder, eds., "Governor Livingston and the 'Sunshine Patriots,'" *WMQ* 3s, XIII (1956), 394–397.

29. Ruth M. Keesey, "Loyalism in Bergen County, New Jersey," *ibid.*, XVIII (1961), 569–570.

30. Catherine Fennelly, "William Franklin of New Jersey," *ibid.*, VI (1949), 361–382.

31. Peter Laslett, "Sir Robert Filmer: The Man Versus the Whig Myth," *ibid.*, V (1948), 522–523.

32. Nelson, *American Tory*, pp. 85–115.

33. This hypothetical temperamental classification was suggested by the marked contrast of personality in the opposing protagonists described by Robert M. Calhoon and Robert M. Weir, "'The Scandalous History of Sir Egerton Leigh,'" *WMQ* 3s, XXVI (1969), 58.

34. Worthington Chauncey Ford and Gaillard Hunt, eds., *Journals of the Continental Congress, 1774–1789*, 34 vols. (Washington, D.C., 1904–1937), II, 103 (hereafter cited as *JCC*).

35. Douglas Southall Freeman *et al.*, *George Washington: A Biography*, 7 vols. (New York, 1948–1957), III, 539.

36. Elmer James Ferguson, *The Power of the Purse: A History of American Public Finance, 1776–1790* (Chapel Hill, 1961), pp. 3–24, explains the prewar experience.

37. Nicholas B. Wainwright, ed., "'A Diary of Trifling Occurrences': Philadelphia, 1776–1778, by Sarah Logan Fisher," *Pennsylvania Magazine of History and Biography*, LXXXII (1958), 420–421; *Pennsylvania Packet*, February 11, 1777.

38. John C. Miller, *The Triumph of Freedom, 1775–1783* (Boston, 1948), pp. 456–464, has a more detailed account than space allows here.

39. Varnum to Laurens, November 29, 1778, Papers CC, Roll 104.

40. Washington to Laurens, November 5, 1779, in John C. Fitzpatrick, ed., *The Writings of George Washington from the Original Manuscript Sources*, 39 vols. (Washington, D.C., 1931–1944), XVII, 73.

41. *Pennsylvania Packet*, December 2, 1779, Resolution of October 2.

42. R. V. Harlow, "Aspects of Revolutionary Finance, 1775–1783," *American Historical Review*, XXXV (1929–1930), 46–68, is a good brief summary of the problem.

43. The table for Massachusetts may be found in *Providence Gazette*, November 1, 1780.

44. Marguerite M. McKee, "Service of Supply in the War of 1812," *Quartermaster Review*, VI (1927), 11; the first section, pp. 6–19, deals with supply problems of the War for Independence.

Notes

45. Ferguson, *Power of the Purse*, pp. 48–56.
46. Davis R. Dewey, *Financial History of the United States*, 9th ed. (New York, 1924), pp. 33–54.
47. This remark was by "Leonidas" in the *Boston Independent Chronicle*, August 5, 1779.
48. S. Sydney Bradford, "Hunger Menaces the Revolution, December 1779–January 1780 (Morristown, N.J.)," *Maryland Historical Magazine*, LXI (1966), 1–23, is a lively account.
49. Ferguson, *Power of the Purse*, pp. 57–69.
50. *Ibid.*, pp. 25–47.
51. Don Higginbotham, "American Historians and the Military History of the American Revolution," *American Historical Review*, LXX (1964–1965), 18–34, is quite the best critical review of the literature.
52. James A. Huston, *The Sinews of War: Army Logistics, 1775–1953* (Washington, D.C., 1966), pp. 3–85, covers the supply problems of the War for Independence.
53. How each state met its land requirements is explained in Paul V. Lutz, "Land Grants for Service in the Revolution," *New-York Historical Society Quarterly*, XLVIII (1964), 221–235.
54. Bernhard Knollenberg, *Washington and the Revolution: A Reappraisal* (New York, 1940), devotes pp. 106–121 to Washington and New England.
55. He bared his troubles at length in Washington to President of the Congress, September 24, 1776, Fitzpatrick, *Writings of Washington*, VI, 106–116.
56. Maurer Maurer, "Military Justice Under General Washington," *Military Affairs*, XXVIII (1964–1965), 8–16.
57. "the Spirit of inlistment [*sic*] is no more," Pendleton to Woodford, May 15, 1777, in David John Mays, ed., *The Letters and Papers of Edmund Pendleton*, 2 vols. (Charlottesville, Va., 1967), I, 209.
58. Arthur J. Alexander, "How Maryland Tried to Raise Her Continental Quotas," *Maryland Historical Magazine*, XLII (1947), 184–196, affords a good illustration.
59. Allen Bowman, *The Morale of the American Revolutionary Army* (Washington, D.C., 1943), pp. 13–17, 29–38.
60. Sidney Kaplan, "Rank and Status Among the Massachusetts Continental Officers," *American Historical Review*, LVI (1950–1951), 318–326.
61. *JCC*, June 16, 1775, II, 93–95, 94 n.–95 n.
62. Washington to President of the Congress, October 4, 1776, Fitzpatrick, *Writings of Washington*, VI, 153.
63. Washington to President of the Congress, February 11, 1777, *ibid.*, VII, 133–134.
64. Morris to Bingham, February 16, 1777, in Edmund C. Burnett, ed., *Letters of Members of the Continental Congress, 1774–1789*, 8 vols. (Washington, D.C., 1921–1936), II, 259–260 (hereafter cited as *LCC*).
65. *JCC*, March 13, 1777, VII, 174.
66. *Ibid.*, September 14, 1777, VIII, 743–744.
67. *Ibid.*, September 15, 1777, 746.
68. *Ibid.*, July 31, 1777, 592–593.
69. John McA. Palmer, "America's Debt to a German Soldier," *Harper's Monthly Magazine*, CLVII (1928), 456–466, is a pleasant piece but overstates Steube's part.
70. Sherman to Wooster, June 23, 1775, *LCC*, I, 142.
71. Benjamin Quarles, *The Negro in the American Revolution* (Chapel Hill,

1961), is definitive; Richard B. Morris, "Class Struggle and the American Revolution," *WMQ* 3s, XIX (1962), 19; Miller, *Triumph of Freedom*, pp. 508–512, briefly sketches the story of the black soldier.

72. Washington to Schuyler, August 20, 1775, Fitzpatrick, *Writings of Washington*, III, 437, states his fear that their presence would work against the congressional policy of neutrality.

73. *JCC*, July 12, 1775, II, 174–177.

74. Higginbotham, "American Historians and Military History," pp. 31–32.

75. Bowman, *Morale*, pp. 62–92.

76. Louis Morton, "The Origins of American Military Policy," *Military Affairs*, XX (1958), 75–82; John W. Shy, "A New Look at Colonial Militia," *WMQ* 3s, XX (1963), 175–185; Robert C. Pugh, "The Revolutionary Militia in the Southern Campaign," *ibid.*, XIV (1957), 154–175.

77. Washington to President of the Congress, September 21, 1775, Fitzpatrick, *Writings of Washington*, III, 512.

78. C. L. Hatch, *The Administration of the American Revolutionary Army* (Cambridge, Mass., 1904), pp. 86–124, is old but not outdated.

79. Kenneth R. Rossman, *Thomas Mifflin and the Politics of the American Revolution* (Chapel Hill, 1952), pp. 151–160; *Boston Independent Chronicle*, February 17, 1780.

80. Washington to President of the Congress, December 12, 1778, Fitzpatrick, *Writings of Washington*, XIII, 383.

81. Quoted in McKee, "Service of Supply," p. 9.

82. *Pennsylvania Packet*, December 27, 1781.

83. Washington to President of the Congress, June 23, 1779, Fitzpatrick, *Writings of Washington*, XV, 328–329; Durand Echeverria and Orville T. Murphy, eds., "The American Revolutionary Army: A French Estimate in 1777," *Military Affairs*, XXVII (1963), 1–7.

84. *JCC*, July 15, 1775, II, 184–185; Donald E. Reynolds, "Ammunition Supply in Revolutionary Virginia," *Virginia Magazine of History and Biography*, LXXIII (1965), 56–77.

85. Miller, *Triumph of Freedom*, pp. 72–74; Bowman, *Morale*, pp. 39–45, considers bravery and cowardice.

86. Richard B. Morris, *Government and Labor in Early America* (New York, 1946), pp. 279–309.

87. Fred Shelley, "Ebenezer Hazard: America's First Historical Editor," *WMQ* 3s, XII (1955), 53; Bache to Hancock, January 18, 1777, Papers CC, Roll 75.

88. Howard Lewis Applegate, "The Medical Administrators of the American Revolutionary Army," *Military Affairs*, XXV (1961), 1–10.

89. *Pennsylvania Packet*, December 12, 1780.

90. Rush to Morgan, July 17, 1779, Papers CC, Roll 77.

91. Washington to President of the Congress, November 1, 1777, Fitzpatrick, *Writings of Washington*, IX, 482–483; Olive Anderson, "The Treatment of Prisoners of War in Britain During the American War of Independence," *Institute of Historical Research Bulletin*, XXVIII (1955), 63–83. An undated, unsigned memorandum (23 pp.), listing acts of Congress and names of exchanged prisoners in chronological order through 1782, is in Papers CC, Roll 72.

92. Washington to President of the Congress, September 4, 1778, Fitzpatrick, *Writings of Washington*, XII, 400; Washington to Morris, January 8, 1783, *ibid.*, XXVI, 20; Catherine Snell Crary, "The Tory and the Spy: The Double Life of James Rivington," *WMQ* 3s, XVI (1959), 61–72.

93. A spare, factual narrative of the subject is found in Harry M. Ward, *The Department of War, 1781–1795* (Pittsburgh, 1962), pp. 1–38.

Notes

94. Robert E. Burns, "Ireland and British Military Preparations for War in America in 1775," *Cithara*, II (1963), 42–61; Elisha P. Douglass, "German Intellectuals and the American Revolution," *WMQ* 3s, XVII (1960), 200–218; Margarete Woelfel, ed., "Memoirs of a Hessian Conscript: J. G. Seumes' Reluctant Voyage to America," *ibid.*, V (1948), 553–570.

95. G. H. Gutteridge, "Lord George Germain in Office," *American Historical Review*, XXXIII (1927–1928), 23–43; Wallace Brown, ed., "Viewpoints of a Pennsylvania Loyalist," *Pennsylvania Magazine of History and Biography*, XCI (1967), 419–420; Jack M. Sosin, "The Use of Indians in the War of the American Revolution: A Re-Assessment of Responsibility," *Canadian Historical Review*, XLVI (1965), 101–121.

96. Walter Dorn, *Competition for Empire, 1740–1763* (New York, 1940), has a superb analysis of eighteenth-century militarism; see particularly pp. 80–84, 99–102.

97. Gerald S. Graham, "Considerations on the War of American Independence," *Institute of Historical Research Bulletin*, XXII (1949), 22–34, presents the case for the thesis that the British *lost* a very difficult war, which was not really *won* by the other side.

98. See a surgeon's admiring description of enemy mortar fire in Charles E. Hatch, Jr., and Thomas M. Pitcairn, eds., *Yorktown, Climax of the Revolution* (Washington, 1941), p. 9.

CHAPTER 7: Toward Independence, 1776

1. Edmund Cody Burnett, ed., *Letters of Members of the Continental Congress, 1774–1789*, 8 vols. (Washington, D.C., 1921–1936), I, 345 n. (hereafter cited as *LCC*).

2. Duane to Stirling, March 1, 1776, *ibid.*, I, 369.

3. *New-York Gazette and Weekly Chronicle*, September 29, 1776.

4. J. E. Tyler, ed., "An Account of Lexington in the Rockingham MSS. at Sheffield," *William and Mary Quarterly*, 3d ser., X (1953), 107 (hereafter cited as *WMQ* 3s).

5. Richard Smith, Diary, *LCC*, I, 379, 393.

6. Dorothy Burne Goebel, "The 'New England Trade' and the French West Indies, 1763–1774: A Study in Trade Policies," *WMQ* 3s, XX (1963), 356–372, makes much use of hitherto unexploited French economic documents.

7. Smith, Diary, January 9, 1776, *LCC*, I, 304.

8. Samuel Flagg Bemis, *The Diplomacy of the American Revolution* (New York, 1935), pp. 16–28.

9. Georges E. Lemaître, *Beaumarchais* (New York, 1949), attempts a psychoanalysis of its subject.

10. Worthington Chauncey Ford and Gaillard Hunt, eds., *Journals of the Continental Congress, 1774–1789*, 34 vols. (Washington, D.C., 1904–1937), November 29 and December 11, 1775, III, 391–392, 423 (hereafter cited as *JCC*).

11. Smith, Diary, February 29, 1776, *LCC*, I, 368–369.

12. Reed to Washington, March 15, 1776, *LCC*, I, 373 n.

13. Deane to Mumford, October 15, 1775, *ibid.*, I, 230.

14. *JCC*, April 6, 1776, IV, 257–259.

15. Quoted in John C. Miller, *The Triumph of Freedom, 1775–1783* (Boston, 1948), p. 274.

16. "A Continental Farmer," *Pennsylvania Packet*, June 3, 1776; Charles H.

Notes

Lincoln, *The Revolutionary Movement in Pennsylvania, 1760–1776* (Philadelphia, 1901), pp. 261–262, 261 n.–262 n.

17. J. Adams to Warren, April 22, 1776, reprinted in many places; easily accessible in Samuel Eliot Morison, ed., *Sources and Documents Illustrating the American Revolution*, 2d ed. (Oxford, 1929), pp. 146–147.

18. Charles Francis Adams, ed., *The Works of John Adams*, 10 vols. (Boston, 1856), III, 46.

19. Widely available in Henry Steele Commager, ed., *Documents of American History*, 7th ed. and earlier eds. (New York, 1963), I, 99.

20. Duane to R. Livingston, December 20, 1775, *LCC*, I, 282.

21. *Providence Gazette*, November 4, 1775.

22. *JCC*, May 15, 1776, IV, 357–358.

23. Adams, *Works of John Adams*, II, 490.

24. Quoted in Morison, "Prelude to Independence: The Virginia Resolutions of May 15, 1776," *WMQ* 3s, VIII (1951), 488.

25. Lee to L. Carter, June 2, 1776, *LCC*, I, 468–469.

26. Included in Commager, *Documents*, I, 100.

27. *JCC*, June 10, 1776, V, 428–429.

28. For Jefferson's notes, see *ibid.*, VI, 1087–1093; for Adams's summary, Adams to Winthrop, June 23, 1776, *LCC*, I, 502.

29. Roger Champagne, "New York Politics and Independence, 1776," *New-York Historical Society Quarterly*, XLVI (1962), 281–303.

30. Julian P. Boyd, ed., *The Papers of Thomas Jefferson*, 17 vols. (Princeton, 1950–), III, 67; IV, 221; V, 3, 604.

CHAPTER 8: Independent, Invaded, Intractable

1. Julian P. Boyd, ed., *The Papers of Thomas Jefferson*, 17 vols. (Princeton, 1950–), I, 337–340.

2. As much as anyone could wish to know about the history of the text of the Declaration of Independence, in line by line exegesis, is found in Edward Dumbauld, *The Declaration of Independence and What It Means Today* (Norman, Okla., 1950), although there is rather less than one would expect on "what it means today."

3. Wilbur Samuel Howell, "The Declaration of Independence and Eighteenth Century Logic," *William and Mary Quarterly*, 3d ser., XVIII (1961), 463–484 (hereafter cited as *WMQ* 3s).

4. Worthington Chauncey Ford and Gaillard Hunt, eds., *Journals of the Continental Congress, 1774–1789*, 34 vols. (Washington, D.C., 1904–1937), July 15, 1776, V, 560 (hereafter cited as *JCC*).

5. Adams's description is quoted in George H. Ryden, "Caesar Rodney," *Dictionary of American Biography* (hereafter cited as *DAB*).

6. *JCC*, July 19, 1776, V, 590–591.

7. Quoted in Clifford Chesley Hubbard, "William Ellery," *DAB*.

8. Jefferson's notes of the debate are in Boyd, *Papers of Jefferson*, I, 309–315.

9. E. Rutledge to Jay, June 8, 1776, Edmund Cody Burnett, ed., *Letters of Members of the Continental Congress, 1774–1789*, 8 vols. (Washington, D.C., 1921–1936), I, 476–477 (hereafter cited as *LCC*).

10. Charles Warren, "The Doctored Letters of John Adams," *Proceedings of the Massachusetts Historical Society*, LXVIII, 1944–1947 (Boston, 1952), 160–170.

Notes

11. Stella F. Duff, "The Case Against the King: The *Virginia Gazette* Indicts George III," *WMQ* 3s, VI (1949), 383–397; Pauline Maier, "John Wilkes and American Disillusionment with Britain," *WMQ* 3s, XX (1963), 373–395.

12. Dudley Fitts and Robert Fitzgerald, trans., *Sophocles' Antigone* (New York, 1939; reprint ed., 1967), p. 17.

13. Charles A. Barker, "Maryland Before the Revolution," *American Historical Review*, XLVI (1940–1941), 11–12.

14. Harold J. Laski, "Liberty," *Encyclopaedia of the Social Sciences*, 15 vols. (New York, 1930–1935), is a good springboard into the pool of speculation mixed with historical analysis of this important but not easily defined concept.

15. Arthur M. Schlesinger, Sr., "The Lost Meaning of 'The Pursuit of Happiness,'" *WMQ* 3s, XXI (1964), 325–327.

16. Richard B. Morris, "Class Struggle and the American Revolution," *WMQ* 3s, XIX (1962), 3–29, is a good recent antidote for the poison of historical monism.

17. Douglas Southall Freeman *et al.*, *George Washington: A Biography*, 7 vols. (New York, 1948–1957), IV, 127, quoting McCurtin's Journal, p. 40.

18. Ira D. Gruber, "Lord Howe and Lord George Germain, British Politics and the Winning of American Independence," *WMQ* 3s, XXII (1965), 225–243, is a fine essay on which, in this chapter, the author leans heavily and gratefully.

19. Washington to President of the Congress, April 22, 1776, in John C. Fitzpatrick, ed., *The Writings of George Washington from the Original Manuscript Sources*, 39 vols. (Washington, D.C., 1931–1944), IV, 500–504.

20. Clinton to Harvey, September 1, 1776, Freeman, *Washington*, IV, 178 n., 177 n.

21. Washington to President of the Congress, August 26, 1776, Fitzpatrick, *Writings of Washington*, V, 491.

22. L. H. Butterfield, "Psychological Warfare in 1776: The Jefferson-Franklin Plan to Cause Hessian Desertions," *Proceedings of the American Philosophical Society*, XCIV (1950), 233–241.

23. See Washington's report of September 8, 1776, Fitzpatrick, *Writings of Washington*, VI, 27–33.

24. *Providence Gazette*, November 13, 1779.

25. Washington to President of the Congress, September 2, 1776, Fitzpatrick, *Writings of Washington*, VI, 4–7.

26. *Boston Independent Chronicle*, August 2, 1776.

27. Bartlett to Whipple, September 3, 1776, *LCC*, II, 66–67.

28. *JCC*, September 6, 1776, V, 738.

29. John Adams to Abigail Adams, September 6, 1776, *LCC*, II, 75.

30. Adams, *ibid.*, 93 n.–94 n.

31. *JCC*, September 17, 1776, V, 765–766.

32. E. H. Tatum, ed., *The American Journal of Ambrose Serle, 1776–1778* (San Marino, Calif., 1940), July 15, 1776, p. 45.

33. Edmond George Petty-Fitzmaurice, *The Life of William, Earl of Shelburne*, 2d and rev. ed., 2 vols. (London, 1912), II, 1–2.

34. Quoted in Gruber, "Lord Howe and Lord George Germain," p. 238.

CHAPTER 9: Diplomatic Dawn and Military Dusk

1. Committee of Secret Correspondence to Franklin, Deane, A. Lee, December 21, 1776, Papers of the Continental Congress, 1774–1789, Microcopy No.

247, National Archives, Washington, D.C., Roll 105 (hereafter cited as Papers CC, Roll . . .).

2. Worthington Chauncey Ford and Gaillard Hunt, eds., *Journals of the Continental Congress, 1774–1789*, 34 vols. (Washington, 1904–1937), June 12, 1776, v, 433 (hereafter cited as *JCC*).

3. *Ibid.*, July 18 and September 17, 1776, v, 576–589, 768–779.

4. Imperfect Secret Journal, i, September 17, 1776, Papers CC, Roll 20.

5. *JCC*, October 16, 1776, vi, 884.

6. John J. Meng, ed., *The Despatches and Instructions of Conrad Alexandre Gérard, 1778–1780* (Baltimore, 1939), p. 68.

7. *JCC*, December 23, 1776, vi, 1036–1037.

8. *Ibid.*, December 30, 1776, 1054–1058.

9. *Ibid.*, September 26, 1776, v, 827.

10. *Ibid.*, September 28, 1776, 833–834.

11. Franklin and R. Morris memorandum, later signed in concurrence by R. Lee and Hooper, October 1, 10, and 11, 1776, in Edmund Cody Burnett, ed., *Letters of Members of the Continental Congress, 1774–1789*, 8 vols. (Washington, D.C., 1921–1936), ii, 110–111 (hereafter cited as *LCC*).

12. Franklin to Mazzei, August(?), 1776, *LCC*, ii, 65.

13. Quoted in John H. Latané and David W. Wainhouse, *History of American Foreign Policy* (New York, 1941), p. 11.

14. Robert L. Kahn, ed., "An Account of a Meeting with Benjamin Franklin at Passy on October 9, 1777: From George Forster's English Journal," *William and Mary Quarterly*, 3d ser., xii (1955), 473 (hereafter cited as *WMQ* 3s).

15. See references under "Franklin" in the index of any of the numerous volumes of selections from the writings of John Adams.

16. Hancock to Thomas, May 24, 1776, *LCC*, i, 463.

17. For the designs of the ships of war used in this micro-campaign, see Howard I. Chapelle, *The History of the American Sailing Navy* (New York, 1949), pp. 100–110.

18. Arnold to Schuyler, October 15, 1776, Papers CC, Roll 172.

19. *Pennsylvania Packet*, August 8, 1778.

20. A. T. Mahan, *Major Operations of the Navies in the War of American Independence* (London, 1913), pp. 6–7. A weakness of Mahan's logical symmetry is that the French were mounting a naval expedition to the West Indies, where pickings could be rich, before they knew of Burgoyne's disaster.

21. The question is fully aired in Bernhard Knollenberg, *Washington and the Revolution: A Reappraisal* (New York, 1940), pp. 129–139.

22. Gerry to Trumbull(?), November 26, 1776, *LCC*, ii, 164.

23. Washington to President of the Congress, November 6, 1776, in John C. Fitzpatrick, ed., *The Writings of George Washington from the Original Manuscript Sources, 1745–1799*, 39 vols. (Washington, D.C., 1931–1944), vi, 248–250.

24. Quoted in John C. Miller, *The Triumph of Freedom, 1775–1783* (Boston, 1948), p. 141.

25. The words are Gordon C. Turner's in a review in *WMQ* 3s, x (1953), 245.

26. *Connecticut Gazette and Universal Intelligencer* (New London), January 3, 1777.

27. Many editions, first in the periodical press in "The American Crisis," No. 1, *Pennsylvania Packet*, December 27, 1776.

28. Warren to S. Adams, December 29, 1776, *Warren-Adams Letters, Being Chiefly a Correspondence Among John Adams, Samuel Adams, and James*

Notes

Warren, Massachusetts Historical Society, Collections, LXXII–LXXIII (Boston, 1917–1925), LXXIII, 441–442.

29. *JCC*, December 9, 10, 11, and 12, 1776, VI, 1015, 1018–1020, 1023, 1027.

30. Treasury Office Papers, Baltimore, December 21, 1776, Papers CC, Roll 145.

31. Quoted in Page Smith, *John Adams*, 2 vols. (Garden City, N.Y., 1962), I, 313–314.

32. Morris to Jay and to Langdon, January 12, 1777, *LCC*, II, 214.

33. Washington to John Augustine Washington, December 18, 1776, Fitzpatrick, *Writings of Washington*, VI, 398.

34. Washington to President of the Congress, December 20, 1776, *ibid.*, 400–409.

35. *JCC*, December 12 and 27, 1776, VI, 1027, 1045–1046.

36. S. Adams to Warren, January 1, 1777, *LCC*, II, 202.

37. Washington to President of the Congress, January 1, 1777, Fitzpatrick, *Writings of Washington*, VI, 461.

38. Quoted in Mahan, *Major Operations*, p. 48.

39. Washington's report is in Fitzpatrick, *Writings of Washington*, VI, 441–444.

40. Morris, Clymer, and Walton to the Congress, January 5, 1777, Papers CC, Roll 150.

41. Washington to President of the Congress, January 19, 1777, Fitzpatrick, *Writings of Washington*, VII, 29–30.

CHAPTER 10: The Year the British Might Have Won—1777

1. Worthington Chauncey Ford and Gaillard Hunt, eds., *Journals of the Continental Congress, 1774–1789*, 34 vols. (Washington, D.C., 1904–1937), June 14, 1776, VIII, 464 (hereafter cited as *JCC*). The word "thirteen" before the words "United States" was not in the first approved draft, but was inserted in the Corrected Journal.

2. Rumsey to Johnson, May 1, 1777, Edmund Cody Burnett, ed., *Letters of Members of the Continental Congress, 1774–1789*, 8 vols. (Washington, D.C., 1921–1936), II, 350 (hereafter cited as *LCC*).

3. Washington to President of the Congress, August 3, 1777, in John C. Fitzpatrick, ed., *The Writings of George Washington from the Original Manuscript Sources*, 39 vols. (Washington, D.C., 1931–1944), IX, 8–9.

4. *Pennsylvania Evening Post*, July 1, 1777.

5. Washington to President of the Congress, July 25, 1777, Fitzpatrick, *Writings of Washington*, VIII, 470.

6. *JCC*, September 17, 1777, VIII, 751–753.

7. Washington to President of the Congress, September 11, 1777, Fitzpatrick, *Writings of Washington*, IX, 207.

8. John to Abigail Adams, September 30, 1777, *LCC*, II, 504.

9. Washington to President of the Congress, October 7, 1777, Fitzpatrick, *Writings of Washington*, IX, 321–323.

10. Same to same, November 1, 1777, *ibid.*, 476–477.

11. Francis Hopkinson, "Battle of the Kegs" (1778), in George F. Horner and Robert A. Bain, eds., *Colonial and Federalist American Writing* (New York, 1966), p. 423.

12. *Rivington's Royal Gazette* (New York), October 11, 1777.

13. A. G. Bradley, ed., *The Journal of Nicholas Cresswell, 1774–1777*, 2d ed. (New York, 1928), entry of July 13, 1777, p. 257.

14. *JCC*, September 14, 1777, VIII, 742.

15. *Ibid.*, September 27 and 30, October 1, 1777, 755–756.

16. John to Abigail Adams, August 19, 1777, *LCC*, II, 455.

17. Don R. Gerlach, "Philip Schuyler and 'The Road to Glory': A Question of Loyalty and Competence," *New-York Historical Society Quarterly*, XLIX (1965), 343–345.

18. Quoted in John C. Miller, *The Triumph of Freedom, 1775–1783* (Boston, 1948), p. 189.

19. General Arthur St. Clair, *New-York Gazette and Weekly Mercury*, September 1, 1777.

20. Williams to Trumbull, August 6, 1777, *LCC*, II, 441.

21. The reputation of Gates is re-examined in Bernhard Knollenberg, *Washington and the Revolution: A Reappraisal* (New York, 1940), pp. 1–20, 102–105.

22. Quoted in Miller, *Triumph of Freedom*, p. 183.

23. Duane to R. Livingston, September 3(?), 1777, *LCC*, II, 473–474.

24. Marvin L. Brown, ed., *Baroness von Riedesel and the American Revolution: Journal and Correspondence* (Chapel Hill, 1965), pp. 55–56.

25. Washington to R. H. Lee, October 28, 1777, in Worthington C. Ford, ed., "Washington at the Crisis of the Revolutionary War," *Century Magazine*, LXXXI (1910–1911), 663. This letter was not reproduced in Fitzpatrick's edition of the *Writings*, although listed in the *Reader's Guide to Periodical Literature, 1910–1914* (1915). Ford categorically affirmed its authenticity, and was as well qualified as anyone to testify on the subject.

26. *Providence Gazette*, November 1, 1777.

27. *JCC*, X, 33.

28. Roberdeau to Wharton, November 10, 1777, *LCC*, II, 547, 547 n.

29. Knollenberg, *Washington and the Revolution*, pp. 140–150.

30. Brown, *Baroness von Riedesel*, p. 64.

31. Gates to Laurens, December 3, 1777, Papers of the Continental Congress, 1774–1789, Microcopy No. 247, National Archives, Washington, D.C., Roll 70.

32. Washington to President of the Congress, October 22–23, 1778, Fitzpatrick, *Writings of Washington*, XIII, 132.

33. The fall of the Howes is explained in Ira D. Gruber, "Lord Howe and Lord George Germain, British Politics and the Winning of American Independence," *William and Mary Quarterly*, 3d ser., XXII (1965), 238–243.

CHAPTER 11: Hard Words and Cold Comfort, 1777–1778

1. Washington to Arnold, January 20, 1778, in John C. Fitzpatrick, ed., *The Writings of George Washington from the Original Manuscript Sources*, 39 vols. (Washington, D.C., 1931–1944), X, 325.

2. Washington to Board of War, January 3, 1778, *ibid.*, X, 253–254.

3. Albigence Waldo, "Valley Forge, 1777–1778, Diary of Surgeon Albigence Waldo, of the Connecticut Line," *Pennsylvania Magazine of History and Biography*, XXI (1897), entry of December 14, p. 306.

4. Washington, Circular Letter, December 29, 1777, Fitzpatrick, *Writings of Washington*, X, 224.

5. Carson I. A. Ritchie, ed., "A New York Diary of the Revolutionary War,"

Notes

New-York Historical Society Quarterly, L, (1966), 232–234, includes entries made during Howe's stay at Philadelphia.

6. Washington to President of the Congress, December 23, 1777, Fitzpatrick, *Writings of Washington*, X, 192–198.

7. Waldo, "Diary," entry of December 29, p. 315.

8. Washington, "Thoughts upon a Plan . . ." [March 31, 1778(?)], in Fitzpatrick, *Writings of Washington*, XI, 185–194.

9. Edmund Cody Burnett, *The Continental Congress* (New York, 1941; reprint ed., 1964), pp. 267–297, concerning the Conway Cabal, as well as elsewhere in the book, leaves the impression that the Congress was often a handicap to Washington, rather than his employer.

10. Worthington Chauncey Ford and Gaillard Hunt, eds., *Journals of the Continental Congress, 1774–1789*, 34 vols. (Washington, D.C., 1904–1937), June 12, 1776, V, 434–435 (hereafter cited as *JCC*).

11. R. H. Lee to Washington, October 20, 1777, in Edmund C. Burnett, ed., *Letters of Members of the Continental Congress, 1774–1789*, 8 vols. (Washington, D.C., 1921–1936), II, 527–528 (hereafter cited as *LCC*).

12. James A. Huston, *The Sinews of War* (Washington, D.C., 1966), pp. 6–8. Burnett, *Continental Congress*, p. 289, believes that Gates and Mifflin were so well known as anti-Washington plotters that they dared not visit his camp.

13. Washington to Gates (re Conway), February 9, 1778, Fitzpatrick, *Writings of Washington*, X, 437–441.

14. Washington to President of the Congress, December 22 and 23, 1777, *ibid.*, X, 183–188, 192–198.

15. *JCC*, November 27, 1777, IX, 971–972.

16. "General Return," February 20, 1778, and "Observations," February 16, 1778, Papers of the Continental Congress, 1774–1789, Microcopy Number 247, National Archives, Washington, D.C., Roll 183 (hereafter cited as Papers CC, Roll . . .).

17. See Burnett, *Continental Congress*, pp. 290–295, for this viewpoint.

18. R. H. Lee to Washington, October 20, 1777, *LCC*, II, 527–528.

19. *JCC*, December 13, 1777, IX, 1023–1026.

20. Sergeant to Lovell, November 20, 1777, *LCC*, II, 570 n.

21. Lovell to Gates, November 27, 1777, *ibid.*, 570.

22. Lyman H. Butterfield, "The Milliner's Mission in 1775; Or, the British Seize a Treasonable Letter from Dr. Benjamin Rush," *William and Mary Quarterly*, 3d ser., VIII (1951), 198.

23. Lyman H. Butterfield, ed., *Letters of Benjamin Rush*, 2 vols. (Princeton, 1951), I, 154–192, contains this flow of letters from October 1, 1777, to January 22, 1778.

24. Washington to Henry, March 28, 1778, Fitzpatrick, *Writings of Washington*, XI, 164–165.

25. Summarized in Henry Laurens to John Laurens, October 16, 1777, *LCC*, II, 521–522. John Laurens was an officer at Washington's headquarters.

26. Willard M. Wallace, *Appeal to Arms: A Military History of the American Revolution* (New York, 1951), p. 176.

27. Burnett, *Continental Congress*, pp. 279–297, quotation on p. 297.

28. Bernhard Knollenberg, in *Washington and the Revolution: A Reappraisal* (New York, 1940), began afresh to study the alleged Conway Cabal with disciplined skepticism, and came away confirmed in doubt. There has been no significant systematic defense of the conspiracy theory since. See particularly pp. 65–92.

29. The standard work is Merrill Jensen, *The Articles of Confederation* (Madison, 1940; reprinted with third Preface, dated January 1959). The remainder of this chapter owes so much to Jensen's work that further citation would be cumbrous.

30. *Boston Independent Chronicle*, August 7, 1777.

31. For the French correspondent's discussion of "these republics" as late as February 5, 1778, see *ibid.*

32. *Ibid.*, February 20, 1777. The anonymous author was commenting on Speech from the Throne, November 4, 1776.

33. This parallel explanation is drawn from Burnett, *Continental Congress,* pp. 215–219.

34. Murray G. Lawson, "Canada and the Articles of Confederation," *American Historical Review,* LVIII (1952–1953), 39–54.

35. Claude Halstead Van Tyne, *The War of Independence: American Phase* (Boston, 1929), p. 310.

36. *JCC*, October 7, 1777, IX, 779–782.

37. Burnett, *Continental Congress,* p. 250.

38. Rumsey to Daniel of St. Thomas Jenifer, November 24, 1776, *LCC*, II, 162–163.

39. Papers CC, Roll 9.

40. The textual history of the Articles of Confederation may be studied in Papers CC, Roll 61, which includes the first long-hand drafts and printed texts, both much amended in several handwritings.

41. Richard M. Gummere, "John Dickinson, the Classical Penman of the Revolution," *Classical Journal,* LII (1952), 81–88.

CHAPTER 12: Foreign Entanglements and Embraces, 1778

1. Quoted in Max Savelle, "The American Balance of Power and European Diplomacy," in Richard B. Morris, ed., *The Era of the American Revolution* (New York, 1939), p. 164.

2. Worthington Chauncey Ford and Gaillard Hunt, eds., *Journals of the Continental Congress, 1774–1789,* 34 vols. (Washington, D.C., 1904–1937), December 30, 1776, VI, 1055 (hereafter cited as *JCC*).

3. Enclosure referring to November 1777, in Holker to Congress, June 16, 1778, Papers of the Continental Congress, 1774–1789, Microcopy 247, National Archives, Washington, D.C., Roll 124 (hereafter cited as Papers CC, Roll . . . , with microcopy number added where it varies from 247).

4. A. Lee to Congress, August 7, 1777, with several enclosures authenticated as to handwriting, Papers CC, Roll 110.

5. Julian P. Boyd, "Silas Deane: Death by a Kindly Teacher of Treason?" *William and Mary Quarterly,* 3d ser., XVI (1959), 165–187, 319–342, 515–550 (hereafter cited as *WMQ* 3s).

6. For examples, see 219 pages in 1779, in Papers CC, Roll 109.

7. The French and English texts of the treaties are in *JCC*, May 4, 1778, XI, 419–455.

8. *JCC*, May 2, 1778, XI, 417–418.

9. *Ibid.*, May 4, 1778, 457–458.

10. Lafayette to Laurens, May 1, 1778, in Edmund C. Burnett, ed., *Letters of*

Notes

Members of the Continental Congress, 1774–1789, 8 vols. (Washington, D.C., 1921–1936), III, 215 n. (hereafter cited as *LCC*).

11. *Massachusetts Spy* (Worcester), April 30, 1778.

12. *Ibid.,* April 16, 1778.

13. *Providence Gazette*, November 28, 1778.

14. *JCC*, May 4, 1778, XI, 438.

15. The subject is touched on in Merrill D. Peterson, "Thomas Jefferson and Commercial Policy, 1783–1793," *WMQ* 3s, XXII (1965), 587–588.

16. Diary, Samuel Holten, September 12, 1778, *LCC*, III, 407.

17. *JCC*, September 11 and 14, 1778, XII, 901, 908.

18. Caille to Congress, September 6, 1779, Papers CC, Microcopy 332, Roll 5.

19. S. Adams to Cooper, January 19, 1779, *LCC*, IV, 36–37.

20. John J. Meng, ed., *Despatches and Instructions of Conrad Alexandre Gérard, 1778–1780* (Baltimore, 1939), pp. 53, 59 n., 87.

21. *Connecticut Packet* (New London), January 15, 1779; reprinted from *Pennsylvania Packet*, December 15, 1778.

22. Edmund S. Morgan, "The Puritan Ethic and the American Revolution," *WMQ* 3s, XXIV (1967), 25–33.

23. L. H. Butterfield *et al.,* eds., *Diary and Autobiography of John Adams*, 4 vols. (Cambridge, Mass., 1961), II, 345.

24. *Pennsylvania Packet*, January 9, 1779.

25. *Boston Independent Chronicle*, February 4, 1779.

26. *Rivington's Royal Gazette* (New York), May 3, 1780.

27. Quoted in Robert A. East, *Business Enterprise in the American Revolutionary Era* (New York, 1938), p. 196.

28. J. Adams to Gerry, July 9, 1778, in C. F. Adams, ed., *The Works of John Adams*, 10 vols. (Boston, 1856), III, 177–181.

29. *Pennsylvania Packet*, August 6, 1778.

30. G. H. Guttridge, ed., "Adam Smith on the American Revolution," *American Historical Review*, XXXVIII (1932–1933), 719, 720. In fairness to Smith it should be added that he was speaking of pliability *after* reunion.

31. Richard B. Morris, *The Peacemakers: The Great Powers and American Independence* (New York, 1965), p. 148.

32. *JCC*, April 22, 1778, X, 374–380.

33. Gadsden to Drayton, June 1, 1778, in Richard Walsh, ed., *The Writings of Christopher Gadsden, 1746–1805* (Columbia, S.C., 1966), pp. 127–128.

34. Carlisle, Clinton, Eden, and Johnstone, June 16, 1778, *Boston Independent Chronicle*, August 6, 1778.

35. *JCC*, August 11, 1778, XI, 770–774.

36. McKean to Mrs. McKean, June 17, 1778, *LCC*, III, 301; Reed to Mrs. Reed, July 21, 1778, *ibid.*, 346.

37. John F. Roche, "Was Joseph Reed Disloyal?" *WMQ* 3s, VIII (1951), 406–417.

38. Laurens to Gates, June 13, 1778, *LCC*, III, 289.

39. McKean to Rodney, June 17, 1778, George H. Ryden, ed., *Letters to and from Caesar Rodney, 1756–1784* (Philadelphia, 1933), p. 273.

40. *Boston Independent Chronicle*, August 6, 1778.

41. McKean to Mrs. McKean, June 9, 1778, *LCC*, III, 284.

42. *JCC*, June 17, 1778, XI, 614–615.

43. *Ibid.*, October 30, 1778, XII, 1081.

44. *Pennsylvania Packet*, August 8, 1778.

Notes

CHAPTER 13: A Maritime Dimension Added, 1778–1779

1. The accumulation of these Continental warships is well treated in Howard I. Chapelle, *The History of the American Sailing Navy* (New York, 1949), pp. 79–100.

2. Stephen T. Powers, "The Decline and Extinction of American Naval Power, 1781–1787," Ph.D. thesis, University of Notre Dame, 1964.

3. Hancock to Washington, June 14, 1776, in Edmund Cody Burnett, ed., *Letters of Members of the Continental Congress, 1774–1789*, 8 vols. (Washington, D.C., 1921–1936), I, 488–489 (hereafter cited as *LCC*).

4. Report of the Marine Committee, July 25, 1777 (adopted), Miscellaneous Papers, Papers of the Continental Congress, 1774–1789, National Archives, Washington, D.C., Microcopy 332, Roll 6 (hereafter cited as Papers CC, Roll . . .).

5. The best life is Samuel Eliot Morison, *John Paul Jones* (Boston, 1959).

6. Worthington Chauncey Ford and Gaillard Hunt, eds., *Journals of the Continental Congress, 1774–1789*, 34 vols. (Washington, D.C., 1904–1937), March 23, 1776, IV, 229–230 (hereafter cited as *JCC*).

7. *Ibid.*, December 23, 1776, VI, 1036.

8. My conclusion is based on observation of the ship models collected by the United States Naval Academy.

9. Fleming to Jefferson, August 10, 1779, *LCC*, IV, 360–361.

10. Huntington to Trumbull, Root to Wadsworth, September 9, 1779, *ibid.*, 413–414.

11. Lewis to Sayre, August 10 and September 4, 1779, *ibid.*, 362.

12. Carmichael to Committee for Foreign Affairs, May 25, 1780 (from Aranjuez), Papers CC, Microcopy 247, Roll 116. (Later references to Papers CC are all from Microcopy 247.)

13. Montmorin, quoted in Andrew C. McLaughlin, *The Confederation and the Constitution, 1783–1789* (New York, 1905), p. 10.

14. Pollock's records are in Pollock to President of the Congress, September 18, 1782, Papers CC, Roll 64.

15. Papers CC, Roll 71.

16. The episode is illuminated in G. S. Brown, "The Anglo-French Naval Crisis, 1778: A Study of Conflict in the North Cabinet," *William and Mary Quarterly*, 3d ser., XIII (1956), 3–25.

17. The best account of this self-delusive British self-entrapment is William B. Willcox, "British Strategy in America, 1778," *Journal of Modern History*, XIX (1947), 97–121.

18. R. Lee to F. Lee, July 12, 1778, *LCC*, III, 325–326.

19. Washington to President of the Congress, July 22, 1778, in John C. Fitzpatrick, ed., *The Writings of George Washington from the Original Manuscript Sources*, 39 vols. (Washington, D.C., 1931–1944), XII, 209–213.

20. *London Gazette*, November 10, 1778; reprinted in *Rivington's Royal Gazette* (New York), March 10, 1779.

21. Laurens to d'Estaing, September 10, 1778, *LCC*, III, 406.

22. S. Adams to Warren and to Savage, September 12 and 14, 1778, *ibid.*, 409–411.

23. Marine Committee to Franklin, July 19(?), 1779, *LCC*, IV, 328–330; Lovell to Franklin, July 16, 1779, *ibid.*

Notes

24. Jones to Franklin, May 18, 1778, Papers CC, Roll 185.
25. McKean to Atlee, July 7, 1778, *LCC*, III, 321–322.
26. Laurens to Lowndes, July 15, 1778, *ibid.*, 332–333.
27. Major General James Pattison (Artillery), in Carson I. A. Ritchie, ed., "A New York Diary of the Revolutionary War," *New-York Historical Society Quarterly*, L (1966), 262.
28. Washington to President of the Congress, July 1, 1778, Fitzpatrick, *Writings of Washington*, XII, 139–146.
29. Lee to President of the Congress, received January 10, 1780, Papers CC, Roll 177.
30. Gérard to Vergennes (translated by this author), July 18, 1779, in John J. Meng, ed., *Despatches and Instructions of Conrad Alexandre Gérard, 1778–1780* (Baltimore, 1939), p. 798.
31. Washington to President of the Congress, May 3, 1779, Fitzpatrick, *Writings of Washington*, XIV, 484–485.
32. *Pennsylvania Evening Post*, July 3, 1779.
33. Laurens to Henry, July 24, 1778, *LCC*, III, 349.
34. R. Lee to F. Lee, July 27, 1778, *ibid.*, 351.
35. Duane for the committee to confer with Washington, to President of the Congress, January 25, 1779, *LCC*, IV, 41–42.
36. John Fell, Diary, July 26, and Laurens to Hamilton, July 29, 1779, *ibid.*, 344, 347.

CHAPTER 14: Backward at Home, Forward Abroad, 1779–1780

1. *Connecticut Gazette and Universal Intelligencer* (New London), January 16, 1778.
2. The quoted phrase is from Piers Mackesy, *The War for America, 1775–1783* (Cambridge, Mass., 1964), p. 491.
3. *Pennsylvania Packet*, February 9, 1779.
4. Worthington Chauncey Ford and Gaillard Hunt, eds., *Journals of the Continental Congress, 1774–1789*, 34 vols. (Washington, D.C., 1904–1937), February 23, 1779, XIII, 241–244 (hereafter cited as *JCC*).
5. An excellent account is Richard B. Morris, *The Peacemakers: The Great Powers and American Independence* (New York, 1965), Chapter I.
6. John Adams to President of the Congress, December 3, 1778, received March 4, 1779, Papers of the Continental Congress, 1774–1789, Microcopy 247, National Archives, Washington, D.C., Roll 111 (hereafter cited as Papers CC, Roll . . . ; all citations below are from Microcopy 247).
7. Lovell to Gates, June 9, 1779, in Edmund Cody Burnett, ed., *Letters of Members of the Continental Congress, 1774–1789*, 8 vols. (Washington, D.C., 1921–1936), IV, 254 (hereafter cited as *LCC*).
8. Gérard's part is described in the editor's introduction to John J. Meng, ed., *Despatches and Instructions of Conrad Alexandre Gérard, 1778–1780* (Baltimore, 1939), pp. 101–121.
9. *JCC*, August 14, 1779, XIV, 959–960.
10. *JCC*, September 25–27, 1779, XV, 1107–1113.
11. Washington to President of the Congress, March 1, 1779, in John C. Fitzpatrick, ed., *The Writings of George Washington from the Original Manuscript Sources*, 39 vols. (Washington, D.C., 1931–1944), XIV, 165–166.

12. William Gilmore Simms, *The Life of Francis Marion*, 10th ed. (New York, 1844), pp. 87–91; quotation from p. 88.

13. See, for example, letters of Houston and McKean, November 12 and 13, 1779, *LCC*, IV, 517, 518.

14. *JCC*, November 17, 1779, XV, 1284.

15. Washington to President of the Congress, September 7, 1779, in Fitzpatrick, *Writings of Washington*, XVI, 240–241. For Clinton's thoughts at the time, see *ibid.*, 241 n.

16. See letters of May 4, 5, and 9, 1780, *LCC*, V, 125, 126–127, 130–131.

17. *JCC*, June 13 and 23, 1780, XVII, 508, 554.

18. Gertrude Richards, "New Letters of George Washington to Benjamin Lincoln," *Harvard Library Bulletin*, X (1956), 39–72, suggests further study.

19. Julian P. Boyd, ed., *The Papers of Thomas Jefferson*, 17 vols. (Princeton, 1950–), III, IV, V, *passim*, is replete with this kind of data.

20. *JCC*, June 13, 14, and 17, 1780, XVII, 508, 510–511, 523–525.

21. Walker to Weedon, July 11, 1780, *LCC*, V, 256.

22. Madison to Pendleton, November 7, 1780, *ibid.*, 438.

23. President of the Congress to Luzerne, December 20, 1780, *ibid.*, 494–495.

24. Benjamin Hunningher, "Dutch-American Relations During the Revolution," *New-York Historical Society Quarterly*, XXXVII (1937), 170–184, tells the story well and briefly.

25. Minutes of the Late Committee for Foreign Affairs, Respecting Mr. Dumas, Papers CC, Roll 121.

26. *Pennsylvania Evening Post*, July 21, 1780.

27. *Massachusetts Spy* (Worcester), April 5, 1781.

28. H. A. Barton, "Sweden and the War of American Independence," *William and Mary Quarterly*, 3d ser., XXXIII (1966), 408–430.

29. Richard Graewe, "The American Revolution Comes to Hannover," *ibid.*, XX (1963), 246–250.

30. Morris, *Peacemakers*, Chapter IV.

CHAPTER 15: The Worst of Times, 1780–1781

1. General Charles Lee's description of Mrs. Gates, quoted in John C. Miller, *The Triumph of Freedom, 1775–1783* (Boston, 1948), p. 521.

2. Washington to Jay, April 14, 1779, in John C. Fitzpatrick, ed., *The Writings of George Washington from the Original Manuscript Sources*, 39 vols. (Washington, D.C., 1931–1944), XIV, 385.

3. De Kalb to Gates, July 16, 1780, Papers of the Continental Congress, 1774–1789, National Archives, Washington, D.C., Microcopy 247, Roll 174 (hereafter cited as Papers CC, Roll . . .).

4. Gates to President of the Congress, August 20, 1780, *ibid.*

5. Lovell to Holten, September 10, 1780, in Edmund Cody Burnett, ed., *Letters of the Continental Congress, 1774–1789*, 8 vols. (Washington, D.C., 1921–1936), V, 367 (hereafter cited as *LCC*).

6. George W. Corner, ed., *The Autobiography of Benjamin Rush* (Princeton, 1948), p. 156.

7. Carl Van Doren, *Secret History of the American Revolution* (New York, 1941), has the best account of the Arnold affair.

8. Willard M. Wallace, *Traitorous Hero: The Life and Fortunes of Benedict*

Notes

Arnold (New York, 1954), is a very satisfying biography. See pp. 174–191 for Arnold's difficulties with Pennsylvania and the Congress.

9. A Philadelphia writer in *New-York Gazette and Weekly Mercury*, September 7, 1778.

10. Arnold to Huntington, October 6 and later, 1779, *LCC*, IV, 476 n.–477 n.; S. Holten, Diary, entry October 6, 1779, *ibid.*, 476.

11. Arnold to Huntington, July 17, 1780, Papers CC, Roll 179.

12. "Thoughts on a British Attempt on West Point" [July 1779], in Fitzpatrick, *Writings of Washington*, XVI, 26–28.

13. Clinton to Germain, October 11 and 20, 1780, "Treason of Benedict Arnold," *Pennsylvania Magazine of History and Biography*, XXII (1898), 411–412.

14. Committee at Headquarters to Trumbull, June 1, 1780, *LCC*, V, 179–180.

15. Hamilton to Greene, September 25, 1780, Papers CC, Roll 175.

16. Quoted in Edward Channing, *A History of the United States*, 6 vols. (New York, 1905–1925), III, 307.

17. President of the Congress to Greene, September 27, 1780, *LCC*, V, 393.

18. Same to Governor of Connecticut, October 17(?), 1780, *ibid.*, 421.

19. E.g., Lovell to Peabody and to Holten, October 3, 1780, *ibid.*, 402, 402 n.

20. On September 30; *Pennsylvania Packet*, October 3, 1780.

21. Corner, *Autobiography of Rush*, p. 158.

22. Washington to J. Laurens, October 13, 1780, Fitzpatrick, *Writings of Washington*, XX, 173.

23. Board of War to the Congress, January 21, 1780, Papers CC, Roll 159.

24. Washington to President of the Congress, March 17, 1780, Fitzpatrick, *Writings of Washington*, XVIII, 121–122.

25. Same to same, May 5, 1780, *ibid.*, 330.

26. *New-York Gazette and Weekly Mercury*, September 11, 1780.

27. Washington to President of the Congress, May 8, 1781, Fitzpatrick, *Writings of Washington*, XXII, 60.

28. Same to same, April 10, 1778, *ibid.*, XI, 235–236.

29. Same to Committee of Conference, February 27, 1779, *ibid.*, XIV, 159.

30. Same to President of the Congress, August 11, 1779, *ibid.*, XVI, 78–80.

31. Same to same, April 3, 1780, *ibid.*, XVIII, 208–209.

32. Same to Committee of Cooperation, June 11, 1780, *ibid.*, 505–506.

33. Same to President of the Congress, June 18, 1780, *ibid.*, XIX, 27.

34. Same to Committee of Cooperation, August 17, 1780, *ibid.*, 391–394.

35. Same to President of the Congress, September 8, 1780, *ibid.*, XX, 14–15.

36. Papers CC, Roll 48.

37. February 20, 1780, Papers CC, Roll 42.

38. "The Memorial of the . . . General Officers," August 1780, Papers CC, Roll 57.

39. Washington to President of the Congress, February 17, 1780, Fitzpatrick, *Writings of Washington*, XVIII, 20–21.

40. Same to Lewis, July 6, 1780, *ibid.*, XIX, 130–133.

41. Same to President of the Congress, August 20, 1780, *ibid.*, 410–413.

42. Same to Sullivan, December 17, 1780, *ibid.*, XX, 488–491.

43. Same to Harrison, December 18 and 30, 1778, *ibid.*, XIII, 462–468, seems to mark the beginning of Washington's recorded discontent with Congressmen.

44. Quoted in Robert C. Alberts, *The Golden Voyage: The Life and Times of William Bingham, 1752–1804* (Boston, 1969), p. 98.

45. *Massachusetts Spy* (Worcester), April 1, 1779.

46. Letter dated June 29, 1780, at Philadelphia, in *Boston Independent Chronicle*, August 3, 1780.

47. Washington to President of the Congress, January 6, 1781, Fitzpatrick, *Writings of Washington*, XXI, 66.

48. Cornell to W. Greene, January 7, 1781, *LCC*, V, 514.

49. Madison to Pendleton, January 16, 1781, *ibid.*, 529.

50. Joseph Reed and Brigadier James Potter, "Proposals," January 7, 1781, *ibid.*, 519 n.

51. Sullivan to President of the Congress, January 8, 1781, *ibid.*, 518.

52. Worthington Chauncey Ford and Gaillard Hunt, eds., *Journals of the Continental Congress, 1774–1789*, 34 vols. (Washington, D.C., 1904–1937), January 24, 1781, XIX, 79–83; quotation on p. 81.

53. Washington to President of the Congress, February 3, 1781, Fitzpatrick, *Writings of Washington*, XXI, 178–179.

54. The story is well told in Carl Van Doren, *Mutiny in January* (New York, 1943).

55. Andrew Adams to Lyman, August 17, 1778, *LCC*, III, 378.

56. *Rivington's Royal Gazette* (New York), March 7, 1781.

57. Root to Trumbull, February 20, 1781, *LCC*, V, 576.

58. J. Breckinridge to L. Breckinridge, June 7, 1781, in L. H. Harrison, ed., "Young Mr. Breckinridge Experiences War, Pestilence, and Inflation, 1781," *William and Mary Quarterly*, 3d ser., IX (1952), 217.

59. E. James Ferguson, "Business, Government, and Congressional Investigations," *ibid.*, XVI (1959), 293–318, is an excellent study of the subject.

60. Robert A. East, *Business Enterprise in the American Revolutionary Era* (New York, 1938), explains the activity of the commercial community.

61. Ford and Hunt, *Journals of the Continental Congress*, June 4, 1781, XX, 598.

62. Washington to Morris, July 13, 1781, Fitzpatrick, *Writings of Washington*, XXII, 365, 365 n.

63. Hamilton to Morris, April 30, 1781, in Harold E. Syrett and Jacob E. Cooke, eds., *The Papers of Alexander Hamilton*, 15 vols. (New York, 1961–), II, 604–635; Morris to Hamilton, May 26, 1781, *ibid.*, 645–646.

64. The standard life is Clarence L. Versteeg, *Robert Morris, Revolutionary Financier* (Philadelphia, 1954).

65. Davis Rich Dewey, *Financial History of the United States*, 12th ed. (New York, 1936), p. 35. Dewey's book, in the format of a college text, is a deceptively unassuming masterpiece which seems destined to endure.

CHAPTER 16: Of Real Estate and Nationalism, 1780–1781

1. The text is most widely available in Henry Steele Commager, ed., *Documents of American History*, 2 vols. (New York, many editions and dates), I.

2. Jean H. Vivian, "Military Land Bounties During the Revolutionary and Confederation Periods," *Maryland Historical Magazine*, LXI (1966), 231–256.

3. Larry R. Gerlach, "Firmness and Prudence: Connecticut, the Continental Congress, and the National Domain, 1776–1786," *Connecticut Historical Society Bulletin*, XXXI (1966), 65–68.

4. Richard P. McCormick, *Experiment in Independence, New Jersey in the Critical Period, 1781–1789* (New Brunswick, N.J., 1950), pp. 218–220.

Notes

5. Thomas P. Abernethey, *Western Lands and the American Revolution* (New York, 1937), is a standard work.

6. Richard B. Morris, *The American Revolution Reconsidered* (New York, 1967), makes a point of this.

7. George E. Lewis, *The Indiana Company, 1763–1798* (Glendale, Cal., 1941), is a complete and exhaustive case study.

8. Paul W. Gates, "Tenants of the Log Cabin," *Mississippi Valley Historical Review*, XLIX (1962–1963), 3–5. After statehood, Kentucky found its grant-acreage totaling four times the area of the state.

9. Quoted in John C. Miller, *The Triumph of Freedom, 1775–1783* (Boston, 1948), p. 656.

10. Richard K. Murdock, ed., "A French Report on Vermont, [October] 1778," *Vermont History*, XXXIV (1966), 217–225.

11. Christopher Collier, "Roger Sherman and the New Hampshire Grants," *ibid.*, XXX (1962), 211–219.

12. Robinson to Allen, March 30, 1780, February 2, 1781, Papers of the Continental Congress, 1774–1789, Microcopy 247, National Archives, Washington, D.C., Roll 181 (hereafter cited as Papers CC, Roll ...).

13. Allen to Huntington, March 9, 1781, *ibid.*

14. Chilton Williamson, *Vermont in Quandary: 1763–1785* (Montpelier, 1949), tells the whole story.

15. Jay to Clinton, September 2, 1779, in Edmund Cody Burnett, ed., *Letters of Members of the Continental Congress, 1774–1789*, 8 vols. (Washington, D.C., 1921–1936), IV, 400 (hereafter cited as *LCC*).

16. Randolph to Nelson, November 7, 1781, *LCC*, VI, 259.

17. Duane, Floyd, and McDougall, March 1, 1781, in Worthington Chauncey Ford and Gaillard Hunt, eds., *Journals of the Continental Congress, 1774–1789*, 34 vols. (Washington, D.C., 1904–1937), XIX, 208–210 (hereafter cited as *JCC*).

18. Merrill Jensen, "The Creation of a National Domain, 1781–1784," *Mississippi Valley Historical Review*, XXVI (1939–1940), 323–342.

19. Irving Brant, "Madison, the 'North American,' on Federal Power," *American Historical Review*, LX (1954–1955), 50.

20. Randolph to Nelson, November 7, 1781, *LCC*, VI, 259–261.

21. Brant, "Madison, the 'North American,'" p. 51.

22. *JCC*, March 1, 1781, XIX, 213–223, gives the text of the Articles with all necessary critical apparatus.

23. Brant, "Madison, the 'North American,'" p. 51.

24. *JCC*, February 7, 1781, XIX, 126–128.

25. Thomas Rodney, Diary, entry March 1, 1781, and letter to Mrs. Rodney, March 1, 1781, *LCC*, VI, 1.

26. Merrill E. Jensen, *The Articles of Confederation* (Madison, Wis., 1940; reprint ed., 1959), is the standard work. Use of the reprinted edition is desirable because of its preface, dated January 3, 1959.

27. *Ibid.*, pp. 239–245.

28. Papers CC, Rolls 53–57.

29. E. James Ferguson, "The Nationalists of 1781–1783 and the Economic Interpretation of the Constitution," *Journal of American History*, LVI (1956–1957), 241–261, well explains how Continental finance gave impetus to nationalism.

30. Quoted in *ibid.*, p. 246.

31. Alexander Hamilton, *The Federalist*, No. 15, in Jacob E. Cooke, ed., *The Federalist* (Middletown, Conn., 1961), p. 92. Cooke's is the best text, al-

though published before attributions of authorship were established to the satisfaction of all.

32. Robert J. Taylor, "Trial at Trenton," *William and Mary Quarterly*, 3d ser., XXVI (1969), 521–547.

33. Papers CC, Roll 184.

34. Papers CC, Roll 35.

35. *Pennsylvania Packet*, January 4, 1780.

36. *New-York Gazette*, September 2, 1782.

37. Stanley Elkins and Eric McKitrick, "The Founding Fathers, Young Men of the Revolution," *Political Science Quarterly*, LXXVI (1961), 202–203, is a very satisfying essay.

38. Elizabeth Cometti, "The Civil Servants of the Revolutionary Period," *Pennsylvania Magazine of History and Biography*, LXXV (1951), 159–169.

CHAPTER 17: The Long Lane to Yorktown, 1780–1781

1. Walker to Weedon, October 24, 1780, in Edmund C. Burnett, ed., *Letters of Members of the Continental Congress, 1774–1789*, 8 vols. (Washington, D.C., 1921–1936), V, 427 n. (hereafter cited as *LCC*).

2. Captured letter dated March 30, 1781, in *Rivington's Royal Gazette* (New York), May 2, 1781.

3. Jac Weller, "The Irregular War in the South," *Military Affairs*, XXIV (1960), 124–136.

4. The standard and only really useful biography is Theodore George Thayer, *Nathanael Greene* (New York, 1960).

5. Van Dyke to Rodney, March 29, 1781, *LCC*, VI, 38 n.

6. Washington to President of the Congress, June 7, 1781, in John C. Fitzpatrick, ed., *The Writings of George Washington from the Original Manuscript Sources*, 39 vols. (Washington, D.C., 1931–1944), XXII, 172–173.

7. *Pennsylvania Packet*, June 12, 1781.

8. Washington to President of the Congress, August 2, 1781, Fitzpatrick, *Writings of Washington*, XXII, 445–448.

9. *New-York Gazette*, September 3, 1781.

10. Washington to Morris, August 17, 1781, Fitzpatrick, *Writings of Washington*, XXIII, 11–12.

11. Morris to Washington, August 22, Washington to Morris, September 7, 1781, Fitzpatrick, *Writings of Washington*, XXIII, 12 n., 95.

12. Evelyn M. Acomb, ed., *The Revolutionary Journal of Baron Ludwig von Closen* (Chapel Hill, 1958), p. 120.

13. Continental Army veteran Lem Cook, reminiscing in 1864 at age 105, *Life*, May 31, 1948.

14. Edward M. Riley, ed., "St. George Tucker's Journal of the Siege of Yorktown, 1781," *William and Mary Quarterly*, 3d ser., V (1948), 387.

15. *Rivington's Royal Gazette* (New York), October 31, 1781.

16. Washington to President of the Congress, October 19, 1781, Fitzpatrick, *Writings of Washington*, XXIII, 241–244.

17. Burke to Middleton, October 19, 1781, *LCC*, VI, 249 n.

18. *Ibid.*, 248 n.–249 n.

19. Acomb, *Journal of Closen*, p. 167.

20. Worthington Chauncey Ford and Gaillard Hunt, eds., *Journals of the*

Notes

Continental Congress, 1774–1789, 34 vols. (Washington, D.C., 1904–1937), XXI, 1071.

21. President of the Congress to Washington, October 31, 1781, *LCC*, VI, 252–253.

22. Madison to Pendleton, October 30, 1781, in William T. Hutchinson and William M. E. Rachal, eds., *The Papers of James Madison*, 5 vols. (Chicago, 1962–), III, 296.

23. *Ibid.*

24. Connecticut delegates to Trumbull, October 25, 1781, *LCC*, VI, 251.

25. Livermore to Weare, October 30, 1781, *ibid.*

26. Elias Boudinot, *ibid.*, 249 n.

27. *Pennsylvania Packet*, November 1, 1781.

28. *Providence Gazette*, November 3, 1781.

29. *Ibid.*, November 10, 1781.

30. *Rivington's Royal Gazette*, November 7, 1781.

31. William B. Willcox, "The British Road to Yorktown: A Study in Divided Command," *American Historical Review* (1946–1947), LII, 1–35.

32. Solomon M. Lutnick, "The Defeat at Yorktown: A View from the British Press," *Virginia Magazine of History and Biography*, LXXII (1964), 471–478.

33. Washington, Circular to the States, January 31, 1782, Fitzpatrick, *Writings of Washington*, XXIII, 478.

34. Washington, Memorandum, May 1, 1782, *ibid.*, XXIV, 194–215.

35. Washington to Secretary for Foreign Affairs, April 23, 1781, *ibid.*, XXIV, 155–156.

36. Washington to Secretary at War, March 21, 1782, *ibid.*, XXIV, 83–86.

37. Washington to Lafayette, January 4–5, 1782, *ibid.*, XXIII, 429–431.

38. Washington to President of the Congress, October 27–29, 1781, *ibid.*, XXIII, 297.

CHAPTER 18: Free, Sovereign, and Independent States

1. See, for example, a Massachusetts letter reprinted from the London *Evening Post*, April 1781, *Boston Independent Chronicle*, August 9, 1781.

2. *Rivington's Royal Gazette* (New York), May 1, 1782.

3. The story of making the peace is so well told in Richard B. Morris, *The Peacemakers: The Great Powers and American Independence* (New York, 1965), as to make further citation superfluous.

4. Madison to E. Randolph, May 14, 1782, in Edmund Cody Burnett, ed., *Letters of Members of the Continental Congress, 1774–1789*, 8 vols. (Washington, D.C., 1921–1936), VI, 350–351 (hereafter: *LCC*).

5. *Pennsylvania Packet*, June 1, 1782.

6. Madison to E. Randolph, May 14, 1782, *LCC*, VI, 350–351.

7. Quoted in George Dangerfield, *Chancellor Robert R. Livingston of New York, 1746–1813* (New York, 1960), p. 114.

8. T. Rodney to C. Rodney, June 14, 1781, *LCC*, VI, 119–120.

9. *Massachusetts Spy* (Worcester), April 11, 1782.

10. H. Laurens, Jr., to Hanson, March 28, 1782, Papers of the Continental Congress, 1774–1789, Microcopy No. 247, National Archives, Washington, D.C., Roll 117. Young Laurens scrambled his dates herein, but they can be decoded.

11. Stephen G. Kurtz, "The Political Science of John Adams: A Guide to

His Statecraft," *William and Mary Quarterly*, 3d ser., xxv (1968), 605–613 (hereafter cited as *WMQ* 3s).

12. J. Adams to Jefferson, February 3, 1821, in Lester J. Cappon, ed., *The Adams-Jefferson Letters*, 2 vols. (Chapel Hill, 1959), ii, 571. There is no reason to believe he had another opinion earlier in life.

13. Herbert E. Klingelhofer, ed., "Matthew Ridley's Diary During the Peace Negotiations of 1782," *WMQ* 3s, xx (1960), 102.

14. Worthington Chauncey Ford and Gaillard Hunt, eds., *Journals of the Continental Congress*, 34 vols. (Washington, D.C., 1904–1937), June 11, 1781, xx, 662–627 (hereafter cited as *JCC*).

15. French views of the Northern interest are exhaustively considered in William E. O'Donnell, *The Chevalier de La Luzerne* (Bruges, 1938), pp. 69–86.

16. Madison to Pendleton, October 22, 1782, *LCC*, vi, 515.

17. Shelburne to Oswald, July 22, 1782, Edmond George Petty-Fitzmaurice, *The Life of William, Earl of Shelburne*, 2d and rev. ed., 2 vols. (London, 1912), ii, 169.

18. Gilman to Weare, December 17, 1782, *LCC*, vi, 562.

19. *JCC*, April 11, 1783, xxiv, 240.

20. *Ibid.*, April 15, 1783, 244–251, contains the text.

CHAPTER 19: Independence Won

The history of the treaty which acknowledged the independence of the United States is definitively told in Richard B. Morris, *The Peacemakers: The Great Powers and American Independence* (New York, 1965), on which this chapter leans so heavily as to make detailed citation impossible.

1. Vergennes to Franklin, December 15, and Franklin to Vergennes, December 17, 1782, in Francis Wharton, ed., *Revolutionary Diplomatic Correspondence of the United States*, 6 vols. (Washington, 1889), vi, 140, 142.

2. Vergennes to Luzerne, July 21, 1783, quoted in William E. O'Donnell, *The Chevalier de La Luzerne*, (Bruges, 1938), p. 236.

3. Peters to Gates, March 13, 1783, in Edmund Cody Burnett, ed., *Letters of Members of the Continental Congress, 1774–1789*, 8 vols. (Washington, D.C., 1921–1936), vii, 79 (hereafter cited as *LCC*).

4. Boudinot to Washington, March 17, 1783, *ibid.*, 83.

5. Mifflin to Dickinson, January 14, 1784, *ibid.*, 410–411.

6. Quoted in Andrew C. McLaughlin, *The Confederation and the Constitution, 1783–1789* (New York, 1905), pp. 29–30.

7. Dora Mae Clark, "British Opinion of Franco-American Relations, 1775–1795," *William and Mary Quarterly*, 3d ser., iv (1947), 307 (hereafter cited as *WMQ* 3s).

8. Piers Mackesy, "British Strategy in the War of American Independence," *Yale Review*, lii (1962–63), 557.

9. George III to Shelburne, November 10, 1782, in Edmond George Petty-Fitzmaurice, *The Life of William, Earl of Shelburne*, 2d and rev. ed., 2 vols. (London, 1912), ii, 203.

10. Hamilton to Washington, March 24, 1783, *LCC*, vii, 94–95.

11. Benjamin Lincoln, "Monthly Extract From the General Returns . . . for the Year 1782," March 1783, Papers of the Continental Congress, 1774–1789,

Notes

Microcopy No. 247, National Archives, Washington, D.C., Roll 163 (hereafter cited as Papers CC, Roll . . .).

12. Washington to Morris, June 16, 1782, in John C. Fitzpatrick, ed., *The Writings of George Washington from the Original Manuscript Sources, 1745–1799*, 39 vols. (Washington, D.C., 1931–1944), XXIV, 351.

13. Washington to Lincoln, October 2, 1782, *ibid.*, XXV, 226–229.

14. Washington to Jones, December 14, 1782, *ibid.*, 430–431.

15. "A Hint to the Author of Common Sense," *Pennsylvania Packet*, December 7, 1782.

16. Worthington C. Ford and Gaillard Hunt, eds., *Journals of the Continental Congress, 1774–1789*, 34 vols. (Washington, D.C., 1904–1937), January 25 and February 25, 1783, XXIV, 93–96, 145–148, the text carried by McDougall: 291–293 (hereafter cited as *JCC*).

17. *LCC*, VII, xi.

18. *JCC*, April 29, 1783, XXIV, 297. The papers related to this disaffection are collected in *ibid.*, 291–311. Major John Armstrong, Jr., is thought to have been the author of the Newburgh addresses (there were two). Edmund Cody Burnett, *The Continental Congress* (New York, 1941; reprint ed., 1964), p. 567, doubts that Armstrong could write well enough. This is a subjective judgment which provokes another—that Armstrong could write much better than Burnett, and much better than most eighteenth-century Americans.

19. Washington to President of the Congress and to Jones, March 12, 1783, Fitzpatrick, *Writings of Washington*, XXVI, 211–212, 213–216.

20. Hamilton to Washington, March 17, 1783, *LCC*, VII, 85–87.

21. Washington to Hamilton, April 4, 1783, Fitzpatrick, *Writings of Washington*, XXVI, 291–293.

22. Washington to Hamilton, March 4, 1783, *ibid.*, 185–188.

23. *JCC*, October 18, 1783, XXV, 703.

24. Armstrong to Gates, April 29, 1783, *LCC*, VII, 155 n.

25. Armstrong to Gates, May 30, 1783, *ibid.*, 175 n.

26. *JCC*, June 21, 1783, XXIV, 410.

27. The 1783 Philadelphia menace is concisely described in Virginia Delegates to Harrison, June 24, 1783, *LCC*, VII, 196–197.

28. Armstrong to Gates, June 26, 1783, *ibid.*, 200 n.

29. Rush to Montgomery, July 2, 1783, *ibid.*, 201 n.–202 n.

30. *JCC*, November 3, 1783, XXV, 802.

31. Washington, "Farewell Orders," November 2, 1783, Fitzpatrick, *Writings of Washington*, XXVII, 222–227.

32. *JCC*, December 20, 22, and 23, 1783, XXV, 818, 819–820, 837–839.

33. Howell to Greene, December 24, 1783, *LCC*, VII, 398–399.

34. McHenry to Caldwell, December 23, 1783, *ibid.*, 394.

35. Paine, "The American Crisis," No. 2, *Pennsylvania Packet*, February 4, 1777.

36. Henry J. Young, "Treason and Its Punishment in Revolutionary Pennsylvania," *Pennsylvania Magazine of History and Biography*, XC (1966), 287–313.

37. Richard D. Younger, "Grand Juries and the American Revolution," *Virginia Magazine of History and Biography*, LXIII (1955), 267–268.

38. Bradley Chapin, "Colonial and Revolutionary Origins of the American Law of Treason," *WMQ* 3s, XVII (1960), 16–17.

39. Declaration, Board of Directors, Associated Loyalists, December 20, 1780, William Franklin, President, Papers CC, Roll 200.

40. Louise B. Dunbar, "The Royal Governors in the Middle and Southern Colonies on the Eve of the Revolution," in R. B. Morris, ed., *The Era of the American Revolution* (New York, 1939), pp. 214–268.

41. Richard D. Brown, "The Confiscation and Disposition of Loyalists' Estates in Suffolk County, Massachusetts," *WMQ* 3s, xxi (1964), 534–550.

42. Richard C. Haskett, "Prosecuting the Revolution," *American Historical Review*, lix (1953–54), 578–587.

43. Robert S. Lambert, "The Confiscation of Loyalist Property in Georgia, 1782–1786," *WMQ* 3s, xx (1963), 80–94.

44. *JCC*, November 27, 1777, ix, 971.

45. Washington to President of the Congress, June 3, 1777, Fitzpatrick, *Writings of Washington*, viii, 172–175, 174 n.

46. Frederick B. Wiener, *Civilians Under Military Justice* (Chicago, 1967), pp. 113–122, gives an account of the episode.

47. *Boston Independent Chronicle*, August 8, 1782.

48. *Connecticut Gazette and Universal Intelligencer* (New London), January 3, 1783.

49. New York Delegates to Clinton, April 23, 1783, *LCC*, vii, 149.

50. Duane to Clinton, August 21, 1783, and later letters on the same subject, *ibid.*, 272–273.

51. A. Lee to Monroe, August 23, 1783, *ibid.*, 277.

52. *Boston Independent Chronicle*, February 13, 1783.

53. *Rivington's Royal Gazette* (New York), May 1, 1779.

54. Washington to Lincoln, November 6, 1782, Fitzpatrick, *Writings of Washington*, xxv, 322.

55. Washington, General Orders, August 19, 1782, *ibid.*, 42.

56. Washington to Morris, September 4, 1782, *ibid.*, 124.

57. *Jackson v. The Dolphin*, Forman, Claimant, the Revolutionary War Prize Cases, Microcopy No. 162, National Archives, Washington, D.C., Case 91, Roll 11. For the remark about firewood, Sherwood to M'Lane, December 4, 1782, see *ibid*.

58. *Rivington's Royal Gazette*, March 1, 1783.

59. *Providence Gazette*, November 8, 1783.

60. "Inspection Roll of Negroes," April 23 to November 19, 1783, Miscellaneous Papers, Continental Congress, Microcopy 332, National Archives, Washington, D.C., Roll 7.

CHAPTER 20: Why It Came Out as It Did

1. *The Gentleman's Magazine*, xxx (1760), 136, 188.

A NOTE ON SOURCES

Selected Bibliography

Manuscripts

The only widely available manuscript sources for the congressional history of the war are the microfilm publications of the National Archives: specifically, Microcopy Number 162, Revolutionary War Prize Cases; Microcopy Number 247, Papers of the Continental Congress, 1774–1789 (a tremendous bulk); and Microcopy Number 332, Miscellaneous Papers, Continental Congress.

Newspapers

The newspapers printed in America during the War for Independence were provincial and localist. Except for documents issued by the Continental Congress, which are more easily consulted in the *Journals* (see below), they rarely touched on the war as a whole. When they did, it was in the manner of cheerleaders; they expounded the philosophy of rebellion against tyrants and urged readers to stand fast against British seductions. If approached cautiously, each newspaper will sooner or later produce something of value, but on balance only two are essential to the student: the *Pennsylvania Packet*, of Philadelphia and York, was, off and on, the court gazette of the Congress, and the *New-York Gazette* of 1775, which became *Rivington's Royal Gazette* after Rivington replaced his smashed press in 1777, spoke out for loyalism.

Official Documents

The great official documentation of the central direction of the war is Worthington C. Ford and Gaillard Hunt, eds., *Journals of the Continental Congress, 1774–1789*, 34 vols. (Washington, D.C., 1904–1937). Equally useful for documenting the diplomacy is Francis Wharton, ed., *The Revolutionary Diplomatic Correspondence of the United States*, 6 vols. (Washington, 1889). John J. Meng usefully edited the *Despatches and Instructions of Conrad Alexandre Gérard, 1778–1780* (Baltimore, 1939), the first French minister to the United States.

Personal Papers

A vast collection of congressional correspondence, glossed with extracts from persons close to the delegates, is Edmund Cody Burnett, ed., *Letters of Members of the Continental Congress, 1774–1789*, 8 vols. (Washington, D.C., 1921–1936). John C. Fitzpatrick edited *The Diaries of George Washington, 1748–1799*, 4 vols. (Boston, 1925) and *The Writings of George Washington from the Original Manuscript Sources*, 39 vols. (Washington, D.C., 1931–1944), which lack, of course, the in-letters. Gilbert Chinard, *George Washington as the French Knew Him: A Collection of Texts* (Princeton, 1940), is a remarkably eulogistic collection. Julian P. Boyd, ed., *The Papers of Thomas Jefferson*, 17 vols. (Princeton, 1950–), an editorially perfect monument, fortunately spans the years to the 1790's, as do the excellent texts of Harold C. Syrett and Jacob E. Cooke, eds., *The Papers of Alexander Hamilton*, 15 vols. (New York, 1961–), and William T. Hutchinson and W. M. E. Rachal, eds., *The Papers of James Madison*, 5 vols. (Chicago, 1962–). A similar Franklin corpus is in process but has not reached the war years; until this is finished the reader can make do with John Bigelow, ed., *The Works of Benjamin Franklin*, 12 vols. (New York, 1904). There is an explosion of Adams texts: Lester J. Cappon, ed., *The Adams-Jefferson Letters*, 2 vols. (Chapel Hill, 1959); L. H. Butterfield *et al.*, eds., *Diary and Autobiography of John Adams*, 4 vols. (Cambridge, Mass., 1961), and the same scholars' *The Adams Papers, Adams Family Correspondence . . . 1761 . . . 1778*, 2 vols. (Cambridge, 1963). *The Warren-Adams Letters*, Massachusetts Historical Society Collections, LXXII–LXXIII (1917–1925), includes Samuel Adams and James Warren. Other older Adams collections are available, but Butterfield and company will be replacing them soon in perfected form.

Benjamin Rush has merited attention, as shown in George W. Corner, ed., *The Autobiography of Benjamin Rush* (Princeton, 1948), and L. H. Butterfield, ed., *Letters of Benjamin Rush*, 2 vols. (Princeton, 1951).

Less central but very instructive are the following long personal collections: A. G. Bradley, ed., *The Journal of Nicholas Cresswell, 1774–1777*, 2d ed. (New York, 1928); Marvin L. Brown, ed., *Baroness von Riedesel and the American Revolution: Journal and Correspondence* (Chapel Hill, 1965); P. S. Foner, ed., *The Complete Writings of Thomas Paine*, 2 vols. (New York, 1945), which is not really "complete"; David John Mays, ed., *The Letters and Papers of Edmund Pendleton, 1734–1803*, 2 vols. (Charlottesville, Va., 1967); Kenneth Roberts, ed., *March to Quebec: Journals of the Members of Arnold's Expedition* (New York, 1940), a work which ought to be emulated often; George H. Ryden, ed., *Letters to and from Caesar Rodney, 1756–1784* (Philadelphia, 1933); E. H. Tatum, ed., *The American Journal of Ambrose Serle, 1776–1778* (San Marino, Calif., 1940), the diary of William Howe's secretary.

Biography

Practically every American of importance to the War for Independence is sketched in the *Dictionary of American Biography*. British members of the cast are in the *Dictionary of National Biography*. Of book-length biographies only a sampling can be presented.

A Note on Sources

Washington has attracted the most authors: Curtis P. Nettels, *George Washington and American Independence* (Boston, 1951) emphasizes, and may exaggerate, Washington's influence on the independence movement; Douglas Southall Freeman *et al.*, *George Washington: A Biography*, 7 vols. (New York, 1948–1957), rivals the Washington Monument in size and intent; Bernhard Knollenberg, *Washington and the Revolution: A Reappraisal* (New York, 1940), and *George Washington: The Virginia Period, 1732–1775* (Durham, N.C., 1964), tries to approach his subject dispassionately.

Rebels in uniform are interestingly treated in Samuel Eliot Morison, *John Paul Jones* (Boston, 1959); William Gilmore Simms, *The Life of Francis Marion*, 10th ed. (New York, 1844), a fine example of the On-to-Valhalla! school of early American historiography; Theodore George Thayer, *Nathanael Greene* (New York, 1960); and Willard M. Wallace, *Traitorous Hero: The Life and Fortunes of Benedict Arnold* (New York, 1954).

Some useful biographies of civilian rebels are E. P. Alexander, *A Revolutionary Conservative: James Duane of New York* (New York, 1938); Herbert S. Allan, *John Hancock* (New York, 1948); R. S. Boardman, *Roger Sherman, Signer and Statesman* (Philadelphia, 1938); George Adams Boyd, *Elias Boudinot* (Princeton, 1952); Irving Brant, *James Madison, the Virginia Revolutionist* (Indianapolis, 1941); George Dangerfield, *Chancellor Robert R. Livingston of New York* (New York, 1960); Don R. Gerlach, *Philip Schuyler and the American Revolution in New York* (Lincoln, Neb., 1964)—Schuyler, of course, being a soldier too; Dumas Malone, *Jefferson, the Virginian* (Boston, 1948); Kenneth R. Rossman, *Thomas Mifflin and the Politics of the American Revolution* (Chapel Hill, 1952)—Mifflin was a general through the 1770's; Page Smith, *John Adams*, 2 vols. (Garden City, N.Y., 1962), the first life to be written from the lately released Adams papers; Clarence L. Versteeg, *Robert Morris* (Philadelphia, 1954).

The outside agitators, both military and civil, have had less attention, but see John R. Alden, *General Gage in America* (Baton Rouge, 1948); Alfred Owen Aldridge, *Man of Reason: The Life of Thomas Paine* (Philadelphia, 1959), the life of one who conspired with Franklin to cross an ocean in order to incite riots; Edmond George Petty-Fitzmaurice, *The Life of William, Earl of Shelburne*, 2d and rev. ed., 2 vols. (London, 1912), too often neglected; Ross J. S. Hoffman, *Edmund Burke, New York Agent* (Philadelphia, 1956); William E. O'Donnell, *The Chevalier de La Luzerne, French Minister to the U.S., 1779–1784* (Bruges, 1938), which complements Meng's *Gérard*, above, and Burnett's *Continental Congress*, below; Arnold Whitridge, *Rochambeau* (New York, 1965), the only work on Rochambeau in English; Franklin and Mary Wickwire, *Cornwallis: The American Adventure* (Boston, 1970); William Willcox, *Portrait of a General: Sir Henry Clinton in the War of Independence* (New York, 1964).

Other Secondary Works

General. The standard general history of these years is the excellent John R. Alden, *The American Revolution, 1775–1783* (New York, 1954), and a good book to pair with it is John C. Miller, *The Triumph of Freedom, 1776–1783* (Boston, 1948). An indispensable anthology of many seminal essays is Richard B. Morris, ed., *The Era of the American Revolution* (New York, 1939; reprint ed., 1965). Old but respected is Claude Halstead Van Tyne, *The War of Independence, American Phase* (Boston, 1929).

The Revolutionary Spirit. All stages and levels of the intellectual and emotional ferment of the war years may be seen in the following literary sampling: Alice M. Baldwin, *The New England Clergy and the American Revolution* (Durham, N.C., 1928); Weldon A. Brown, *Empire or Independence: A Study in the Failure of Reconciliation, 1774–1783* (University, La., 1941); Philip Davidson, *Propaganda and the American Revolution, 1763–1783* (Chapel Hill, 1941); Elisha P. Douglass, *Rebels and Democrats* (Chapel Hill, 1955); Edward Dumbauld, *The Declaration of Independence and What It Means Today* (Norman, Okla., 1950), a line-by-line exegesis, but not much on "what it means today"; Edmund S. Morgan, ed., *The American Revolution: Two Centuries of Interpretation* (Englewood Cliffs, N.J., 1965), a good bouquet of the blossoms of historical metaphysics; Richard B. Morris, *The American Revolution Reconsidered* (New York, 1967); William H. Nelson, *The American Tory* (Oxford, 1961); Claude H. Van Tyne, *The Loyalists in the American Revolution* (New York, 1902; reprint ed., 1959)—a classic.

Military Affairs. The battlefield has had the closest attention of any aspect of the subject, and on both sides. In any short selective list the following demand inclusion: Troyer Anderson, *The Command of the Howe Brothers During the American Revolution* (New York, 1936); C. K. Bolton, *The Private Soldier Under Washington* (New York, 1902); Allen Bowman, *The Morale of the American Revolutionary Army* (Washington, D.C., 1943), a too-little-known account of the surprisingly large number of mutinies and quasi-mutinies, and preventive measures; Howard I. Chapelle, *The History of the American Sailing Navy* (New York, 1949), rather technical but indispensable; C. L. Hatch, *The Administration of the American Revolutionary Army* (Cambridge, Mass., 1904), good but so general as to leave room for several much-needed narrower studies within the field; James A. Huston, *The Sinews of War: Army Logistics, 1775–1953* (Washington, D.C., 1966), devotes its first eighty-five pages to the War for Independence, and discusses it very clearly; Piers Mackesy, *The War for America, 1775–1783* (Cambridge, Mass., 1964), being British, comes closer to giving proper attention to the burden of West Indian warfare, which is the only really neglected sub-topic of the military story; Carl Van Doren, *Mutiny in January* (New York, 1943) and *Secret History of the American Revolution* (New York, 1941), narrates the most serious mutiny and the most important treasonable defection (Arnold's), respectively; by lucky accident of alphabet one may lump together Willard M. Wallace, *Appeal to Arms* (New York, 1951), and Christopher Ward, *The War of the Revolution* (completed by John R. Alden), 2 vols. (New York, 1952), which are the two best straight military histories of the war—the chief difference between them being that Ward's is about thrice as long and detailed; Frederick Bernays Wiener, *Civilians Under Military Justice: The British Practice Since 1689, Especially in North America* (Chicago, 1967), is British history, but half the book concerns the court-martial jurisdiction of the British Army in North America, 1765–1783.

Colonies, States, Sections. These sub-units of the continental effort deserve separate treatment, since each colony and state had its own American Revolution. Nevertheless they overlap the continental revolution, and an introductory knowledge of the relation between local and continental problems can be gained from W. W. Abbot, *The Royal Governors of Georgia, 1754–1775* (Chapel Hill, 1959); Thomas P. Abernethey, *Western Lands and the American Revolution* (New York, 1937), a fully articulated story; John R. Alden, *The*

A Note on Sources

South in the Revolution, 1763-1789 (Baton Rouge, 1957); Richard P. McCormick, *Experiment in Independence: New Jersey in the Critical Period, 1781-1789* (New Brunswick, N.J., 1950); Bernard Mason, *The Road to Independence: The Revolutionary Movement in New York, 1773-1777* (Lexington, Ky., 1966).

Founding the Republic. There are three essential books on the attempt to conduct continental affairs as though governed by a central authority: Edmund Cody Burnett, *The Continental Congress* (New York, 1941; reprint ed., 1964), which has been described by a constitutional scholar as "a great unread book"; Merrill E. Jensen, *The Articles of Confederation* (Madison, Wis., 1940, but use the 1959 reprint edition with a third preface); Andrew C. McLaughlin, *The Confederation and the Constitution* (New York, 1905), a very durable classic.

The Economics of the War. Robert A. East, *Business Enterprise in the American Revolutionary Era* (New York, 1938); E. James Ferguson, *The Power of the Purse: A History of American Public Finance, 1776-1790* (Chapel Hill, 1961); Curtis P. Nettels, *The Emergence of a National Economy, 1775-1815* (New York, 1962). These three authors come as close to creating order out of chaos as humankind can.

The Wartime Society. Written history, almost of necessity, has a tendency toward sensationalism, because it deals with change—the more abrupt, the more interesting. But wars and crises rarely touch large masses simultaneously, and a refreshing corrective for sensationalism is Jackson Turner Main, *The Social Structure of Revolutionary America* (Princeton, 1965), which shows placidity as general, and turbulence as exceptional. A large neglected fraction of the population begins to get deserved attention in Benjamin Quarles, *The Negro in the American Revolution* (Chapel Hill, 1961).

Diplomacy. Samuel Flagg Bemis, *The Diplomacy of the American Revolution* (New York, 1935; reprint ed., 1957), is the standard work; Richard B. Morris, *The Peacemakers: The Great Powers and American Independence* (New York, 1965), an exhaustive account of the making of the peace which legitimized American independence, is a book which will be unsurpassed in the foreseeable future; Gerald Stourzh, *Benjamin Franklin and American Foreign Policy* (Chicago, 1954), is excellent (i.e., excels) in every meaning of the word.

Periodical Literature

Because the American Revolution has been so well studied, there are hundreds of quite valuable short documentary publications and secondary essays. Of the serial publications in which such matter appears, the following ten were most useful to me, in order of frequency of use: *William and Mary Quarterly*, third series, which alone contributed about 44 per cent of my entries; *American Historical Review*, which contributed 10.5 per cent; *Journal of American History* (including its earlier title, *Mississippi Valley Historical Review*); *Virginia Magazine of History and Biography; Military Affairs; Maryland Historical Magazine; New-York Historical Society Quarterly; Pennsylvania Magazine of History and Biography; Political Science Quarterly; South Carolina Historical Magazine*. Another fifteen or twenty periodicals of real value to the study could also be named.

INDEX

Index

Index

Index

Index

Index

Index

A NOTE ON THE AUTHOR

Marshall Smelser was born in Joliet, Illinois, and studied at Quincy College and Harvard University, where he received a Ph.D. He has spent most of his teaching career at the University of Notre Dame, where he is now Professor of History. Mr. Smelser's other books include *The Democratic Republic, 1801–1815; The Congress Founds the Navy;* and *American Colonial and Revolutionary History.* His articles, reviews, and poems have appeared in *Harper's* and the *New Yorker,* as well as in learned journals.